The Business Student Writer's Manual and Guide to the Internet

The Business Student Writer's Manual and Guide to the Internet

Thomas P. Bergman
Stephen M. Garrison
Gregory M. Scott
University of Central Oklahoma

PRENTICE HALL, Upper Saddle River, New Jersey 07458

Acquisitions Editor: *Don Hull*
Associate Editor: *John Larkin*
Editorial Assistant: *Paula D'Introno*
Editor-in-Chief: *James Boyd*
Marketing Manager: *Debbie Clare*
Production Editor: *Maureen Wilson*
Managing Editor: *Dee Josephson*
Manufacturing Buyer: *Diane Peirano*
Manufacturing Supervisor: *Arnold Vila*
Manufacturing Manager: *Vincent Scelta*
Composition: *Digitype*

Library of Congress Cataloging-in-Publication Data

Bergman, Thomas P.
   The business student writer's manual and guide to the internet /
Thomas P. Bergman, Stephen M. Garrison, Gregory M. Scott.
     p.   cm.
   Includes bibliographical references and index.
   ISBN 0-13-598004-6
   1. Business writing—Handbooks, manuals, etc. 2. Internet
(Computer network)—Handbooks, manuals, etc. I. Garrison, Stephen
M. II. Scott, Gregory M. III. Title.
HF5718.3.B474 1998
808′.066651—dc21
                                     97-41483
                                         CIP

Prentice-Hall International (UK) Limited, *London*
Prentice-Hall of Australia Pty. Limited, *Sydney*
Prentice-Hall Canada Inc., *Toronto*
Prentice-Hall Hispanoamericana, S.A., *Mexico*
Prentice-Hall of India Private Limited, *New Delhi*
Prentice-Hall of Japan, Inc., *Tokyo*
Pearson Education Asia Pte. Ltd., *Singapore*
Editora Prentice-Hall do Brasil, Ltda., *Rio de Janeiro*

Printed in the United States of America
10 9 8 7 6 5 4 3 2

Contents

Preface

The business college at our school recently formed a board of advisors. Board members include corporate presidents, major stockholders, human resource directors, and a wide range of other business leaders. When one of our instructors asked the board members what sort of student they most wanted to see apply for a job, their number one response was "someone who is a good communicator, both in writing and in person." The book you are now holding offers you practical help in mastering the communications skills that will qualify you for the position you are aiming for after graduation. But this book is not just about communications. It is also about performing better on all of your class assignments and getting higher grades in all of your business courses.

We realize that, despite their best efforts, your professors simply do not have the time to answer all of the questions you will have about completing your business class projects. This book will be invaluable to you as you complete all of the fundamental assignments you will be asked by your business professors to complete. We have included step-by-step instructions for writing a research paper, a business plan, a marketing plan, a survey report, and a case analysis. We have also included help for accounting students who are assigned specialized writing projects. Studying the relevant chapter before beginning each writing assignment will enable you to work more efficiently and with greater confidence, producing the very best report of which you are capable.

Other chapters offer different kinds of help. If, for example, you are not overly fond of group projects—and group projects are a fact of the business student's life—Chapter 8 can help you to come to terms with them and—who knows?—maybe even enjoy them. Chapter 9 then shows you how to go about preparing for the presentation that you will probably have to make to your class once you have completed a group project.

Our chapter on computer-assisted research includes lots of nuts-and-bolts instruction, beginning with the basics of using e-mail and other Internet/Web tools. We teach you how to use the tools you have at your school, which may not always have access to top-of-the-line machines and software. If you already know how to Web surf but still have trouble finding information on the World Wide Web, check out Chapter 10 for information about how to get moving on the information highway.

If you have not already done so, now is the time to discover what an extraordinarily satisfying experience it can be to write well. This book will help you make that discovery. Keep it handy, refer to it often, and remember to enjoy your school experience. These are the good old days.

TO THE PROFESSOR

We regularly bemoan the fact that our business students cannot write as well as we or their employers would like. Some of us try hard to help our students learn to write better, but when we do, we find that we must take precious time away from the content of the business course we are supposed to be teaching in order to teach writing skills our students should already know!

If this sounds like your situation, this book can help. When you use *The Business Student Writer's Manual and Guide to the Internet* as an accompaniment to your course text, you can simply direct students to prepare a business plan as presented in Chapter 12 or a case analysis as described in Chapter 14. Each of the writing assignments addressed in the book is described in detail, with lots of conceptual information to help students understand the purpose of the assignment and formatting instructions to help them make their final presentations as professional as possible. The chapters on writing are probably unlike any you have seen before. We have approached writing as a *skill used to acquire knowledge* as well as a way to convey knowledge.

The chapters in Part Two provide a step-by-step approach to conducting research and provide lists and descriptions of sources, both electronic and print, useful to business students. In Chapter 6 we present answers to the relatively new questions on how to cite Internet and World Wide Web sources. We also explain the proper usage of the registered trademark symbol "®," and suggest that students adopt the practice of honoring the ownership of these valuable business icons by identifying registered trade and service marks as such, especially where student papers are likely to be published on the Web.

Part Three focuses on group work, oral presentations, and the Internet. The chapter on oral presentations includes an assignment to prepare an *oral presentation plan*. This project forces students to thoroughly prepare for their class presentations through the novel approach of designing a presentation for delivery by another student group. Part Four covers business plans, survey reports, marketing plans, case analyses, and the written assignments usually found in the financial disciplines.

This book is much more than just a writing guide. Your business students will learn to communicate better, use the tools they need to complete the projects you assign, and better understand the purposes of these projects. This of this book as your assistant. It will reduce your need for hand-outs, and free up precious class time. It will help you do your job.

The Business Student
Writer's Manual
and Guide to the Internet

INTRODUCTION

The Many Disciplines of Business

THE ROLE OF BUSINESS IN SOCIETY

If you are new to the disciplines of business . . .

Welcome to an exciting, multifaceted new perspective on our world. If you are like most of us, you have been raised to be a consumer—an enlightened consumer, perhaps, but a consumer still. Once you cross the threshold into the disciplines of business you will enter the world of the *producer*. In this world, the focus is on creating the goods and services demanded by our fellow humans. This is, in fact, the ultimate purpose of business.

As a society, we have agreed to allow businesses to meet our needs for goods and services and, in return, to receive a profit limited only by the conditions under which the business person chooses to operate. The very term "business" implies profit, and so it is not surprising that many people in business see their purpose to be the earning of great sums of money. The fact is, however, the accumulation of wealth is incidental to the primary task of the business person to provide goods and services to the community. Profit just happens to be the motivator of choice at this moment in history.

Novices to the world of business are sometimes put off by the rather tawdry notion that money is to be their payoff for a life's work. Many factors in our society condition us to think that, for most people, the earning of money usually involves the compromising of some deeper dream. This way of thinking suggests that we too often become shackled to our jobs, which in turn rob us of freedom and spirit.

To those who think this way about the business world, consider this: the various disciplines of business make possible the lives we all desire. While economists devise plans for distributing goods and services throughout the society, accountants, financiers, managers, and marketing experts do the work of executing those plans. This work is necessary for the continued functioning of our world, and it can offer a lifetime of appealing challenges to the creative mind.

COMMUNICATION IN THE DIVERSE DISCIPLINES OF THE BUSINESS WORLD

Over the past several hundred years, businessmen and women have amassed a great deal of knowledge about how best to perform the myriad tasks required of them. For efficiency's sake, they have subdivided this knowledge into several major disciplines:

accounting, business law, communications, finance, management, and marketing. In many business schools today, economics has moved from its traditional home in Liberal Arts into the School of Business. We should be careful, though, when discussing where economics belongs; many economists are uneasy with their new home in the business school.

Each of the separate business disciplines bears its own personality derived from the discipline's focus. But despite the differences, there are certain needs and goals all the disciplines of the business world share. One of the most crucial of these shared needs is writing skill. To the question, "Why write well?" the business person, no matter what discipline he or she is in, immediately responds, "Because it improves your bottom line!" Let us look at some of the characteristic writing skills needed in the various business disciplines.

Accounting

The job of the accountant is to observe what others in a business concern have done, to record accurately the financial effects of those observed actions, to report to others in the business what has occurred, and to provide advice about the best methods of performing each of these tasks, preferably before the business has acted in error. In addition, the accountant performs the crucial task of designing and implementing methods of controlling access to the assets of the business so as to safeguard them and insure their proper use in furthering one of the vital goals of the business—maximizing profit.

In the accountant's world, communications must be as accurate as it is humanly possible to make them. A misplaced decimal point may mean the difference between a bonus and bankruptcy. An inaccurate description in the footnote to the annual financial statement may trigger a calamitous fall in the company stock price or a lawsuit filed by one of the many federal regulatory agencies whose job it is to ensure compliance with disclosure laws.

Money is always serious business. This means that, when it comes to accounting communications, clarity is the guiding principle. No flash, no panache. Just the facts, accurately, concisely, precisely conveyed, in a manner that can leave no doubt as to the one and only meaning of the communication.

It is this drive for accuracy in communication that characteristically gives students in accounting courses the greatest headaches. But as you work and rework formulas and financial statements in your classroom, remember this: one day a company's future—and the well-being of all its employees—may rely on the habits you are cultivating now.

Business Law

In business law, as the name clearly implies, the emphasis is on the construction and interpretation of legal phrases. There is absolutely no tolerance for ambiguity, unless, of course, the legal intent is best served by ambiguity in a particular agreement. Each word in each phrase must be measured and weighed for all possible interpretations. A legal document is usually revised a number of times before it is produced in final form. Experienced attorneys who have seen their agreements tested in court are especially careful in their use of precise language.

Experience?

A famous and successful business person was once asked to what he attributed his great success in business. He responded, "Good ideas." The questioner, unsatisfied, pressed with, "Well, sure, but to what do you attribute your good ideas?" The businessman responded, "Experience." "Okay," said the questioner, still not satisfied, "How do you get experience?" "Bad ideas," came the response.

Attorneys do their best work with an eye to the future. If they do their job well, the agreements signed today will act in ways that help prevent strife among their business clients down the road. When the attorneys fail to craft agreements that accurately capture the intent of the parties (assuming the parties of both parts are forthright in their goals and do not have hidden agendas), everyone loses. Even the attorneys lose: who needs an attorney whose agreements cause conflict?

For the business law student, writing assignments tend mainly to be analyses of legal situations. The emphasis in such an assignment is on the clarity with which the student can capture the elements of the applicable law as they maintain in the case at hand. To be successful in writing for business law, the student must master the skills required to craft accurate sentences that clearly express often complex ideas. Clarity is crucial, but the student must also master the three main tools of analysis—comparison, contrast, and synthesis—in order to identify the specific information that needs to be presented with clarity.

Communications

Form Over Substance?

In the officers' monthly newsletter, the outcome of the baseball game between the officers and the enlisted men was reported as follows: ". . . the officers came in second, while the enlisted men came in next to last."

In the world of business, especially in the field of public relations, the way a message is conveyed is often more important than the message itself. Unlike the preceding disciplines we have discussed, in which creativity in language is actually discouraged, in business communications it is highly desirable, if not mandatory. For this reason the discipline of business communications requires as its starting point a comprehensive knowledge of spelling, grammar, and punctuation, followed by a solid grounding in the fundamentals of format, style, and phrasing.

A common argument concerning the use of art in business writing goes something like this: "My ideas are what should be valued. I would rather not work for someone who values form over substance." It is a reasonable sounding position, but it fails to recognize just how competitive the world of business really is. For each job, there is usually a large number of applicants, and many of these will be fully qualified. This means that the recruiter has the opportunity to select the employee who is not only qualified but possessed of other attributes—such as skill in the creative use of language—as well. It goes without saying that, in order to impress a potential employer in the world of business communication, you need to be able to demonstrate command of a confident, appealing prose style.

Finance

In the discipline of finance, as in accounting, cleverness in wording is not a primary goal. The tools used in financial analyses are primarily mathematical, a fact which greatly reduces the need for communication, among peers, in the written language. This does not at all mean, however, that language skills are not important to finance. Ultimately someone must communicate the results of the number crunching efforts of the finance department to those outside the discipline. This task, if done well, requires an extraordinary sort of writing skill, one that, unfortunately, is often hard to find among finance experts. Too often, the response of the business executive looking through a financial report filled with numbers and charts and graphs is to demand that someone explain all the gobbledygook.

It takes a talented communicator to translate the numerical information generated by the finance department's professionals into understandable language, couched in terms meaningful to the reader. Because the typical reader is the business executive, such rare communications experts will find themselves pushed far and fast up the ladder of success in business. In business as in most other human endeavors, rarity adds value.

Management

Of all the business disciplines, management is the most diverse, and so are the writing skills required of managers. Managers may function in the area of human resources (formerly called personnel), where they may be called on to draft an employee handbook, compile a set of job descriptions, or even write a union contract. In the bids and quotes department, the manager may be responsible for the final issuance of a complex bid proposal that must convey the particular strengths and competencies of the company to the prospective customer. In still another capacity, plant or department managers find themselves writing a mind-boggling variety of types of letters, as well as the many standard reports required by upper management.

As the manager climbs toward the top level of the organization, writing skills become ever more important. At the lowest level of management, the individual will typically deal with a range of issues from a few thousand dollars in value to perhaps a few tens of thousands. Rarely will this supervisor be given discretion over greater issues that may even affect the ability of the firm to survive. At the top of the heap, though, the manager deals almost daily with the big issues. These frequently involve much greater sums of money, often running into the hundreds of millions and having a powerful effect on the viability of the firm.

There are no upper level managers who cannot effectively communicate their ideas. If you aspire to this level, it is vital that you acquire excellent communications skills before leaving the university. Once on the job, every piece of writing you produce will become an inextricable piece of your career history and may well affect your chances for advancement in the firm.

Marketing

Novice business persons frequently treat marketing as though it consists of just two elements: advertising and personal selling. The reality is that marketing is central to every successful business today. Marketing professionals are intimately involved in product development, manufacturing, packaging design, quality control, shipping, and, of course, advertising.

Since the beginning of the Industrial Revolution in the last century, marketing has evolved through three distinct phases. In the first phase, marketing simply meant producing the product. The demand for manufactured goods greatly exceeded the ability of the emerging industrial sector to supply them. During this phase, all the business person had to focus on was making production ever more efficient so that more goods could be produced.

In phase two of marketing's evolution, production capacity caught up with demand, resulting in flat sales trends and minimal growth for the firms that produced goods. A new marketing strategy came into being: the concept of *selling*. This strategy required businesses to work at finding ways to differentiate their products from those of competing firms. Although in most cases the differences between competing products were cosmetic rather than functional, they nevertheless provided an army of sales professionals with the tools to persuade customers to buy from their firms. The crucial skill for these salespeople was the ability to create a sense of need in the mind of the customer.

Finally, as the population of consumers became better educated, primarily through television, the modern phase of marketing began. Able now to distinguish cosmetic differences from functional differences, consumers have become far more demanding of value for their money. This trend has forced marketers to begin the development of a product by determining what functions the customer really wants. This task has fallen naturally to the marketing professionals, who have become ever more involved in decisions made throughout the company, from the conceptual stages of product design through delivery of the products.

The marketing professional must master several different types of writing. He or she must be competent in the development and implementation of such analytical tools as surveys and focus group studies. These tools require skills in developing probing, unambiguous questions designed to elicit accurate and complete answers to questions that define customer need. Once the data are obtained, the marketer must write a report that can be understood by the executive managers who make crucial decisions regarding the ultimate product design.

Marketers must also be adept at writing problem solving reports that may involve any or all of the functions of the business, from production through delivery and post-purchase contacts with the customer. These reports can be politically sensitive, since they require the marketer to investigate different company departments where he or she may be viewed as an interloper who "has no business down here." In such a situation, the skill with which a report is phrased becomes extremely important for company morale as well as for sales.

A third type of writing performed by the marketer, and the most traditional type, is advertising copy. Writing advertising copy is an art unto itself. Here hyperbole becomes the norm, and art clearly dominates function. Even the rules of grammar are often set aside for the more pressing goal of transmitting an idea dynamically. The concept guiding all writing in marketing is *to design the message to fit the customer's need.* Marketers must be creative enough and skillful enough to appeal to a variety of types of readers, from technical experts in product design to corporate psychologists helping develop new products to general managers who integrate products into sales strategies.

Those of you interested in a marketing position will not be expected by potential employers to possess skill in writing ad copy immediately. You will be required, however, to demonstrate an ability to analyze the needs of an audience—and your first audience will be the recruiter, usually an experienced marketing writer, who evaluates your job application.

Economics

Of all the business disciplines, economics is the most esoteric, concerned primarily with the realm of ideas and theory. The economist must learn to convey extraordinarily complicated ideas clearly, often to readers unfamiliar with such ideas. Economists tend to fall into one of two career categories. The first category covers jobs in the public sector, positions offered by government or quasi-governmental organizations in which the tasks performed are mainly theoretical analysis and development. This sort of job requires the ability to conduct research using sophisticated analytical tools—both quantitative and qualitative—and to write traditional academic research reports, complete with citations and bibliography. Yes, if you become an economist in the public sector, you will have a chance to use the research paper skills that you labored over in your college career.

The other career category open to economists is the private sector. The economist who enters the business world will need the skills of his public-sector counterpart and, in addition, an ability to translate the high-level language traditionally used in academic writings into a more pragmatic style that can clarify a sophisticated analysis for the business executive.

A very real danger awaits the highly trained economist in the business world. Many business managers are quite sensitive to the disparity between their own educational background and that of the economist who works down the hall in the same company. This sensitivity must be taken into consideration in the economist's style of writing, which must be able to convey very complex ideas, indicate all of the underlying rationales for these ideas, and point out their implications for the business, all the while appearing neither condescending to the manager nor overly academic.

The keys to successful writing for the business economist are: (1) the ability to communicate in the vocabulary of the reader, and (2) the ability to express ideas concisely. The second task is the more difficult. Economic ideas are inherently difficult to grasp. Probably the most useful writing skill an economist can possess is a gift for using analogy to illustrate complicated ideas.

Summary

Here is a final, basic rule that applies to writing in all of the disciplines of business: there is absolutely no tolerance for structural writing errors. There can be no spelling errors, no grammatical errors, no punctuation errors. One of the best habits a business writer can acquire is the habit of skillful editing.

The first chapters of this manual will lead you through the composition process in a way designed to help you acquire all the habits you will need to produce successful writing in the business disciplines. The later chapters will give you practice in the kinds of writing you will have to produce, not only in your college courses but beyond them, in the brave new world of business.

CHAPTER 1

Writing as Communication

1.1 WRITING TO LEARN

Writing is a way of ordering your experience. Think about it. No matter what you are writing—it may be a paper for your Fundamentals of Management class, a short story, a limerick, a grocery list—you are putting pieces of your world together in new ways and making yourself freshly conscious of these pieces. This is one of the reasons writing is so hard. From the infinite welter of data that your mind continually processes and locks in your memory, you are selecting only certain items significant to the task at hand, relating them to other items, and phrasing them in a new coherence. You are mapping a part of your universe that has hitherto been unknown territory. You are gaining a little more control over the processes by which you interact with the world around you.

This is why the act of writing, no matter what it leads to, is never insignificant. It is always *communication*, if not with another human being, then with yourself. It is a way of making a fresh connection with your world.

Writing, therefore, is also one of the best ways to *learn*. This statement, at first, may sound odd. If you are an unpracticed writer, you may share a common notion that the only purpose writing can have is to express what you already know or think. In this view, any learning that you as a writer might do has already been accomplished by the time your pen meets the paper; your task is to inform and even surprise the reader. But if you are a practiced writer, you know that at any moment as you write, you are capable of surprising *yourself*. And it is surprise that you look for: the shock of seeing what happens in your own mind when you drop an old, established opinion into a batch of new facts or bump into a cherished belief from a different angle. Writing synthesizes new understanding for the writer. E. M. Forster's famous question, "How do I know what I think until I see what I say?" is one that all of us could ask. We make meaning as we write, jolting ourselves by little, surprising discoveries into a larger and more interesting universe.

The Role of Writing in Business

The help that writing gives us with learning and with controlling what we learn is one of the major reasons why your business instructors will require a great deal of writing from you. Learning the complex and diverse world of the business professional takes more than a passive ingestion of facts or a passion for numbers. You have to understand the theories and practices of the business world well enough to be able to adapt them to a variety of different circumstances and environments. The manager of an ice cream store with five employees in a Colorado shopping mall will face challenges somewhat different from those confronting the chief accountant of a smoke-laden foundry in the rust belt of Ohio, where two unions represent 14,000 of the foundry's workers. When you write in a marketing class or a business law class, you are entering into the world of the business person in the same way he or she does — testing theory against fact, fact against belief.

Writing is the entryway into business. Virtually everything that happens in business happens on paper first. Business plans are wrestled into shape before their contents enable the business leaders to choose a set of strategies to be followed by the firm. All significant business speeches are written before they are spoken. And in business, the stakes are often very high for the many who are affected by activities of a given company. Often, in business as elsewhere, gaining recognition for our ourselves and our ideas depends less upon what we say than upon how we say it. Accurate and persuasive writing is absolutely vital to the business leader and to those who aspire to lead.

Learning by Writing

Here is a way to test the notion that writing is a powerful learning tool: rewrite the notes you have taken from a recent class lecture. It does not matter which class; it can be history, chemistry, advertising. Choose a difficult class, if possible, one in which you are feeling somewhat unsure of the material, and one for which you have taken copious notes.

As you rewrite, provide the *transitional elements* (the connecting phrases, like *in order to, because of, and, but, however*) that you were unable to supply in class because of the press of time. Furnish your own examples or illustrations of the ideas expressed in the lecture.

This experiment forces you to supply necessary coherence out of your own thought processes. See if the loss of time it takes you to rewrite the notes is not more than compensated for by a gain in your understanding of the lecture material.

Challenge Yourself

There is no way around it: writing is a struggle. Did you think you were the only one to feel this way? Take heart! Writing is hard for everybody, great writers included. Bringing order into the world is never easy. Isaac Bashevis Singer, winner of the 1978 Nobel Prize in literature, once wrote, "I believe in miracles in every area of life *except* writing. Experience has shown me that there are no miracles in writing. The only thing that produces good writing is hard work" (qtd. in Lunceford and Connors 1992, 2).

Hard work is evident in the following words from Herbert Hoover. The passage is carefully designed to remind the reader of the many benefits of our economic system. How does the passage make you feel about the role of business in your life?

From the savings made by greater efficiency in production—that is, in the time we have saved from other occupations—we have added the automobile and the good road, the movies, the radio and the phonograph directly to the standard of living. We have increased the diffusion of electric light, power, telephone, plumbing, better housing, and a dozen other things. Some feel that in all this we are deadening the soul of man by machine production and standardization. . . . I may observe that the man who has a standard telephone, a standard bathtub, a standard electric light, a standard radio, and one and a half hours' more daily leisure is more of a man and has a fuller life and more individuality than he has without the tools for varying his life. (Kent 1985, 135)

One reason that writing is difficult is that it is not actually a single activity at all but a process consisting of several activities that can overlap each other, with two or more sometimes operating *simultaneously* as you labor to organize and phrase your thoughts. (We will discuss these activities later in this chapter.) The writing process tends to be sloppy for everyone, an often frustrating search for meaning and for the best way to articulate that meaning.

Frustrating though that search may sometimes be, it need not be futile. Remember this: the writing process makes use of skills which we all have. The ability to write, in other words, is not some magical competence bestowed on the rare, fortunate individual. While few of us may achieve the proficiency of Isaac Singer or Herbert Hoover, we are all capable of phrasing thoughts clearly and in a well-organized fashion. But learning how to do so takes *practice*.

The one sure way to improve your writing is to write.

One of the toughest but most important jobs in writing is to maintain enthusiasm for your writing project. Such commitment may sometimes be hard to come by, given the difficulties inherent in the writing process, and that can be made worse when the project assigned is unappealing at first glance. How, for example, can you be enthusiastic about having to write a paper analyzing the Lincoln Electric Company when you have never even heard of that firm and can see no sense in analyzing a company you have never heard of before, located in a place you doubt you will ever even visit?

One of the worst mistakes that unpracticed student writers sometimes make is to fail to assume responsibility for keeping themselves interested in their writing. No matter how hard it may seem at first to drum up interest in your topic, *you have to do it*—that is, if you want to write a paper you can be proud of, one that contributes useful material and a fresh point of view to the topic. One thing is guaranteed: if you are bored with your writing, your reader will be, too. So what can you do to keep your interest and energy level high?

Challenge yourself. Think of the paper not as an assignment for a grade, but as a piece of writing that has a *point* to make. To get this point across persuasively is the real reason why you are writing, *not* the simple fact that a teacher has assigned you a project.

> **Question:** If someone were to ask you why you are writing your paper, what would you answer? If your immediate, unthinking response is, "Because I've been given a writing assignment," or "Because I want a good grade," or some other nonanswer along these lines, your paper may be in trouble.
>
> If, on the other hand, your first impulse is to explain the challenge of your main point—"I'm writing to show how one company can exercise leadership throughout its industry and even beyond, no matter what its size or where that company happens to be located"—then you are thinking usefully about your topic.

Maintain Self-confidence

Having a sense of confidence in your ability to write well about your topic is essential for good writing. This does not mean that you will always know what the end result of a particular writing activity will be. In fact, you have to cultivate your ability to tolerate a high degree of uncertainty while weighing evidence, testing hypotheses, experimenting with organizational strategies and wording. Be ready for temporary confusion, for seeming dead ends, and remember that every writer faces these obstacles. It is from your struggle to combine fact with fact, to buttress conjecture with evidence, that order arises.

Do not be intimidated by the amount and quality of work already done in your field of inquiry. The array of opinion and evidence that confronts you in the published literature can be confusing. But remember that no important topic is ever exhausted. *There are always gaps*—questions that have not yet been satisfactorily explored either in the published research on a subject or in the prevailing popular opinion. It is in these gaps that you establish your own authority, your own sense of control.

Remember that the various stages of the writing process reinforce each other. Establishing a solid motivation strengthens your sense of confidence about the project, which in turn influences how successfully you organize and write. If you start out well, using good work habits, and give yourself ample time for the various activities to gel, you should produce a paper that will reflect your best work, one that your audience will find both readable and useful.

1.2 THE WRITING PROCESS

The Nature of the Process

As you engage in the writing process, you are doing many different things at once. While planning, you are no doubt defining the audience for your paper at the same time that you are thinking about the paper's purpose. As you draft the paper, you may organize your next sentence while revising the one you have just written. Different parts of the writing process overlap, and much of the difficulty of writing is that so many things happen at once. Through practice—in other words, through *writing*—it is possible to learn how to control those parts of the process that can be controlled and to encourage those mysterious, less controllable activities.

No two people go about writing in exactly the same way. It is important for you to recognize routines—modes of thought as well as individual exercises—that help you negotiate the process successfully. And it is also important to give yourself as much time as possible to complete the process. Procrastination is one of the writer's greatest enemies. It saps confidence, undermines energy, destroys concentration. Working regularly, keeping as close as possible to a well-thought-out schedule, often makes the difference between a successful paper and an embarrassment.

Although the various parts of the writing process are interwoven, there is naturally a general order to the work you have to do. You have to start somewhere! What follows is a description of the various stages of the writing process—*planning, drafting, revising, editing, proofreading*—along with suggestions about how to get the most out of each.

Planning

Planning includes all activities that lead up to the writing of the first draft. These activities differ from person to person. Some writers, for instance, prefer to compile a formal outline before writing that draft. Some writers perform brief writing exercises to jumpstart their imaginations. Some draw diagrams; some doodle. Later on we'll look at a few individual starting strategies, and you can determine which may be of help to you.

Now, however, let us discuss some early choices that all writers must make about their writing during the planning stage. These choices concern *topic, purpose*, and *audience*, elements helping to make up the *writing context*, the terms under which we all write. Every time you write, even if you are writing a diary entry or a note to the milkman, these elements are present. You may not give conscious consideration to all of them in each piece of writing that you do, but it is extremely important to think carefully about them when writing a business paper. Some or all of these defining elements may be dictated by your assignment, yet you will always have a degree of control over them.

Selecting a Topic

No matter how restrictive an assignment may seem to be, there is no reason to feel trapped by it. Within any assigned subject you can find a range of topics to explore. What you are looking for is a topic that engages your *own* interest. Let your curiosity be your guide. If, for example, in a Human Resources class you have been assigned the subject of employment law, then guide yourself to find some issue concerning employment law that interests you. (How has the requirement under the *Americans With Disabilities Act* that persons with AIDS be hired without discrimination been implemented in such sensitive industries as daycare for children and food services? What is the current status of minorities in the workforce, following 30 years of Affirmative Action?) Any good topic comes with a set of questions; you may well find that your interest picks up if you simply begin asking questions.

One strong recommendation: ask your questions *on paper*. Like most other mental activities, the process of exploring your way through a topic is transformed when you write down your thoughts as they come instead of letting them fly through your mind unrecorded. Remember the old adage from Louis Agassiz: "A pen is often the best of eyes" (1958, 106).

While it is vital to be interested in your topic, you do not have to know much about it at the outset of your investigation. In fact, having too heartfelt a commitment to a topic can be an impediment to writing about it; emotions can get in the way of objectivity. Better often to choose a topic that has piqued your interest yet remained something of a mystery to you: a topic discussed in one of your classes, perhaps, or mentioned on television or in a conversation with friends.

Narrowing a Topic

The task of narrowing your topic offers you a tremendous opportunity to establish a measure of control over the writing project. It is up to you to hone your topic to just the right shape and size to suit both your own interests and the requirements of the assignment. Do a good job of it, and you will go a long way toward guaranteeing yourself sufficient motivation and confidence for the tasks ahead of you. Do it wrong, and somewhere along the way you may find yourself directionless and out of energy.

Generally, the first topics that come to your mind will be too large to handle in your research paper. For example, the topic of business on the World Wide Web has generated a tremendous number of published news articles and reports recently by experts in the field. Despite all the attention turned toward this topic, however, there is still plenty of room for you to investigate it on a level that has real meaning to you and that does not merely recapitulate the published research. What about an analysis of how one new strategy, that of Amazon.com, Inc. <http://www.amazon.com>, an entirely Web based book retailer, is affecting the strategies of its more traditional competitors?

The problem with most topics is not that they are too narrow or too completely explored; it is that they are too rich. There are so many useful ways to address the topic that choosing the best focus is often difficult. Take some time to narrow your topic. Think through the possibilities that occur to you, and, as always, jot down your thoughts.

Narrowing Topics

The following topics were assigned to undergraduate students in a Small Business Management class. Their task was to write a 5-to-10 page report on one of the topics. Following each topic are examples of ways in which students narrowed it to make manageable paper topics.

General Topic	Paper Topic
Franchising	Franchising as an alternative strategy for expansion
Family businesses	Managing the succession process in a family-owned business
Marketing	Small business on the World Wide Web
Financing	Love money: obtaining start-up money from the family

---

Exercise

Without taking time to research them, see what kinds of viable narrowed topics you can make from the following general topics:

corporate takeover defensive strategies	management information systems
franchising	accounting rule changes
employee turnover	affirmative action hiring policies
venture capital	employee compensation
cash management	business valuation

Example:

general topic: venture capital

narrowed topics:
 how venture capital firms are formed
 differing funding criteria of the various types of venture capital firms
 the long-term costs of using venture capital to capitalize a business

---

Finding a Thesis

As you plan, be on the lookout for an *idea* that would serve as your *thesis*. A thesis is not a fact, which can be verified by data, but a hypothesis worth discussing, an argument with more than one possible conclusion. Your thesis sentence will reveal to your reader not only the argument you have chosen, but also your orientation toward it and the conclusion that your paper will attempt to prove.

In looking for a thesis, you are doing many jobs at once:

1. You are limiting the amount and kind of material that you must cover, making it manageable.

2. You are also increasing your own interest in the narrowing field of study.

3. You are working to establish your paper's purpose, the *reason* why you are writing about your topic. (If the only reason you can see for writing is to earn a good grade, then you probably won't!)

4. You are establishing your notion of who your audience is and what sort of approach to the subject might best catch their interest.

In short, you are gaining control over your writing context. For this reason, it is a good idea to come up with a thesis early on, a *working thesis*, which will very probably change as your thinking deepens but which will allow you to establish a measure of order in the planning stage.

The thesis sentence

The introduction of your paper will contain a sentence that expresses the task that your paper intends to accomplish. This *thesis sentence* communicates your main idea, the one you are going to prove or defend or illustrate. It sets up an expectation in the reader's mind that is your job to satisfy. But a thesis sentence is more than just the statement that informs your reader of your goal: it is a valuable tool to help you narrow your focus and confirm in your own mind your paper's purpose.

Developing a Thesis

In a Small Business Management class, students were assigned a 15-page paper to be written on a relevant topic of the student's choice. One student, Tommy Wu, decided to investigate franchising.

Tommy's first working thesis: "Franchising is a common business strategy."

The problem with this thesis, as Tommy quickly found out, was that it was not an idea that could be argued, but a fact easily corroborated by the sources Tommy began to consult. As he read articles from a variety of publications such as *The Wall Street Journal, Inc. Magazine, Business Week,* and various reports on the franchising industry prepared by the Small Business Administration and the Department of Commerce, Tommy began to get interested in the question of just why a business executive would choose to use a franchising strategy rather than simply building company-owned stores as most businesses have traditionally done.

Tommy's second working thesis: "Franchising offers many advantages in support of a rapid expansion strategy."

This thesis narrows the topic somewhat and gives Tommy an opportunity to use material gleaned from his research, but there is still no real comment attached to it. It still states a bare fact, easily proved. At this point, Tommy became interested in the still narrower topic of how franchising agreements often cause conflict, even to the point of litigation, between the franchiser company and disgruntled store owner franchisees. He found that the major issues in contention were the restrictions placed on the franchisees and the often exaggerated claims of profit potential made as an inducement to buy into the organization. As Tommy explored the arguments made by franchisers and franchisees, he began to feel that franchisers derived their most important advantage from their opportunity to deal with relatively unsophisticated business people.

Tommy's third working thesis: "Franchising is the modern version of indentured servitude for the novice business person."

Note how this thesis narrows the focus of Tommy's paper still further than the other two while also presenting an arguable hypothesis. This thesis tells Tommy what he has to do in his paper, just as it tells his reader what to expect.

At some time during your preliminary thinking on a topic, you should consult the library to see how much published work has already been done, and using the CD-ROM based business indexes is a great way to start. These sources can be searched by key word or phrase, and all of them will include an abstract with each listing of a published article or book. Making a preliminary computer search or a more traditional library search offers you at least two benefits:

1. It acquaints you with a body of writing that will become very important in the research phase of the paper.

2. It gives you a sense of how your topic is generally addressed by the community of scholars you are joining. Is the topic as important as you think it is? Has there already been so much research on the topic as to make your inquiry, in its present formulation, irrelevant? These questions can be answered by turning to the literature.

As you go about determining your topic, remember that one goal of business writing in college is to enhance your own understanding of business, to build an accurate model of the way our business systems work and what your role in a system might be, given a choice of business career. Let this goal be a help to you: aim your research into those subject areas that you know are important to your understanding of each of the disciplines of business.

Defining a Purpose

There are many ways to classify the purposes of writing, but, in general, most writing is undertaken either to inform or to persuade an audience. The goal of informative or *expository* writing is, simply, to impart information about a particular subject, while the aim of *persuasive* writing is to convince your reader of your point of view on an issue. The distinction between expository and persuasive writing is not hard and fast. Most writing in business has elements of both exposition and persuasion. Most effective writing, however, has a clearly chosen focus of either exposition or persuasion. Business plans (Chapter 12), for example, are designed to persuade, while case analyses (Chapter 14) are meant to inform. When you begin writing, consciously select a primary aim of exposition or persuasion, and then set out to achieve that goal.

To Explain or to Persuade. . .

Can you tell from the titles of these two papers, both written on the same topic, which is an **expository** and which a **persuasive** paper?

1. Business Law: Twenty Years of Evolution in Principle
2. Whatever Happened to *Caveat Emptor*?

Taking up again the subject of venture capital, let us assume that you have been required to write a paper explaining how venture capital firms operate. If you are writing an expository paper, your task could be to describe in as coherent and impartial way as possible the methods by which each type of venture capital firm is created, how it obtains its investment funds, and then how each type of venture capital firm determines which investments it will make.

If, however, your paper attempts to convince your reader that venture capital firms, through favored treatment under the current law, are positioned to earn obscene profits at the expense of the entrepreneurs who create new businesses, you are now writing to persuade, and your strategy is radically different. Persuasive writing seeks to influence the opinions of its audience toward its subject.

Writing assignments in business classes may blur the distinction between expository and persuasive writing. You may be called upon to analyze the business strategies of a firm, evaluate the impact of newly implemented government programs or laws, speculate on the future impact of the NAFTA Treaty, identify or define problems within a range of fields, suggest solutions, and predict results. It is very important to spend planning time sharpening your sense of purpose.

Learn what you want to say. By the time of your final draft, you must have a very sound notion of the point you wish to argue. If, as you write that final draft, someone were to ask you to state your thesis, you should be able to give a satisfactory answer with a minimum of delay and no prompting. If, on the other hand, you have to hedge your answer because you cannot easily express your thesis, you may not yet be ready to write a final draft. You may have to write a draft or two or engage in various prewriting activities in order to arrive at a secure understanding of your task.

Question: Two writers have been asked to state the thesis of their papers. Which writer better understands the writing task?

Writer 1: "My paper is about the North American Trade Agreement."

Writer 2: "My paper argues that the North American Trade Agreement will inevitably reduce the average standard of living of citizens of both the U.S. and Canada, to the benefit of the citizens of Mexico."

Watch out for bias! There is no such thing as pure objectivity. You are not a machine. No matter how hard you may try to produce an objective paper, the fact is that every choice you make as you write is influenced to some extent by your personal beliefs and opinions. What you tell your readers is *truth* is influenced, sometimes without your knowing, by a multitude of factors: your environment, upbringing, and education; your attitude toward your audience; your political affiliation; your race and gender; your career goals and your ambitions for the paper you are writing. The influence such factors produce can be very subtle, and it is something you must work to identify in your own writing as well as in the writing of others in order not to mislead or be misled. Remember that one of the reasons why you write is *self-discovery.* The writing you will do in business classes—as well as the writing you will do for the rest of your life—will give you a chance to discover and confront honestly your own views on your subjects. Responsible writers keep an eye on their own biases and are honest with their readers about them.

Defining Your Audience

In any class that requires writing from you, it may sometimes be difficult to remember that the point of your writing is not simply to jump through the technical hoops imposed by the assignment. The point is *communication*—the transmission of your knowledge and your conclusions to the reader in a way that suits you. Your task is to pass to your reader the spark of your own enthusiasm for your topic. Readers who were indifferent to your topic should look at it in a new way after reading your paper. This is the great challenge of writing: to enter into your reader's mind and leave behind new knowledge, new questions.

It is tempting to think that most writing problems would be solved if the writer could view the writing as if it had been produced by another person. The discrepancy between the understanding of the writer and that of the audience is the single greatest impediment to accurate communication. To overcome this barrier you must consider your audience's needs. By the time you begin drafting, most if not all of your ideas have begun to attain coherent shape in your mind, so that virtually any words in which you try to phrase those ideas will reflect your thought accurately—*to you.* Your reader, however, does not already have in mind the conclusions that you have so painstakingly achieved. If you omit from your writing the material that is necessary to complete your readers' understanding of your argument, they may well not be able to supply that information themselves.

The potential for misunderstanding is present for any audience, whether it is made up of general readers, experts in the field, or your professor, who is reading, in part, to see how well you have mastered the constraints that govern the relationship between writer and reader. Make your presentation as complete as possible, bearing in mind your audience's knowledge of your topic.

Know Your Audience

LEE IACOCCA FOR PRESIDENT!

Primarily because of his role in orchestrating the federal bailout of Chrysler Corporation during the mid-1980s, Lee Iacocca became very well known. Many people came to identify with Iacocca and his down-home, no-nonsense ideas about business and government. By 1988 he had received over 10,000 letters urging him to run for president. His response to his would-be supporters was a gracious decline, but no matter what he said about his intentions to run, his supporters couldn't seem to get the message.

> At first, the more I said I would not run, the more they said I must be running. I tried all kinds of responses. I started with General Sherman—you know: "If nominated I will not accept; if elected I will not serve." All that brought was lots of cartoons of me sitting in a Sherman tank making the proclamation. Then I said I would like to be President, but only if I were appointed. Real smartass! That didn't work. I tried "The only thing I'm running for is my life." That didn't work either. Then I really messed up. I began telling audiences I wouldn't run because I'm not a politician. The audiences leaped to their feet and applauded like crazy. That's exactly what they wanted—a nonpolitician. I dropped that line in a hurry. Next, I appeared on the same program as Dr. Ruth. I touted her as my running mate. I said we'd make a terrific ticket—I'd tell them what to do, and she'd tell them how! (Iacocca 1989, 285)

MESSAGES IN INTERNATIONAL MARKETING

When American soft drink companies first began to market their drinks overseas, they frequently found out just how much difference there was in the interpretations those from a different culture placed on their advertising messages. Coca-Cola found out that their slogan "Come Alive," translated into some languages, means "Arise From the Dead!" Even the colors used in their advertisements had a profound effect. In Hong Kong and The People's Republic of China, white symbolizes death, but in Brazil, the symbolic color for death is purple. (Dunn and Barban 1986, 770).

Invention Strategies

We have discussed methods of selecting and narrowing the topic of a paper. As your focus on a specific topic sharpens, you naturally begin to think about the kinds of information that will go into the paper. In the case of papers not requiring formal research, that material comes largely from your own recollections. Indeed, one of the reasons why instructors assign such papers is to convince you of the incredible richness of your memory, the vastness and variety of the "database" you have accumulated and which, moment by moment, you continue to build.

So vast is your horde of information that it can sometimes be difficult to find within it the material that would best suit your paper. In other words, finding out what you already know about a topic is not always easy. *Invention*, a term borrowed from classical rhetoric, refers to the task of discovering, or recovering from memory, such information. As we write, all of us go through some sort of invention procedure that helps us explore our topic. Some writers seem to have little problem coming up with material; others need more help. Over the centuries writers have devised different exercises that can help locate useful material housed in memory. We shall look at a few of these briefly.

Freewriting

Freewriting is an activity that forces you to get something down on paper. There is no waiting around for inspiration. Instead, you set yourself a time limit—three minutes, five minutes—and write for that length of time *without stopping*, not even to lift the pen from the paper or your hands from the keyboard. You can freewrite on a typewriter or a computer. Focus on the topic, and don't let the difficulty of finding relevant material stop you from writing. If necessary, you may begin by writing, over and over, some seemingly useless phrase, like, "I cannot think of anything to write about," or, perhaps, the name of your topic. Eventually, something else will occur to you. (It is surprising how long a three-minute freewriting can seem to last!) At the end of the freewriting, look over what you have produced for anything you might be able to use. Much of the writing will be unusable, but there may be an insight or two that you did not know you possessed.

In addition to its ability to recover usable material for your paper, freewriting has a couple of other benefits attached to it. First, it takes little time, which means you may repeat the exercise as often as you like. Second, it breaks down some of the resistance that stands between you and the act of writing. There is no initial struggle to find something to say; you just *write*.

Freewriting

The teacher in Sally Hernandez' Fundamentals of Management class assigned her a paper to write focusing on some aspect of family-owned businesses. Sally, who felt her understanding of the topic was slight, tried to get her mind started on the job of finding a topic that interested her with a three-minute freewriting. Thinking about family businesses, Sally wrote steadily for three minutes without lifting her pen from the paper. Here is the result of her freewriting:

Well, let's see — How common are family businesses? Do I know any?? Do the members get along? I bet my brother and I wouldn't. Is there freeloading by some black sheep? Do some kids rebel? Seems like they might if dad is a tyrant. They also seem to have it pretty good; the whiners. I would like it a lot if I stood to inherit. How does this nepotism affect the non-family members? If junior is coming through the ranks, can an outsider ever hope to get the good positions in such a business? How do the girls in the family fare? Wonder how many women run family-owned businesses?

Brainstorming

Brainstorming is simply making a list of ideas about a topic. It can be done quickly and at first without any need to order items into a coherent pattern. The point is to write down everything that occurs to you quickly and as briefly as possible, using individual words or short phrases. Once you have a good-sized list of items, you can group them according to relationships that you see among them. Brainstorming, then, allows you to uncover both ideas stored in your memory and useful associations among those ideas.

Brainstorming

A professor in a marketing class asked his students to write a 700-word paper describing a comprehensive new strategy for marketing snack food items to college students. Ann Mathias, a student in the class, started thinking about the assignment by brainstorming. First, she simply wrote down anything that occurred to her:

Marketing Snack Foods to Students

chips and candy	healthy foods	vending options
soda pop	beer!	international students
servicing distribution points	manned counters	hours of operation
sources of supply	prices	competition
getting the word out	sanitation	refunds and exchanges
getting permission to enter	where to locate	special promotions

Thinking through her list, Ann decded to rearrange it into the four elements of the marketing mix: product, price, place, and promotion. At this point she decided to discard some items that were redundant or did not seem to have much potential. As you can see, Ann had some questions about where some of her items would fit.

Product

chips and candy

healthy foods

soda pop

beer ?

international students' preferences

vending options ?

competition ?

Price

prices

competition ?

refunds and exchanges

Place (Distribution)

serving distribution points

manned counters

hours of operation

getting permission to enter

where to locate

vending options

competition ?

Promotion

getting the word out

vending options ?

competition ?

At this point, Ann decided that her strongest inclination was to explore the strategy of installing portable manned carts offering healthy snack items in several convenient locations across campus.

Asking Questions

It is always possible to ask most or all of the following questions about any topic: *Who? What? When? Where? Why? How?* These questions force you to approach the topic as a journalist does, setting it within different perspectives which can then be compared.

Asking Questions

For a class in labor relations, a professor asked her class to write a paper describing the impact of right-to-work-laws on the unionizing efforts of the major industrial unions. Here are some questions that a student in the class might logically ask to begin thinking toward a thesis.

> *Who* is represented by the unions, who are the union leaders?
>
> *What* are the primary and secondary goals of the unions?
>
> *What*, exactly, do the right-to-work laws prohibit and allow?
>
> *When* did these laws first begin to be enacted?
>
> *Where* are the right-to work states? (Is there a geographical pattern that could help explain why some states have chosen to enact these laws while others have not?)
>
> *How* have the laws worked out where they have been in effect for some time? (How have the union membership levels and the numbers of closed shops fared under right-to-work?)
>
> *When* might the right-to-work laws become universal, if ever? (When might the forces pushing the enactment of right-to-work laws become weakened and the trend reverse?)
>
> *Why* do states choose to pass right-to-work laws? (What is their goal in doing so? Do they achieve their goals?)
>
> *Who* is pushing for right-to-work? (And who is against it, other than the unions, of course?)

Can you think of other questions that would make for useful inquiry?

Maintaining Flexibility

As you engage in invention strategies you are also performing other writing tasks. You are still narrowing your topic, for example, as well as making decisions that will affect your choice of tone or audience. You move forward on all fronts, each decision you make influencing the others. This means you must be flexible enough in your understanding of the paper's development to allow for slight course adjustments, alterations in your understanding of your goal. Never be so determined to prove a particular theory that you fail to notice when your own understanding of it changes. *Stay objective.*

Organizing Your Writing

A paper that has all the facts but gives them to the reader in an ineffective order will confuse rather than inform or persuade. While there are various methods of grouping ideas, none is potentially more effective than outlining. Unfortunately, no organizing process is more often misunderstood.

Outlining for Yourself

There are really two jobs that outlining can do. First, it can serve as a means of forcing you, the writer, to gain a better understanding of your ideas by arranging them according to their interrelationships. There is one primary rule of outlining: ideas of equal weight are placed on the same level within the outline. This rule requires you to determine the relative importance of your ideas. You have to decide which ideas are of the same type or order and into which subtopic each idea best fits.

If, in the planning stage, you carefully arrange your ideas in a coherent outline, your own grasp of your topic will be greatly enhanced. You will have linked your ideas logically together and given a skeleton to the body of the paper. This sort of subordinating and coordinating activity is difficult, however, and sometimes inexperienced writers begin to write their first draft without an effective outline, hoping for the best. That hope is usually unfulfilled, especially in complex papers involving research.

Organizing Thoughts

Scott, a student in an entrepreneurship class, researched the phenomenon of women entrepreneurs and came up with the following facts and theories. Number them in logical order.

❑ A growing number of women have been entering the formal workplace during the past 20 years.

❑ Changing social roles and economic imperatives have reduced the ability of women to stay home with their children.

❑ The Small Business Administration formally issued guidelines favoring women and minorities in their applications for services, during the early 1980s.

❑ College and University schools of business have seen enrollments in traditionally all-male disciplines completely reversed in gender. This is especially true in accounting and human relations courses.

❑ The economy is becoming more global and more competitive.

Outlining for Your Reader

The second job that an outline does is to serve as a reader's blueprint to the paper, summarizing its points and their interrelationships. A busy policymaker can quickly get a sense of your paper's goal and the argument you have used to promote it by consulting your outline. The clarity and coherence of the outline helps to determine how much attention your audience will give to your ideas.

Your instructors in your business classes will give you a great deal of help with the arrangement of your material into an outline to accompany your paper. Sometimes, as in the formal case analysis presented in Chapter 14, a pre-formatted outline will be provided. But while you must pay close attention to the requirements of the accompanying outline, do not forget how powerful a tool an outline can be in the early planning stages of your paper.

Formal Outline Pattern

Following this pattern accurately during the planning stage of your paper helps to guarantee that your ideas are placed logically:

Thesis sentence (prefaces the organized outline)

I. First main idea
   A. First subordinate idea
      1. Reason, example, or illustration
      2. Reason, example, or illustration
         a. Detail supporting reason #2
         b. Detail supporting reason #2
         c. Detail supporting reason #2
   B. Second subordinate idea
II. Second main idea

Notice that each level of the paper must have more than one entry; for every *A* there must be at least a *B* (and, if required, a *C, D,* etc.), and for every *1* there must be a *2*. This arrangement forces you to *compare ideas*, looking carefully at each one to determine its place among the others. The insistence on assigning relative values to your ideas is what makes your outline an effective organizing tool.

The Patterns of Business Papers

The structure of any particular type of business paper is governed by a formal pattern. When rigid external controls are placed on their writing, some writers tend to feel that their creativity is impeded by a kind of "paint-by-numbers" approach to structure. It is vital to the success of your paper that you never allow yourself to be overwhelmed by the pattern rules for a particular type of paper. Remember that such controls are placed on papers not to limit your creativity but to make the paper immediately and easily useful to its intended audience. It is as necessary to write clearly and confidently in a business plan or an article critique as in a term paper for English literature, a résumé, a short story, or a job application letter.

Drafting

The Rough Draft

After the planning comes the writing of the first draft. Using your thesis and outline as direction markers, you must now weave your amalgam of ideas, researched data, and persuasion strategies into logically ordered sentences and paragraphs. Though adequate prewriting may facilitate the drafting, it still will not be easy. Writers establish their own individual methods of encouraging themselves to forge ahead with the draft, but here are some tips to bear in mind.

1. Remember that this is a *rough draft*, not the final draft. At this stage, it is not necessary that every word you write be the best possible choice. Do not put that sort of pressure on yourself; you must not allow anything to slow you down now. Writing is not like sculpting in stone, where every chip is permanent; you can always go back to your draft later and add, delete, reword, rearrange. *No matter how much effort you have put into planning, you cannot be sure how much of this first draft you will eventually keep.* It may take several drafts to get one that you find satisfactory.

2. Give yourself sufficient time to write. Don't delay the first draft by telling yourself there is still more research to do. You cannot uncover all the material there is to know on a particular subject, so don't fool yourself into trying. Remember that writing is a process of discovery. You may have to begin writing before you can see exactly what sort of final research you need to do. Remember that there are other tasks waiting for you after the first draft is finished, so allow time for them as you determine your writing schedule.

It is also very important to give yourself time to write because the more time that passes after you write a draft, the better your ability to view it with greater objectivity. It is very difficult to evaluate your writing accurately soon after you complete it. You need to cool down, to recover from the effort of putting all those words together. The "colder" you get on your writing, the better able you are to read it as if it were written by someone else and thus acknowledge the changes you will need to make to strengthen the paper.

3. *Stay sharp*. It is important to keep in mind the plan you created for yourself as you narrowed your topic, composed a thesis sentence, and outlined the material. But if you begin feel a strong need to change the plan a bit, do not be afraid to do so. Be ready for surprises dealt you by your own growing understanding of your topic. Your goal is to record your best thinking on the subject as accurately as possible.

Language Choices

To be convincing, your writing has to be *authoritative*. That is, you have to sound as if you have complete confidence in your ability to convey your ideas in words. Sentences that sound stilted or suffer from weak phrasing or the use of clichés are not going to win supporters for the aims that you express in your paper. So a major question becomes: How can I sound confident?

Here are some points to consider as your work to convey to your reader that necessary sense of authority.

Level of formality

Tone is one of the primary methods by which you signal to the reader who you are and what your attitude is toward him and toward your topic. Your major decision is which level of language formality is most appropriate to your audience. The informal tone you would use in a letter to a friend might well be out of place in a paper on "Decision Support Systems" written for your management information systems professor. Remember that tone is only part of the overall decision that you make about how to present your information. Formality is, to some extent, a function of individual word choices and phrasing. Is it appropriate to use contractions like *isn't* or *they'll*? Would the strategic use of a sentence fragment for effect be out of place? The use of informal language, the personal *I*, and the second person *you* is traditionally forbidden—for better or worse—in certain kinds of writing. Often part of the challenge of writing a formal paper is simply how to give your prose impact while staying within the conventions.

Jargon

One way to lose readers quickly is to overwhelm them with jargon—phrases that have a special, usually technical meaning within your discipline but which are unfamiliar to the average reader. The very occasional use of jargon may add an effective touch of atmosphere, but anything more than that will severely dampen a reader's enthusiasm for the paper. Often a writer uses jargon in an effort to impress the reader by sounding lofty or knowledgeable. Unfortunately, all jargon usually does is cause confusion. In fact, the use of jargon usually indicates the writer's lack of connection to his audience.

Business writing is a haven for jargon. Perhaps writers of annual stockholder reports and business plans believe their readers are all completely attuned to their terminology. It may be that these writers occasionally hope to obscure damaging information or potentially risky strategies in confusing language. Or the problem could simply be fuzzy thinking on the writer's part. Whatever the reason, the fact is that business papers too often sound like prose made by machines to be read by machines.

Students may feel that, in order to be accepted as business professionals, their papers should conform to the practices of their published peers. *This is a mistake.* Remember that it is *never* better to write a cluttered or confusing sentence than a clear one, and that burying your ideas in jargon defeats the effort that you went through to form them.

Spot the Jargon

What words in the following sentence, from a published book on the stock market, are jargon? Can you rewrite the sentence to clarify its meaning?

> The rise of the over-the-counter exchange has brought thousands of secondary issues that were once traded by the obscure "pink sheet" method—where you never knew if you were getting a fair price—into a reliable and efficient computerized marketplace. (Lynch 1989, 286)

Clichés

In the heat of composition, as you are looking for words to help you form your ideas, it is sometimes easy to plug in a *cliché*—a phrase that has attained universal recognition by overuse. (*Note*: Clichés differ from jargon in that clichés are part of the general public's everyday language, while jargon is specific to the language of experts in a particular field.) Our vocabularies are brimming with clichés:

It's raining *cats and dogs*.

That issue is *dead as a doornail*.

It's time for the plant manager to *face the music*.

Angry voters *made a beeline* for the ballot box.

The problem with clichés is that they are virtually meaningless. Once colorful means of expression, they have lost their color through overuse, and they tend to bleed energy and color from the surrounding words. When revising, replace clichés with fresh wording that more accurately conveys your point.

Descriptive language

Language that appeals to readers' senses will always engage their interest more fully than language that is abstract. This is especially important for writing in disciplines that tend to deal in abstracts, such as finance, management information systems, and business law. The typical business paper, with its discussions of abstract theory, strategic alternatives, or points of law, is usually in danger of floating off on a cloud of abstractions, with each paragraph drifting farther away from the felt life of the reader. Whenever appropriate, appeal to your readers' sense of sight, hearing, taste, touch, or smell.

Which of These Two Sentences Is More Effective?

1. The report by the OSHA inspection team noted several serious violations.
2. The report by the OSHA inspection team noted that (1) the air in the plant was nearly unbreathable and burned the eyes, (2) a forklift truck carrying 20,000 pounds of scrap metal had tipped precariously as it rattled through a pothole in the floor, and (3) two employees had been hospitalized in the past year for receiving electrical shocks from ungrounded receptacles.

Sexist language

Language can be a very powerful method of either reinforcing or destroying cultural stereotypes. By treating the sexes in subtly different ways in your language, you may unknowingly be committing an act of discrimination. A common example is the use of the pronoun *he* to refer to a person whose gender has not been identified. Some writers, faced with the pronoun dilemma illustrated above, alternate the use of male and female personal pronouns; others use the plural to avoid the need to use a pronoun of either gender:

> SEXIST: A manager should always treat his employees with respect.
> NONSEXIST: A manager should always treat his or her employees with respect.
> NONSEXIST: Managers should always treat their employees with respect.

> SEXIST: Man is a political animal.
> NONSEXIST: People are political animals.

Remember that language is more than the mere vehicle of your thought. Your words shape perceptions for your reader. How *well* you say something will profoundly affect your reader's response to *what* you say. Sexist language denies to a large number of your readers the basic right to fair and equal treatment. Make sure your writing is not guilty of this subtle form of discrimination.

Revising

Revising is one of the most important steps in assuring that your essay is a success. While unpracticed writers often think of revision as little more than making sure all the *i*'s are dotted and *t*'s are crossed, it is much more than that. Revising is *reseeing* the essay, looking at it from other perspectives, trying always to align your view with the view that will be held by your audience. Research in composition indicates that we are actually revising all the time, in every phase of the writing process as we reread phrases, rethink the placement of a item in an outline, or test a new topic sentence for a paragraph. Subjecting your entire hard-fought draft to cold, objective scrutiny is one of the hardest activities to master in the writing process, but it is absolutely necessary. You have to make sure that you have said everything that needs to be said clearly and in logical order. One confusing passage, and the reader's attention is deflected from where you want it to be. Suddenly the reader has to become a detective, trying to figure out why you wrote what you did and what you meant by it. You don't want to throw such obstacles in the path of understanding.

Here are some tips to help you with revision.

1. ***Give yourself adequate time for revision.*** As discussed above, you need time to become "cold" on your paper in order to analyze it objectively. After you have written your draft, spend some time away from it. Try to reread it as if it had been written by someone other than yourself.

2. ***Read the paper carefully.*** This is tougher than it sounds. One good strategy is to read it aloud or to have a friend read it aloud while you listen. (Note, however, that friends are usually not the best critics. They are rarely trained in revision techniques and are often unwilling to risk disappointing you by giving your paper a really thorough examination.)

3. ***Have a list of specific items to check.*** It is important to revise in an orderly fashion, in stages, looking first at large concerns, such as the overall structure, then rereading the paper for problems with smaller elements such as paragraph organization or sentence structure.

4. ***Check for unity*** — the clear and logical relation of all parts of the essay to its thesis. Make sure that every paragraph relates well to the whole of the paper and is in the right place.

5. ***Check for coherence.*** Make sure there are no gaps between the different parts of the argument. Look to see that you have adequate *transition* everywhere it is needed. Transitional elements are markers indicating places where the paper's focus or attitude changes. Transitional elements can be one word long — *however, although, unfortunately, luckily* — or as long as a sentence or a paragraph: *In order to fully appreciate the importance of honoring a rigid seniority system of promotion, it is necessary to examine briefly the history of the unions' battle with management for the right to represent workers.*

   Transitional elements rarely introduce new material. Instead, they are direction pointers, either indicating a shift to new subject matter or signaling how the writer wishes certain material to be interpreted by the reader. Because you, the writer, already know where and why your paper changes direction and how you want particular passages to be received, it can be very difficult for you to catch those places in your paper where transition is needed.

6. ***Avoid unnecessary repetition.*** There are two types of repetition that can annoy a reader, repetition of content and repetition of wording.

   Repetition of content occurs when you return to a subject that you have already discussed. Ideally, you should deal with a topic *once*, memorably, and then move on to your next topic. Organizing a paper is a difficult task, however, that usually occurs through a process of enlightenment in terms of purposes and strategies, and repetition of content can happen even if you have made use of prewriting strategies. What is worse, it can be difficult for you to be aware of the repetition in your own writing. As you write and revise, remember that any unnecessary repetition of content in your final draft is potentially annoying to your readers, who are working to make sense of the argument they are reading and do not want to be distracted by a passage repeating material they have already encountered. You must train yourself, through practice, to look for material that you have repeated unnecessarily.

   Repetition of wording occurs when you overuse certain phrases or words. This can make your prose sound choppy and uninspired, as the following examples demonstrate:

   The AICPA's report on accounting reform will surprise a number of people. A number of people will want copies of the report.

The chairman said at a press conference that he is happy with the last quarter's production level. He will circulate the news to the local news agencies in the morning. He will also make sure that the city planning commission has copies.

I became upset when I heard how the committee had voted. I called the chairman and expressed my reservations about the committee's decision. I told him I felt that he had let the teachers and students of the state down. I also issued a press statement.

The last passage illustrates a condition known by composition teachers as the *I-syndrome.* Can you hear how such duplicated phrasing can hurt a paper? Your language should sound fresh and energetic. Before you turn in your final draft, be sure to read through your paper carefully, looking for such repetition.

Not all repetition is bad, however. You may wish to repeat a phrase for rhetorical effect or special emphasis: *I came. I saw. I conquered.* Just make sure that any repetition in your paper is intentional, placed there to produce a specific effect.

Editing

Editing is sometimes confused with the more involved process of revising. But editing happens later, after you have wrestled through your first draft—and maybe your second and third—and arrived at the final draft. Even though your draft now contains all the information you want to impart and has arranged the information to your satisfaction, there are still many factors to check, such as sentence structure, spelling, and punctuation.

It is at this point that an unpracticed writer might be less than vigilant. After all, most of the work on the paper is finished, since the "big jobs" of discovering material and organizing and drafting it have been completed. *But watch out!* Editing is as important as any other part of the writing process. Any error which you allow in the final draft will count against you in the mind of the reader. This may not seem fair, but even a minor error—a misspelling or the confusing placement of a comma—will make a much greater impression on your reader than perhaps it should. Remember: everything about your paper is *your* responsibility, including performing even the supposedly little jobs right. Careless editing undermines the effectiveness of your paper. It would be a shame if all the hard work you put into prewriting, drafting, and revising were to be damaged because you carelessly allowed a comma splice!

Most of the tips given above for revising hold for editing as well. It is best to edit in stages, looking for only one or two kinds of errors each time you reread the paper. Focus especially on errors that you remember committing in the past. If, for instance, you know you have a tendency to misplace commas, go through your paper looking at each comma carefully. If you have a weakness for writing unintentional sentence fragments, read each sentence aloud to make sure that it is indeed a complete sentence. Have you accidentally shifted verb tenses anywhere, moving from past to present tense for no reason? Do all the subjects in your sentences agree in number with their verbs? Now is the time to find out.

Watch out for *miscues*—problems with a sentence that the writer simply does not see. Remember that your search for errors is hampered in two ways:

1. As the writer, you hope *not* to find any errors with your writing. This desire can cause you to miss mistakes when they do occur.

2. Since you know your material so well, it is easy, as you read, to unconsciously supply missing material — a word, a piece of punctuation — as if it is present.

How difficult is it to see that something is missing in the following sentence:

> Unfortunately, business leaders often have too little regard their customers.

We can guess that the missing word is probably *for*, which should be inserted after *regard*. It is quite possible, however, that the writer of the sentence, as he reads it, will supply the missing *for* automatically, as if it were on the page. This is a miscue, which can be hard for writers to spot because they are so close to their material.

Editing is the stage where you finally answer those minor questions that you put off earlier when you were wrestling with wording and organization. Any ambiguities regarding the use of abbreviations, italics, numerals, capital letters, titles (When do you capitalize the title "president," for example?), hyphens, dashes (usually created on a typewriter or computer by striking the hyphen key twice), apostrophes, and quotation marks have to be cleared up now. You must also check to see that you have used the required formats for footnotes, endnotes, margins, and page numbers.

Guessing is not allowed. Sometimes unpracticed writers who realize that they don't quite understand a particular rule of grammar, punctuation, or format often do nothing to fill that knowledge gap. Instead they rely on guesswork and their own logic — which is not always up to the task of dealing with so contrary a language as English — to get them through problems that they could solve if only they referred to a writing manual. Remember that it does not matter to the reader why or how an error shows up in your writing. It only matters that you have dropped your guard. You must not allow a careless error to undo the good work that you have done.

In business the stakes are often very high. If the readers of the business plan you have written in support of your application for a $750,000 loan stumble across a grammatical error in your executive summary, their opinion of you may be so damaged as to tip the delicate balance of their judgment to reject your loan request.

Catching Mistakes

One tactic for catching mistakes in sentence structure is to read the sentences aloud, starting with the last one in the paper and then moving to the next-to-last, then the previous sentence, thus going backward through the paper (reading each sentence in the normal, left-to-right manner, of course) until you reach the first sentence of the introduction. This backwards progression strips each sentence of its rhetorical context and helps you to focus on its internal structure.

Proofreading

Before you hand in your final version of the paper, it is vital that you check it over one more time to make sure there are no errors of any sort. This job is called *proofreading* or *proofing*. In essence, you are looking for many of the same things you checked for during editing, but now you are doing it on the last draft, which is about to be submitted to your audience. Proofreading is as important as editing: you may have missed an error that you still have time to find, or an error may have been introduced when the draft was recopied or typed for the last time. Like every other stage of the writing process, proofreading is your responsibility.

At this point, you must check for typing mistakes: transposed or deleted letters, words, phrases, or punctuation. If you have had the paper professionally typed, you still must check it carefully. Do not rely solely on the typist's proofreading. If you are creating your paper on a computer or a word processor, it is possible for you unintentionally to insert a command that alters your document drastically by slicing out a word, line, or sentence at the touch of a key. Make sure such accidental deletions have not occurred.

Above all else, remember that your paper represents you. It is a product of your best thought, your most energetic and imaginative response to a writing challenge. If you have maintained your enthusiasm for the project and worked through the different stages of the writing process honestly and carefully, you should produce a paper you can be proud of, one that will serve its readers well.

CHAPTER 2

Writing Competently

2.1 GRAMMAR AND STYLE

The Competent Writer

Good writing places your thoughts in your reader's mind in exactly the way you want them to be there. Good writing tells your reader just what you want her to know without telling her anything you do not wish to say. That may sound odd, but the fact is, writers have to be careful not to let unwanted messages to slip into their writing. Look, for example, at the passage below, taken from a paper analyzing the impact of a worker-retraining program in the writer's state. Hidden within the prose is a message which jeopardizes the paper's success. Can you detect the message?

What's Wrong Here?

Recent articles written on the subject of dislocated workers have had little to say about the particular problems dealt with in this paper. Since few of these articles focus on the problem at the state level.

Chances are, when you reached the end of the second "sentence," you sensed something missing, a gap in logic or coherence, and your eye ran back through both sentences to find the place where things went wrong. The second sentence is actually not a sentence at all. It does have certain features of a sentence—a subject, for example ("few"), and a verb ("focus")—but its first word ("Since") *subordinates* the entire clause that follows, taking away its ability to stand on its own as a complete idea. The second "sentence," which is properly called a *subordinate clause*, merely fills in some information about the first sentence, telling us *why* recent articles about dislocated workers fail to deal with problems discussed in the present paper.

The sort of error represented by the second "sentence" is commonly called a sentence *fragment*, and it conveys to the reader a message that no writer wants to send: that the writer either is careless or—worse—has not mastered the language he is using. Language errors such as fragments, misplaced commas, or shifts in verb tense cause the reader to lose concentration. The writing loses effectiveness.

Remember: Whatever goal you set for your paper, whether you want it to persuade, describe, analyze, or speculate, you must also set another goal: *to display lan-*

guage competence. Without it, your paper will not completely achieve its other aims. Language errors spread doubt like a virus; they jeopardize all the hard work you have done on your paper.

You Say "Potato", Quayle Says "Potatoe"

Anyone who doubts that language competence is important should remember the beating that Dan Quayle took in the press when he was Vice President of the United States for misspelling the word "potato" at a Trenton, New Jersey, spelling bee on 15 June 1992. His error caused a storm of humiliating publicity for the hapless Quayle, adding to an impression of his general incompetence.

Correctness Is Relative

Although they may seem minor, the fact is that the sort of language errors we are discussing—which are often called *surface errors*—can be extremely damaging in certain kinds of writing. Surface errors come in a variety of types, including misspellings, punctuation problems, grammar errors, and the inconsistent use of abbreviations, capitalization, or numerals. These errors are an affront to your reader's notion of correctness—and therein lies one of the biggest problems with surface errors. Different audiences tolerate different levels of correctness. You already know that you can get away with surface errors in a letter to a friend, who will not judge you harshly for them, while those same errors in a job application letter might eliminate you from consideration for the job. Correctness depends to an extent upon context.

Another problem with correctness is that the rules governing correctness shift over time. Certain language practices that would have been considered errors by your grandparents' generation—the splitting of an infinitive, for example, or the ending of a sentence with a preposition—are taken in stride today by most readers.

So how do you write correctly when the rules shift from person to person and over time? Here are some tips.

Consider Your Audience

One of the great risks of writing is that even the simplest of choices you make regarding wording or punctuation can sometimes prejudice your audience against you in ways that may seem unfair.

For example, look again at the old grammar "rule" forbidding the splitting of infinitives. After decades of counseling students *to **never** split* an infinitive (something this sentence has just done), composition experts now concede that a split infinitive is *not* a grammar crime. But suppose you have written a business plan trying to convince your client's board of directors of the need to expand production in a certain area and half the board members—the people you wish to convince—remember their eighth-grade grammar teacher's outdated warning about splitting infinitives. How will they respond when you tell them, in your introduction, that the expansion you are proposing is necessary *to **eventually** expand* sales in new markets? How much of their attention have you suddenly lost because of their automatic recollection of a non-rule? It is possible, in other words, to write correctly and still offend your readers' notions of language competence.

Make sure that you tailor the surface features of your writing to the level of competency that your readers require. When in doubt, take a conservative approach. The same goes for the level of formality you should assume. Your audience might be just as distracted by contractions as by a split infinitive.

Aim for Consistency

When dealing with a language question for which there are different answers—such as whether or not to place a comma after the second item in a series of three ("The manager's speech addressed absenteeism, sales reports, and the hiring situation.")—always use the same strategy. If, for example, you avoid splitting one infinitive, avoid splitting *all* infinitives in your paper.

Have Confidence in What You Already Know About Writing!

It is easy for unpracticed writers to allow their occasional mistakes to depress them about their writing ability. The fact is, most of what we know about writing is right. We are all capable, for example, of phrasing utterances that are grammatically sound, even if we cannot list the grammar rules by which we achieve coherence. Most writers who worry about their chronic errors have fewer than they think. Becoming distressed about errors makes writing more difficult.

Grammar

As various composition theorists have pointed out, the word "grammar" has several definitions. One meaning for grammar is "the formal patterns in which words must be arranged in order to convey meaning." We learn these patterns very early in life and use them spontaneously without thinking about them. Our understanding of grammatical patterns is extremely sophisticated, despite the fact that few of us can actually cite the rules by which the patterns work. Patrick Hartwell tested grammar learning by asking native English speakers of different ages and levels of education, including high school teachers, to arrange these words in natural order:

| French | the | young | girls | four |

Everyone he asked could produce the natural order for this phrase: "the four young French girls." Yet none of Hartwell's respondents said they knew the rule that governs the order of the words (Hartwell 1985, 111).

Eliminate Chronic Errors

If just thinking about our errors has a negative effect on our writing, then how do we learn to write more correctly? Perhaps the best answer is simply to write as often as possible. Give yourself practice in putting your thoughts into written shape, and get lots of practice in revising and proofing your work. And as you write and revise, be honest with yourself—and be patient. Chronic errors are like bad habits; getting rid of them takes time.

You probably know of one or two problem areas in your writing that you could have eliminated but have not done so. Instead, you have "fudged" your writing at the critical points, relying upon half-remembered formulas from past English classes or trying to come up with logical solutions to your writing problems. (*Warning:* The English language does not always work in a way that seems logical.) You simply may have decided that comma rules are unlearnable or that you will never understand the difference between the verbs *lay* and *lie*. And so you guess, and get the rule wrong a good part of the time. What a shame, when just a little extra work would give you mastery over those few gaps in your understanding and boost your confidence as well.

Instead of continuing with this sort of guesswork, instead of living with the gaps, why not face the problem areas now and learn the rules that have heretofore escaped you? What follows is a discussion of those surface features of a paper where errors most commonly occur. You will probably be familiar with most if not all of the rules discussed, but there may be a few you have not yet mastered. Now is the time to do so.

2.2 PUNCTUATION

Apostrophes

An apostrophe is used to show possession; when you wish to say that something belongs to someone or to another thing, you add either an apostrophe and an s or an apostrophe alone to the word that represents the owner.

When the owner is *singular* (a single person or thing), the apostrophe precedes an added *s*:

> According to President Anderson*'s* secretary, the news broadcast has been canceled.
>
> The union*'s* lawyers challenged the company*'s* policy in court.
>
> Somebody*'s* briefcase was left in the auditorium.

The same rule applies if the word showing possession is a plural that does not end in *s*:

> The women*'s* club sponsored several student interns in local firms.
>
> Children*'s* rights to a safe workplace in the Far East has recently become a hot issue.

When the word expressing ownership is a *plural* ending in *s*, the apostrophe follows the *s*:

> The new vice president was discussed at the secretarie*s'* luncheon.

There are two ways to form the possessive for two or more nouns:

1. To show joint possession (both nouns owning the same thing or things), the last noun in the series is possessive:

> The controller and her staff's memo was distributed this morning.

2. To indicate that each noun owns an item or items individually, each noun must show possession:

> The vice-president's and the secretary's reports presented very different recommendations based on the same set of facts.

The importance of the apostrophe is obvious when you consider the difference in meaning between the following two sentences:

> Be sure to pick up the manager's things on your way to the airport.

> Be sure to pick up the managers' things on your way to the airport.

In the first of these sentences, you have only one manager to worry about, while in the second, you have at least two!

Capitalization

Here is a brief summary of some hard-to-remember capitalization rules:

1. You may, if you choose, capitalize the first letter of the first word in a sentence which follows a colon. Make sure, however, to use one pattern consistently throughout your paper:

> Our instructions are explicit: *Do* not allow anyone into the conference without an identification badge.

> Our instructions are explicit: *do* not allow anyone into the conference without an identification badge.

2. Capitalize *proper nouns* (nouns naming specific people, places, or things) and *proper adjectives* (adjectives made from proper nouns). A common noun following the proper adjective is usually not capitalized, nor is a common adjective preceding the proper adjective (such as *a, an,* or *the*):

Proper Nouns	*Proper Adjectives*
Poland	Polish workers
Iraq	the Iraqi business leader
Shakespeare	a Shakespearean tragedy

Proper nouns include:
Names of famous monuments and buildings: the Washington Monument, the Empire State Building, the Library of Congress
Historical events, eras, and certain terms concerning calendar dates: the Civil War, the Dark Ages, Monday, December, Labor Day
Parts of the country: North, Southwest, Eastern Seaboard, the West Coast, New England

NOTE: When words like *north, south, east, west, northwest* are used to designate direction rather than geographical region, they are not capitalized: "We drove *east* to Boston and then made a tour of the *East Coast*."

Words referring to race, religion or nationality: Islam, Muslim, Caucasian, White (*or* white), Oriental, Negro, Black (*or* black), Slavic, Arab, Jewish, Hebrew, Buddhism, Buddhists, Southern Baptists, the Bible, the Koran, American
Names of languages: English, Chinese, Latin, Sanskrit
Titles of corporations, institutions, businesses, universities, organizations: Dow Chemical, General Motors, the National Endowment for the Humanities, University of Tennessee, Colby College, Kiwanis Club, American Association of Retired Persons, the Oklahoma State Senate

NOTE: Some words once considered proper nouns or adjectives have, over time, become common, such as *french fries, pasteurized milk, arabic numerals, italics, panama hat.*

Titles of individuals may be capitalized if they precede a proper name; otherwise, titles are usually not capitalized.

The committee honored Vice-President Jones.

The committee honored the vice-president from Diawa, Inc.

We phoned Doctor Jessup, who arrived shortly afterward.

We phoned the doctor, who arrived shortly afterward.

A story on Queen Elizabeth's health appeared in yesterday's paper.

A story on the queen's health appeared in yesterday's paper.

When Not to Capitalize

In general, you do not capitalize nouns when your reference is nonspecific. For example, you would not capitalize the phrase *the manager*, but you would capitalize *Manager Smith*. The second reference is as much a title as it is a mere term of identification, while the first reference is a mere identifier. Likewise, there is a difference in degree of specificity between the phrase *the state department of commerce* and *the Oklahoma Department of Commerce.*

NOTE: The meaning of a term may change somewhat depending on capitalization. What, for example, might be the difference between a *Democrat* and a *democrat*? When capitalized, the word refers to a member of a specific political party; when not capitalized, the word refers to someone who believes in the democratic form of government.

Capitalization depends to some extent on the context of your writing. For example, if you are writing a staffing plan for an existing company, you may capitalize words and phrases—*Board of Directors, Chairman of the Board, the Institute*—that would not be capitalized in a paper written for a more general audience. Likewise, in some contexts it is not unusual to see titles of certain powerful officials capitalized even when not accompanying a proper noun: The President took few members of his staff to Camp David with him.

Colons

We all know certain uses for the colon. A colon can, for example, separate the parts of a statement of time (4:25 a.m.), separate chapter and verse in a Biblical quotation (John 3:16), and close the salutation of a business letter (Dear Mr. Keaton:). But the colon has other, less well known uses that can add extra flexibility to sentence structure.

The colon can introduce into a sentence certain kinds of material, such as a list, a quotation, or a restatement or description of material mentioned earlier:

LIST
The committee's research proposal promised to do three things: (1) establish the extent of the problem, (2) examine several possible solutions, and (3) estimate the cost of each solution.

QUOTATION
In her first response to our proposal, Ms. Harris challenged us with these words: "How will your company's expansion plan make a difference in the life of our city?"

RESTATEMENT OR DESCRIPTION
Ahead of us, according to the City Planning Commission Director, lay the biggest job of all: convincing her group of the plan's benefits.

Commas

The comma is perhaps the most troublesome of all marks of punctuation, no doubt because its use is governed by so many variables, such as sentence length, rhetorical emphasis, or changing notions of style. The most common problems are outlined below.

The Comma Splice

A comma splice is the joining of two complete sentences with only a comma:

A plant closing is not just an event affecting those inside the company, many stakeholders throughout the region are also affected.

An unemployed worker who has been effectively retrained is no longer an economic problem for the community, he has become an asset.

It might be possible for the city to assess fees on the sale of real estate, however, such a move would be criticized by the community of real estate developers.

In each of these passages, two complete sentences (also called *independent clauses*) have been spliced together by a comma, which is an inadequate break between two sentences.

One foolproof way to check your paper for comma splices is to read carefully the structures on both sides of each comma. If you find a complete sentence on each side, and if the sentence following the comma does not begin with a coordinating conjunction (*and, but, for, nor, or, so, yet*), then you have found a comma splice.

Simply reading the draft through to try to "hear" the comma splices may not work, since the rhetorical features of your prose—its "movement"—may make it hard to detect this kind of sentence completeness error. There are five commonly used ways to correct comma splices.

1. Place a period between the two independent clauses:

INCORRECT: A business owner receives many benefits from his or her affiliation with a franchiser group, there are disadvantages as well.

CORRECT: A business owner receives many benefits from his or her affiliation with a franchiser group. There are disadvantages as well.

2. Place a comma and a coordinating conjunction (*and, but, for, or, nor, so, yet*) between the sentences:

INCORRECT: The councilman's speech described the major differences of opinion over the economic situation, it also suggested a possible course of action.

CORRECT: The councilman's speech described the major differences of opinion over the economic situation, *and* it also suggested a possible course of action.

3. Place a semicolon between the independent clauses:

INCORRECT: Some people feel that the federal government should play a larger role in establishing safety standards in the workplace, many others disagree.

CORRECT: Some people feel that the federal government should play a larger role in establishing safety standards in the workplace; many others disagree.

4. Rewrite the two clauses of the comma splice as one independent clause:

INCORRECT: Television ads played a big part in the advertising campaign, however they were not the deciding factor in the market share increase.

CORRECT: Television ads played a large but not a decisive role in the market share increase.

5. Change one of the independent clauses into a dependent clause by beginning it with a *subordinating word* (for example, *although, after, as, because, before, if, though, unless, when, which,* and *where*), which prevents the clause from being able to stand on its own as a complete sentence.

INCORRECT: The union election was held last Tuesday, there was poor employee participation.

CORRECT: *When* the union election was held last Tuesday, there was poor employee participation.

Comma Missing in a Compound Sentence

A *compound sentence* is composed of two or more independent clauses—two complete sentences. When these two clauses are joined by a coordinating conjunction, the conjunction should be preceded by a comma to signal the reader that another independent clause follows. (This is method number 2 for fixing a comma splice described above.) When the comma is missing, the reader is not expecting to find the second half of a compound sentence and may be distracted from the text.

As the following examples indicate, the missing comma is especially a problem in longer sentences or in sentences in which other coordinating conjunctions appear. Notice how the comma sorts out the two main parts of the compound sentence, eliminating confusion:

Example one:	The maintenance supervisor promised to repair the forklift and investigate the problem and then he walked away.
With the comma added:	The maintenance supervisor promised to repair the forklift and investigate the problem, and then he walked away.
Example two:	The water board can neither make policy nor enforce it nor can its members serve on area companies' boards of directors.
With the comma added:	The water board can neither make policy nor enforce it, nor can its members serve on area companies' boards of directors.

An exception to the rule arises in shorter sentences, where the comma may not be necessary to make the meaning clear:

> The customer called back and he thanked us for our offer.

It is never wrong, however, to place a comma after the conjunction between the independent clauses. If you are the least bit unsure of your audience's notion of "proper" grammar, it is a good idea to take the conservative approach and use the comma:

> The customer called back, and he thanked us for our offer.

Commas with Restrictive and Nonrestrictive Elements

A *nonrestrictive element* is part of a sentence—a word, phrase, or clause—that adds information about another element in the sentence without restricting or limiting the meaning of that element. While this information may be useful, the nonrestrictive element is not needed for the sentence to make sense. To signal its inessential nature, the nonrestrictive element is set off from the rest of the sentence with commas.

Failure to indicate the nonrestrictive nature of an element by using commas can cause confusion. See, for example, how the presence or absence of commas affects our understanding of the following sentence:

> The plant manager was talking with the policeman, who won the outstanding service award last year.

> The plant manager was talking with the policeman who won the outstanding service award last year.

Can you see that the comma changes the meaning of the sentence? In the first version of the sentence, the comma makes the information that follows it incidental: *The plant manager was talking with the policeman, who happens to have won the service award last year.* In the second version of the sentence, the information following the word *policeman* is important to the sense of the sentence; it tells us, specifically, *which* policeman—presumably there are more than one—the plant manager was addressing. Here the lack of a comma has transformed the material following the word *policeman* into a *restrictive element*, meaning one necessary to our understanding of the sentence.

Be sure that in your paper you make a clear distinction between nonrestrictive and restrictive elements by setting of nonrestrictive elements with commas.

Commas in a Series

A series is any two or more items of a similar nature that appear consecutively in a sentence. The items may be individual words, phrases, or clauses. In a series of three or more items, the items are separated by commas.

> *The senator, the mayor,* and *the company president* all attended the ceremony.

> Because of the new zoning regulations, *all trailer parks must be moved out of the neighborhood, all retail businesses must apply for recertification and tax status, and the two local manufacturers must move.*

The final comma in the series, the one before *and*, is sometimes left out, especially in newspaper writing. This practice, however, can make for confusion, especially in longer, complicated sentences like the second example in above. Here is the way that sentence would read without the final, or *serial*, comma:

> Because of the new zoning regulations, *all trailer parks must be moved out of the neighborhood, all retail businesses must apply for recertification and tax status and the two local manufacturers must move.*

Notice that without a comma the division between the second and third items in the series is not clear. This is the sort of ambiguous structure that can cause a reader to backtrack and lose concentration. You can avoid such confusion by always including that final comma. Remember, however, that if you do decide to include it, do so *consistently*; make sure it appears in every series in your paper.

Dangling Modifiers

A *modifier* is a word or group of words used to describe, or modify, another word in the sentence. A *dangling modifier* appears either at the beginning or ending of a sentence and seems to be describing some word other than the one the writer obviously intended. The modifier therefore "dangles," disconnected from its correct meaning. It is often hard for the writer to spot a dangling modifier but the reader can—and will—find them, and the result can be disastrous for the sentence, as the following examples demonstrate:

INCORRECT: *Flying low over Lubbock,* the new plant was seen.
CORRECT: *Flying low over Lubbock,* we saw the new plant.
INCORRECT: *Worried at the cost of the program,* elements of the plan were eliminated in committee.
CORRECT: *Worried at the cost of the program,* the committee eliminated elements of the plan.

CORRECT: The committee members eliminated elements of the plan *because they were worried at the cost of the program.*
INCORRECT: *To lobby for litigation reform,* a lot of effort went into the t.v. ads.
CORRECT: The business lobby group put a lot of effort into the t.v. ads advocating litigation reform.
INCORRECT: *Stunned,* the television broadcast the fired president's announcement of his departure.
CORRECT: The television broadcast the stunned president's departure announcement.

Note that in the first two incorrect sentences, the confusion is largely due to the use of *passive-voice verbs:* "the new plant *was seen,*" "elements of the plan *were eliminated.*" Often, though not always, a dangling modifier results because the actor in the sentence—*we* in the first sentence, *the committee* in the second—is either distanced from the modifier or obliterated by the passive voice verb. It is a good idea to avoid passive voice unless you have a specific reason for using it.

One way to check for dangling modifiers is to examine all modifiers at the beginnings or endings of your sentences. Look especially for *to be* phrases ("*to lobby*") or for words ending in *-ing* or *-ed* at the start of the modifier. Then see if the modified word is close enough to the phrase to be properly connected.

Parallelism

Series of two or more words, phrases, or clauses within a sentence should have the same grammatical structure; this is called *parallelism.* Parallel structures can add power and balance to your writing by creating a strong rhetorical rhythm, as illustrated in this quote from J. P. Morgan: "You are affluent when you buy what you want, do what you wish, and don't give a thought to what it costs." (qtd. in Adler 1985, 56).

We find a special satisfaction in balanced structures and so are more likely to remember ideas phrased in parallelisms than in less highly ordered language. For this reason, as well as for the sense of authority and control that they suggest, parallel structures are common in business writing.

Faulty Parallelism

If the parallelism of a passage is not carefully maintained, the writing can seem sloppy and out of balance. Scan your writing to make sure that all series and lists have parallel structure. The following examples show how to correct faulty parallelism:

INCORRECT: The board of directors promises not only *to reorganize* the manufacturing division, but also the *giving of raises* to all remaining employees. [Connective structures such as *not only . . . but also*, and *both . . . and* introduce elements that should be parallel.]
CORRECT: The board of directors promises not only *to reorganize* the manufacturing division, but also *to give raises* to all remaining managers.
INCORRECT: The cost *of doing nothing* is greater than the cost *to renovate* the production facility.
CORRECT: The cost *of doing nothing* is greater than the cost *of renovating* the production facility.

INCORRECT: Here are the items on the executive committee's agenda: 1) *to discuss* the new property tax, 2) *to revise* the wording of the job announcement, 3) *a* vote on the vice president's request for another assistant.

CORRECT: Here are the items on the committee's agenda: 1) *to discuss* the new property tax, 2) *to revise* the wording of the job announcement, 3) *to vote* on the vice president's request for another assistant.

Fused (Run-on) Sentence

A *fused sentence* is one in which two or more *independent clauses* (passages that can stand as complete sentences) have been joined together without the aid of any suitable connecting word, phrase, or punctuation. There are several ways to correct a fused sentence:

INCORRECT: The committee members were exhausted they had debated for two hours.

CORRECT: The committee members were exhausted. They had debated for two hours. [The clauses have been separated into two sentences.]

CORRECT: The committee members were exhausted; they had debated for two hours. [The clauses have been separated by a semicolon.]

CORRECT: The committee members were exhausted, having debated for two hours. [The second clause has been rephrased as a dependent clause.]

INCORRECT: Our business plan impressed the committee it also convinced them to reconsider their action.

CORRECT: Our business plan impressed the committee and also convinced them to reconsider their action. [The second clause has been rephrased as part of the first clause.]

CORRECT: Our business plan impressed the committee, and it also convinced them to reconsider their action. [The clauses have been separated by a comma and a coordinating word.]

While a fused sentence is easily noticeable to the reader, it can be maddeningly difficult for the writer to catch. Unpracticed writers tend to read through the fused spots, sometimes supplying the break that is usually heard when sentences are spoken. To check for fused sentences, read the independent clauses in your paper *carefully*, making sure that there are adequate breaks among all of them.

Pronoun Errors

Its Versus It's

Do not make the mistake of trying to form the possessive of *it* in the same way that you form the possessive of most nouns. The pronoun *it* shows possession by simply adding an *s*:

The attorney argued the case on *its* merits.

The word *it's* is a contraction, meaning *it is*:

> *It's* the most expensive program ever launched by the marketing department.

What makes the *its/it's* rule so confusing is that most nouns form the singular possessive by adding an apostrophe and an *s*:

> The *union's* announcement startled the employees.

When proofreading, any time you come to the word *it's*, substitute the phrase *it is* while you read. If the phrase makes sense, you have used the correct form. If you have used the word *it's*:

> The newspaper article was misleading in *it's* analysis of the lawsuit.

Then read it as *it is*:

> The newspaper article was misleading in *it is* analysis of the lawsuit.

If the phrase makes no sense, substitute *its* for *it's*:

> The newspaper article was misleading in *its* analysis of the lawsuit.

Vague Pronoun Reference

Pronouns are words that stand in place of nouns or other pronouns that have already been mentioned in your writing. The most common pronouns include *he, she, it, they, them, those, which,* and *who.* You must make sure that there is no confusion about the word to which each pronoun refers:

> The mayor said that *he* would support our proposed site plan if the city council would also back *it.*

The word that is replaced by the pronoun is called its *antecedent.* To check the accuracy of your pronoun references, ask yourself this question: *to what does the pronoun refer?* Then answer the question carefully, making sure that there is not more than one possible antecedent.

Consider the following example:

> Several area business owners decided to defeat the new zoning ordinance. *This* became the focal point of a vicious battle between area residents and local business leaders.

To what does the word *This* refer? The immediate answer seems to be the word *ordinance* at the end of the previous sentence. But it is more likely the writer was referring to the attempt of the business owners to defeat the ordinance, but there is no word in the first sentence that refers specifically to this action. The reference is unclear. One way to clarify the reference is to change the beginning of the second sentence:

> Several area business owners decided to defeat the new zoning ordinance. *Their attack on the ordinance* became the focal point of a vicious battle between area residents and local business leaders.

This point is further demonstrated by the following sentence:

> When the chairman of the board of directors of Chrysler Corporation decided to hire Lee Iacocca to head the company, *he* had little idea of the crisis that lay ahead.

To whom does the word *he* refer? It is unclear whether the writer is referring to the chairman or to Lee Iacocca. One way to clarify the reference is simply to repeat the antecedent instead of using a pronoun:

> When the chairman of the board of directors of Chrysler Corporation decided to hire Lee Iacocca to head the company, *Iacocca* had little idea of the crisis that lay ahead.

Pronoun Agreement

A pronoun must agree in gender and in number with its antecedent, as the following examples demonstrate:

> Alice Johnson said that *she* appreciated our department's support in the project.
>
> One supervisor asked Sam what *he* would have done if the department personnel had not supported *him*.
>
> Having listened to our proposal, the customer agreed to respond to *it* within a week.
>
> Engineers working on the bridge said *they* were pleased with the schedule so far.

Certain words, however can be troublesome antecedents, because they may look like plural pronouns but are actually singular:

anyone	anybody	each	either	everybody
everyone	nobody	no one	somebody	someone

A pronoun referring to one of these words in a sentence must be singular, too.

> INCORRECT: *Each* of the women in the department brought *their* children.
> CORRECT: *Each* of the women in the department brought *her* children.
> INCORRECT: Has *everybody* received *their* paycheck?
> CORRECT: Has *everybody* received *his* or *her* paycheck? [The two gender-specific pronouns are used to avoid sexist language.]
> CORRECT: Have *all the employees* received *their* paychecks? [The singular antecedent has been changed to a plural one.]

A Shift in "Person"

It is important to avoid shifting unnecessarily among first person (*I, we*), second person (*you*), and third person (*she, he, it, one, they*) unnecessarily. Such shifts can cause confusion:

INCORRECT: *Most people* [third person] who apply for a job find that if *you* [second person] tell the truth during *your* interview, *you* will be more likely to be hired.

CORRECT: *Most people* who apply for a job find that if *they* tell the truth during *their* interviews, *they* are more likely to be hired.

INCORRECT: *One* [first person] cannot tell whether *they* [third person] are cut out for entrepreneurship until *they* actually try to start a business.

CORRECT: *One* cannot tell whether *one* is cut out for entrepreneurship until *one* actually tries to start a business.

Quotation Marks

It can be difficult to remember when to use quotation marks and where they go in relation to other marks of punctuation. When faced with these questions, unpracticed writers often try to rely on logic rather than on a rule book, but the rules do not always seem to rely on logic. The only way to make sure of your use of quotation marks is to *memorize* the rules. Luckily, there are not many.

The Use of Quotation Marks

Use quotation marks to enclose direct quotations that are not longer than four typed lines:

> In response to the downsizing of automobiles in the early 1970s, Henry Ford II, Chairman of the Board of Ford Motor Company, said, "Minicars produce miniprofits" (qtd. in Jackman 1984, 131).

Longer quotes are placed in an indented, double-spaced block, *without* quotation marks:

> But where is the entrepreneur to get the money? The Arthur Young Accounting Firm responds:
> > Beyond digging into one's own pocket or the pockets of family and friends—which always risks more than just money—there is a network of informal investors (sometimes called angels) who are willing to put their money into new businesses. Some don't have enough funds to get into a venture capital fund but still like the risk of venture-type investments. Others like to take a more hands-on approach to their investment decisions. A few may even be gizmo-driven dilettantes looking for the next Rube Goldberg-type invention. (Siegel, Schultz, and Ford 1987, 25)

Use single quotation marks to set off quotations within quotations:

> "I intend," said the company president, "to use in my speech a line from Frost's poem, 'The Road Not Taken.' "

NOTE: When the interior quote occurs at the end of the sentence, both single and double quotation marks are placed outside the period.

Use quotation marks to set off titles of the following:

short poems (those not printed as a separate volume)

short stories

articles or essays

songs

episodes of television or radio shows

Use quotation marks to set off words or phrases used in special ways.

1. To convey irony:

   The so-called "conservative" congress has done nothing but increase spending and raise taxes.

2. To indicate a technical term:

   To "reconcile" is to determine the actual cash balance by considering items which have not yet been reflected in the bank's statement and those which have not yet been recorded in the cash accounting records. You should reconcile your cash account at least monthly. [Once the term is defined, it is not placed in quotation marks again.]

Quotation Marks in Relation to Other Punctuation

Place commas and periods *inside* closing quotation marks:

"My fellow workers," said the president, "there are tough times ahead of us."

Place colons and semicolons *outside* closing quotation marks:

In his report on the effect of imports, the agent warned against "an insidious threat"; he was referring to the loss of blue-collar jobs.

There are several victims of the company's decision to "right-size": the workers, the small business owners, and the vendors.

Use the context to determine wither to place question marks, exclamation points, and dashes inside or outside closing quotation marks. If the punctuation is part of the quotation, it goes *inside* the quotation mark:

"When will the committee make up its mind?" asked the office manager.

The workers shouted, "Think of our families!" and "No more layoffs!"

If the punctuation is not part of the quotation, place it *outside* the quotation mark:

Which business leader said, "They can have any color they want, as long as it's black"? [Although the quote was a complete sentence, you do not place a period after it. There can only be one piece of terminal punctuation, or punctuation that ends a sentence.]

Semicolons

The semicolon is another little used punctuation mark that you should learn to incorporate into your writing strategy because of its many potential applications. For example, a semicolon can be used to correct a comma splice:

INCORRECT: The union representatives left the meeting in good spirits, their demands were met.

CORRECT: The union representatives left the meeting in good spirits; their demands were met.

INCORRECT: Several guests at the seminar had lost their invitations, however, we were able to seat them, anyway.

CORRECT: Several guests at the seminar had lost their invitations; however, we were able to seat them, anyway. [Conjunctive adverbs like *however*, *therefore*, and *thus* are not coordinating words (such as *and, but, or, for, so, yet*) and cannot be used with a comma to link independent clauses. If the second independent clause begins with a *however*, it must be preceded by either a period or a semicolon.]

As you can see from the second example above, connecting two independent clauses with a semicolon instead of a period strengthens their relationship.

Semicolons can also separate items in a series when the series items themselves contain commas:

The newspaper account of the lawsuit stressed the theft, which is clearly minor; the fire, though it probably had nothing to do with the failure of the division; and the charges of price fixing, which may have been the only real violation worth a lawsuit.

Avoid misusing semicolons. For example, use a comma, not a semicolon, to separate an independent clause from a dependent clause:

INCORRECT: Students from the college volunteered to answer phones during the pledge drive; which was set up to generate money for their new student-owned business.

CORRECT: Students from the college volunteered to answer phones during the pledge drive, which was set up to generate money for their new student-owned business.

Do not overuse semicolons. Although they are useful, too many semicolons in your writing can distract your reader's attention. Avoid monotony by using semicolons sparingly.

Sentence Fragments

A fragment is an incomplete part of a sentence that is punctuated and capitalized as if it were an entire sentence. It is an especially disruptive error, because it obscures the connections that the words of a sentence must make in order to complete the reader's understanding.

Students sometimes write fragments because they are concerned that a particular sentence is growing too long and needs to be shortened. Remember that cutting the length of a sentence merely by adding a period somewhere often creates a fragment. When checking your writing for fragments, it is essential that you read each sentence carefully to determine whether it has: (1) a complete subject and a verb, and (2) a subordinating word before the subject and verb, which makes the construction a subordinate clause rather than a complete sentence.

Types of Sentence Fragments

Some fragments lack a verb.

INCORRECT: The chairperson of our committee, having received a letter from the general manager. [The word *having*, which can be used as a verb, is here being used as a gerund introducing a participial phrase. *Watch out* for words that look like verbs but are being used in another way.]

CORRECT: The chairperson of our committee received a letter from the general manager.

Some fragments lack a subject:

INCORRECT: Our study shows that there is broad support for the new product line. And for the old product line as well.

CORRECT: Our study shows that there is broad support for the new product line and for the old product line as well.

Some fragments are subordinate clauses:

INCORRECT: After the latest price changes came out. [This clause has the two major components of a complete sentence: a subject (*changes*) and a verb (*came*). Indeed, if the first word (*After*) were deleted, the clause would be a complete sentence. But that first word is a *subordinating word*, which prevents the following clause from standing on its own as a complete sentence. *Watch out* for this kind of construction. It is called a *subordinate clause*, and it is *not* a sentence.]

CORRECT: After the latest price changes came out, the order department was swamped with cancellations. [A common method of revising a subordinate clause that has been punctuated as a complete sentence is to connect it to the complete sentence to which it is closest in meaning.]

INCORRECT: Several smelting company owners asked for copies of the trade group's report. Which called for reform of the Environmental Protection Agency.

CORRECT: Several smelting company owners asked for copies of the trade group's report, which called for reform of the Environmental Protection Agency.

Spelling

All of us have problems spelling certain words that we have not yet committed to memory. But most writers are not as bad at spelling as they believe they are. Usually it is that handful of words that the individual finds troubling. It is important to be as sensitive as possible to your own particular spelling problems—and to keep a dictionary handy. There is no excuse for failing to check spelling.

What follows are a list of commonly confused words and a list of commonly misspelled words. Read through the lists, looking for those words which tend to give you trouble. If you have any question about the spelling of a word, *consult your dictionary.*

COMMONLY CONFUSED WORDS

accept/except

advice/advise

affect/effect

aisle/isle

allusion/illusion

an/and

angel/angle

ascent/assent

bare/bear

breath/breathe

brake/break

buy/by

capital/capitol

choose/chose

cite/sight/site

complement/compliment

conscience/conscious

corps/corpse

council/counsel

dairy/diary

descent/dissent

desert/dessert

device/devise

die/dye

dominant/dominate

elicit/illicit

eminent/immanent/
   imminent

envelop/envelope

every day/everyday

fair/fare

formally/formerly

forth/fourth

hear/here

heard/herd

hole/whole

human/humane

its/it's

know/no

later/latter

lay/lie

lead/led

lessen/lesson

loose/lose

may be/maybe

miner/minor

moral/morale

of/off

passed/past

patience/patients

peace/piece

personal/personnel

plain/plane

precede/proceed

presence/presents

principal/principle

quiet/quite

rain/reign/rein

raise/raze

reality/realty

respectfully/respectively

reverend/reverent

right/rite/write

road/rode

scene/seen

sense/since

stationary/stationery

straight/strait

taught/taut

than/then

their/there/they're

threw/through

too/to/two

track/tract

waist/waste

waive/wave

weak/week

weather/whether

were/where

which/witch

whose/who's

your/you're

COMMONLY MISSPELLED WORDS

a lot

acceptable

accessible

accommodate

accompany

accustomed

acquire

against

annihilate

apparent

arguing/argument

authentic

before

begin/beginning

believe

benefited

bulletin

business

cannot

category

condemn

committee

courteous

definitely

dependent

desperate

develop

different

disappear

disappoint

easily

efficient

equipped

exceed

existence

experience

environment

exercise

fascinate

finally

foresee

forty

fulfill

gauge

guaranteed

guard

harass

hero/heroes

humorous

hurried/hurriedly

hypocrite

ideally

immediately

immense

incredible

innocuous

intercede

interrupt

irrelevant

irresistible

irritate

knowledge

license

likelihood

maintenance

manageable

meanness

mischievous

missile

necessary

nevertheless

no one

noticeable
noticing
nuisance
occasion/occasionally
occurred/occurrences
omission
omit
opinion
opponent
parallel
parole
peaceable
performance
pertain
practical
preparation
probably
professor
prominent
pronunciation
process
psychology
publicly
pursue/pursuing
questionnaire
realize
receipt
received
recession
recommend
referring
religious
remembrance
reminisce
repetition
representative
rhythm
ridiculous
roommate

satellite
scarcity
scenery
secede/secession
science
secretary
senseless
separate
sergeant
shining
significant
sincerely
skiing
stubbornness
studying
succeed/success
successfully
susceptible
suspicious
technical
temporary
tendency
therefore
tragedy
truly
tyranny
unanimous
unconscious
undoubtedly
until
vacuum
valuable
various
vegetable
visible
without
women
writing

CHAPTER 3

Organizing the Research Process

3.1 GAINING CONTROL OF THE RESEARCH PROCESS

The research paper is where all your skills as an interpreter of details, an organizer of facts and theories, and a writer of clear prose come together. In the business disciplines, the research paper is primarily a learning tool, the use of which is limited mainly to college courses. Once you have left the confines of the university, memos, formal and informal reports, and business plans will become the primary means by which you will organize and convey information to others in the business community. But while business people do not usually organize their information in the format of an academic research paper, they do perform research. And the research process is virtually the same no matter what presentation format is used.

Students new to the writing of research papers sometimes find themselves intimidated by the job ahead of them. After all, the research paper adds what seems to be an extra set of complexities to the writing process. As any other expository or persuasive paper does, a research paper must present an original thesis using a carefully organized and logical argument. But a research paper investigates a topic that is outside the writer's own experience. This means that writers must locate and evaluate information that is new, in effect educating themselves as they explore their topics. A beginning researcher sometimes feels overwhelmed by the basic requirements of the assignment or by the authority of the source material being investigated.

As you begin a research project, it may be difficult to establish a sense of control over the different tasks you are undertaking. You may have little notion of where to search for a thesis or even for most helpful information. If you do not carefully monitor your own work habits, you may find yourself unwittingly abdicating responsibility for the paper's argument by borrowing it wholesale from one or more of your sources.

Who is in control of your paper? The answer must be *you*—not the instructor who assigned you the paper, and certainly not the published writers and interviewees whose opinions you solicit. If all your paper does is paste together the opinions of others, it has little use. It is up to you to synthesize an original idea from a judicious evaluation of your source material. While there are, of course, many elements of your paper about which you are unsure at the beginning of your research project—for example, you will probably not yet have a definitive thesis sentence or even much understanding of the shape of your argument—you *can* establish a measure of control over the process you will go through to complete the paper. And if you work regularly and systematically, keeping yourself open to new ideas as they present themselves, your sense of control will grow.

Here are some suggestions to help you establish and maintain control of your paper.

1. ***Understand your assignment.*** It is possible for a research assignment to come to grief simply because the writer did not read the assignment carefully. Considering how much time and effort you are about to put into your project, it is a very good idea to make sure you have a clear understanding of what it is your instructor wants you to do. *Be sure to ask your instructor about any aspect of the assignment that is unclear to you—but only after you have read it carefully.* Recopying the assignment in your own handwriting is a good way to start, even though your instructor may have given the assignment to you in writing. Make sure, before you dive into the project, that you have considered the following questions.

2. ***What is your topic?*** The assignment may give you a great deal of specific information about your topic, or you may be allowed considerable freedom in establishing one for yourself. In an auditing class in which you are studying issues affecting the internal control function, your professor might give you a very specific assignment—a paper, for example, examining the risks to which an auditor who fails to identify weaknesses in the internal control function during the conduct of an audit is exposed—or she may allow you to choose for yourself the issue that your paper will address. You need to understand the terms, set up in the assignment, by which you will design your project.

3. ***What is your purpose?*** Whatever the degree of latitude you are given in the matter of your topic, pay close attention to the way in which your instructor has phrased the assignment. Is your primary job to *describe* the impact of a current employment law or to *take a stand* on it? Are you to *compare* two alternative business strategies, and if so, to what end? Are you to *classify, persuade, survey, analyze?* Look for such descriptive terms in the assignment in order to determine the *purpose* of the project.

4. ***Who is your audience?*** Your own orientation to the paper is profoundly affected by your conception of the audience for whom you are writing. Granted, your number one reader is your instructor, but who else would be interested in your paper? Are you writing for the business leaders of a community? a plant manager or his supervisors? a prospective entrepreneur? A paper describing the impact on business of the Americans With Disabilities Act may justifiably contain much more technical jargon for an audience of human resources professionals than for a planning commission made up of local business and civic leaders.

5. ***What kind of research are you doing?*** You will do one if not both of the following kinds of research:

   a. *Primary research,* which requires you to discover information first-hand, often through the conducting of interviews or surveys (see Chapter 11 for a discussion of surveys). In primary research, you are collecting and sifting through raw data—data that have not already been interpreted by researchers—that you will then study, select, arrange, and speculate on. This raw data may be the opinions of experts or people on the street, historical documents, the published letters of a famous management theorist, or material collected from other researchers. It is important to set up carefully the methods by which you collect your data. Your aim is to gather the most accurate information possible, from which sound observations may be made later, either by you or by other writers using the material you have uncovered.

   b. *Secondary research,* which uses published accounts of primary materials. While the primary researcher might survey a marketplace for buyers' attitudes about telemarketing, the secondary researcher will use the material from the survey to support a particular thesis. Secondary research, in other words, focuses on interpretations of raw data. Most of your college papers will be based on your use of secondary sources.

Primary Source	*Secondary Source*
A published collection of Frederick Taylor's letters	A journal article arguing that the tone of Taylor's letters illustrates Taylor's frustration in trying to get his theory of scientific management accepted
An interview with the president of the AFL-CIO	A character study of the president based on the interview
Material from a survey	A paper basing its thesis on the results of the survey

6. ***Keep your perspective.***   Whichever type of research you perform, you must keep your results in perspective. There is no way in which you, as a primary researcher, can be completely objective in your findings. It is not possible to design a survey that will net you absolute truth, nor can you be sure that the opinions you gather in interviews reflect the accurate and unchanging opinions of the people you question. Likewise, if you are conducting secondary research, you must remember that the articles and journals you are reading are shaped by the aims of their writers, who are interpreting primary materials for their own ends. The farther you get from a primary source, the greater the possibility for distortion. Your job as a researcher is to be as accurate as possible, and that means keeping in view the limitations of your methods and their ends.

3.2 EFFECTIVE RESEARCH METHODS

In any research project there will be moments of confusion, but you can prevent confusion from overwhelming you by establishing an effective research procedure. You need to design a schedule for the project that is as systematic as possible, yet flexible enough so that you do not feel trapped by it. A schedule will help keep you from running into dead ends by always showing you what to do next. At the same time, the schedule helps you to retain the presence of mind necessary to spot new ideas, new strategies, as you work.

Give Yourself Plenty of Time

You may feel like delaying your research for many reasons: unfamiliarity with the library, the press of other tasks, a deadline that seems comfortably far away. But do not allow such factors to deter you. Research takes time. Working in a library seems to speed up the clock, so that the hour you expected it to take you to find a certain source becomes two hours. You must allow yourself the time it takes not only to find material but to read it, assimilate it, set it in context with your own thoughts. If you delay starting, you may well find yourself distracted by the deadline, having to keep an eye on the clock while trying to make sense of a writer's complicated argument.

The following schedule lists the steps of a research project in the order in which they are generally accomplished. Remember that each step is dependent upon the others, and that it is quite possible to revise earlier decisions in the light of later discoveries. After some background reading, for example, your notion of the paper's purpose may change, a fact that may, in turn, alter other steps. One of the strengths of a good schedule is its flexibility. Note that this schedule lists tasks for both primary and secondary research; you should use only those steps that are relevant to your project.

Research Schedule

Task	Date of Completion
Determine topic, purpose, audience	_____
Do background reading in reference books	_____
Narrow your topic; establish a tentative hypothesis	_____
Develop a working bibliography	_____
Write for needed information	_____
Read and evaluate written sources, taking notes	_____
Determine whether to conduct interviews or surveys	_____
Draft a thesis and outline	_____
Write a first draft	_____
Obtain feedback (show draft to instructor, if possible)	_____
Do more research, if necessary	_____
Revise draft	_____
Correct bibliographical format of paper	_____
Prepare final draft	_____
Proofread	_____
Proofread *again*, looking for characteristic errors	_____
Deadline for final draft	_____

Do Background Reading

Whether you are doing primary or secondary research, you need to know what kinds of work have already been done in your field of study. A good way to start is by consulting general reference works, though you do not want to overdo it (see below). Chapter 4 lists specialized reference works focusing on topics of interest to business students and professionals. You might find help in such volumes even for specific, local problems, such as how to minimize the negative publicity of a plant closing or how to choose a promotional strategy for a new regional shopping center.

WARNING: Be very careful not to rely too exclusively on material taken from general encyclopedias, such as *Encyclopedia Britannica* or *Colliers Encyclopedia*. You may wish to consult one for an overview of a topic with which you are unfamiliar, but students new to research are often tempted to import large sections, if not entire articles, from such volumes, and this practice is not good scholarship. One major reason why your instructor has required a research paper from you is to let you experience the kinds of books and journals in which the discourse of business is conducted. Encyclopedias are good places for instant introductions to subjects; some encyclopedias even include bibliographies of reference works at the ends of their articles. But to write a useful paper you will need much more detailed information about your subject. Once you have learned what you can from a general encyclopedia, move on to other sources.

A primary rule of source hunting is to *use your imagination.* Determine what topics relevant to your study might be covered in general reference works. If, for example, you are looking for introductory readings to help you with the aforementioned research paper on promotional strategies for shopping centers, you might look into such specialized reference tools as an introduction to marketing text book or, even better, a text used in Promotional Strategy, an advanced marketing class. The brief discussions of your topic in such text books are often supported by a list of published sources providing more detailed information.

Narrow Your Topic and Establish a Working Thesis

Before exploring outside sources, you should find out what you already know or think about your topic, a job that can only be accomplished well in writing. You might wish to investigate your own attitude toward your topic by using one or more of the prewriting strategies described in Chapter 1. You might also be surprised by what you know—or don't know—about the topic. This kind of self-questioning can help you discover a profitable direction for your research.

For a research paper in a course in Entrepreneurship, Patricia Harrison was given the general topic of studying the people who choose entrepreneurship as a vocation. She narrowed her topic to a study of entrepreneurial traits. Here is the course her thinking took as Patricia looked for ways to limit the topic effectively and find a thesis:

GENERAL TOPIC	Entrepreneurial Traits
POTENTIAL TOPICS	Entrepreneurs: What They Were Like as Children
	How School Affects Entrepreneurs
	Family Influences on Entrepreneurs
	Personal Traits That Predict Success in Entrepreneurship
WORKING THESIS	Public education discourages entrepreneurship as it prepares children for lives as employees.

Specific methods for discovering a thesis are discussed in Chapter 1. It is unlikely that you will come up with a satisfactory thesis at the beginning of your project. You need a way to guide yourself through the early stages of research toward a main idea that is both useful and manageable. Having in mind a *working thesis*—a preliminary statement of your purpose—can help you select material that is of greatest interest to you as you examine potential sources. The working thesis will probably evolve as your research progresses, and you should be ready to accept such change. You must not fix on a thesis too early in the research process, or you may miss opportunities to refine it.

Develop a Working Bibliography

As you begin your research, you will look for published sources—essays, books, interviews with experts in the field—that may help you. This list of potentially useful sources is your *working bibliography.* There are many ways to develop this bibliography. The cataloging system in your library will give you titles, as will specialized published bibliographies in your field. (Some of these bibliographies are listed in Chapter 4.) The general reference works in which you did your background reading may also list such sources, and each specialized book or essay you find will itself have a bibliography of sources its writer used which may be useful to you, as discussed earlier.

It is from your working bibliography that you will select the items for your final bibliography, which will appear in the final draft of your paper. Early in your research you do not know which of the sources will help you and which will not, but it is important to keep an accurate description of each entry in your working bibliography so that you will be able to tell clearly which items you have investigated and which you will need to consult again. Establishing the working bibliography also allows you to practice using the bibliographical format you are required to follow in your final draft. As you make your list of potential sources, be sure to include all the information about each one in the proper format, using the proper punctuation. (Chapter 6 describes and gives models of appropriate bibliographical formats.)

Write for Needed Information

In the course of your research you may need to consult a source that is not immediately available to you. Working on the entrepreneurship paper, for example, you might find that a packet of potentially useful information is available from the Small Business Administration or from a public interest group in Washington. Or you may discover that a needed book is not held by your university library or by any other local library. Or you may learn that an elementary school entrepreneurship program has been implemented in the school system of another state. In such situations, it may be tempting to disregard potential sources because of the difficulty of consulting them. If you ignore this material, however, you are not doing your job.

It is vital that you take steps to acquire the needed material. In the first case above, you can simply write the Washington agency or interest group; in the second, you may use your library's interlibrary loan procedure to obtain a copy of the book; in the third, you can track down the administrator responsible for the entrepreneurship program, by mail or by phone, and ask for information. Remember that many businesses and government agencies want to share their information with interested citizens; some have employees or entire departments whose job is to facilitate communication with the public. Be as specific as possible when asking for information by mail. It is a good idea to outline your own project, in no more than a few sentences, in order to help the respondent determine the types of information that will be useful to you.

Never let the immediate unavailability of a source stop you from trying to consult it. And be sure to begin the job of locating and acquiring such long-distance source material as soon as possible to allow for the various delays that often occur.

Evaluate Written Sources

Fewer research experiences are more frustrating than trying to recall information found in a source that you can no longer identify. You must establish an efficient method of examining and evaluating the sources listed in your working bibliography. Suggestions for compiling an accurate record of your written sources are described below.

Determine Quickly the Potential Usefulness of a Source

For books, you can read the front material (the introduction, foreword, and preface) looking for the author's thesis; you can also examine chapter headings, dust jackets, and indexes. A journal article should announce its intention in its introduction, which in most cases will be a page or less in length. This sort of preliminary examination should tell you whether a more intensive examination is worthwhile. *Whatever you decide about the source, copy its title page,* making sure that all important publication information (including title, date, author, volume number, and page numbers) is included. Write on the photocopied page any necessary information that is not printed there. Without such a record, later on in your research you may forget that you have consulted a text, in which case you may find yourself repeating your examination of it.

When you have determined that a potential source is worth closer inspection, explore it carefully. If it is a book, determine whether you should invest the time needed to read it in its entirety. Whatever the source, make sure you understand not only its overall thesis, but also each part of the argument that the writer sets up to illustrate or prove the thesis. You need to get a feel for the shape of the writer's argument, how the subtopics form (or do *not* form) a logical defense of the main point. What do you think of the writer's logic and the examples used? Coming to an accurate appraisal may take more than one reading.

As you read, try to get a feel for the larger argument in which this source takes its place. Its references to the works of other writers will show you where else to look for additional material and indicate the general shape of scholarly opinion concerning your subject. If you can see the source you are reading as only one element in an ongoing dialogue instead of an attempt to have the last word on the subject, then you can place its argument in perspective.

Use Photocopies

Periodicals and most reference works cannot be checked out of the library. Before the widespread placement of photocopy machines, students could use these materials only in the library, jotting down information on note cards. While there are advantages to using the note card method (see below), photocopying saves you time in the library and allows you to take the source information in its original shape home, where you can decide how to use it at your convenience.

If you do decide to make copies of source material, you should do the following:

- Be sure to follow all copyright laws.
- Have the exact change for the photocopy machines. Do not trust the change machines at the library. They are usually battle-scarred and cantankerous.
- Record all necessary bibliographical information on the photocopy. If you forget to do this, you may find yourself making an extra trip to the library just to get an accurate date of publication or page numbers.

Remember that photocopying a source is not the same thing as examining it. You will still have to spend time going over the material, assimilating it in order to use it accurately. It is not enough merely to have the information close to hand or even to read it through once or twice. You must *understand it thoroughly.* Be sure to give yourself time for this kind of evaluation.

The note card: A thing of the past? In many ways note cards are an old-fashioned method of recording source material, and for unpracticed researchers they may seem an unwieldy and unnecessary step, since the information jotted on them—one fact per card—will eventually have to be transmitted again, in the research paper. However, before you decide to bury the note-card system once and for all, consider its advantages:

1. Using note cards is a way of forcing you to think productively as you read. In translating the language of the source material into the language of your notes, you are assimilating the material more completely than you would by merely reading it.

2. Note cards give you a handy way to arrange and rearrange your facts, looking for the best possible organization for your paper. Not even a computer gives you the flexibility of a pack of note cards as you try to order your paper.

Determine Whether Interviews or Surveys Are Needed

If your project calls for primary research, you may need to interview experts on your topic or to conduct a survey of opinions among a select group, using a questionnaire. Be sure to prepare yourself as thoroughly as possible for any primary research. Here are some tips:

Conducting an Interview

Establish a purpose for each interview, bearing in mind the requirements of your working thesis. In what ways might your interview benefit your paper? Write down your formulation of the interview's purpose. Estimate its length, and inform your subject. Arrive for your scheduled interview on time and dressed appropriately. Be courteous.

Learn as much as possible about your topic by researching published sources. Use this research to design your questions. If possible, learn something about the backgrounds of the people you interview. This knowledge may help you to establish rapport with your subjects and will also help you tailor your questions. Take with you to the interview a list of prepared questions. However, be ready during the interview to depart from your scheduled list in order to follow any potentially useful direction that the questioning may take.

Take notes. Make sure you have extra pens. Do not use a tape recorder because it will inhibit most interviewees. If you must use audio tape, *ask for permission from your subject* before beginning the interview. Follow up your interview with a thank-you letter and, if feasible, a copy of the paper in which the interview is used.

Designing and Conducting a Survey

Chapter 11 discusses instructions for designing and conducting a survey.

Draft a Thesis and Outline

No matter how thoroughly you may hunt for data or how fast you read, you will not be able to find and assimilate every source pertaining to your subject, especially if it is popular or controversial, and you should not prolong your research unduly. You must bring this phase of the project to an end—with the option of resuming it later if the need arises—and begin to shape both the material you have gathered and your thoughts about it into a paper. During the research phase of your project, you have been thinking about your working thesis, testing it against the material you have discovered and considering ways to improve it. Eventually, you must formulate a thesis that sets out an interesting and useful task, one that can be satisfactorily managed within the length limits of your assignment and that effectively employs much, if not all, of the material you have gathered.

Once you have formulated your thesis, it is a good idea to make an outline of the paper. In helping you to determine a structure for your paper, the outline is also testing the thesis, prompting you to discover the kinds of work your paper will have to do to complete the task set out by the thesis. Chapter 1 discusses the structural requirements of the formal and the informal outline. (If you have used note cards, you may want to start outlining by organizing your cards according to the headings you have given them and looking for logical connections among the different groups of cards. Experimenting with structure in this way may lead you to discoveries that will further improve your thesis.)

No thesis or outline is written in stone. There is still time to improve the structure or purpose of your paper even after you have begun to write your first draft, or, for that matter, your final draft. Some writers actually prefer to write a first draft of the paper before outlining, then study the draft's structure in order to determine what revisions need to be made. *Stay flexible*, always looking for a better connection, a sharper wording of your thesis. All the time you are writing, the testing of your ideas continues.

Write a First Draft

Despite all the preliminary work you have done on your paper, you may feel a resistance to beginning your first draft. Integrating all your material, your ideas, into a smoothly flowing argument is indeed a complicated task. It may help to think of your first attempt as only a *rough draft*, which can be changed as necessary. Another strategy for reducing the reluctance to starting is to begin with the part of the draft that you feel most confident about instead of with the introduction. You may write sections of the draft in any order, piecing the parts together later. But however you decide to start writing—**START.**

Obtain Feedback

It is not enough that *you* understand your argument; others have to understand it, too. If your instructor is willing to look at your rough draft, you should take advantage of the opportunity and pay careful attention to any suggestions for improvement. Other readers may be of help, though having a friend or a relative read your draft may not be as helpful as having it read by someone who is knowledgeable in your field. In any event, be sure to evaluate carefully any suggestions you receive for improvement. Remember, the final responsibility for the paper rests with you.

3.3 ETHICAL USE OF SOURCE MATERIAL

You want to use your source material as effectively as possible. This will sometimes mean that you should quote from a source directly, while at other times you will want to express source information in your own words. At all times, you should work to integrate the source material skillfully into the flow of your written argument.

When to Quote

You should quote directly from a source when the original language is distinctive enough to enhance your argument or when rewording the passage would lessen its impact. In the interest of fairness, you should also quote a passage to which your paper will take exception. Rarely, however, should you quote a source at great length (longer than two or three paragraphs). Nor should your paper, or any lengthy section of it, be merely a string of quoted passages. The more language you take from the writings of others, the more the quotations will disrupt the rhetorical flow of your own words. Too much quoting creates a choppy patchwork of varying styles and borrowed purposes in which sense of your own control over your material is lost.

Placing Quotations in Relation to Your Own Writing

When you do use a quotation, make sure that you insert it skillfully. According to several authoritative bibliographical format sources, quotations of four lines or fewer should be integrated into your text and set off with quotation marks:

> "In the last analysis," Alice Thornton argued in 1990, "we cannot afford not to embark on a radical program of fiscal reform" (12).

Quotations longer than four lines should begin on a new line and be double-spaced and indented five spaces from the left-hand margin:

> Blake's outlook for the solution to the city's problem of abandoned buildings is anything but optimistic:
> > If the trend in demolitions due to abandonments continues, the cost of doing nothing may be too high. The three-year period from 1988 to 1991 shows an annual increase in demolitions of roughly twenty percent. Such an upward trend for a sustained period of time would eventually place a disastrous hardship on the city's resources. And yet the city council seems bent on following the tactic of inaction. (1993, 8)

Acknowledge Quotations Carefully

Failing to signal the presence of a quotation skillfully can lead to confusion or choppiness:

> The U.S. Secretary of Labor believes that worker retraining programs have failed because of a lack of trust within the American business culture. "The American business community does not visualize the need to invest in its workers" (Winn 1992, 11).

The first sentence in the above passage seems to suggest that the quote that follows comes from the Secretary of Labor. Note how this revision clarifies the attribution:

According to reporter Fred Winn, the U.S. Secretary of Labor believes that worker retraining programs have failed because of a lack of trust within the American business culture. Summarizing the Secretary's view, Winn writes, "The American business community does not visualize the need to invest in its workers" (1992, 11).

The origin of each quote must be signaled within your text at the point where the quote occurs, as well as in the list of works cited, which follows the text. Chapter 6 describes documentation formats that are commonly approved in business writing.

Quote Accurately

If your quotation introduces careless variants of any kind, you are misrepresenting your source. Proofread your quotations very carefully, paying close attention to such surface features as spelling, capitalization, italics, and the use of numerals.

Occasionally, in order either to make a quotation fit smoothly into a passage, to clarify a reference, or to delete unnecessary material, you may need to change the original wording slightly. You must, however, signal any such change to your reader. Some alterations may be noted by brackets:

> "Several times in the course of the interview, the president of RJT, Inc., said that his stand [on closing the local operation] remains unchanged" (Johnson 1997, 2).

Ellipses indicate that words have been left out of a quote.

> "The last time the firm showed a profit for three quarters in a row . . . was back in 1982" (Samuels 1996, 143).

When you integrate quoted material with your own prose, it is unnecessary to begin the quote with ellipses.

> Benton raised eyebrows with his claim that "nobody in the controller's office knows how to tie a shoe, let alone construct a budget" (Jennings 1997, 12).

Paraphrasing

Your writing has its own rhetorical attributes, its own rhythms and structural coherence. Inserting several quotations into a section of your paper can disrupt the patterns you establish in your prose and diminish its effectiveness. Paraphrasing, or recasting source material in your own words, is one way to avoid the choppiness that can result from a series of quotations.

Remember that a paraphrase is to be written in *your* language; it is not a near copy of the source writer's language. Merely changing a few words of the original does justice to no one's prose and frequently produces stilted passages. This sort of borrowing is actually a form of plagiarism. To integrate another's material into your writing fully, *use your own language.*

Paraphrasing may actually increase your comprehension of source material, because in recasting a passage you will have to think very careful about its meaning, more carefully, perhaps, than you might if you merely copied it word for word.

Avoiding Plagiarism

Paraphrases require the same sort of documentation as direct quotes. The words of a paraphrase may be yours, but the idea belongs to someone else. Failure to give that person credit, in the form of references within the text and in the bibliography, may make you vulnerable to a charge of plagiarism.

Plagiarism is the use of someone else's words or ideas without proper credit. While some plagiarism is deliberate, produced by writers who understand that they are guilty of academic thievery, much of it is unconscious, committed by writers who are not aware of the varieties of plagiarism or who are careless in recording their borrowings from sources. Plagiarism includes:

- Quoting directly without acknowledging the source
- Paraphrasing without acknowledging the source
- Constructing a paraphrase that closely resembles the original in language and syntax

One way to guard against plagiarism is to keep careful notes of when you have directly quoted source material and when you have paraphrased—making sure that the wording of the paraphrases is yours. Make sure that all direct quotes in your final draft are properly set off from your own prose, either with quotation marks or in indented blocks.

Students often minimize, or even dismiss the importance of plagiarism. "So what's the big deal?" In the academic world, and in the world of the professional business person, the work product is more often than not an idea. The academician generates theories, systems, and procedures. The business professional creates operations, finance, and marketing strategies. All of these are "just ideas," but on the basis of his idea to create a sporty, low-priced car, Lee Iacocca ascended to the presidency in two of the greatest corporations in the world. His idea—the Ford Mustang—became one of the most successful automobiles ever conceived.

Today, more than ever, we live in a world of ideas. The quality of your ideas will determine, more than any other output you produce, the level to which you will rise during your working life. Most people would never even consider stealing another's product when that product is tangible, a cleverly designed computer or sound system, for example. Likewise, we should consider the ideas of others to be unavailable for us to take without giving credit to the owner.

What kind of paraphrased material must be acknowledged? Basic material that you find in several sources need not be acknowledged by a reference. For example, it is unnecessary to cite a source for the information that IBM is a leading manufacturer of computer hardware and software, because this is a fact that is commonly known. However, Professor Jackson's opinion, published in a recent article, that IBM is currently in serious decline and may even go out of business within ten years is not a fact but a theory based on Jackson's research and defended by her. If you wish to make use of Jackson's opinion in a paraphrase, you need to give her credit for it, as you should the judgments and claims from any other source.

Any information that is not widely known, whether factual or open to dispute, should be documented. This includes statistics, graphs, tables, and charts taken from a source other than your own primary research.

CHAPTER 4

Sources of Information

4.1 HOW INFORMATION IS USED IN THE DISCIPLINES OF BUSINESS

In Chapter 3 we presented a systematic approach to the task of planning and writing research papers in the field of business. In this chapter we will give you a lot of information about finding sources for the kinds of information that go into business papers. Chances are you are reading this now because your instructor has given you a research paper to write, and you are ready to start the process of looking for sources. But before we plunge into the data, if you have not already done so, take a little more time to prepare. Do you have a written statement of purpose? Do you have a research question in mind? Do you know specifically what data you are looking for, what questions you need to answer?

If you cannot answer these basic questions, your research efforts are quite likely to end in frustration. There is a veritable mountain of data out there. Without a purpose to guide your use of it, however, data is literally meaningless. It is your purpose that turns data into information. Once you have determined specifically what your research task is, your efforts to mine the data stores of the library and the Internet will gratify you in ways you can only imagine. All that resource material out there contains power, and it can be yours to command-but not until you have a specific purpose. So now, before you go looking through Chapter 4, go back and read Chapter 3. Then, when you are ready, dive right in!

In most business classes, your textbooks will offer much of the information you need for your assignments. Often, however, you will be called upon to research specific companies, industries, business opportunities, strategies, issues, or other business topics. These outside projects are designed to give you practice in researching, organizing, and writing a variety of reports; and they introduce you to relevant data sources, many of which you will find useful throughout your business career.

In this chapter, we have categorized a wealth of information sources in a way that you should find useful. As you already know, having spent considerable time preparing research papers for your classes, data does not cooperate. In the five sections that follow, we have listed sources that are likely to be most fruitful for students seeking information of a particular sort. Of course, each source might well be useful to those seeking information of another kind altogether. To help you identify how focused or general a source may be, we have adopted a system of one to five stars (*). One star indicates that source is very narrowly focused and you can expect to find only information relevant to the topic under which that source is listed. Five stars means you can expect to find information that might be helpful for any of your business research purposes.

The star system will help you to identify quickly sources that may be of the most value to your present project. We suggest that you first visit the sources you need in the section that best describes your task, then, visit the four- and five-star sources listed under the other headings, checking out additional sources you find within the other sections and within the sources you visit, until you find the information you need.

Remember, research takes time. Before you begin to visit any sources, whether print or electronic, read the section in Chapter 10 about conducting searches on the Internet. The time you spend preparing for your quest will pay large dividends in efficiency and completeness in your data-gathering efforts. Your preparation for data searches is particularly important when you are preparing to visit Internet sources because these sites are extraordinarily distracting. Preparing this listing took longer than other chapters in this book because there is so much to see and so many places to visit that we had a hard time keeping our focus, just as we predict you will. If you have not yet visited hyperspace, you are in for a real treat.

Many of the sources listed are redundant. For example, there are several sources of financial ratios. We have included several because every library is different in its holdings. By listing a number of sources that offer essentially the same information, we hope to include at least one that you will be able to find at your school.

In printed discussions of Internet websites, it can sometimes be difficult determining which typographical marks close to a website name are actually part of the site name instead of simply part of the sentence. For clarity, we have enclosed the name of each website within angle brackets. Bear in mind that the brackets themselves are not part of the website name. Remember that any punctuation occurring close to a site name but *outside* the brackets is also not part of the name. For example, neither the brackets nor the period at the end of the following sentence are part of the site name mentioned:

Last night I started my Internet search at <http://www.bnet.att.com/>.

One final note: To demonstrate the incredible richness of the Internet, we used it to compile most of the information that makes up the rest of this chapter. We have placed plus signs (+) at the ends of entries to indicate the Internet sources from which many of the reviews in our list came. Here is a key to the review sources, along with the dates on which we accessed them:

+ Reviews marked with a single plus sign came from the "Industry Research Desk":

<http://www.virtualpet.com/industry/howto/search.htm>,

accessed March 19, 1997.

++ Reviews marked with two plus signs came from "Finding Industry Information":

<http://www.pitt.edu/~buslibry/industries.html>,

accessed March 19, 1997.

+++ Reviews marked with three plus signs came from "ABI/INFORM":

<http://infoshare1.princeton.edu:2003/online/databases/descriptions/abi_inform.html>,

accessed March 19, 1997.

++++ Reviews marked with four plus signs came from "NYPL How to Find U.S. Company Information":

<http://gopher.nypl.org/research/sibl/company/companyinfo.html#introduction>,

accessed March 19, 1997.

Reviews that are not marked by any plus signs originated with us.

4.2 GENERAL BUSINESS SOURCES

Nearly all useful business information is organized according to The Standard Industrial Classification System.

- **Standard Industrial Classification Manual.** Do you know how your business or industry is classified? Before attempting any serious business research you must find out how the various information sources classify your business or industry. Look in this manual. Every library has a copy. Or you can look up your classification on the Web at

<http://www.fedmarket.com/sic/index.html> or

<http://www.wave.net/upg/immigration/sic_index.html>.

- **New Standard Industrial Classifications Manual**

<http://www.ntis.gov/business/sic.htm>.

A new classification system called the North American Industry Classification System (NAICS) has been devised to apply to products and services that move across national borders under the North American Free Trade Agreement (NAFTA). If you are studying import/export, check out this brand new classification system on the Web.

General Business Starting Places on the Web

***** *Yahoo* <http://www.yahoo.com/Business/>

The very best starting point if you are not yet focused on specific questions, this Yahoo site can link you to every kind of business data on the Internet. Also see Yahoo Directories <http://www.yahoo.com/Business_and_Economy/Companies/Directories/> for company and specific industry directories.

**** *Business Bookmarks* <http://www.bnet.att.com/>

This site includes many links to specific business and industry sources. The regional links you can find here are of great value when you are looking for city-specific hard and soft data. Business Bookmarks is mainly oriented to business professionals.

Indexes of Business Periodicals and Documents

***** *ABI/Inform* (CD-ROM Database)

One of the most popular business databases in North America, this CD-ROM-based information source contains over 300,000 abstracts of articles published in over

800 business journals. Approximately 4,000 new abstracts and citations are added each month. +++

***** *Business Periodicals Index* (Print and CD-ROM Database)

This dual-medium source covers nearly 350 journals in business and economics. Types of journals listed include general business magazines, financial publications, personnel management, and a selection of trade journals. ++

***** *Dow Jones News Retrieval Service* (Online Private Database)

This online, *fee-based* service includes over 3,000 publications, newspaper, magazine articles and newswires, current and historical stock quotes, and company data. ++++

***** *Dun & Bradstreet Web Server* <http://www.dbisna.com/>

This site includes a "News & Views" feature and a "Business Trends" section containing recent articles, press releases and survey results. ++++

***** *F & S Index* (Print & Electronic Database)

This index provides detailed coverage of more than 750 trade journals, newspapers, government documents, and special studies. ++

* *Fortune Magazine* <http://pathfinder.com/@@yRf1fAcA1Qfs5KjR/fortune/index.html>

Fortune Magazine's website contains many Links to *Fortune* lists organized by country, industry, and company. ++++

***** *General Business File* (CD-ROM)

Citations and full text articles in this CD-ROM site pertain to business management, industry reports, company reports, and financial analysis. ++++

***** *NEXIS* (Online Private Database)

This online, *fee-based* service contains the full texts of articles from hundreds of newspapers (including *The New York Times*), periodicals, newsletters, and wire services. It is updated daily. ++++

***** *Wall Street Journal Index* (Print, CD-ROM, and Web)

The Wall Street Journal is widely acclaimed as the official chronicle of American business activity. Each year's index is divided into two volumes, one citing company-specific articles, and the other general news. ++ Also see the *fee-based WSJ* website for much broader on-line searches that can locate many business publications. <http://www.wsj.com/>.

***** *Wilson Business Abstracts* (CD-ROM)

Indexing business magazines, this CD-ROM source covers all subjects in business and economics. ++++

Lists of All Periodicals in Print

***** *Ulrich's International Periodicals Directory*

A directory of 62,000 periodicals covering all subject areas, this print-based source is great for locating hard-to-find trade publications. Once you find the trade publication, contact the editor for information on indexing sources so you can find the articles you need.

***** *Working Press of the Nation*

You can use this directory of periodicals in the same way as *Ulrich's* above. They are similar.

Small Business Information Sources

Some sources specialize in small business. Don't stop with these, but they may contain information not included in the more general business sources.

- *Business Dateline* (CD-ROM)
  Full text articles from more than 180 regional business journals, daily newspapers, and business wire services are included in this CD-ROM database. It is particularly useful for smaller companies. ++++
- *The Entrepreneur and Small Business Problem Solver: An Encyclopedic Reference and Guide*
- *Small Business Index*
  This index lists pamphlets, books, and articles that deal with various aspects of starting and operating a small business, arranged by type of business.
- *Small Business Reporter*
  Each issue of this periodical is dedicated to a particular type of small business or some aspect of small business in general.
- *Small Business: Look Before You Leap: A Catalog of Sources of Information to Help You Start and Manage Your Own Small Business*
- *Small Business Sourcebook*
  This print resource profiles many different types of small businesses. It gives a good overview of selected small businesses, with leads to additional sources and financial ratio information.

Sources of Sources

If you have not found a better starting point, try these sources of sources:

- *A Business Information Guide Book*
- *Business Information: How to Find It, How to Use It*
- *Business Information Sources*
- *Business Services and Information: The Guide to the Federal Government*
- *Encyclopedia of Associations*
- *Encyclopedia of Business Information*

Trade associations can offer a wealth of information on their industries. Write or call for help.

- *Encyclopedia of Business Information Sources*
- *National Trade and Professional Associations of the United States*
- *Statistics Sources*
- *Where to Find Business Information: A Worldwide Guide for Everyone Who Needs the Answers to Business Questions*

4.3 MARKETING INFORMATION SOURCES

*   *1990 U.S. Census Lookup* <http://cedr.lbl.gov/cdrom/doc/lookup_doc.html>

Allowing direct access to virtually all 1990 U.S. Bureau of Census data, this website lets you customize data searches to answer your specific questions.

*   *F&S Plus Text Predicasts* (CD-ROM)

(U.S. & International)—This marketing research index for companies and industries includes both abstracts and full texts of research articles. The print version comes in two volumes: *F&S Index International Annual and F&S Index United States Annual.* ++++

*   *Market Share Reporter*

Most of the data in this print source, which covers products and service categories in industries, comes from trade journals, newsletters, and magazines. Some data is based on analysts' reports as published in the *Investext* database. ++

*   *Predicats Forecasts*

Organized by product code, this print source leads users to publications offering projections of business and economic activities and provides a summary of data from these publications. ++

**   *Small Business Marketing: A Selected and Annotated Bibliography*
*   *United States Patent and Trademark Office* <http://www.uspto.gov/>

Search the patent and trademark archives. Learn about patents and trademarks as legal rights.

Discussions of Trading Areas

Following are several websites that let you identify the extent of your trading area, then print material to include in your marketing or business plan.

- *Census TMS Home Page* <http://tiger.census.gov/>
  This site allows you to create maps of any area of the U.S. You decide exactly where and what you want to show on the map. Zoom in and out to create exactly the map you want.
- *MapBlast Map Maker* <http://www.mapblast.com/>
- *Planet Earth Home Page State Maps* <http://www.nosc.mil/planet_earth/states.html>

- *Univ. of Texas Electronic Maps* <http://www.lib.utexas.edu/Libs/PCL/Map_collection/Map_collection.html>
- *Yahoo Maps* <http://www.vicinity.com/yahoo/>
  Input an address and see it on a U.S. street map.

4.4 INFORMATION ABOUT SPECIFIC INDUSTRIES AND COMPANIES

Check out these search strategy sites on the Web! They offer lots of links and citations to other sources on the Web and in print. Many of the other sources we have listed are linked from these sites, especially the last two. When performing on-line searches, beginning with one of these sites can save you a lot of searching and URL typing.

- *Finding Industry Information* <http://www.pitt.edu/~buslibry/industries.html>
  This site presents a search strategy and many print sources to help you find industry and company-specific data.
- *Industry Research Desk* <http://www.virtualpet.com/industry/>
  If you need specific industry or specific company information, there literally is no better place on Earth to find it than this site. Prepare to be amazed—and educated!
- *NYPL How to Find U.S. Company Information* <http://gopher.nypl.org/research/sibl/company/companyinfo.html>
  The New York Public Library guide to finding company information is an incomparable source of all sorts of information.

Industry Information

*   *Computer Select* (CD-ROM)

Covering more than 150 computer industry periodicals, this database focuses on hardware, software, electronics, engineering, and communications. It also includes computer hardware and software product information and short company profiles from data sources. ++++

*   *Encyclopedia of American Industries*

Providing comprehensive information on a wide range of industries, this print source describes industry background, organizational structure, current conditions, and industry leaders. ++

*   *Finance, Insurance, & Real Estate USA*

With more than 2,600 company listings, print resource provides comprehensive data on financial industries, including financial performance data; trends in establishments, employment, and payroll; state rankings; and detailed state industry data. ++

*   *Manufacturing USA*

This fifteen-year data series includes listings for nearly 25,000 companies, giving detailed information on 459 manufacturing industries, including data on establishment, employment, compensation, production and capital expenditures, shipments, and trends. ++

*   *Service Industries USA*

This print source gives comprehensive data on 2,100 services grouped into 151 industries. It combines federal statistics with a variety of statistics on establishments, employment, revenue, ownership, and occupation. Size, structure, and cost patterns of each industry are provided. Data is presented on national through city levels. ++

**   *Standard & Poor's Industry Surveys*

Focusing on the current situation and outlook, this resource offers concise investment profiles for a broad range of industries. Coverage is extensive and includes some summary data on major companies in each industry. ++

*   *U.S. Industrial Outlook*

Published by the Dept. of Commerce, this source gives brief profiles of industries and includes a description of the current business situation and five-year prospects. ++

Company Information

Many companies have been written up in case studies published in strategic marketing books or journals. Those studies can be quite useful. Look for cases on the company you are researching, their competitors, and their industry.

- *Case On-Line Information System* <telnet://ecch.babson.edu> (Login Name=COLIS)
  This site allows you to research over 10,000 academic cases.
- *Harvard Business School Case Studies Index* <gopher://hbscat.harvard.edu/>
  This site provides abstracts of cases and details about how to order the full cases.
- *MIS Case Studies* <http://www.cox.smu.edu/mis/cases/home.html>
  Source: +

Here are other resources offering a range of information on companies:

*   *American Big Business Directory* (CD-ROM)

This database specializes in information on the 140,000 U.S. companies with 100 or more employees. It includes names of over 430,000 executives. You can search this database by job title, primary SIC code, manufacturers, stock exchange. ++++

*   *American Business Disc* (CD-ROM)

This database contains addresses and sales information for 10 million U.S. companies, searchable by state, city, zip code, and area code. ++++

*   *American Manufacturers Directory* (CD-ROM)

Each entry in this database, which lists over 120,000 manufacturers with 25 or more employees, includes the company name, the complete address, the phone number, an executive name and title, up to 3 SIC codes, the number of employees, and the sales volume. ++++

*   *Brands and Their Companies/Companies and Their Brands*

This print resource is useful if you are not sure whether the name you have is the name of a company or a brand name. ++++

     *   *CompaniesOnline Search* <http://www.companiesonline.com>

A portion of the Dunn and Bradstreet credit report database is now available for *free*. Full Dunn and Bradstreet credit reports can be requested on companies through Dunn and Bradstreet on the web for $20 each. +

     *   *Corporate Affiliations Plus* (CD-ROM)

Updated annually, this directory provides information for over 16,000 major U.S. and foreign corporations and their subsidiaries, divisions, and affiliates. The print version is entitled *Directory of Corporate Affiliations*. ++++

     *   *Corptech Directory of Technology Companies* <http://www.corptech.com/providrs.htm>

This website provides descriptive information on over 40,000 U.S. high technology companies, including many small, privately-owned computer software and hardware firms, and many biotechnology firms. It also includes company rankings. ++++

     *   *Directory of Companies Required to File Annual Reports with the Securities and Exchange Commission*

     *   *Dun's Business Locator* (CD-ROM)

Focusing on the current year, this database lists addresses and type of business for over 10 million companies from Dun and Bradstreet Information Services' business database. You can search by company name only. ++++

     *   *Dun's Million Dollar Disc* (CD-ROM)

This database targets large public and private companies, giving address, phone, sales volume, number of employees, SIC code, key officers, board of directors, DUNS number, ownership date, bank, accounting firm, and state of incorporation. The print version is entitled *Million Dollar Directory: America's Leading Public & Private Companies*.

     *   *Dun's Service Market Disc* (CD-ROM)

This resources offers information on 205,000 U.S. service companies and is searchable by sales, SIC code, number of employees, zip code, area code, state, county, and city. Companies are listed alphabetically, geographically, and by industry SIC code. The print version is titled *Dun's Directory of Service Companies*. ++++

     *   *Dun's Small Business Sourcing File* (CD-ROM)

This source lists over 250,000 small businesses, including minority and female-owned businesses, searchable by SIC code, business type, and geographic area. ++++

     *   *Dun's Regional Directory*

Area companies are listed alphabetically and by industry SIC code. ++++

     *   *Hoover's Handbook of American Business*

This source prints profiles of over 500 public and private corporations and some large nonprofit organizations. ++++

* *Hoover's Guide to Private Companies*

Five hundred major private U.S. enterprises are profiled. ++++

* *Hoover's Guide to the Top New York Companies*

This resource profiles top New York area public and private companies. ++++

* *Hoover's Online* <http://www.hoovers.com/>

The corporate directory located on this site can be searched by ticker symbol, company name, location, industry, and sales. This database profiles publicly listed U.S. companies traded on the three major stock exchanges and more than 1,200 of America's largest private companies. There are also many links to other useful resources. ++++

* *International Directory of Company Histories*

Organized by industry, this multi-volume set describes firms from every major industry, from advertising to waste management, providing detailed information on the historical development of the world's largest and most influential public, private, and state-controlled companies. ++++

* *Look Up USA* <http://www.abii.com/>

You can look up any business in the U.S. and get its address and phone number, plus credit rating information. This site is constantly updated but contains information only as current as the most recent *Yellow Pages* for each location.

* *Moody's Complete Corporate Index*
* *Networth's "The Insider: Public Companies"* <http://networth.galt.com/www/home/equity/irr/>

This site provides a list of links to company websites.

* *Notable Corporate Chronologies*

This print resource provides a chronological history for more than 1,150 corporations worldwide. ++++

* *Open Market Commercial Sites Index* <http://www.directory.net/dir/directory.html>

On this site you will find a list of links to company websites.

* *Owners and Officers of Private Companies*

Basic information, including financial figures for more than 46,000 leading private U.S. companies, is provided in this print source. ++++

* [SBA Reports] <gopher://gopher.umsl.edu:70/11/library/govdocs/indpro/>

The Small Business Administration provides extensive profiles for a few of the typical "mom and pop" businesses.

* *Standard Directory of Advertisers and Agencies*

This directory gives information about the advertisers and advertising methods of a wide range of companies. Information includes each company's advertising agency, the media used, and appropriation amounts. There is a CD-ROM version: *Advertiser & Agency Red Book Plus.* ++++

*   *Standard & Poor's Register of Corporations, Directors and Executives* (Print and CD-ROM)

Focusing on public and private companies, this database gives basic information for each of its subjects, including accounting firm, primary bank, and law firm. Vol. 2 contains addresses and brief biographies of company directors and executives. ++++

*   *Thomas Register of American Manufacturers* (Print and CD-ROM, Web version: <http://www.thomasregister.com:8000/>)

Use the company profiles volumes for basic information. ++++

*   *Ward's Business Directory of U.S. Private and Public Companies*

For the companies profiled, *Ward's* lists address, phone, fax, sales volume, number of employees, SIC code, year founded, and key officers. ++++
The following sources provide information on industry operating norms needed to perform a *ratio analysis.* (See Chapter 14 for a discussion of financial ratio analysis.)

- *Business Ratios by Gates*
- *Almanac of Business and Industrial Financial Ratios*
- *Financial Studies of the Small Business*
- *Industry Norms and Key Business Ratios*

This book explains the ratios. Also see our Chapter 14 for an explanation of selected ratios.

- *Quarterly Financial Report for Manufacturing, Mining and Trade Corporations*
- *Robert Morris Associates. RMA Annual Statement Studies*
- *S & P's Analysts Handbook; Composite Corporate Per Share Data, by Industries*

4.5 BUSINESS AND EMPLOYMENT LAW SOURCES

Many legal issues are discussed in corporate reports produced by the companies in the industry. (See the sections entitled "Information About Specific Industries and Companies" and "Financial and Economic Data Sources" in this chapter for access to corporate annual, 10K, and 10Q reports.)

*   *American Legal Reports*

A several hundred volume set, this work consists of reports written about specific issues and is printed in a series, the current one of which is the fifth. Paper indexes are provided. You will be able to find reports on almost any industry. The reports consist of discussions of cases (with case references) about specific issues. It is an excellent reference. +

*   *Index to Legal Periodicals* (Print and CD-ROM)
*   *Federal Court Finder* <http://www.law.emory.edu/FEDCTS/>

This site locates federal courts and provides decisions from some of them. +

*   *PACER* <http://www.uscourts.gov/PubAccess.html>

This *fee-based*, on-line system offers current court records searchable on-line.

**   *Public Affairs Information Service (PAIS)*

This print source covers the public policy literature of law, business, economics, finance, international relations and trade, government, and other social sciences. ++

*   *U.S. Court of Appeals 10th Circuit* <http://www.law.emory.edu/10circuit/>

On this site you will find information on the cases in the 10th circuit court's jurisdiction.

4.6 FINANCIAL AND ECONOMIC DATA SOURCES

*   *Best's Insurance Reports*

This source offers financial information on thousands of insurance companies, including ratings of financial conditions. ++++

*   *Capital Changes Reporter*

For public companies, this print source provides a chronological list of dividends, stock splits, name changes, mergers, acquisitions, and other changes in corporate capital and debt structure. ++++

*   *Compact D/SEC* (CD-ROM)

This SEC database, from Disclosure, offers historical and current business and financial information covering over 11,000 public companies in the U.S. It includes directory information, officers and directors, management information, balance sheets, and price/earning ratios. ++++

*   *Compustat PC Plus* (CD-ROM)

This database gives the following types of Security and Exchange Commission reports: Annual Reports, 10K, proxy, and company profiles for businesses listed on the New York Stock Exchange and the American Stock Exchange only. ++++

****   *EDGAR* <http://www.sec.gov/edgarhp.htm>

From the EDGAR Database you can retrieve SEC filings (including 10K's, 10Q's, Annual Reports, and Prospectuses) for approximately 3,500 U.S. public corporations. The site is made available through the EDGAR development project at the NYU Stern School of Business. ++++

****   *Laser Disclosure* (CD-ROM)

This database gives full text images (including graphics) of 10K Reports, Annual Reports, and other financial statements. ++++

** *Moody's Industry Review*

Covering 4,000 companies in almost 150 industries, this review profiles companies ranked within industry by five financial characteristics (revenue, net income, total assets, cash and marketable securities, and long-term debt) and five ratios (profit margin, return on capital, return on assets, P/E, and dividend yield). You will also find EPS, book value, and 12-stock price summaries. ++

* *Moody's Manuals*

Consult Moody's Complete Corporate Index to know which Moody's Manual to use. Each company listing provides an abstract of the financial statement and debt structure, a brief history, and a description of subsidiaries and properties. ++++

** *National Trade Data Bank (NTDB)*

A collection of many different databases on CD-ROM, the NTDB includes economic and demographic statistics for many countries, *A Basic Guide to Exporting, Foreign Trade Data, The Foreign Traders Index* (a directory of companies interested in dealing with U.S. companies), export opportunity reports, and much more. ++ This material is available on-line for an individual fee of $150 per year. Your school may also own a site license to the database. Ask your professor.

Tip: The *INQUERY Search Demonstration Page* <http://ciir.cs.umass.edu/demo/> lets you search for information on older NTDB databases. Select "Market Research" as your target database in the query page.

* *PC Quote Online* <http://www.pcquote.com/>

Check this site for real-time stock quotes, ticker-symbol lookup, and free search for breaking news on a company.

* *Standard & Poor's Corporation Records*

This multi-volume set provides short histories and descriptions of public corporations listed on the AMEX, NYSE, and the larger unlisted and regional exchanges. The Daily News volume should be checked for current information about dividends, splits, mergers, etc. ++++

* *Standard & Poor's Stock Reports* (CD-ROM)

Financial information for public companies listed here includes PE ratios, dividend, beta and earnings data, and S & P bond ratings. Updated quarterly, this resource is also available in print. Both current and historical trend data are included. ++++

*** *Streetlink* <http://www.streetlink.com/>

Check this site for the latest quarterly reports from many public companies and press releases. ++++

* [10K REPORTS] (Microfiche)

Selected 10K and Annual Reports on microfiche for publicly traded companies may be available in your library. Ask your librarian. ++++

**   *Value Line Investment Survey*

For about 1,700 stocks, This print source, published weekly, provides financial fundamentals, plus opinions about investment worthiness, rankings for safety, and forecasts of future performance. ++++

***   *Wall Street Research Net* <http://www.wsrn.com/home/companyResearch.html>

Type in the company name or stock symbol and WSRN will retrieve links to their home page, current stock quote, stock graph, SEC filings, press releases, company news, company profile, and more. ++++

CHAPTER 5

Formats

5.1 GETTING STARTED

Your format makes your paper's first impression. Justly or not, accurately or not, the format of your paper announces your professional competence—or lack of competence. A well executed format implies that your paper is worth reading. More important, however, a proper format brings information to your readers in a familiar form that has the effect of setting their minds at ease. Your paper's format, therefore, should impress your reader with your academic competence as a business professional by following accepted format standards. Like the style and clarity of your writing, your format communicates messages that are often more readily and profoundly received than the content of the document itself.

The format described in this chapter is in conformance with standards generally accepted in the disciplines of business and includes instructions for the following elements:

- General page format
- Title page
- Abstract
- Executive summary
- Table of contents
- List of tables, figures
- Text
- Reference page
- Appendix

Except for special instructions from your course instructor, follow the format directions in this manual exactly.

5.2 GENERAL PAGE FORMAT

Business paper assignments should be typed or computer printed on 8 ½-by-11 inch premium white bond paper, 20-pound or heavier. Do not use any other color or size except to comply with special instructions from your instructor, and do not use an off-white or poor quality (draft) paper. Business papers that are worth the time to write are worthy of good paper.

Always submit to your instructor an original typed or computer (preferably laser or inkjet) printed manuscript. Do not submit a photocopy! Always print a second copy to keep for your own files in case the original is lost.

Margins, except for theses and dissertations, should be one inch on all sides of the paper. Unless otherwise instructed, all paper submissions should be *double-spaced* in a 12-point word processing font or typewriter pica type. Typewriter elite type may be used if another is not available. Select a font that is plain and easy to read, such as Helvetica, Arial, Courier, Garamond, or Times Roman. Do not use script, stylized, or elaborate fonts.

Page numbers should appear in the upper right-hand corner of each page, one inch from the right side and one-half inch from the top of the page, beginning immediately after the title page. Numbering should proceed consecutively beginning with the title page, although no page number should appear on either the title page or the first page of text. You may, if you wish, use lowercase roman numerals (i, ii, iii, iv, v, vi, vii, viii, ix, x, etc.) for pages that precede the first page of text, such as the table of contents and table of figures. If you use roman numerals for these pages, place each numeral at the center of the bottom of the page.

Ask your instructor about bindings. In the absence of further directions, *do not bind* your paper or enclose it within a plastic cover sheet. Place one staple in the upper left corner, or use a paper clip at the top of the paper. Note that a paper to be submitted to a journal for publication should not be clipped, stapled, or bound in any form.

5.3 TITLE PAGE

The following information will be centered on the title page:

- Title of paper
- Name of writer
- Course name, section number, and instructor
- College or university
- Date

As the sample title page shows, the title should clearly describe the problem addressed in the paper. If the paper discusses the impact of the *Americans With Disabilities Act,* for example, the title "Profit Impact of the *Americans With Disabilities Act*" is professional, clear, and helpful to the reader. "The *Americans With Disabilities Act,*" "New Legislation," or "Politics and Profits" are all too vague to be effective. Also, the title should not be "cute." A cute title may attract attention for a play on Broadway, but it will detract from the credibility of a paper in all business disciplines—yes, even in marketing. "New Invention Fails to Solve Inadequate Solid Waste Disposal Problems" is professional. "Down in the Dumps" is not.

In the disciplines of business you will be called upon to write not only traditional term papers but also a number of specialized formal reports. Three such reports discussed in this manual, *business plans, marketing plans,* and *case analyses,* require the use of a *cover sheet* rather than a title page. There is little difference between the

A Comparison of the Management Styles of Henry Ford
and Ross Perot

by

Howard Jones

Strategic Management

MNGMT 4892

Dr. Bart Chekhowsky

University of the Foothills

January 26, 1997

two; in order to allow report readers to communicate quickly with the writers, a cover sheet includes the writer's place of employment and his or her (or their) telephone number(s). The company for which you work will probably specify the format of your cover sheet.

5.4 ABSTRACT

An abstract is a brief summary of a paper written primarily to allow potential readers to know the paper's subject matter to see if the paper contains information of sufficient interest for them to read the paper. People conducting research want specific kinds of information, and they often read dozens of abstracts looking for papers that contain information relevant to their research topic. Abstracts have the designation "Abstract" centered near the top of the page. Next, the title appears, also centered, followed by a paragraph that precisely states the paper's topic, research and analysis methods, and results and conclusions. An abstract should be written in one paragraph which does not exceed 150 words. Remember that an abstract is not an introduction. Instead, it summarizes your paper. An example of an abstract appears below.

Abstract

Business Concepts of the Novice Entrepreneur

The author, an experienced teacher of entrepreneurship, believes that novice entrepreneurs fail in their first business creation efforts because they possess a number of flawed or missing business concepts. To investigate these concepts, the author conducted an ethnographic study using a qualitative approach. The author employed a triangulation method of data collection, interviewing three separate sources. In addition, the author drew upon his own experiences in arriving at the tentative conclusions presented and discussed in the paper. The paper synthesizes six faulty concepts from the interview data collected.

5.5 EXECUTIVE SUMMARY

A paper will ordinarily have either an abstract or an executive summary. Rarely will one paper have both. Like an abstract, an executive summary summarizes the content of a paper but does so in more detail. Whereas abstracts are read by people who are doing research, executive summaries are more likely to be read by people who need some or all of the information in the paper in order to make a decision. Many people, however, will read the executive summary to fix clearly in mind the organization and results of a paper before reading the paper itself. Equipped with the content that the executive summary provides, readers then understand the whole paper as they read it in its entirety. An example of an executive summary is printed below.

Executive Summary

The MGB, Ltd., parts manufacturing plant located in Singapore has experienced a number of problems including missed due dates, high employee turnover, and unacceptably low quality. An investigation of the situation by Bob Chalmers, Assistant Production Manager at the Canton, Ohio, facility and Sheri Rupp, Division Quality Coordinator, has yielded a number of explanations for the observed difficulties.

The Singapore plant was brought on line in 1978 and has experienced periods of stable productivity, interspersed with chaotic interruptions similar to that now underway. Past efforts to address the problems by replacing managers have had little effect. In some cases, replacing the manager has even exacerbated the problems.

The Singapore plant is critical to the operations of MGB, Ltd. because it offers the only source of low cost labor for the parts it supplies to the other divisional production facilities. Efforts to secure outside vendors have failed due to a number of problems including high cost, low quality, proprietary equipment requirements, and the inherent complexity of the parts manufacturing processes required.

The specific findings from our investigation include the following:

1. The missed due dates result mainly from the other two problems. When a low quality batch has to be reworked, plant output is naturally curtailed. The low quality seems to be mainly the result of poorly trained new hires who have been, of necessity, hired to replace exiting workers.

2. Employee turnover appears to be the result of many factors, which can be divided into two categories: external environmental factors that we cannot control and internal factors that we can control.

3. Low quality has two components: poorly trained workers making mistakes that result in reduced quality of output, and poor quality materials that, when allowed to enter the system, make defective parts more likely.

Our analysis suggests that the Singapore plant consider implementing several changes to address the three problem areas. First, the area of quality need not be addressed directly until the high turnover and the missed due dates are solved. We suspect that solving the first two will also go a long way toward solving the third.

A consultant should be hired who can assist management in accurately predicting the effects of political conflicts as they emerge. Most of the external environmental changes that affect worker turnover are either changes in the law, such as different curfews and/or travel permit restrictions, or changes in the economy that result from political action, such as currency exchange rate effects and import/export restrictions that cause rapid inflation.

The consultant will help management devise contingency plans to address imminent threats, rather than being caught flat-footed as in the past. Worker training should be formalized and made more efficient. This should also include a major effort at cross-training. These efforts will go a long way toward assisting plant management in insuring that a core of well-trained workers is always available.

Once these recommendations have been implemented, quality can again be addressed directly if required.

5.6 TABLE OF CONTENTS

A table of contents does not provide as much information as an outline but does include the titles of the major divisions and subdivisions of a paper. Tables of contents are not normally required but may be included in student papers or papers

Table of Contents

presented at professional meetings. They are normally required, however, in books, theses, and dissertations. The table of contents should reflect the headings used in the text. It should consist of the chapter or main section titles with one additional level of titles.

5.7 LISTS OF TABLES AND FIGURES

A list of tables or list of figures contains the titles of the tables or figures included in the paper in the order in which they appear, along with their page numbers. You may list tables, illustrations, and figures together under the title "figures" (and title them all "figures" in the text), or if you have a list with more than one-half page of entries, you may have separate lists of tables, figures, and illustrations. The format for all such tables should correspond to that of the example below.

```
List of Figures

1. Population Growth in Five U.S. Cities 1980-1986...  1

2. Number of Businesses by State, 1980 and 1990 ......  3

3. Economic Indicators January to June 1991 .........  6

4. Number of Business Failures by State, 1980
   and 1990 ............................................ 11

5. International Trade 1880-1890 ..................... 21

6. Gross Domestic Product, Nova Scotia, 1900-1960 .... 22

7. California Business Regulatory Expenditures
   1960-1980 .......................................... 35

8. Housing Starts in the Midwest .................... 37

9. Albuquerque Hotel Industry, 1978 ................. 39

10. Quality Control Developments Following the
    World War II Era ................................. 40
```

½"

3

½"

1"   1"

as they relate to being in business and solving business-related problems? To answer this question I have taken a viewpoint that my constructs, presented below, which are supported by data from two or more sources are likely to be more generally accurate than those supported by only one source. Those constructs which were contradicted have not been presented here.

I contend that novice entrepreneurs, of which Sam is one example, possess at least some of the erroneous concepts described briefly below. I have interpreted Sam's actions and ideas, together with data from the two other sources, to support my contention. Following the description of the concepts identified, each concept is then discussed in detail in the sections which follow, beginning with the most pervasive, and, I believe, the most important.

The six constructs that emerged from analysis and synthesis of the qualitative data are as follows:

1. *If You Agree with Me, We Must Both Be Right!* This concept results in actions taken to ratify a personally held set of beliefs and makes an objective analysis of a business proposal more difficult.

2. *Ignorance Is Bliss.* Lack of knowledge has a profound effect on the actions of the novice entrepreneur. This concept can be divided into three sub-categories as follows: a) "I know this will work so don't bother me with your negative attitude." There is a tendency to ignore the possibility that negative information exists. b) "Since I can't solve the problem, I don't believe anyone else can either." Lacking knowledge of a problem solution causes one to think no one else has a solution either. c) "Anybody can do that!" There is a strong tendency to oversimplify.

3. *Make a Plan? Hell, I'm Going to Do Something!* Planning, as a mature business concept, is almost entirely missing in the work of the novice entrepreneur.

4. *It's Not My Fault!* Novices tend to attribute problems to external factors.

5. *Try It. You'll Like It!* Novices have a selling concept rather than a more mature marketing concept.

6. *Hope Springs Eternal!* This concept, that I can succeed if only I keep trying, is the condition (if there is one) required for business success. Because education does often come from experience, persistence is almost sufficient by itself.

1"

5.8 TEXT

Ask your instructor for the number of pages required for the paper you are writing. The text should follow the directions explained in Chapters 1 and 2 of this manual and should conform to the format of the facsimile page shown below. Note that the facsimile page is double-spaced. Most professional business writing is single-spaced, but while you remain a student, your papers will be critiqued and graded. By double-spacing, you allow your professor the room needed to write comments where they can be most beneficial to you.

Chapter Headings

Your papers should include no more than three levels of headings:

- *Primary*, which should be centered, with each word except articles, prepositions, and conjunctions capitalized.
- *Secondary*, which begin at the left margin, also with each word except articles, prepositions, and conjunctions capitalized.
- *Tertiary*, which should be written sentence style (with only the first word and proper nouns capitalized) with a period at the end, underlined. The following illustration shows the proper use of headings:

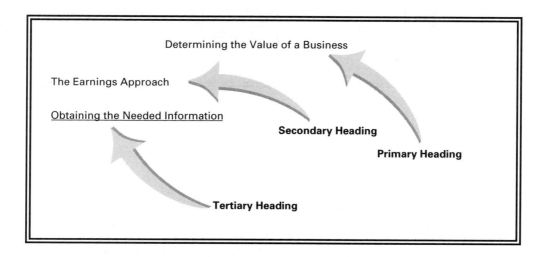

Tables

Tables in the text are used to show relationships among data in order to help the reader come to a conclusion or understand something. Tables that show simple results or "raw" data should be placed in an appendix. Tables should not reiterate the content of the text. They should say something new, and they should stand on their own. That is, the reader should be able to understand your table without reading the text.

Clearly label the columns and rows in your table. The source of the information in the table should be shown immediately below the table, not in a footnote or end note. The following diagram provides an example of a properly formatted table.

Table 1. Population Change in Ten U.S. Cities 1980–1986

City	1986 Rank	1980 Population	1986 Population	Percentage Change 1980 to 1986
New York	1	7,071,639	7,262,700	2.7
Los Angeles	2	2,968,528	3,259,300	9.8
Chicago	3	3,005,072	3,009,530	.2
Houston	4	1,611,382	1,728,910	7.3
Philadelphia	5	1,688,210	1,642,900	-2.3
Detroit	6	1,203,369	1,086,220	-9.7
San Diego	7	875,538	1,015,190	16.0
Dallas	8	904,599	1,003,520	10.9
San Antonio	9	810,353	914,350	12.8
Phoenix	10	790,183	894,070	13.1

Source: U.S. Bureau of the Census, County and City Data Book 1988.

Illustrations and Figures

Illustrations such as charts and graphs are frequently included in the body of business papers and in the appendices where they are necessary to explain the content. If illustrations are necessary, do not paste or tape photocopies of photographs or similar materials to the pages of the text or the appendix. Instead, photocopy each one on a separate sheet of paper and center each illustration, along with its typed title, within the normal margins of the paper. Oversized materials such as maps, product literature, and financial statements can be handled in one of three ways. Crop the desired material during the photocopy process so that it will fit on the standard page, reduce the material so that it will fit on a standard page, or use an 11" x 17" page folded as shown in Figure 1 below. Note that the format of the following illustrations conforms to the format you should use for illustrations embedded in the body of the report. The format of the titles of each illustration should be the same as the format for tables and figures.

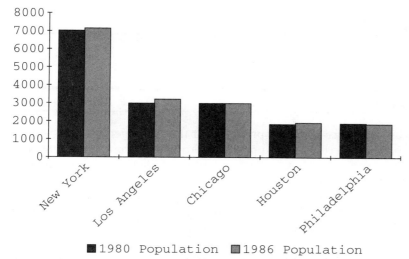

Source: U.S. Bureau of the Census, County and City Data Book 1988 (1988).

Figure X. Population Growth in Five U.S. Cities 1980-1986

FIGURE 1. Folding Oversized Illustrations.

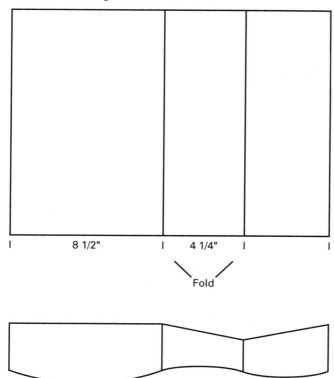

5.9 REFERENCE PAGE

The format for references is discussed in Chapter 6.

5.10 APPENDICES

Appendices are reference materials provided for the convenience of the reader at the back of the paper, after the text. Appendices provide information that supplements the important facts contained in the text and may include maps, charts, tables, and selected documents. Do not place in your appendix materials that are merely interesting or decorative. Include only items that will answer questions raised by the text or are necessary to explain the text. Follow the guidelines for formats for illustrations, tables, and figures when adding material in an appendix. At the top center of the page, label your first appendix "Appendix A," your second appendix "Appendix B," and so on. Do not append an entire government report, journal article, or other publication, but only the portions of such documents that are necessary to support your paper. The source of the information should always be evident on the appended pages. A sample appendix page is given below.

Appendix A

Table 1. Population Change in Ten U.S. Cities 1980–1986

City	1986 Rank	1980 Population	1986 Population	Percentage Change 1980 to 1986
New York	1	7,071,639	7,262,700	2.7
Los Angeles	2	2,968,528	3,259,300	9.8
Chicago	3	3,005,072	3,009,530	.2
Houston	4	1,611,382	1,728,910	7.3
Philadelphia	5	1,688,210	1,642,900	-2.3
Detroit	6	1,203,369	1,086,220	-9.7
San Diego	7	875,538	1,015,190	16.0
Dallas	8	904,599	1,003,520	10.9
San Antonio	9	810,353	914,350	12.8
Phoenix	10	790,183	894,070	13.1

Source: U.S. Bureau of the Census, County and City Data Book 1988 (1988).

CHAPTER 6

Citing Sources

6.1 PRELIMINARY DECISIONS

One of your most important jobs as a research writer is to document your use of source material carefully and clearly. Failure to do so will cause your reader confusion, damage the effectiveness of your paper, and perhaps make you vulnerable to a charge of plagiarism. Proper documentation is more than just good form. It is a powerful indicator of your own commitment to scholarship and the sense of authority that you bring to your writing. Good documentation demonstrates your expertise as a researcher and increases your reader's trust in you and your work.

Unfortunately, as anybody who has ever written a research paper knows, getting the documentation right can be a frustrating, confusing job, especially for the writer who is not familiar with the citation system. Positioning each element of a single reference citation accurately can require what seems an inordinate amount of time looking through the style manual. Even before you begin to work on the specific citations, there are important questions of style and format to answer.

What to Document

Direct quotes must always be credited, as well as certain kinds of paraphrased material. Information that is basic—important dates, universally acknowledged facts or opinions—need not be cited. Information that is not widely known, whether fact or opinion, should receive documentation. A sentence stating that Henry Ford established the Ford Motor Company, for example, does not need a bibliographical citation. A sentence which relates one scholar's opinion about Henry Ford's attitude toward the unions in the early 1900s, however, does require a reference.

What if you are unsure as to whether a certain fact is widely known? You are, after all, very probably a newcomer to the field in which you are conducting your research. When in doubt, supply the documentation. It is better to over-document than to fail to do justice to a source.

The Choice of Style

While the question of which documentation style to use may be decided for you by your instructor, others may allow you a choice. There are several styles available, each designed to meet the needs of researchers in particular fields. The reference systems approved by the Modern Language Association (MLA) and the American Psychological Association (APA) are often used in the humanities and the social sciences and could serve the needs of the business writer. At present, however, there is no consensus in the business world as to which documentation style best serves the needs of the discipline. In the absence of such a consensus, this manual offers two styles, one traditional and one innovative, that are appropriate for business papers:

- The Author-Date System
- The Student Citation System

We will describe both systems in detail below and provide model references for each.

The Importance of Consistency

Whichever style and format you use, the most important rule is to *be consistent*. Sloppy referencing undermines your reader's trust and does a disservice to the writers whose work you are incorporating into your own argument. And from a purely practical standpoint, inconsistent referencing can severely damage your grade.

Using the Style Manual

Read through the following pages before trying to use them to structure your notes. Unpracticed student researchers tend to ignore this section of the style manual until the moment the first note has to be worked out, and then they skim through the examples looking for the one example that perfectly corresponds to the immediate case in hand. But most style manuals do not include every possible documentation model, so the writer must piece together a coherent reference out of elements from several models. Reading through all the models before using them gives you a feel for where to find different aspects of models as well as for how the referencing system works in general.

6.2 THE AUTHOR-DATE SYSTEM

Several bibliographical authorities use a variation of the author-date system. The author-date formats prepared in this manual especially for the use of business students follow the conventions established in the fourteenth edition of *The Chicago Manual of Style (CMS)*, which is perhaps the most universally approved of all documentation authorities. Where helpful, section numbers for relevant passages in the *CMS* appear in parentheses. For example, *CMS* (15.367) refers to section 367 of Chapter 15 of the *CMS*, a section which shows how to cite source material taken from the United States Constitution.

The Author-Date System: The Textual Note

An author-date reference has two components. The first is a note placed in parentheses within the text of the paper near where the source material appears. In order not to distract the reader from the argument, this textual note is as brief as possible, containing just enough information to refer the reader to the second component of the reference: a full citation in the bibliography that follows the text.

Usually the minimum information necessary in the textual note is the author's name—meaning the name by which the source is alphabetized in the bibliography—and the date of the publication of the source. As indicated by the models below, this information can be given in a number of ways. *Note:* Models of bibliographical entries that correspond to these parenthetical text references are given in the next section of this chapter.

Author, Date, and Page in Parentheses

> Several critics found the manager's remarks to be, in the words of one, "hopelessly off the mark and dangerously incendiary" (Northrup 1997, 28).

Note that, when it appears at the end of a sentence, the parenthetical reference is placed inside the period.

Page and Chapter in Notes

A text citation may refer to an entire book or an entire article, in which case you need not include page numbers. However, you will sometimes need to cite specific page and chapter numbers, which follow the date, and are preceded by a comma and, in the case of a chapter, the abbreviation *chap.* Note that you do not use the abbreviation *p.* or *pp.* when referring to page numbers.

Page Numbers

> Rudd (1998, 84–86) provides a brief but coherent description of the bill's evolution.

Chapter Numbers

> Collins (1997, chaps. 9, 10) discusses at length the structure of the business plan.

Author and Date in Text

The following example focuses the reader's attention on Northrup's article:

> For a highly critical review of the manager's performance, see Northrup 1997 (28).

Author in the Text, Date, and Page in Parentheses

Here the emphasis is on the author, for only Northrup's name is within the grammar of the sentence:

> Northrup (1997, 28) called the manager's remarks "hopelessly off the mark and dangerously incendiary."

Source with Two Authors

> The administration's efforts at reforming the hiring system are drawing more praise than condemnation (Younger and Petty 1996).

Notice that the names are not necessarily arranged alphabetically. Use the order that the authors themselves sanctioned on the title page of the book.

Source with Three Authors

> Most of the farmers in the region support the cooperative's new pricing plan (Moore, Macrory, and Traylor 1998, 132).

Source with Four or More Authors

Place the Latin phrase *et al.*, meaning "and others," after the name of the first author. Note that the phrase appears in roman type, not italics, and is followed by a period:

> According to Herring et al. (1994, 42), five builders backed out of the project due to doubts about the local economy.

Source with No Ascertainable Author

If you cannot determine the author of your source, begin the textual note with the title of the article or book. Do not use the phrase "anonymous" to designate the author. Note that the date of publication comes behind the title and that the methods for designating a book title (italics) or article title (quotation marks) are maintained. You may also use a shortened form of the title. The complete title of the book in the following model is *The Burden of Change: The Richard Longfeld Legacy:*

> Longfeld insisted that all managers be trained in group psychology (*Burden of Change* 1965).

> It may be that the company's market plan had been sabotaged by a rival company ("See No Evil" 1968, 7).

More Than One Source

Note that the references are arranged alphabetically:

> Several commentators have supported the board's decision to expand the ruling (Barrere 1995; Grady 1995; Payne 1994).

Two Authors with the Same Last Name

Use a first initial to differentiate two authors with the same last name.

> Few consumers will appreciate the new price cuts (L. Grady 1998, 5). The president may not be right in thinking his new policy will stimulate sales (B. Grady 1998, 45).

Two Works by the Same Author

If two references by the same author appear in the same note, place a comma between the publication dates:

> George (1996, 1998) argues for sweeping tax reform on the national level.

If the two works were published in the same year, differentiate them by adding lowercase letters to the publication dates. Be sure to add the letters to the references in the bibliography too:

> The commission's last five annual reports pointed out the same weaknesses in the structure of the city government (Estrada 1998a, 1998b).

Reprints

It is sometimes significant to note the date when an important text was first published, even if you are using a reprint of that work. In this case, the date of the first printing appears in brackets before the date of the reprint:

> During that period, there were three advertising strategies that were deemed potentially useful to corporate executives (Adams [1964] 1988, 12).

Classic Texts

You may use the author-date system to structure notes for classic texts, such as the Bible, standard translations of ancient Greek works, or numbers of the *Federalist Papers*, by citing the date and page numbers of the edition you are using. Or you may refer to these texts by using the systems by which they are subdivided. Since all editions of a classic text employ the same standard subdivisions, this reference method has the advantage of allowing your reader to find the citation in any published version of the text. For example, you may cite a biblical passage by referring to the particular book, chapter, and verse, all in roman type, with the translation given after the verse number:

> "But the path of the just is as the shining light, that shineth more and more unto the perfect day" (Proverbs 4:18 King James Version).

The *Federalist Papers* may be cited by their standard numbers:

> Madison addresses the problem of factions in a republic (Federalist 10).

Newspaper Articles

According to the *CMS* (16.117), references to daily newspapers should be handled within the syntax of your sentence:

> In a 10 August 1997 editorial, the *New York Times* painted the new regime in glowing colors.

> An article entitled "Hoag on Trial," written by Austin Fine and published in the *Tribune* on 24 November 1996, took exception to Manager Hoag's remarks.

Usually, according to the CMS, references to newspaper items are not included in the bibliography. If you wish to include such references, however, there is a model of a bibliography entry in the next section of this chapter.

Public Documents

You may cite public documents using the standard author-date technique. The *CMS* (15.322-411, 16.148-79) gives detailed information on how to cite public documents published by the national, state, county, or city governments, as well as those published by foreign governments. Corresponding bibliography entries appear in the next section.

Congressional journals

Parenthetical text references to either the *Senate Journal* or the *House Journal* start with the journal title in place of the author, the session year, and, if applicable, the page:

> Manager Jones endorsed the proposal as reworded by Manager Edward's committee (*Senate Journal* 1997, 24).

Congressional debates

Congressional debates are printed in the daily issues of the *Congressional Record*, which are bound biweekly and then collected and bound at the end of the session. Whenever possible, you should consult the bound yearly collection instead of the biweekly compilations. Your parenthetical reference should begin with the title *Congressional Record* (or *Cong. Rec.*) in place of the author's name and include the year of the congressional session, the volume and part of the *Congressional Record*, and finally the page:

> Rep. Valentine and Rep. Beechnut addressed the question of funding for secondary hiring (Cong. Rec. 1930, 72, pt. 8: 9012).

Congressional reports and documents

References to these reports and documents, which are numbered sequentially in one- or two-year periods, include the name of the body generating the material, the year, and the page:

> Rep. Slavin promised from the floor to answer the charges against him within the next week (U.S. House 1997, 12).

NOTE: Any reference that begins with *U.S. Senate* or *U.S. House* may omit the *U.S.*, if it is clear from the context that you are referring to the United States. Whichever form you use, be sure to use it *consistently*, in both the notes and the bibliography.

Bills and resolutions

According to the *CMS* (15.347-48), bills and resolutions, which are published in pamphlets called "slip bills," on microfiche, and in the *Congressional Record*, are not always given a parenthetical text reference and a corresponding bibliography entry. Instead, the pertinent reference information appears in the syntax of the sentence. If, however, you wish to cite such information in a text reference, the form depends on the source from which you took your information:

> *Citing to a Slip Bill*
>
> The recent ruling prohibits consular officials from rejecting visa requests out of hand (U.S. Senate 1996).
>
> The recent ruling prohibits consular officials from rejecting visa requests out of hand (*Visa Formalization Act of 1996*).

You may cite either the body that authored the bill or the title of the work itself. Whichever method you choose, remember to begin your bibliography entry with the same material.

> *Citing to the* Congressional Record
>
> The recent ruling prohibits consular officials from rejecting visa requests out of hand (U.S. Senate 1996, S7658).

The number following the date and preceded by an *S* (for Senate; *H* for House) is the page in the *Congressional Record*.

Laws

As with bills and resolutions, laws (also called statutes) are not necessarily given a parenthetical text reference and a bibliography entry. Instead, the identifying material is included in the text. If you wish to make a formal reference for a statute, you must structure it according to the place where you found the law published. Initially published separately in pamphlets, as slip laws, statutes are eventually collected and incorporated, first into a set of volumes called *U.S. Statutes at Large* and later into the *United States Code*, a multivolume set that is revised every 6 years. You should use the latest publication.

Citing to a Slip Law
You should either use *U.S. Public Law*, in roman type, and the number of the piece of legislation, or the title of the law:

> Congress stipulates that any book deposited for copyright in the Library of Congress that suffers serious damage or deterioration due to age be rebound in library cloth (U.S. Public Law 678, 16-17).

> Congress stipulates that any book deposited for copyright in the Library of Congress that suffers serious damage or deterioration due to age be rebound in library cloth (*Library of Congress Book Preservation Act of 1997*, 16-17).

Citing to the Statutes at Large
Include the page number after the year:

> Congress stipulates that any book deposited for copyright in the Library of Congress that suffers serious damage or deterioration due to age be rebound in library cloth (*Statutes at Large* 1997, 466).

Citing to the United States Code

> Congress stipulates that any book deposited for copyright in the Library of Congress that suffers serious damage or deterioration due to age be rebound in library cloth (*Library of Congress Book Preservation Act of 1997*, U.S. Code. Vol. 38, Sec. 1562).

United States Constitution
According to the *CMS* (15.367), references to the United States Constitution include the number of the article or amendment, the section number, and the clause, if necessary:

> The president has the power, in extraordinary circumstances, either to convene or to dismiss Congress (U.S. Constitution, art. 3, sec. 3).

It is not necessary to include the Constitution in the bibliography.

Executive department documents
A reference to a report, bulletin, circular, or any other type of material issued by the executive department starts with the name of the agency issuing the document, although you may use the name of the author, if known:

> Recent demographic projections suggest that city growth will continue to be lateral for several more years, as businesses flee downtown areas for the suburbs (Department of Labor 1984, 334).

Legal references
Supreme Court
As with laws, court decisions are rarely given their own parenthetical text reference and bibliography entry, but are instead identified in the text. If you wish to use a for-

mal reference, however, you may place within the parentheses the title of the case, in italics, followed by the source (for cases after 1875 this is the *United States Supreme Court Reports*, abbreviated U.S.), which is preceded by the volume number and followed by the page number. You should end the first reference to the case that appears in your paper with the date of the case, in brackets. You need not include the date in subsequent references:

> The judge ruled that Ms. Warren did have an obligation to offer assistance to the survivors of the wreck, an obligation which she failed to meet (*State of Nevada* v. *Goldie Warren* 324 U.S. 123 [1969]).

Before 1875, Supreme Court decisions were published under the names of official court reporters. The reference below is to William Cranch, *Reports of Cases Argued and Adjudged in the Supreme Court of the United States, 1801-1815*, 9 vols. (Washington, D.C., 1804-17). The number preceding the clerk's name is the volume number; the last number is the page:

> The first case in which the Supreme Court ruled a law of Congress to be void was *Marbury* v. *Madison*, in 1803 (1 Cranch 137).

For most of these parenthetical references, it is possible to move some or all of the material outside the parentheses simply by incorporating it in the text:

> In 1969, in *State of Nevada* v. *Goldie Warren* (324 U.S. 123), the judge ruled that an observer of a traffic accident has an obligation to offer assistance to survivors.

Lower Courts

Decisions of lower federal courts are published in the *Federal Reporter.* The note should give the volume of the *Federal Reporter* (*F.*), the series, if it is other than the first (*2d*, in the model below), the page, and, in brackets, an abbreviated reference to the specific court (the example below is to the Second Circuit Court) and the year:

> One ruling takes into account the bias that often exists against the defendant in certain types of personal injury lawsuits (*United States* v. *Sizemore*, 183 F. 2d 201 [2d Cir. 1950]).

Publications of government commissions

According to the *CMS* (15.368), references to bulletins, circulars, reports, and study papers that are issued by various government commissions should include the name of the commission, the date of the document, and the page:

> This year saw a sharp reaction among large firms to the new tax law (Securities and Exchange Commission 1985, 57).

Corporate authors

Because government documents are often credited to a corporate author with a lengthy name, you may devise an acronym or a shortened form of the name and indicate in your first reference to the source that this name will be used in later citations:

> Government statistics over the last year showed a continuing leveling of the inflation rate (*Bulletin of Labor Statistics* 1997, 1954; *hereafter BLS*).

The practice of using a shortened name in subsequent references to any corporate author, whether a public or private organization, is sanctioned in most journals, including the *American Business Review*, and approved in the CMS (15.252). Thus, if you refer often to the *U.N. Monthly Bulletin of Statistics*, you may, after giving the publication's full name in the first reference, use a shortened form of the title — perhaps an acronym such as *UNMBS* — in all later cites.

Publications of state and local governments

According to the CMS (15.377), references to state and local government documents are similar to those for the corresponding national government sources:

> In arguing for the legality of cockfighting, Manager Lynd actually suggested that the "sport" served as a deterrent to crime among the state's young people (Oklahoma Legislature 1995, 24).

The *CMS* (16.178) restricts bibliographical information concerning state laws or municipal ordinances to the running text.

Interviews

According to the *CMS* (16.127, 130), citations to interviews should be handled within the syntax of a sentence rather than in parentheses. The *CMS* states that interviews need not be listed in the bibliography but may be included if you or your instructor wishes. Model bibliography formats for such material appear in the bibliography section of this chapter.

Published interview

> In a March 1997 interview with Selena Fox, Simon criticized the use of private funds to build such city projects as the coliseum.

No parenthetical reference is necessary in the above citation because sufficient information is given for the reader to find the complete citation, which will be alphabetized under Simon's name in the bibliography.

Unpublished interview conducted by the writer of the paper

> In an interview with the author on 23 April 1997, Dr. Kennedy expressed her disappointment with the new court ruling.

If you are citing material from an interview that you conducted, you should identify yourself as the author and give the date of the interview.

The Author-Date System: Bibliography

In a paper using the author-date system of referencing, the parenthetical text references point the reader to the full citations in the bibliography. This bibliography, which always follows the text, is arranged alphabetically according to the first element in each citation. Usually this element is the last name of the author or editor, but in the absence of such information, the citation is alphabetized according to the title of the work, which is then the first element in the citation (*CMS* 16.41).

The bibliography is double-spaced throughout, even between entries. As with most alphabetically arranged bibliographies, there is a kind of reverse indentation system: after the first line of a citation, all subsequent lines are indented five spaces.

Capitalization

This manual advocates the use of standard, or "headline style," capitalization rules for titles in the bibliographical citations. In this style, all first and last words in a title, and all other words *except* articles (*a, an, the*), coordinating words (*and, but, or, for, nor*), and all prepositions are capitalized. The *CMS* (15.73.3), however, uses a "down" style (or sentence style) of capitalization, in which "only the first word of the main title and the subtitle and all proper nouns and proper adjectives" are capitalized. You should check with your instructor to see which capitalization style you should use. In keeping with its general policy, this manual gives examples using the format.

Books

One author

> Northrup, Alan K. 1997. *Living High off the Hog: Recent Pork Barrel Legislation in the Senate.* Cleveland: Johnstown.

First comes the author's name, inverted, then the date of publication, followed by the title of the book, the place of publication, and the name of the publishing house. For place of publication, do not identify the state unless the city is not well known. In that case, use postal abbreviations to denote the state (*OK, AR*).

Periods are used to divide most of the elements in the citation, although a colon is used between the place of publication and publisher. Custom dictates that the main title and subtitle are separated by a colon, even though a colon may not appear in the title as printed on the title page of the book.

Two authors

Only the name of the first author is reversed, since it is the one by which the citation is alphabetized:

> Spence, Michelle, and Kelly Rudd. 1996. *Hiring and the Law.* Boston: Tildale.

Three authors

> Moore, J. B., Jeannine Macrory, and Natasha Traylor. 1998. *Down on the Farm: Renovating the Farm Loan.* Norman, OK: Univ. of Oklahoma Press.

According to the *CMS* (15.161), you may abbreviate the word *University* if it appears in the name of the press:

Four or more authors

> Herring, Ralph, et al. 1994. *Funding City Projects.* Atlanta: Jessup Institute for Policy Development.

No ascertainable author

Do not use the phrase "anonymous" to designate author whose name cannot be determined; instead, begin your citation with the title of the book, followed by the date. You may move initial articles (a, an, the) to the end of the title:

> *Burden of Change: The Richard Longfeld Legacy, The.* 1965. San Luis Obispo, CA: Blakeside.

Editor, compiler, or translator as author

When no author is listed on the title page, the *CMS* (16.46) calls for you to begin the citation with the name of the editor, compiler, or translator:

> Trakas, Dylan, comp. 1998. *Making the Road-Ways Safe: Essays on Highway Preservation and Funding.* El Paso: Del Norte Press.

Editor, compiler, or translator with author

Place the editor, compiler, or translator's name after the title, prefaced, according to the *CMS* (16.47), by the appropriate phrase: *Ed., Comp., or Trans.:*

> Pound, Ezra. 1953. *Literary Essays.* Ed. T. S. Eliot. New York: New Directions.

> Stomper, Jean. 1973. *Grapes and Rain.* Trans. John Picard. New York: Baldock.

Untranslated book

If your source is in a foreign language, it is not necessary, according to the *CMS* (15.118), to translate the title into English. Use the capitalization format of the original language (see in *CMS* 9).

> Picon-Salas, Mariano. 1950. *De la Conquesta a la Indipendéncia.* Mexico D.F.: Fondo de Cultura Económica.

If you wish to provide a translation of the title, do so in brackets or parentheses following the title. Set the translation in roman type, and capitalize only the first word of the title and subtitle, proper nouns, and proper adjectives:

> Wharton, Edith. 1916. *Voyages au front* (Visits to the Front). Paris: Plon.

Two or more works by the same author

According to the *CMS* (15.66, 16.28), the author's name in all citations after the first may be replaced, if you wish, by a three-em dash (six strokes) of the hyphen:

> Russell, Henry. 1978. *Famous Last Words: Notable Supreme Court Cases of the Last Five Years.* New Orleans: Liberty Publications.
> ———. 1988. *Great Court Battles.* Denver: Axel & Myers.

Chapter in a multiauthor collection

> Gray, Alexa North. 1998. Foreign policy and the foreign press. In *Current Media Issues*, ed. Barbara Bonnard. New York: Boulanger.

The parenthetical text reference may include the page reference:

(Gray 191, 195–97)

You *must* repeat the name if the author and the editor are the same person:

Farmer, Susan A. 1995. "Tax Shelters in the New Dispensation: How to Save Your In come." In *Making Ends Meet: Strategies for the Nineties*, ed. Susan A. Farmer. Nashville: Burkette and Hyde.

Author of a foreword or introduction
There is no need, according to the *CMS* (16.5 1), to cite the author of a foreword or introduction in your bibliography, unless you have used material from that author's contribution to the volume. In that case, the bibliography entry is listed under the name of the author of the foreword or introduction. Place the name of the author of the work itself after the title of the work:

Farris, Carla. 1998. Foreword to *Marital Stress among the Professoriat: A Case Study*, by Basil Givan. New York: Galapagos.

The parenthetical text reference cites the name of the author of the foreword or introduction, not the author of the book:

(Farris 1998)

Subsequent editions
If you are using an edition of a book other than the first, you must cite the number of the edition or the status, such as *Rev. ed.* for Revised edition, if there is no edition number:

Hales, Sarah. 1994. *The Coming Water Wars*. 2d ed. Pittsburgh: Blue Skies.

Multivolume work
If you are citing a multivolume work in its entirety, use the following format:

Graybosch, Charles. 1988–89. *The Rise of the Unions*. 3 vols. New York: Starkfield.

If you are citing only one of the volumes in a multivolume work, use the follow- ing format:

Ronsard, Madeleine. 1996. *Monopolies. Vol. 2 of A History of Capitalism*. Ed. Joseph M. Sayles. Boston: Renfrow.

Reprints

Adams, Sterling R. [1964] 1988. *How to Win an Election: Promotional Campaign Strategies*. New York: Starkfield.

Modern editions of classics
It is not necessary to give the date of original publication of a classic work:

Burke, Edmond. 1987. *Reflections on the Revolution in France.* Ed. J.G.A. Pocock. Indi
anapolis: Hackett.

Remember, if the classic text is divided into short, numbered sections (such as
the chapter and verse divisions of the Bible), you do not need to include the work in
your bibliography unless you wish to specify a particular edition.

Periodicals

Journal articles

Journals are periodicals, usually published either monthly or quarterly, that specialize
in serious scholarly articles in a particular field.

Journal with Continuous Pagination

Most journals are paginated so that each issue of a volume continues the numbering
of the previous issue. The reason for such pagination is that most journals are bound
in libraries as complete volumes of several issues; continuous pagination makes it easier to consult these large compilations:

Hunzecker, Joan. 1987. "Teaching the Toadies: Cronyism in Municipal Politics." *Review
of Local Politics* 4:250–62.

Note that the name of the journal, which is italicized, is followed without punctuation
by the volume number, which is itself followed by a colon and the page numbers.
There should be no space between the colon and the page numbers, which are *inclusive.* Do not use *p.* or *pp.* to introduce the page numbers.

Journal in Which Each Issue is Paginated Separately

Skylock, Browning. 1991. "'Fifty-Four Forty or Fight!': Sloganeering in Early America." *American History Digest* 28 (3): 25–34.

The issue number appears in parentheses immediately following the volume number.
Place one space between the colon and the page numbers.

Magazine articles

Magazines, which are usually published weekly, bimonthly, or monthly, appeal to the
popular audience and generally have a wider circulation than journals. *Newsweek* and
Scientific American are examples of magazines.

Monthly Magazine

The name of the magazine is separated from the month of publication by a comma.
According to the *CMS* (15.231), you may omit inclusive page numbers in a magazine
reference, but if you choose to include them, use a comma to separate them from the
date of the issue, as in the second example below:

Stapleton, Bonnie. 1981. "How It Was: On the Sales Trail with Og Mandino." *Lifetime
Magazine,* April.

Weekly or Bimonthly Magazine

The day of the issue's publication appears before the month:

Bruck, Connie. 1997. "The World of Business: A Mogul's Farewell." *The New Yorker,*
18 October, 12–15.

Newspaper articles

The *CMS* (16.117) says that bibliographies usually do not include entries for articles from daily newspapers. If you wish to include such material, however, here are two possible formats:

> *New York Times.* 1997. Editorial, 10 August.
>
> Fine, Austin. 1996. "Hoag on Trial." *Carrollton (Texas) Tribune*, 24 November.

Note that *The* is omitted from the newspaper's title, as it is for all English language newspapers (*CMS* 15.242). If the name of the city in which an American newspaper is published does not appear in the paper's title, it should be appended, in italics. If the city is not well known, the name of the state is added, in italics, in parentheses, as in the second model above. The *CMS* (15.234-42) offers additional suggestions for citations of newspaper material.

Public Documents

Congressional journals

References to either the *Senate Journal* or the *House Journal* begin with the journal's title and include the years of the session, the number of the Congress and session, and the month and day of the entry:

> *U.S. Senate Journal.* 1997. 105th Cong., 1st sess., 10 December.

The ordinal numbers *second* and *third* may be represented as *d* (52d, 103d) or as *nd* and *rd*, respectively.

Congressional debates

> *Congressional Record.* 1930. 71st Cong., 2d sess. Vol. 72, pt. 8.

Congressional reports and documents

> U.S. House. 1997. *Report on Government Efficiency As Perceived by the Public.* 105th Cong., 2d sess. H. Doc. 225.

Bills and resolutions

> Citing to a Slip Bill

> > U.S. Senate. 1996. *Visa Formalization Act of 1996.* 105th Cong. 1st sess. S.R. 1437.

or

> *Visa Formalization Act of 1996. See* U.S. Senate. 1996.

The abbreviation *S.R.* in the first model above stands for *Senate Resolutions*, and the number following is the bill or resolution number. For references to House bills, the abbreviation is *H.R.* Notice that the second model refers the reader to the more complete entry above. The choice of formats depends upon the one you used in the parenthetical text reference.

Citing to the Congressional Record

> Senate. 1997. *Visa Formalization Act of 1997.* 105th Cong., 1st sess., S.R. 1437. *Congressional Record* 135, no. 137, daily ed. (10 December): S7341.

Laws

Citing to a Slip Law

> U.S. Public Law 678. 105th Cong., 1st sess., 4 December 1997. *Library of Congress Book Preservation Act of 1997.*

or

> *Library of Congress Book Preservation Act of 1997.* U.S. Public Law 678. 105th Cong., 1st sess., 4 December 1997.

Citing to the Statutes at Large

> *Statutes at Large.* 1998. Vol. 82, p. 466. *Library of Congress Book Preservation Act of 1997.*

or

> *Library of Congress Book Preservation Act of 1997.* Statutes at Large 82:466.

Citing to the United States Code

> *Library of Congress Book Preservation Act, 1997.* U.S. Code. Vol. 38, sec. 1562.

United States Constitution

According to the *CMS* (16.172), the Constitution is not listed in the bibliography.

Executive department documents

> Department of Labor. 1998. *Report on Urban Growth Potential Projections.* Washington, D.C.: GPO.

The abbreviation for the publisher in the above model, *GPO*, stands for the *Government Printing Office*, which prints and distributes most government publications. According to the *CMS* (15.327), you may use any of the following formats to refer to the GPO:

Washington, D.C.: U.S. Government Printing Office, 1984.

Washington, D.C.: Government Printing Office, 1984.

Washington, D.C.: GPO, 1984.

Washington, 1984.

Washington 1984.

Remember to *be consistent* in using the form you choose.

Legal references

Supreme Court

According to the *CMS* (16.174), Supreme Court decisions are only rarely listed in bibliographies. If you do wish to include such an entry, here is a suitable format:

> *State of Nevada* v. *Goldie Warren*. 1969. 324 U.S. 123.

For a case prior to 1875, use the following format:

> *Marbury* v. *Madison*. 1803. 1 Cranch 137.

Lower Courts

> *United States* v. *Sizemore*. 1950. 183 F. 2d 201 (2d Cir.).

Publications of government commissions

> U.S. Securities and Exchange Commission. 1984. *Annual Report of the Securities and Exchange Commission for the Fiscal Year*. Washington, D.C.: GPO.

Publications of state and local governments

Remember that references for state and local government publications are modeled on those for corresponding national government documents:

> Oklahoma Legislature. 1991. Joint Committee on Public Recreation. *Final Report to the Legislature, 1995,* Regular Session, on Youth Activities. Oklahoma City.

Interviews

According to the *CMS* (16.130), interviews need not be included in the bibliography, but if you or your instructor wants to list such entries, here are possible formats:

Published interview

Untitled Interview in a Book

> Jorgenson, Mary. 1998. Interview by Alan McAskill. In *Hospice Pioneers*. Ed. Alan McAskill, 62–86. Richmond: Dynasty Press.

Titled Interview in a Periodical

> Simon, John. 1997. "Picking the Patrons Apart: An Interview with John Simon." By Selena Fox. *Media Week*, 14 March, 40–54.

Interview on television

> Snopes, Edward. 1998. Interview by Kent Gordon. *Oklahoma Politicians*. WKY Television, 4 June.

Unpublished interview

> Kennedy, Melissa. 1997. Interview by author. Tape recording. Portland, ME, 23 April.

Unpublished Sources

Personal communications
According to the CMS (16.130), references to personal communications may be handled completely in the text of the paper:

> In a letter to the author, dated 16 July 1997, Mr. Bentley admitted the marketing plan was flawed.

If, however, you wish to include a reference to an unpublished communication in the bibliography, you may do so using one of the following models:

> Bentley, Jacob. 1997. Letter to author, 16 July.

> Duberstein, Cindy. 1996. Telephone conversation with the author, 5 June.

> Timrod, Helen. 1997. E-mail to author, 25 April.

Theses and dissertations

> Hochenauer, Klint. 1980. "Populism and the Free Soil Movement." Ph.D. diss. University of Virginia.

> Sharpe, Ellspeth Stanley. 1996. "Black Women in Politics: A Troubled History. " Master's thesis. Oregon State University.

Paper presented at a meeting

> Zelazny, Kim, and Ed Gilmore. 1997. "Art for Art's Sake: Funding the NEA in the Twenty-First Century." Presented at the annual meeting of the Conference of Metropolitan Arts Boards, San Francisco.

Manuscript in the author's possession

> Borges, Rita V. "Mexican-American Border Conflicts, 1915–1970." University of Texas at El Paso. Photocopy.

The entry includes the institution with which the author is affiliated and ends with a description of the format of the work (typescript, photocopy, etc).

Citing sources from the Internet
The need for a reliable Internet citation system continues to grow, but attempts to establish one are hampered by a number of factors. For one thing, there is no foolproof method of clearly reporting even such basic information as the site's author(s), title, or date of establishment. Occasionally authors identify themselves clearly; sometimes they place a link to their home page at the bottom of the site. But it is not always easy to determine exactly who authored a particular site. Likewise, it can be difficult to de-

termine whether a site has its own title or instead exists as a subsection of a larger document with its own title. Perhaps the biggest problem facing Internet researchers is the instability of Internet sites. While some sites may remain in place for weeks or months, many either move to another site—not always leaving a clear path for you to find it—or disappear.

You can watch bibliographical history being made on a day-to-day basis on the Internet, where a number of researchers are working to establish viable electronic citation formats. See what you can find, for example, on the following site on the World Wide Web:

> http://www.fis.utoronto.ca/internet/citation.htm

This site offers links to several pages where bibliographers are coming to grips with the problems of Internet referencing. The 14th edition of the *CMS*, our guide through the last two sections of this chapter, is not of much help when it comes to electronic sources. Therefore, until such time as an authoritative citation system for the Internet is available, we suggest the following simple formats, based in part on the work of other researchers available on the Internet.

Bibliographical reference for a site on the World Wide Web
Place the following information in this order, separating most of the elements with periods: Name of author, reversed (if known). Title of Document (in quotation marks). Edition, revision, or version information. Date of document. Date upon which you last accessed the site (in parentheses). Site address, alone on the next line:

> Page, Melvin E. "A Brief Citation Guide for Internet Sources in History and the Humanities. Ver. 2.1. 20 February 1996.
> <http://www.nmmc.com/libweb/employee/citguide.him> (13 April 1997).

The two symbols < and > which surround the site address are not part of the address; they serve merely to denote the address from the rest of the citation. It is important not to break the often lengthy information string that constitutes the site address, hence the relatively short second line of the citation. Note that there is no period between the > and the access date, in parentheses.

Bibliographical reference for an FTP site

> Dodd, Sue A. "Bibliographic References for Computer Files in the Social Sciences: A Discussion Paper." Rev. May 1990.
> <ftp://ftp.msstate.edu/pub/docs/history/netuse/electronic.biblio.cite> (13 April 1997).

Remember, the one thing that is absolutely required in order to find a site on the Internet is the site address (URL), so make sure that you copy it accurately.

Bibliographical reference for a CD-ROM
A CD-ROM's publisher can usually be identified in the same way as a book's publisher. The following model is for a source with an unascertainable author. Note that it is still necessary to include, in parentheses, the latest date on which you accessed the database:

> *Dissertation Abstracts Ondisc.* 1861-1994. CD-ROM: UMI/Dissertation Abstracts Ondisc. (15 December 1996).

6.3 THE STUDENT CITATION SYSTEM (SCS)

The Student Citation System

As an alternative to the author-date system, you may want to use the Student Citation System (SCS). Before you do so, however, be sure to get your instructor's approval. Why, you may ask, would anyone want another citation system, especially since so many disciplines already have their own (MLA, APA, and others)? It is precisely because college students are currently required to use several different citation systems that the SCS was created. The SCS is the first system specifically designed for use in all undergraduate college courses. Students who use it will be able to use the same system in their English, psychology, sociology, math, science, history, business, and other courses.

How is the SCS different from other citation systems? In addition to the fact that it is designed to be used in courses in all disciplines, the SCS has several other distinctive features: The SCS is made for students, not academicians. It is simpler, has fewer rules to learn, and is easier to type than other systems. The SCS uses the punctuation and syntax of a new grammar that students are quickly learning around the world: the universal language of the Internet. The Internet is rapidly becoming the foremost means of a wide range of research and communication activities. SCS symbols are familiar to anyone who has used the internet: / @ +. They allow citations to be constructed with a minimum of space, effort, and confusion.

General Rules and Rules for Notes

Like other citation systems, the SCS requires that each source citation include (1) a note in the text in which the reference to the source cited occurs, and (2) an entry in a reference page. Notes in the text are always placed at the end of the sentence in which the reference is made. Examine the models that accompany the following list of rules for notes.

	Rule	*Example*
1	Notes in the text always contain, in this order: 1. a forward slash (/> 2. a source reference numeral (1,2,3 etc.) 3. a dot (.) that ends the sentence.	Iacocca demanded immediate action /1. (Notice that there is a space before the /, but no spaces between the / and the 1, or between the 1 and the dot.)
2	Direct quotes and references to materials on a specific page both require a page number.	Iacocca demanded immediate action /1.23. (Note that no spaces occur between the dots and the page number.)
3	You may indicate a range of pages or a page and a range of pages.	Iacocca demanded immediate action /1.23-25. Iacocca demanded immediate action /1.19.23-25.
4	Indicate chapters, sections, parts, and volumes in the note with appropriate abbreviations. Note that there is no dot between the abbreviation and the	Iacocca demanded immediate action /1.c3. Iacocca demanded immediate action /1.s3. Iacocca demanded immediate action /1.pt3. Iacocca demanded immediate action /1.v3.

Rule	Example
number of the chapter, section, part, or volume.	
5 You may cite more than one source in a single note. Separate sources by the / without spaces between any of the characters.	Smith demanded immediate action /1.v3.23/4/13.c6. (This note refers to source 1, volume, 3 page 23; source 4; and source 13, chapter 6.)
6 Once used, reference numbers always refer to the same source. They may be used again to refer to a different quote or idea from that same source.	Iacocca demanded immediate action /1.19. Pickens, who had had a severe headache the evening before, came to join him /5/7. One source reported that they had argued about hiring procedures /1.33. (The second note in this passage refers the reader to two different sources, numbers 5 and 7. The third note is another reference to the first source used in the paper.)
7 Refer to a constitution with article and section number.	Ross Perot fulfilled his obligation to inform his stockholders of the transaction /18.2.3.
8 Refer to passages in the Bible, the Koran, and other ancient texts that are divided into standard verses with the verse citation in the note.	Jake forgot that "the seventh day shall be your Holy day" /6.Exodus 35.2. (This example refers to the book of Exodus, chapter 35, verse 2. The 6 indicates that this is the sixth source cited in the paper. There is a dot between the source number and the verse citation.)

Rules for Reference Pages

General Format Rules

The reference list, entitled "References," is usually the final element in the paper. Its entries are arranged in the order that citations appear in the paper. The references page has standard page margins (one inch from all sides of the paper). All lines are double spaced. Model references pages appear at the end of this chapter.

Rules of Punctuation and Abbreviation

1. Punctuation imitates the format used on the Internet.
2. No spaces occur between entry elements (author, date, and so on) or punctuation marks (/ . + @ ").
3. Dots (.) always follow entry elements with exceptions for punctuation rules 5–6.
4. The number of the source is always followed immediately by a dot.
5. Dots are also used to separate volume and edition numbers in journals.
6. Additional authors are denoted by a plus (+) sign.
7. Subtitles of books and articles are separated from main titles by a colon and a single space: "Crushing Doubt: Pascal's Bleak Epiphany."

8. Book chapters and periodical articles are enclosed in quotation marks (" ").

9. Use the following abbreviations:

c   chapter
comp   compiler
ed   editor
NY   New York (Use postal abbreviations for all states. Note that NY is unique in that when it is used alone it always means New York City. Cite other New York State locations in this form: "Oswego NY." Cite cities in other states like this: "Chicago IL" "Los Angeles CA" "Boston MA.")
pt   part
s   section
sess   session
tr   translator
v   volume
S   September (Months: Ja F Mr Ap My Je Jl Au S Oc N D)
C   College
I   Institute
U   University

10. Use full names instead of initials of authors whenever they are used in the original source. When listing publishers you may use the commonly used names instead of full titles. For example, use "Yale" for "Yale University Press"; use "Holt" for Holt, Rinehart and Winston." Use Internet abbreviations when known, such as "Prenhall" for "Prentice Hall, Inc." When abbreviating universities in dissertation and thesis citations, place no dot between the names of the state or city and the university. For example, use "MaIT" for the Massachusetts Institute of Technology and "UMa" for the University of Massachusetts. Always use the second letter of the state abbreviation, in lower case, to avoid the following type of confusion: "OSU" could be a university in Ohio, Oklahoma, or Oregon.

Rules of Order

Elements are always entered in the order shown in the following list of examples. Not all elements are available for every citation (authors are sometimes not provided), and the table provides directions for these cases. Further, not all entries are appropriate for every citation. For example, cities of publication are not required for magazines. Carefully examine the order of elements in the examples in the table.

Source	*Citation Elements and Examples*
Books One author:	3.Edna Applegate. 1995.My Life on Earth.4th ed. Howard Press. St. Louis MO. Note the order of elements: —Reference number of note (1, 2, 3, etc.), followed by a dot —Author's name —Year of publication —Title of book —Number of edition, if other than the first —Name of publisher —City of publication —State of publication (not necessary for New York City)
Two to three authors:	10. William Grimes+Joan Smith+Alice Bailey.1996.Philosophy and Fire.Harvard.Cambridge MA.

Source	*Citation Elements and Examples*
More than three authors:	42.Lois Mills+others.1989.Revolution in Thought.Agnew.NY.
Editor, compiler, or translator in place of author:	1.Michael Schendler ed. 1992.Kant's Cosmology.Bloom.NY. (Remember that the citation for New York City does not require a state abbreviation.)
Editor, compiler, or translator with author:	9.Elena White.1997.Nietzsche Was Right.Alexander Nebbs tr.Spartan.Biloxi MS.
No author, editor, compiler, or translator:	5.The Book of Universal Wisdom.1993.4ᵗʰ ed.Northfield Publications.Indianapolis IN. (Reverse the placement of the date and title of the book, beginning the entry with the title.)
Separately authored foreword, afterword, or preface as source:	17.Beulah Garvin.1992.Preface.Down in the Hole by James Myerson.Philosopher's Stone Press.Boston MA.
Separately authored chapter, essay, or poem as source:	5.Jack Wittey.1994."Chickens and People." Animal Rights Anthology.3ʳᵈ ed.Gene Cayton comp.Palo Duro Press.Canyon TX.73-90.
One volume in a multivolume work:	9.Astrid Schultz+others.1991.The Myth of the West.v3 of The Development of European Thought.8 vols.Muriel Hodgson ed.University of Rutland Press.Rutland ME.

Encyclopedias

Citation from an encyclopedia that is regularly updated:	24.Ronald Millgate.1985."Mills, John Stuart."Encyclopedia Americana. (The date refers to the edition of the encyclopedia. Cite the name of the article exactly as it appears in the encyclopedia.)
When no name is given for the article's author:	2. "Mills, John Stuart."1946.Hargreave's Encyclopedia.
Ancient texts: Bible, Koran, etc.:	24.Holy Bible.New International Version. (Because the book, chapter, and verse numbers are given in the textual reference, it is not necessary to repeat them here. Remember to cite the traditional divisions of the work instead of the page number and publication information of the specific edition you used.)

Periodicals
Journal articles:

Article with author or authors named:	30.Ellis Michaels+Andrea Long.1996."How We Know: An Exercise in Cartesian Logic."Philosopher's Stone.12.4.213-227. (This citation refers to an article published in a journal entitled *Philosopher's Stone,* volume 12, number 4, pages 213–227.)
Article with no author named:	7."Odds and Ends."1995.Philosopher's Stone.12.4.198–199.

Magazine articles:

Article in a weekly or bi-weekly magazine.	11.Lorraine Bond.1994."The Last Epicurean."Mental Health.6Jn.34–41. (This citation refers to an article published in the June 6, 1994, issue of *Mental Health.*)

Source	*Citation Elements and Examples*
Article in a monthly magazine:	3.Allan Hull.1996."My Secret Struggle."Pathology Digest.Mr. 17-30. (The difference between a citation for a monthly magazine and one for a weekly or bi-weekly magazine is that the former does not include a reference to the specific day of publication.)
Newspapers: Article with named author:	10.Anne Bleaker.1995."Breakthrough in Artificial Intelligence." New York Times.10My.14. (The word *The* is omitted from the newspaper's title.)
Article with unnamed author:	22."Peirce Anniversary Celebration Set."1996.Kansas City Times-Democrat.1Ap.14.
When city is not named in newspaper title:	13.Boyd Finnell.1996."Stoic Elected Mayor."(Eugenia, TX) Daily Equivocator.30D.1. (Place the name of the city, and the abbreviation for the state if the city is not well known, in parentheses before the name of the paper.)
Government documents Agency publications:	28.U.S. Department of Commerce.1996.Economic Projections: 1995-2004.GPO. (Note that, when no author's name is given, the government department is considered the author. Because the Government Printing Office [GPO], the government's primary publisher, is located in Washington,DC, you need not list the city of publication.)
Legislative journals:	31.Senate Journal.1993.103Cong.sess1.D10. (This citation refers to the record, published in the *Senate Journal*, of the first session of the 103rd Congress, held on December 10, 1993.) 8.Congressional Record.71 Cong.sess.2.72.8. (This citation refers to the account, published in the *Congressional Record*, of the second session of the 71st Congress, volume 72, page 8.)
Bills in Congress:	13.U.S. Senate.1997.Visa Formalization Act of 1997.105Cong.sess1.SR.1437. (This citation refers to Senate Resolution 1437, originated in the first session of the 105th Congress. Bills originating in the House of Representatives are designed by the abbreviation HR.)
Laws:	7.U.S. Public Law 678.1993.Library of Congress Book Preservation Act of 1993.U.S. Code.38.1562. (The law referred to in this citation is recorded in section 1562 of volume 38 of the *U.S. Code*.)
Constitutions:	31.U.S. Constitution. 8.MO.Constitution. (This citation refers to the Missouri State Constitution.)
Internet documents:	4.Akiko Kasahara and K-lab,Inc.1995.ArtScape of the Far East: Seminar on the Philosophy of Art.Shinshu.University Nagano.Japan.@http://Pckiso3.cs.Shinshu-u.ac.jp/artscape/index.html.Oct27.96.

Source	*Citation Elements and Examples*
	(The last two items in an Internet citation are always the website at which the document was found, followed by the date accessed.)
Unpublished materials: Interview:	12.Lily Frailey.1994.Interview with Clarence Parker.Santa Fe NM.10Ag.
Thesis or dissertation:	21.Gregory Scott.1973.Mysticism and Politics in the Thought of Bertrand Russell.MA thesis.UVa.
Paper presented at a meeting:	5.Celia Hicks. 1995."What Whitehead Would Say." Conference on the Western Imagination. 14Ja.Boston MA. (The citation includes the name of the conference and the date on which the paper was presented, and ends with the city where the conference took place.)
Manuscript housed in a collection:	32.Jose Sanchez.1953?-1982.Journal.Southwest Collection.Arial Library.Chisum Academy.Canyon TX. (Unpublished manuscripts are sometimes left unnamed and undated by their authors. Use any relevant information supplied by the repository catalogue to complete the citation. When a date is hypothesized, as in the above example, place a question mark after it.)
Manuscript in the author's possession:	14.Jane Fried.1996.Life in California.UTx.Photocopy. (The citation includes the institution with which the author is affiliated and ends with a description of the format of the work: typescript, photocopy, and so on.)

SAMPLE REFERENCES PAGES:

1. Amanda Collingwood.1993.Architecture and Philosophy.Carlington Press.Detroit MI.

2. Tom Barker+Betty Clay, eds.1987.Swamps of Louisiana.Holt.NY.

3. Joan Garth+Allen Sanford.1963."The Hills of Wyoming."Critical Perspectives on Landscape.Prentice Hall.Upper Saddle River NJ.49-75.

4. Hayley Trakas, ed.1994.Russell on Space.3rd ed.Harmony Press.El Paso.TX.

5. Philippe Ariès.1962.Centuries of Childhood: A Social History of Family Life in the Northeastern Region of Kentucky.Robert Baldock tr.Knopf.NY.

6. Jesus Gonzolez.1995."The Making of the Federales."Mexican Stories Revisited.Jules Frank ed.Comanche Press.San Antonio TX.54-79.

7. Carla Harris.1994.Foreword.Marital Stress and the Philosophers: A Case Study by Basil Givan.Galapagos.NY.

8. Jasper Craig.1993."The Flight from the Center of the Cities."Time.10S.67-69.

9. Matthew Moen.1996."Evolving Politics of the Christian Right."PS:Business and Politics.29.3.461-464.

10. Patrick Swick.1996."Jumping the Gun on the Federal Reserve."New York Times.10 My.78.

11. Frances Muggeridge.1993."The Truth is Nowhere."Conundrum Digest.Mr.40-54.

12. Alan McAskill.1994."Interview with Mary Jordan."Hospice Pioneers of New Mexico. Dynasty Press.Enid.OK.62-86.

13. Jane Smith.1997.Interview with Jerry Brown.San Francisco CA.15Oc.

14. Jacob Lynd.1973.Perfidy in Academe: Patterns of Rationalization in College Administrations.Ph.D. diss.UVA.

15. Holy Bible.New King James Version.

16. Paula Thomas.1970-1976.Diary.Museum of the Plains.Fabens TX.

17. U.S. Department of Labor.1931.Urban Growth and Population Projections:1930-1939.GPO.

18. Senate Journal.1993.103Cong.sess1.D10.

19. U.S. Senate.1997.Visa Formalization Act of 1997.105Cong. sess1.SR.1437.

21. Peter Bolen.1995."Creating Designs in Social Systems."The Internet Journal of Sociological Welfare.14.6.http://www.carmelpeak.com.

22. U.S. Public Law 678.1993.Library of Congress Book Preservation Act of 1993.U.S. Code.38.1562. 23.U.S.Constitution.

6.4 USE OF "TM", "SM", AND "®"

These symbols, "TM", "SM", and "®," which you frequently see in technical manuals and advertisements, are devices used by businesses and other organizations to serve notice to the rest of the world that they are claiming exclusive rights to use specific trademarks or service marks. "TM" stands for trademark, "SM" stands for service mark and "®" stands for registered trademark or service mark.

A trademark can be text, e.g., "The Real Thing®," or a symbol, such as one of the many forms the Coca-Cola® logo has taken over the many years of that brand's life. As you may already have guessed, trademarks apply to products, and service marks apply to services. Except for using different abbreviations, they are otherwise treated the same. If the trademark or service mark has been registered with the U.S. Patent office, "®" is used. If the trademark or service mark has not been registered, "TM" or "SM" is used.

Organizations adopt brand names, logos, and other words, phrases, and symbols to help differentiate their offerings from those of competing companies. Accordingly, the owners of these trademarks (and service marks) are quite sensitive to their usage by others. Their fears are well grounded in history. Brand names, if not well protected, can fall into such common use that anyone, including the firm's competitors, can freely use the former brand name. Brand names no longer protected include aspirin, kerosene, and formica, to name just a few. Business professionals must take precautions to insure that every time they use their own trademarks these are always accompanied by the proper symbol. Most businesses go farther, though, sending letters to publishers who fail to include the symbol where the firm's trademarks have been printed and published.

Professional writing standards for publishers require the use of the "®" symbol next to a registered trademark, but, mainly because student papers are not usually widely distributed, *The Chicago Manual of Style* does not call for the use of any of these symbols.

We in the school of business would like to encourage our students to adopt the professional writing practice of identifying registered trademarks as such in their writing, by adding the "®" symbol next to the trademark, as we have throughout this manual. We suggest also that student writers use "TM" or "SM" if used in the source. In this usage, adding the designation is analogous to quoting the words of another. The writer cannot know for sure that the source has a legal right to the claimed property, but, just as the writer cannot know if the quote is accurate in content, the source is accepted at face value. Even though this usage is not required, respecting the property rights that attend a registered trademark is a good idea and a good habit to learn. Further, with the advent of student publishing via the Internet and the Web, the assumption that a student paper will not be widely distributed is no longer justifiable.

NOTE: Most of the sources used as models in this chapter are not references to actual publications.

CHAPTER 7

Making Effective Use of Your Personal Computer

7.1 FEATURES OF WORD PROCESSING PROGRAMS

Just as in so many other fields of endeavor, the computer is revolutionizing scholarship. Card catalogs are disappearing from libraries, replaced by computer terminals and database systems that offer the researcher new ways to acquire information more quickly than ever before. It is possible to access a growing number of periodicals from a computer, and soon a wide variety of types of published sources may be available on the screen, eliminating delays in acquiring material. When you, as a young scholar, have your first journal article accepted for publication, it is quite likely that your editor will request a disk copy of the final draft to accompany the hard copy.

The advantages of using a computer in your own writing are numerous and profound. Most obvious is the sheer ease of typing on a computer, with its word-wrap feature, which does away with the need to strike the "return" key at the end of each line, and its quick, uncomplicated procedures for making changes and corrections. Because you can save a draft on a disk, you need never retype just to make another copy. Graphics and formatting features can help give your paper a professional look. And the language tools included in most word processing software programs offer help with spelling and grammar.

Here is a list of features, available from several word processing programs, that are of real help to researchers. (The names may change slightly from program to program.)

Name of Feature	*What It Does*
Block command	Allows you to mark a section of text in the document in order to perform another operation on that section, such as moving or copying it
Copy command	Makes a copy of a section of text
Footnote/endnote program	Formats text into a footnote or endnote
Grammar checker	Analyzes your language for basic patterns; points out passages that may be awkward or incorrect; may flag slang or colloquialisms
Graphics, tables, charts	Enables you to design tables and charts or import pictures, stored in the word processing program, into your document

Name of Feature	*What It Does*
Header/footer program	Helps with formatting by placing an identifying word or phrase at the top or bottom of a page
Index program	Arranges words that you mark in your text into an alphabetical index file, indicating the page number in the text on which the word occurs
Move command	Moves a passage from one part of your document to another location or from one file to another
Outline program	Rearranges text into standard outline format
Pagination program	Prints page number on each page at the location you choose
Print command	Prints a document
Replace command	Finds a specific word or phrase in your document and replaces it with another
Retrieve command	Retrieves a document from a floppy disk or hard drive
Save command	Stores a document on a floppy disk or a hard drive
Search command	Finds a word or phrase in your document
Spell checker	Checks your spelling against the program's internal dictionary; flags deviations and offers suggestions for respelling the word
Statistics program	Performs functions such as counting the number of words in your document, the number of revisions, and the time you have spent on each
Table of contents	Arranges text that you have identified as headings into a separate table of contents, indicating the page number in the text for each section
Thesaurus	Offers synonyms for a word
Word wrap	Automatically returns the cursor to the left margin when you reach the end of a line

Revision Help

The relative ease of composing on a computer provides two important kinds of assistance for the writer. First, it facilitates *revision,* which many researchers point to as perhaps the most crucial phase of the writing process. Indeed, as Chapter 1 suggests, you cannot write without revising—re-*seeing*, rethinking—as you move from sentence to sentence, paragraph to paragraph. By making it easy to move and change blocks of texts of all sizes, from words to entire documents, the computer breaks down many of our inhibitions concerning revision. As it frees us from constraints, the computer allows us to be bolder, more open to possible improvements of all sorts. The computer in fact may help us to *think* better while we write. It is important, as you compose drafts at the keyboard, that you become sensitive to the ways in which the tremendous flexibility of the computer can enhance your revision skills.

Saving Time

The second major boon of the computer is that it *saves time*. Tasks that once took much time and effort, such as typing and retyping a draft, figuring out the placement of footnotes, or correcting a chronic misspelling throughout the final draft, are either eliminated or made much faster by the computer. This does not mean, however, that you should speed through all phases of a writing project. Certain parts of the writing process—prewriting, planning, drafting—must not be rushed. But there is no reason why mechanical functions, such as tracking down certain words to be changed or merely transcribing a draft, should take up time that could be better spent on other tasks.

7.2 FEATURES OF SPREADSHEETS

The electronic spreadsheet provides the accountant with a very powerful tool. The spreadsheet program lets the user enter data, text, or formulas into "cells" which are organized into rows and columns, as in a chart. Headings describe the contents of columns or rows. The user enters data, usually numbers (as in dollars), into the cells (the point where a row and a column intersect.) The spreadsheet can then be programmed to perform various functions using the data. For example, the spreadsheet can add all of the dollars entered in a particular row or column.

The power of the spreadsheet lies in its ability to carry out automatically all of the accountant's computations in the same sequence the accountant would have done by hand in the past and render the final result, profit, for example, in seconds. Once the spreadsheet has been built, with the row and column headings in place, the accountant need only input the data to receive a virtually instantaneous set of details to answer a particular question about his business. Then, for each new question, the new data can be entered in place of the old and a new result computed in an instant.

Johnson Pneumatics Company, Inc. Pro Forma Income Statements First Quarter, 1996				
	January	February	March	Quarterly Total
Income:				
Sales	$25,000	$30,000	$45,000	$100,000
Cost of Goods Sold	18,750	22,500	33,750	75,000
Gross Profit	$6,250	$7,500	$11,250	$25,000
Expenses:				
Labor	5,000	6,000	9,000	20,000
Rent	600	600	600	1,800
Utilities	350	350	350	1,050
Supplies	235	235	235	705
Depreciation	475	475	475	1,425
Total Expenses	$6,660	$7,660	$10,660	$24,980
Net Profit Before Taxes	($410)	($160)	$590	$20

When compared to today's Excel®, Lotus123®, and Quatro Pro®, early programs like Visicalc® and the first versions of Lotus123® were incredibly slow. But even these old programs were thousands of times faster than the very best accountants working in the days before computers. Today's spreadsheet applications are many times faster than their early precursors, and they are so easy and simple to use that the managers often perform their own financial analyses. For particularly complex analyses, a data processing employee or an accountant may build the original spreadsheet the manager needs, but more and more often the manager is the one who runs the analysis, changing the data as needed to answer relevant questions.

Every student of business needs to learn to use a spreadsheet application program. Like managers and accountants, the financial analyst too will find daily use for a spreadsheet, as will the management information systems employee. Even the human resources worker will need to use a spreadsheet to compute the cost of benefits package changes or the effect of a proposed change in a compensation plan. In fact, the power of the spreadsheet to answer a wide variety of questions quickly makes this tool essential for every professional level employee, no matter what the business discipline. Even business attorneys must account for their time and prepare budgets for their departments.

As a business student, you will receive specific instructions for those assignments requiring the use of a spreadsheet. In many student assignments, however, the spreadsheet is simply used in place of a manual approach to attaining the same objective.

In preparing a case study using a ratio analysis approach, for example, you do not need to use a spreadsheet, but using one can greatly facilitate your analysis. Once you have built the ratio analysis template, you will be able to use it again and again throughout your business education and beyond, depending on the field you land in. For a business plan in which you will include pro forma income statements, cashflow statements, and balance sheets, a spreadsheet will save you many hours of tedious calculation and eliminate an entire category of errors: computers cannot make addition errors! Even in preparing informational reports, such as a report on the implications of a union contract proposal, a spreadsheet can be very helpful, though instructors seldom require spreadsheets for such assignments. Using data relevant to the proposal, modern spreadsheets can display charts and graphs that better present your data, while automating the underlying computations as well. The chart shown below was generated automatically by Excel® and is based on the spreadsheet example presented above.

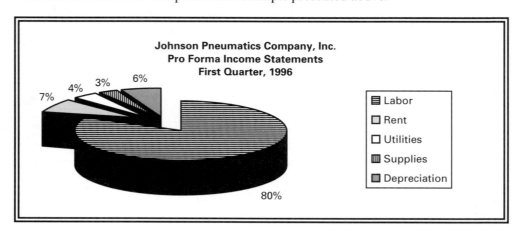

You should take a class that teaches you how to use a spreadsheet as early in your business education as possible, so that you may make use of this powerful tool throughout your education. Gaining practice with spreadsheets will greatly assist you in your professional career.

7.3 FEATURES OF ELECTRONIC PRESENTATION PROGRAMS

While in many disciplines a writing project ends with the delivery of the written document, business presentations frequently require a personal presentation also. This personal presentation can affect the attitude of the audience toward the product—and the promotion prospects of the presenter. A poorly delivered presentation, no matter how wonderful the written document on which it is based, will make a negative impression on all members of the audience, including professors and bosses.

In Chapter 9 you will learn how to prepare for all your business presentations, both as a student and as a business professional. Once the document has been written, your most important tool in preparing a dynamic, hard-hitting presentation of your findings is a PC-based presentation program. This new class of software has become available only within the past few years. Two popular programs are Microsoft Power-Point® and Aldus Persuasion®. These and others like them allow you to prepare fully for your presentations. Good presentation programs offer most or all of the functions listed below to enable you to create slides that can be presented on an overhead projector.

- Automated slide creation (You type in content, the program designs the slides!)
- Fully editable slides
- Many ready-made slide designs and backgrounds
- Choice of electronic "clip-art" to use in customizing slides
- Wide range of screen transition styles (fade out to the next screen, wipe from left to right, etc.)
- Wide range of "build" options to allow presentation of lists, one item at a time
- Embedding of objects in the slides
  - Charts and graphs, based on spreadsheet files (When the spreadsheet is updated, so is the chart or graph in the slide!)
  - Multimedia objects, including video or audio clips
- Full control over timing of the slide show (from manual advance to fully automated slide presentation)
- Ability to view the whole slide show in "thumbnails" (tiny images of each slide) and rearrange or delete slides.
- Wide range of print options
  - Printing of full slides in color or black and white
  - Printing of thumbnails of the slide show for reference
  - Printing of reduced slides with accompanying speaker's notes
  - Printing of reduced slides with accompanying audience notes as handouts
  - Printing of overhead transparency masters to convert the electronic slide show for an overhead projector

Remember, the availability of modern presentation tools raises the level of expectation of all those who will evaluate your presentations. You will find yourself in competition for grades with students who fully utilize all of the computer power at their disposal to create powerful presentations. If you choose not to avail yourself of these tools, you will find that your grades suffer, and once on the job you will find yourself playing "catch up" in learning to use these increasingly essential tools of the business professional. *Don't wait!* Learn to use these powerful and exciting new tools now. Use them throughout your business education, and throughout your career they will provide you with a significant competitive advantage in the world of business.

7.4 CONDUCTING RESEARCH WITH A COMPUTER

When your writing project involves the use of research materials, the computer can really save you time, especially if you establish a sound working pattern that allows you to obtain the benefits of the old, traditional note card system without having to deal with its handicaps. As Chapter 3 points out, jotting notes on individual cards can help you to assimilate the reference material and later organize your paper. The computer allows you to duplicate these processes while eliminating the need of physically copying material from cards into your draft. Here is a research strategy that allows you to make efficient use of your computer:

1. Instead of sitting in the library filling out note cards on noncirculating material, simply photocopy the source. (Actually, this is a good idea no matter what research strategy you use. You never know when you will want to re-check a source.) If all necessary bibliographical information—the name of the journal, the volume number, the date of the issue, and so on—does not appear in the photocopied material, be sure to record that information so that you will have it for your bibliography. (See Chapter 6 for the types of information required for complete citations of different types of sources.)

2. After you return home, stay close to your computer as you examine the photocopies and any other reference material you have acquired. As you find material that you feel may be useful to your paper, make a note—not on a note card but on your computer. The order of the notes in the computer file you are building does not matter at this point, so there is no need to try to organize this material. It *is* necessary, however, that you use some method of linking each note to its source. You might place an abbreviation of the author's name or the title of the work at the beginning or end of your note.

To quote or not to quote: it is at this point that the question comes up of when to quote from your source directly and when to paraphrase. Chapter 1 discusses the advantages and disadvantages of both strategies. No doubt you will want to reproduce some material exactly, but remember that paraphrasing can often lead you to a better understanding of the material and its original context. Whichever method of transcription you use, take care to represent your source material as accurately as possible.

3. Once you have completed taking notes on your sources, print a copy of this file and cut the pages into strips, each bearing a single note. Arrange these slips as you would note cards to help establish the best organization for your paper.

You can save yourself the effort of printing out the file, cutting the notes into strips, and physically arranging the strips by using the **move**, **index**, or **outline** command, which allows you to move material—a word, sentence, paragraph, or larger section—to a new location. This feature is the electronic equivalent of rearranging a pack of note cards.

4. Just as you can rearrange material within a file, so can you move text, using the **copy** feature, from one file to another. This means that you can begin to draft your paper on the screen and, when the need arises, move into that draft the various notes that you have saved in your notes file.

7.5 POSSIBLE PROBLEMS WITH COMPUTERS

A computer is a powerful aid to writing, but it does not guarantee a good paper. Some of the potential difficulties in using a computer are so well known by now as to have become clichés. For many people, just learning how to use a computer or a word processing program, with its confusing manual and welter of subprograms, can be frustrating. So can losing a file. How many times have you heard a computer rookie complain about touching the wrong key and accidentally obliterating a text that he had worked on for hours? Have you ever felt the anger that comes from seeing a file destroyed by a disruption of the electrical system? (To avoid this problem, *save your work often.*)

Another potentially serious difficulty paradoxically stems from one of the great benefits afforded by the computer: the ease with which you can make changes in your computer draft can actually work against you if you allow yourself to develop an interest in change for change's sake. It is possible to become "hooked" on revision, playing at rewriting instead of pressing on with the draft, until your energy and imagination are exhausted, leaving you short of the number of pages you set as your goal. You have to establish a limit for wordplay, a method of working that keeps you focused on the project.

Another problem concerns the fact that you will often be reading your computer draft from an electronic screen. Research has suggested that spotting writing problems, particularly proofreading errors, is more difficult on a monitor than on a piece of paper. (The difficulty is worse for older screens with colored backgrounds than for those that mimic the white background and black lettering of a typed page.) One solution is to print a hard copy of your draft any time you wish to read it. Another way to help guard against error is by running your software's spelling and grammar checkers. *But beware*: these programs will not catch certain kinds of errors, such as typographical mistakes that happen to be actual words, as in the following poem:

THE SPELL CHECKER POEM

I have a spelling checker,
It cam with my PC.
It clearly marks for my revue
Mistakes I cannot sea.
I've run this poem threw it,
I'm sure your pleased to no
It's letter perfect in its weigh
My spell check tolled me sew!
(AUTHOR UNKNOWN)

Likewise, your computer's grammar program is woefully inadequate for making a detailed, useful analysis of your sentence structures and use of words. One prominent program from a few years ago flagged as unnecessarily abstract all words in a draft that ended in *ion*. Unless you *carefully* proof your paper yourself, spelling and grammar errors could mar the effectiveness of your writing.

A Computer is Not a Magic Box

The fallibility of the spelling and grammar checkers points to what may be the most dangerous pitfall of using a computer: you can be lulled into a false sense of security. If you are not careful, you can begin to believe that the writing and formatting of your paper will take less time and effort than a really good job still requires. This is the sort of attitude that causes students to delay working on their papers until deadlines start to loom. Remember: In some ways, writing really is easier and faster with a computer than without one. But writing is still difficult.

Even with a computer, the toughest part of writing a paper is still . . . writing the paper! While a computer can make some parts of the process less tedious, it cannot think for you. It cannot proofread for you. The real work of writing is still yours to do.

CHAPTER 8

Group Project Reports

8.1 GROUP WORK: A FACT OF LIFE FOR THE BUSINESS STUDENT AND PROFESSIONAL

Nearly every time business leaders are asked what they want their job applicants to know how to do, they respond with two skills. First, they want applicants to be able to communicate effectively and competently, both orally and in writing. Second, they nearly always insist that applicants know how to work in groups of their peers when they get to the job. Whether you enjoy group work or not, the fact is that during your business school experience you will frequently find yourself assigned to work in groups to complete assigned projects.

There are several valid reasons why your instructors will divide their classes into groups. Group work is one way to harness the diversity of interests and abilities in the classroom for the benefit of all students. Those students who have little difficulty in comprehending assigned concepts may need practice in mastering the more subtle aspects of group work. Often cast in a leadership role in their groups, these more knowledgeable students learn to apply new skills as they attempt to direct their peers. Students in groups have the chance to learn how to resolve conflicts, negotiate decisions, apportion work effectively, and motivate their peers to perform well. Students who have not yet caught on to the requirements of the assignment often get the tutoring they need from their group peers. The last reason for assigning group projects is that it lessens the workload on the professor, which in turn allows the projects to be much more complex, giving the students a more realistic learning experience, something in everyone's best interest.

Given that you will have no choice but to work with your assigned groups of students, we suggest that you make the best of each experience. To help you get the most out of your group project experiences, consider the observations and suggestions in the sections that follow.

8.2 TUNING IN TO YOUR GROUP'S DYNAMICS

There is a great deal of psychological literature available on group dynamics, and researchers studying group settings have established dozens of group member types. We do not have the time or space to make a detailed study of these classifications, but you probably already know of certain behaviors people adopt in groups that could be seen as typical. Some students, for example, assume leadership roles. Others tend to believe they have nothing significant to offer the group. There are students who rarely speak out in a group because of a fear of rejection. Many students adopt a policy of drifting through group projects, staying in the background, doing little work yet taking credit for the group's achievement. There are other types of students, and it will be important for you not only to learn to deal with all of them but also to determine where you fit among the patterns, so that you can integrate yourself effectively into the group's activities. The important thing to understanding is that, no matter how your group is composed, it is up to all its member to establish a successful pattern of shared action for getting the project done. Learning how to conduct successful group projects is one of the most important goals of your career as a business student. In the business world, being a good group member is a life-or-death skill.

Your Responsibilities to the Group

All members of a group have a responsibility to every other member to contribute their best efforts to each group activity. *Attending group meetings and engaging in the discussion is not sufficient.* Only when every member thoroughly prepares for each group meeting can the highest quality decisions emerge from the group's efforts. If some group members fail to prepare, the decisions made are often worse than they would have been had the group never met. Unprepared members can still be persuasive even when they lack crucial information.

Appropriate Group Work

A common mistake made by student group members is to attempt to do all of the project work during group member meetings. This is a recipe for disaster, because groups are not very good at "doing work." By that we mean that most kinds of work are best done individually. Tasks such as structuring a report and analyzing data require careful contemplation of the available facts, re-reading passages and looking up additional information to enhance understanding. These procedures suffer greatly in group settings, because to reach a balanced synthesis, all of the information must be available within the same mind. Similarly, writing is best done by an individual, working alone.

Well, then, if analysis and writing are best done individually, what is so useful about groups? The power of groups lies in *idea-generation* and in *organizing tasks*. Groups work best when group meetings are used mainly to get everyone organized and to engage in discussions of how to help members solve problems they have encountered in their individual efforts. Analysis and writing are tasks best performed by individual group members working separately.

Idea Generation

Have you ever been assigned to a group in which only one or two members do most of the talking? This is a typical—and usually not very productive—group situation. Ideas suggested by the other members are often trashed almost as quickly as they are expressed, with little consideration actually given to their validity. In such a typical "brainstorming" session, the more reticent group members tend to clam-up, and who can blame them? No one enjoys a psychological beating. The lack of continuing input from the less-outspoken group members in turn deepens the group leaders' belief that the other group members are just a burden to be put up with for the sake of the course grade. For their part, the silent group members expend considerable energy stewing in their own private frustration over what they view as the arrogance of the more outspoken members. They too leave the experience frustrated by the seeming unwillingness of their peers to listen to their ideas or give them a chance to help with the project in more than a menial way.

The first tool we offer to you to help you break down these natural, self-reinforcing and very destructive patterns is a structured approach to generating ideas called *Nominal Group Brainstorming*. The technique is highly structured and should be followed to the letter until you and your fellow group members gain considerable experience in using the approach. Some of the restrictions may seem silly and unnecessary, especially to the more self-confident among you. Take our word for it, adhering strictly to the approach, as presented below, will yield benefits. The more strictly you adhere, the better the outcome of the session is likely to be.

Nominal Group Brainstorming

Nominal Group Brainstorming is a formal approach to idea generation and group decision making that addresses several weaknesses of unstructured brainstorming exercises. This approach helps to avoid the common problem that many good ideas simply never get presented either because members of the group fear a negative reaction or because the available time is dominated by one or two members. When the steps below are followed as described, this approach becomes a powerful tool that can virtually insure that none of the group members' good ideas get overlooked.

Nominal Group Brainstorming is a structured idea generation procedure. It works by encouraging all group members to maintain in their minds a clear separation between the task of *generating* ideas and the task of *evaluating* the ideas. By focusing only on generating ideas at first, the group provides all its members with an opportunity to make suggestions in an atmosphere free of the fear of instantaneous judgment and rejection. The group solicits ideas from its members systematically and encourages every member to contribute. All the members' ideas are placed on the table for consideration by all.

The procedure includes the six steps presented below.

1. Working *silently* and *separately*, each group member generates a written list of alternative solutions to the problem at hand.

2. When the group meeting begins, each member in turn orally presents one idea, *without elaboration*. These very brief single-idea presentations continue through as many rounds as necessary until all members of the group have presented all their ideas. As the presentations continue, new ideas may be sparked by the ideas presented; when his or her turn comes around again, a member might suggest an idea that is a variation of an idea presented earlier by someone else. A designated secretary records each idea presented in the form of a simple list. Remember, *absolutely no evaluation of ideas is allowed during this step*.

3. After the secretary has recorded all the ideas, each one is then explained by its presenter and discussed by the group in the order in which it was first presented. At this point everyone, including the presenter, should feel free to criticize or support any idea on the group list as each is discussed. Each idea must be allowed to stand on its own merits. If a flaw in one of your ideas has occurred to you since you presented it, then your obligation

to the group is to point out the flaw. Group members must avoid a sense of ownership of ideas. All group members should be encouraged to voice their questions and concerns about each idea as it is discussed in this step. Now is the time for evaluation and the full expression of your opinions.

4. Group members vote on each idea in the group's list, ranking the best idea as 5, the worst as 2–4. The voting pattern should be recorded as well as the total score each idea receives. In this round of voting, each member's vote is recorded under his or her name in the space marked "1st vote" in the table below.

5. Ideas receiving odd voting patterns such as all 4s and 5s, except for a single 1, are discussed again. A lone dissenter might have information not possessed by the other group members or might be missing information held by the others. In general, all ideas that indicate strong disagreement among members should be discussed again in this step.

6. A final vote is taken as in step 4; this time the vote is recorded in the space marked "2nd vote" under the member's name. The idea that receives the highest score (the score is equal to the sum of all member's votes) becomes the group's final decision. Ties should be resolved by discussion, with consensus achieved if possible.

A Sample Voting Form is Shown Below

Idea	Member 1	Member 2	Member 3	Member 4	Member 5	Total
Idea Number 1	1st Vote/2nd Vote	1st Vote/2nd Vote	1st Vote/2nd Vote	1st Vote/2nd Vote	1st Vote/2nd Vote	
Idea Number 2	1st Vote/2nd Vote	1st Vote/2nd Vote	1st Vote/2nd Vote	1st Vote/2nd Vote	1st Vote/2nd Vote	

Organizing the Tasks

Probably the most heated arguments arise during discussions of who is to do what in the student group project. We have observed a variety of group leadership systems emerge and either work well or end in disaster. The most important element in finding a group leadership system is to tackle that issue as the group's first order of business. Most of the time group conflict can be greatly reduced by obtaining the agreement of all group members on how decisions will be made.

In general, the final decisions of the group can be selected from the alternatives presented and discussed, using three different approaches. In the *autocratic* approach (usually the worst alternative), one or two members make the decision for all, after either considering or ignoring the input provided by other members (if any). Better is a *democratic* approach, allowing members to vote on the suggestions, with the one receiving the largest number of votes becoming the final group choice. The best approach from the standpoint of maintaining harmony and morale is *consensus*, in which the group discussion continues until all the members agree that one particular choice is the correct one. This is the most difficult of the three approaches, of course, because often a consensus cannot be reached due to conflicting personalities, differing levels of understanding, and hidden motivations of the members. Notwithstanding the difficulties, a sincere effort to achieve consensus will generally pay large dividends and is highly recommended, not only in student projects but throughout your business career as well. As a fall-back approach if efforts at consensus fail, a democratic approach can often get the job finished in a timely fashion.

Adopting the Right Attitude

Discussions in any work group sometimes become quite heated and can lead to hard feelings that get in the way of achieving the purposes of the group. The best way to avoid such conflicts is for all members to discipline themselves to keep the level of discussion well above the personal level. Before criticizing another member's ideas or presenting one's own ideas, a member should always think first, preparing an answer for the logical rebuttal, "What makes you think that?" Often such an explanation can bring to light misconceptions on which the subject idea is predicated and thereby allow the better idea to prevail. Without such explanations, good ideas can be carelessly discarded and inferior ideas adopted for illogical reasons that remain unstated.

A common trap in group work is for a member to become attached to an idea because he or she first presented it. A sense of ownership of ideas works against the goals of the group, encouraging members to become defensive of an idea even when it is shown to be inferior to others. The best way for members to avoid this trap is not to claim ideas as their own in the first place. When a presenter refers to a suggestion as "My idea . . . ," his or her ego naturally becomes involved, and separation of the idea and the ego becomes very difficult. As a result, if the idea is rejected, the member also feels rejected. Instead, it is important to present each idea as simply "*an* idea," not "*my* idea." When a group member presents an idea this way, he or she should feel as free to criticize the idea as any of the other members.

8.3 STEPS IN PREPARING A GROUP ADMINISTRATION PLAN

To help you to prepare for a group project assignment, your instructor may ask you to prepare a formal Group Administration Plan Report. Unless otherwise instructed, follow the steps discussed in this section.

Identify the Course, the Project, and the Group Members

As in all student assignments, you should prepare a suitable cover sheet. Unless otherwise directed, follow the instructions in Chapter 5 for preparing a *Title Page* for this report. The title of the report should be "Group Administration Plan Report." Be sure you include the name of the course, the course number, the professor's name and the names of all group members, and the date.

Describe the Goals and Objectives of the Project

Your professor will ordinarily provide you with detailed information on how to complete your project, including the goals and objectives of the project. Include these in your group administration plan, adding additional detail as you and your group members deem necessary to provide a complete picture of the project. Beyond the explicit goals imposed by the professor, include additional goals and objectives you and your peers may wish to accomplish personally. For example, you may wish to learn more about electronic research, another member might want to get practice in formal report writing, while a third member might wish to delve more deeply into statistical analysis using a newly acquired statistics package. By explicitly stating all of these individual goals, group members may encounter less conflict when the individual project tasks are assigned. Include at least one personal goal for every member of the group.

Describe the Group Administration System

On this one point, if nowhere else, the group members should reach a consensus. As already discussed, your choices for a system to administer the project are *autocratic*, *democratic, consensus building*, or some combination of two or more of these approaches. When this plan is completed all group members will be required to sign it, indicating their commitment to its contents and to the administration system chosen and described in this section. Be sure you really do agree with the approach chosen by your group. If you have difficulty reaching a consensus, you may wish to request the assistance of your professor in resolving your disagreements. Now is the time for intervention and conflict resolution. Do not wait until your grade is at risk near the deadline for the project report to ask for help.

List the Tasks Required by the Project

Once you have determined the administrative approach you plan to use for the project, take time to divide the overall project into its component parts. A business plan may, for example, call for the kind of task list shown below. Often the major parts of the project will already be provided by your professor, and all you need to do is fill in additional detail as necessary.

TASK LIST FOR A BUSINESS PLAN

Task	Assigned To:	Due Date/Meeting Date	
Pre-Investigation Executive Summary		Due:	January 24
Discussion	Group	Meeting:	January 14
Writing	Bob	Due:	January 20
Editing	Group	Meeting:	January 22
Marketing Analysis		Due:	February 16
Discussion	Group	Meeting:	January 24
Research	Sheri, Bob, Tom, Saba	Due:	February 10
Discussion	Group	Meeting:	February 10
Writing	Saba	Due:	February 14
Editing	Group	Meeting:	February 14
Marketing Strategy		Due:	February 28
Discussion	Group	Meeting:	February 16
Research	Sheri, Bob, Tom, Saba	Due:	February 23
Discussion	Group	Meeting:	February 23
Strategy Worksheet	Sheri	Due:	February 26
Discussion	Group	Meeting:	February 26
Editing	Group	Meeting:	February 26
Production/Operations		Due:	March 15
Discussion	Group	Meeting:	February 28

Task	Assigned To:	Due Date/Meeting Date	
Research	Sheri, Bob, Tom, Saba	Due:	March 6
Discussion	Group	Meeting:	March 6
Writing:			
Inventory Plan	Tom	Due:	March 10
Equipment Plan	Saba	Due:	March 10
Facilities Plan	Bob	Due:	March 10
Human Resources	Sheri	Due:	March 10
Crew Planning Chart Spreadsheet	Saba and Sheri	Due:	March 10
Labor Cost Summary Spreadsheet	Saba and Bob	Due:	March 10
Editing	Group	Meeting:	March 13
Financial Plan		Due:	April 15
Discussion	Group	Meeting:	March 15
Writing:			
Capital Budgeting	Sheri	Due:	April 13
Financial Spreadsheets:			
Income Statements	Saba and Bob	Due:	April 13
Cashflow Statements	Saba and Sheri	Due:	April 13
Balance Sheets	Saba and Tom	Due:	April 13
Editing	Group	Meeting:	April 13
Conclusions/Final Plan Revisions		Due:	May 5
Discussion	Group	Meeting:	April 15
Writing	Sheri, Bob, Tom, Saba	Due:	April 30
Final Editing	Group	Meeting:	April 30
		Meeting:	May 3

Identify the Group Member(s) Responsible for Completing Each Task

Note that in our chart group meetings are reserved for discussion and editing. Of course, the first meeting or two are not included and should be dedicated to the development of this administrative report. The other work of the group is done by individual members working alone or in pairs. The reason for having two members working on each component of the spreadsheets, for example, is to allow members with weaker spreadsheet skills to benefit from some tutoring by Saba, a knowledgeable spreadsheet operator. Identifying group members' personal goals helps to identify opportunities for addressing these goals during the project. Failure to lay out these personal goals explicitly means the chances are greater that you will miss an important opportunity for learning.

In dividing up the work, students have a strong tendency to assign tasks on the basis of current ability (let the computer geniuses prepare the spreadsheets and the good writers do the writing). The problem with this approach is that less learning takes place than is possible in your class projects. A much better tack is to identify the motivated among you and assign tasks on that basis. Let the international student do more of the writing as a self-improvement exercise, if better writing skill is his personal goal. Let the home economics major wrestle with an Internet research component, and so forth. Do not fall into the path of least resistance. No pain, no gain. Use the power of your group to support all of the members as they attempt to better themselves. You can always set your due dates so that ample time exists to allow you to edit the international student's writing or to rebuild the history student's spreadsheet if necessary. This way the group members help each other to grow.

List the Dates and Times for All Group Meetings and a Tentative Agenda for Each

In our chart, group meetings are indicated in the "Assigned to" column. These meetings should be formally assigned a time in this report. Usually groups find one or two convenient times and a place to meet that work for everyone. The required meetings are then held at the same time and place. This approach simplifies everyone's scheduling conflicts and reduces the chances of confusion over meeting times and places. Popular times are right before a night class, just after lunch, or even early mornings. You can plan to meet in vacant classrooms when available, in the school or public library, or even in a student lounge.

Once you get to know each other, you may wish to socialize. Out of deference to group members who may have less free time than you do, however, we suggest that you make it a rule always to complete the business part of your meetings before engaging in social activities.

List the Date of Completion for Each Task

Notice that in our chart you should include a specific date on which each part of the project is due. Set these due dates based on the expected difficulty of each part of the project. No doubt in many cases you will not be able to predict accurately the amount of work involved in an assignment before you tackle it. Accordingly, you should make a tentative plan and ask your professor if it looks reasonable. Just stay flexible and revise your plan as needed, based on the problems and speed you observe once you get started.

Make sure every group member is fully prepared to commit to the meeting schedule embodied in the plan. Distributing copies of a comprehensive timetable, agreed to by all, will go a very long way toward helping all the members plan their hectic schedules and minimize the number of conflicts that arise later.

Prepare a Table of Contents and Signature Page

Finally, as for all formal business reports, you must include a table of contents in the final draft and, because this is a group assignment, a signature page. Refer to Chapter 5 for detailed instructions about constructing a table of contents.

When everything is well organized and all members are working hard to produce their part of the project, you will find yourself excited and eager to attend group meetings.

If your group experiences have been typical, however, you are probably experiencing some considerable doubt right now about this plan. Trust us. Try the organized approach. You are in for a real treat. This group experience may well prove to you, finally, that groups are a good thing. You might even come to believe that the outcome of a properly functioning group will nearly always exceed that of a single individual, no matter how many jokes you have heard like this one:

Camel: a horse designed by committee.

CHAPTER 9

Oral Presentations

9.1 FOUNDATIONS FOR AN EFFECTIVE ORAL REPORT

In the business world, oral reports and presentations are nearly as commonplace as are their written counterparts. So, too, you will find that you are frequently required to present your information to a business class in person. We do not choose lightly to incorporate oral presentations in business courses. We know oral presentations cause lots of psychic pain and agony among stage-frightened students. Your business professors believe their primary job is preparing you for successful entry (or re-entry) into the business world. In this world, you will find yourself in front of all kinds of people—fellow workers, subordinates, customers, vendors, community leaders, and bosses. One poor performance in an oral report you are called upon to present to a selected audience while your boss observes can cost you a promotion, a key assignment, or even your position with the company. Knowing this, business professors try to offer students as many opportunities as we can work into the courses to help you all gain experience in presenting your reports orally.

Stage fright afflicts nearly everyone. Yes, even some of your professors frequently suffer bouts of stage fright. Stage fright is primarily fear of the unknown. As you anticipate the speaking engagement, you may expect that your ideas will be rejected. You may expect the audience to present arguments that challenge your facts or conclusions. You may fear that you will forget where you are in your presentation and appear foolish as you fumble for what you wish to say next. You may even fear that the audience members will fail to take you seriously and that they may even laugh at you for any of a hundred reasons. Finally, you may fear that your presentation will be a failure in achieving your goal, whether that be persuasion, convincing your professor that you have expended sufficient effort, or fending off unwanted questions from your fellow students. The secret of overcoming stage fright is preparation, preparation, preparation.

So what does it mean to prepare for an oral presentation? Too many students assume that all they need is a suit and tie, a few note cards (and maybe a a stiff drink!), and they are ready. The truth of the matter is that, like many other challenges in life, the oral presentation itself is simply the tip of the iceberg. You should plan to spend a great deal more time preparing for a presentation than you do in actually delivering it. A professional presenter might spend a full day preparing for a two-hour presentation, not counting the research that may be necessary before the presentation can be constructed. As a student, you should schedule at least four group planning meetings over at least a two-week period to prepare adequately for a 10–20 minute group presentation to your business class. As always in group projects, you will also need to schedule time to prepare your share of the work before attending the group meetings.

Good presentations leave nothing to chance. The topic is carefully considered. Material is thoroughly researched and organized. Suitable accompanying documents are created, the presentation is scripted, and presenters are rehearsed and timed. The result of such complete preparation is an impressive, seemingly effortless performance that goes off without a hitch.

To help you become familiar with the process of preparing for an oral presentation, we have included an assignment to write an oral presentation plan. Based entirely on the plan document, a second student or group will make the actual presentation. If your professor is to grade you on your efforts, separate grades will be given for the oral presentation plan (described in the following section) and for the delivery of the presentation. We suggest that students in one group prepare the oral presentation plan to be delivered by a second group, and vice versa. In that way, each group will gain experience in both phases of an oral presentation, while also learning the value of a thorough presentation plan. By watching your own presentation plan being implemented by another student, you will learn many ways to improve your plans. By attempting to implement a presentation plan written by another, you will learn just how important the details can become. And finally, by separating out these two vitally interactive functions, you will learn to value teamwork as it is really used in the world of your future.

9.2 STEPS IN PREPARING AN ORAL PRESENTATION PLAN

Prepare a Cover Sheet

Construct a cover sheet appropriate to your report. Refer to Chapter 5 for suitable formats for a cover sheet for this report. The cover sheet helps the reader to identify the nature of the report (from the title), who wrote it (include all of the names of students assigned to work on the plan), who the document was prepared for (professor's name, course name and number, and the name of the school), and the date. All of this information is potentially important because every report may be read by someone outside the intended context. Student papers frequently find a life outside academe, and you owe it to any potential reader to provide all of the information they need to properly interpret the contents of any written report you create. (Besides, if you omit any of the information, your professor will probably reduce your score on the assignment!)

Choose a Topic

The topic of your oral report may be one that is specifically assigned (to report on your analysis of a business case, for example), one that allows you to choose from a limited number of topics provided by your professor, or a topic of your choice, given some general constraints. Whatever the topic, your report should begin with a clearly written statement of what the topic of the presentation will be.

Topic: Analysis of the Ford Motor Company Case as presented on pages 124–149, *Cases in Strategic Management*, by Johnson and Callison, Vixen Publishing, 1993.

Topic: The History of Employment Law, 1868–1996.

Topic: A Book Report on *The Last Days of a Halcyon Era: The Rise and Fall of MGT Corp.*, by Erickson and Pell, Dixon Publishing, 1996.

Focusing on a Theme

As in most other business writing projects, a *deductive* approach is preferred over an *inductive* one.

An *inductive* order (to be avoided in most business presentations) is one in which the details are presented first and the conclusion is reserved until a case has been built that will support that conclusion. Business professionals, however, need the punch line first, so give it to them. Leave the drama in your drama class. In business, always lead with your conclusions, and then present the details that led you to that conclusion. This is known as a *deductive* presentation order.

In a murder mystery, the goal is entertainment. Readers are entertained by sorting out puzzling details. One goal of entertainment is to spend available time in such a pleasurable pursuit. By contrast, business professionals have no free time. If they spend any excess time considering information, such as your presentation, because the information is presented so as to impede the audience's accurate and immediate understanding, business professionals tend to react rather negatively: "Why didn't you tell me up front that the project would not meet the financial standards we require? Why did you make me sit all the way through your stinking presentation to find out what you already knew I needed to know! Out! Get out of my sight! You will never see another nickel of my business!"

For the current project, your goal is to provide the presenter with all of the information and attendant documents needed to deliver an effective presentation. This goal is best served by telling your reader what your conclusions are, right up front. In this way, the reader (and later the audience) is better prepared to understand the purpose of each graphic and to accept the reasoning for the script or speaker's notes provided later in the plan.

One acceptable method of presenting your conclusions in the presentation plan is to present a statement of conclusions immediately following the topic statement. A second approach that may work better for some larger, more complex projects is to include an abstract in which you address your conclusions, literature review highlights, methodology, and implications for practice. The abstract should be 100 words or less and is better explained in Chapter 5. If you are in doubt as to which of these approaches to use, consult with your professor. The use of statements of conclusion is illustrated below.

Topic: Analysis of the Ford Motor Company Case.
Pages 124–149, *Cases in Strategic Management*, Johnson and Callison, Vixen Publishing, 1993.

Conclusions: Henry Ford II had become old and complacent by 1975, allowing many of the firm's direct competitors from overseas a free hand in the U.S. markets. With the introduction of the Escort in 1981, though, a new strategy began to take shape that reinvigorated the company. Unfortunately, in pursuit of short term profits, Ford has once again fallen into economic troubles. We suggest changes in marketing, production, and new product development to address these problems. To allow the sweeping changes we believe are needed, we also suggest that Henry Ford II step down for the good of his company.

Topic: The History of Employment Law: 1868–1996.

Conclusions: Employment law has generally followed a path similar to that followed by discrimination law, from no law, which gives all the power to one side, to current law, which gives too much power to the (formerly) weaker side. From first allowing people to work for anybody who would hire them, and the working conditions and pay to remain a private matter between employer and employee, the law has incrementally moved to the current point at which employees often hold more power than is warranted. Under present employment law, employees are free to harass their bosses by calling down the wrath of any number of federal and state enforcement agencies including the Federal Labor Department, the Occupational Safety and Health Administration, the Environmental Protection Agency, and the Equal Employment Opportunity Commission, to name just a few, if the employee simply feels inclined to do so. The absence of any consequences for employees who file their grievances with any of the plethora of enforcement agencies has led to an imbalance that threatens the very existence of many jobs in the U.S. Businesses are rapidly moving jobs to other countries where such employee rights are virtually unknown. The balance of power must be restored or we will all lose.

Topic: A Book Report on *The Last Days of a Halcyon Era: The Rise and Fall of MGT Corp.*, Erickson and Pell, Dixon Publishing, 1996.

Conclusions: MGT Corp. has suffered the ups and downs of the postwar era and managed to survive three five-quarter periods of losses. Jeffrey Smythe, an upstart with nothing going for him but his $340 million inheritance, took the reigns and, to the surprise of nearly everyone, has turned MGT into a shining example of what the corporation of tomorrow must look like if it is to succeed in the increasingly hostile climate of global competition.

Preparing Through Research

Offering up your conclusions before you present your data and the analysis that supports the conclusions does not mean that you should draw your conclusions before you gather data and analyze it. Do not be confused by the order of your plan, which is constructed so as to help the readers better understand how to do their task of delivering the presentation. Once you have identified the topic, your next step is to acquire all of the information you need to complete your analysis and then to reach an appropriate conclusion.

So how much research is enough? Where do you look for information? The answers to these questions depend on the nature of your assignment. If, for example, your task is to analyze a case included in a strategic management text or an advanced accounting or finance text, you will probably have little need to perform research beyond the textbook itself. Even in such seemingly benign circumstances, though, you should always consider other sources. Always a good idea is to review all of the chapters in your textbook that may apply to the case, looking for fundamental concepts that you can use in your analysis of the data and information found in the case itself. The text may also provide several applicable tools that can help with your analysis. Financial tools may include break-even analysis, computation of the economic order quantity, and calculation of a wide range of key business ratios. Marketing concepts may include such aids as *Sales and Marketing Management Magazine*'s definition of buying power, Reilly's Law of Retail Gravitation, or the infamous BCG matrix. Production analyses may call for the application of linear programming or the use of the PERT planning system.

It should not come as a surprise to you that your professors will be greatly pleased to see that you have attempted to apply *appropriate* concepts and tools that they have been trying to beat into you all semester long! (No, this is not sucking up. This is using what you have learned. So, do it.) If your case involves a public company (IBM, MacDonald's, or Wal Mart, for example), you should also try to locate the most current information available to you in order to add whatever additional insights such data may shed on your case analysis. Try, though, to be true to the case analysis assignment by only looking at the later data after completing your analysis based on the data you are given.

In projects that call for your group to seek out all of the relevant information on your own, you should initially treat the project as though it were an ordinary research paper. (See Chapter 3 for lots of good advice about conducting the research process.) Go get all the necessary information, then organize it, then analyze it, and finally, once you have reached a conlusion, begin to develop your presentation plan.

Preparing the Presentation Documents

The documents you may need to prepare for use by the presenter will usually include the plan document itself, currently under discussion, an outline of the presentation showing what graphic aids are to be used and where they are to be used during the presentation, a script or speaker's notes, and any graphic aids you may deem necessary to support the verbal presentation.

An *outline of the presentation* should be provided for use by the presenter, whether you create a complete word-for-word script or just a set of speaker's notes. The outline will help the presenter cement the presentation structure in her mind as she prepares and thereby help her keep from losing her place during the presentation, or, should that awful event occur, help her find it again without a lot of embarrassing fumbling. Drawing on one of our previous examples, an outline for that presentation is shown below. Notice that all of the graphic aids are listed where they will be used to support the oral presentation.

In addition to all the parts of the presentation, you need to indicate the time allocated to each section. As you proceed through the presentation planning process, a key step is trying out your plan. Once the outline is complete, you will need to run through each part, including the use of graphic aids, and time your presentation. In our experience students without a lot of speaking experience tend to grossly under-

or overestimate the time needed. Only by running through the presentation can you re-alistically expect to establish accurate time guidelines for your presenter.

Once you have collected all of the research information available to you, the most common difficulty lies in deciding what to leave out. You absolutely must condense your presentation. Oral presentations are not simply written works read aloud. That would make little sense. After all, nearly everyone can read faster than you can talk. Be-sides, your class periods are not nearly long enough to allow every student group to make such a long-winded presentation, and such presentations are boring. Yes, chop-ping great hunks of your precious research material is difficult, but you can do it. Be ruthless. Do not go overboard, though. We heard of the greatest condensation ever. When asked, "What is the book *War and Peace* about?" the pundit replied, "Russia."

Topic: A Book Report on *The Last Days of a Halcyon Era: The Rise and Fall of MGT Corp.*, Erickson and Pell, Dixon Publishing, 1996.

Conclusions: MGT Corp. has suffered the ups and downs of the postwar era and managed to survive three five-quarter periods of losses. Jeffrey Smythe, an upstart with nothing going for him but his $340 million inheritance, took the reigns and, to the surprise of nearly everyone, has turned MGT into a shining example of what the corporation of tomorrow must look like if it is to succeed in the increasingly hostile climate of global competition in the airline meal in-dustry.

Outline of the Presentation:

Presentation Item	*Time*	*Visual Aid*
Introductions	2 Min.	Title Slide
Topic		Title Slide
Presentation group members		Title Slide
Presentation preparation group members		Title Slide
Statement of conclusions	1	Conclusions Slide
Background	3	
Airline meals then and now		Meal Pictures Slide
Competitors		Graph of Market Shares and Total
The advent of discount fares	2	Graph of Discounters' Share of Mkt.

Technology in meals
  (Why your airline meal always
    tastes like cardboard)
	1	Picture of Meal Production Facility

MGT in the early years	2	Picture of earliest MGT Plant
MGT's 1993 Chapter 11 bankruptcy	3	Graph of MGT Income: 1967–1993
Jeffrey Smythe—biographical sketch	3	Picture: Smythe on Cover of *Time* Quotes from Pundits—1993
Jeffrey's plan for MGT	4	Excerpts from 1993 Annual Report
The critical factors		List of Factors Slide
The role of luck		Picture of Dice with Quote form Smythe
All's well that ends well		Graph of MGT Income: 1967–1996 Quotes from Pundits—1996

Presentation Item	Time	Visual Aid
The future for MGT	2	Quotes from 1996 Annual Report
Restatement of conclusions and rationale	2	Conclusions Slide
Total Time	25 Min.	

Graphic Aids

Include as attachments a complete set of the graphic aid masters that will be used during the presentation (or screen shots of electronic slides). Masters are the printed copies from which transparencies are made. They need not be in color (unless crucial content is embodied in their colors) since they are used for documentation and review purposes only. The real aids will be used during rehearsals and the actual presentation. Several different kinds of graphic aids may be needed to support your presentation including hand-outs, overhead transparencies, 35mm slides, flip-charts, and electronic slides.

Hand-out materials offer several distinct benefits. Participants may feel that they have had a better experience when they leave with tangible evidence of the event. Participants can also enjoy having a permanent record of the information contained in the presentation, as well as a printed copy of contact information should they choose to follow-up at some later time.

Be careful of the timing you choose for distribution of hand-out materials. Participants may choose to focus on the hand-outs rather than on the presentation if hand-outs are distributed too early in the presentation. Of course, in many circumstances, you may have a reason to want the hand-out information in their hands to help participants to understand the presentation. You should carefully consider your intended purpose(s) for distributing materials and choose the time for their distribution to best achieve your purpose.

Overhead transparencies are the workhorse of the presentation world. Modern computers allow students to create sophisticated 8"x10" transparency slides and even print them out in color. The slide material itself is quite expensive (around $.50 per slide), but if you decide to use custom slides, you can readily create your own, printing proofs on plain paper until you are sure that you have exactly the slides you need before printing them on the expensive transparency slides themselves. If you do not have a color printer, you can usually find a local copy shop that can print the slides for you from your disk files, but be prepared for sticker shock. Some shops charge as much as $3.99 for each printed slide. If you do not need color, you can simply print your slide masters on plain paper, then transfer the images to the transparency film using an ordinary copy machine. (Isn't technology wonderful?)

Professional presenters follow many rules in creating their overhead transparency masters. For your student projects, though, the following rules will be sufficient to help you create an effective and appealing presentation.

- Organize your material in a horizontal format. Overhead projectors are designed to present an image that is wider than it is tall. The best slides contain an image that is no greater than 8" high by 10" wide. Images that are smaller than that should conform to the same ratio of height to width (e.g., an image that is 6" high should be about 7.5" wide.)

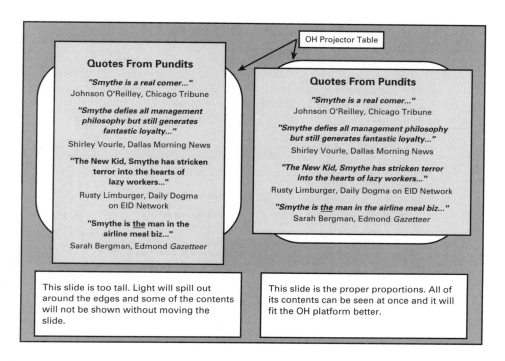

- All of the backlighted surface of the projector should be covered. The outside of the image you want to project should be covered by an opaque material. Failure to effectively block the light that otherwise appears outside your projected image detracts from the appeal of your slide and makes your message harder to read. This also makes your presentation far less professional looking than it could otherwise appear.

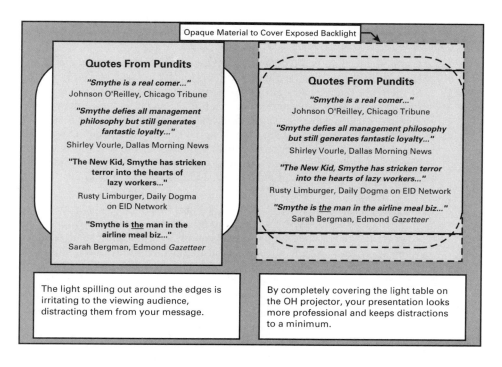

• Arrange the projector and screen so as to minimize *keystoning* (distortion caused by projecting an image onto a screen at an angle). This unwanted effect can be very important when attempting to present to a large audience, because the screen will likely be much larger than that used in presenting your information to a smaller group such as your business class.

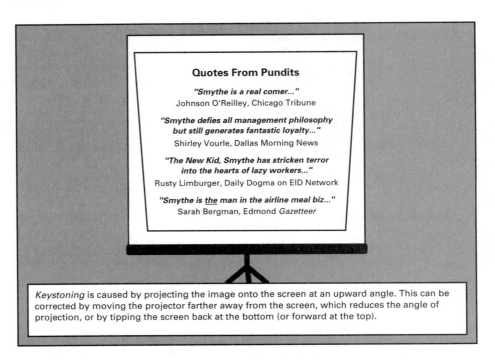

Keystoning Is caused by projecting the image onto the screen at an upward angle. This can be corrected by moving the projector farther away from the screen, which reduces the angle of projection, or by tipping the screen back at the bottom (or forward at the top).

• Use no more than two typefaces on each slide. Modern computers allow anyone to become "font crazy," using a number of fonts mainly because they are available (and some of them are really neat!). For business presentations, do not get too flashy. Remember that your purpose is to convey information. Your presentation materials need to look nice, but stick to conservative fonts such as *Arial* and *Times New Roman*, or other fonts that do not differ dramatically from these old stand-bys. In general, overhead transparencies should contain no type smaller than 14 points. By the time the slide is projected on a screen and the audience is seated at a comfortable range of distances from that screen, type that is smaller than 14 points tends to be very hard to read for those in the back of the room.

• On each slide, use no more than two attributes to add emphasis. Your choices of emphasis attributes include type size (larger type gets more emphasis over smaller type), type style (bold, italics, underlining, capitalization), unusual placement (centering one item when all others are left aligned, or turning an item vertically), and color or shading (brighter colors get more emphasis than do pastels and shades; hot colors such as red and yellow get more emphasis than cold colors such as blue and green; any different color gets more emphasis than other items when all the other items are the same color).

• Use simple backgrounds that do not compete with the message elements. Slides with fancy backgrounds are too often very hard to read. Remember, this presentation is about information content. It is not an art show.

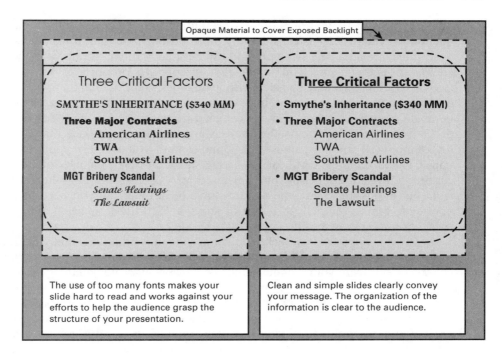

Opaque Material to Cover Exposed Backlight

Three Critical Factors

SMYTHE'S INHERITANCE ($340 MM)

Three Major Contracts
    American Airlines
    TWA
    Southwest Airlines

MGT Bribery Scandal
    Senate Hearings
    The Lawsuit

Three Critical Factors

• **Smythe's Inheritance ($340 MM)**
• **Three Major Contracts**
    American Airlines
    TWA
    Southwest Airlines
• **MGT Bribery Scandal**
    Senate Hearings
    The Lawsuit

The use of too many fonts makes your slide hard to read and works against your efforts to help the audience grasp the structure of your presentation.

Clean and simple slides clearly convey your message. The organization of the information is clear to the audience.

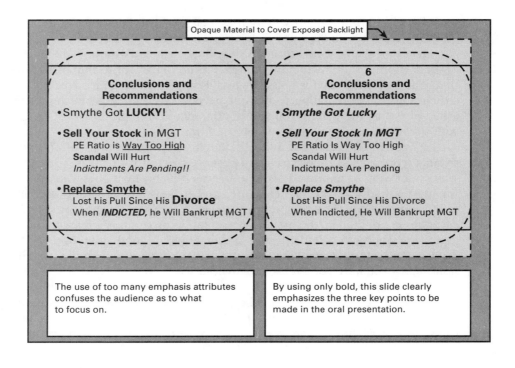

Opaque Material to Cover Exposed Backlight

Conclusions and Recommendations

• Smythe Got **LUCKY!**

• **Sell Your Stock** in MGT
    PE Ratio is <u>Way Too High</u>
    Scandal Will Hurt
    Indictments Are Pending!!

• <u>**Replace Smythe**</u>
    Lost his Pull Since His **Divorce**
    When ***INDICTED,*** he Will Bankrupt MGT

6
Conclusions and Recommendations

• *Smythe Got Lucky*

• *Sell Your Stock In MGT*
    PE Ratio Is Way Too High
    Scandal Will Hurt
    Indictments Are Pending

• *Replace Smythe*
    Lost His Pull Since His Divorce
    When Indicted, He Will Bankrupt MGT

The use of too many emphasis attributes confuses the audience as to what to focus on.

By using only bold, this slide clearly emphasizes the three key points to be made in the oral presentation.

35mm slide shows are better for presenting to large groups. Of course, the production of 35mm slides is considerably more problematic than it usually is for overhead transparencies. The same method can be used, though. Create your slides on the computer, making sure you select the appropriate proportions for these slides (1W:1.5H). Once you are satisfied with your slides, you can take them on disk to a local copy shop where they can either create your slides in-house or send them out to be made elsewhere. Again, you can expect a hefty charge for the slides, on the order of $3–$4 each. With 35mm slides there is an alternative approach that can save you lots of money. If you have access to a 35mm camera, you can print your slides on plain paper, fasten them to a wall or to a copy stand, and take pictures of the slides. Be careful to frame the slides in your viewfinder very carefully. Editing the finished slides is all but impossible. Once the pictures have been taken, all you need to do is have your slide film developed (at a cost of less than $10 for 36 images) and, voila, your presentation is ready to roll.

The one obvious drawback to a 35mm slide presentation is that you need a projector. If this is your choice, you may need to ask your professor for permission to check one out from your campus media center. Be sure, though, that you allow yourself an opportunity to test the projector and learn how to set it up well before the time for your presentation. Lots of little problems can arise, so be prepared.

Electronic presentations consist of a series of slides that are created in one of the presentation programs (e.g., Microsoft Powerpoint® or Corel Presentations®). These powerful programs are easy to learn and easy to use. They allow you to select from a variety of slide templates, complete with colorful backgrounds and snappy graphics. Even the font styles and sizes have been preselected for you. Simply accepting these defaults will virtually guarantee that your presentation will be orderly and attractive. In general, the same rules discussed in the section on overhead transparencies apply to slides in an electronic presentation as well. You will find that the defaults offered generally comply with the rules we have given you.

Some of the best presentation programs, such as Powerpoint®, go a giant step beyond offering slide templates, though. Powerpoint®, for example, includes a function called wizards® that will assist you not only in creating an attractive look, but in structuring the presentation to fit your purpose. By simply answering the questions asked of you by the wizard, you will be offered a proven presentation structure, along with a variety of slide templates to choose from.

Now, let us be clear. Even though the presentation software offers enormous assistance, you can still choose to modify every aspect of your slides. You can still make a mess out of it, or improve it. And no matter which way it goes, you are responsible for the finished product. The computer and its software programs are simply your tools; you are still the craftsperson who must own the finished product. With that caveat in mind, though, the modern presentation program is a marvel that will accelerate your ability to create effective presentations beyond any tool that has ever existed in the history of mankind. Use it—just use it wisely. Take the wizard's suggestions unless you have good reason to do otherwise.

The primary difficulty with electronic presentations is that a sophisticated set of equipment is required to deliver the presentation. The minimum requirements are a computer, an LCD display panel, a high-lumen overhead projector, and a high-reflectivity projection screen. A better setup uses a 3-gun video projector, in place of the LCD panel and the overhead projector. If such equipment is available to you, by all means use it. Be warned, though, with such sophisticated equipment, you absolutely must set it up and practice with it before the day of your presentation. Invariably, you will find out that one or more parts of the system do not work, some connector or cord is missing, or another one or more of a hundred things that can go wrong will go wrong.

If such equipment is not available to you, though, you should still take advantage of the electronic presentation software to create your overhead transparency or 35mm slide masters. The computer programs will allow you to create slides and then print them out to a color printer where you can print onto transparency film, thereby creating your overhead transparencies, or onto plain paper to make masters which can then be copied onto film.

In addition to helping you to structure and design your presentation slides, the programs will also assist you in creating hand-outs, speaker's notes, and even print-outs of miniature slide shots so that you can quickly give your presenter an overview of the presentation. Just as you should be sure you take the responsibility to equip yourself with basic word processing skills while in business school, you should also make sure you learn to use an electronic presentation program. Knowledge of these tools is rapidly becoming a requirement for nearly any business position you may choose to apply for.

A speaker's script or set of notes is the element of the presentation plan that allows you to insure that the delivery achieves your intended result. Of course, if you provide a script, the presenter is left only with control over delivery style, rather than content. Speaker's notes offer much more freedom to the presenter, who must actually create the presentation from just the main ideas provided by you. Your choice of whether to provide a complete word-for-word script or just a set of notes should be decided based on the content being presented and the knowledge base of the presenter. If, for example, you are preparing the presentation plan for delivery by another student or group of students in your same class, a set of notes should be sufficient. If, however, the presenter will be a student in a speech class and the content is business related, you probably will need to provide a complete script. Discuss this choice with your professor.

In general follow these guidelines in creating the document you choose:

- Always type or print the document, using one side of the page only.
- Use 14 point type.
- Double space the text.
- Use 1 1/2" margins all around.
- Number lists of points to be delivered.
- Include, in brackets, instructions for using visual aids or hand-outs.
- Include, in brackets, instructions for important pauses and gestures (if needed).
- Include, in brackets, warnings of items to come on the next page (e.g., "continued").
- Use only a single type style (underline, *italics,* or **bold**) to indicate emphasis. Underlining is probably the safest as it copies well. Bold doesn't always come out in copies. Underlining also does not interfere with readability as italics sometimes can.
- Include bracketed time markers for the presenter to follow.

The more information on style of presentation you give, the more reliable the presenter will be in meeting your expectations. Of course, if you give too much information on style, the presenter may have difficulty keeping up with all the bracketed instructions, causing presentation errors. The best way to determine when you have it right is to try it out. Have a group member or friend try to deliver the presentation, following the script or notes you have provided. This sort of tryout should help you to strike a good balance.

9.3 STEPS IN DELIVERING AN ORAL PRESENTATION

Study the Oral Presentation Plan

Before you attempt to deliver a presentation to your class, you should already have prepared an oral presentation plan, as described in the previous sections of this chapter. If you are following the project outlined in this chapter, you may be preparing for a presentation based on a plan prepared by another student or group in your or another class.

Whichever situation you are in, before you show up to deliver your presentation, you should carefully study your presentation plan. Smooth delivery results from adequate preparation. Professional speakers carefully rehearse their presentations repeatedly, until they have worked out all of the rough spots. Students frequently show up incompletely prepared. The result is gross errors in timing. Do not make that mistake; prepare!

Divide the Work

You will usually find yourself preparing for a business class presentation as a member of a group. In this situation, you will need to work with others to determine who will present what. Too often we observe that the most articulate group member tends to rule in dividing the presentation. A better outcome will be obtained if each student group member presents the portion which best capitalizes on his or her existing expertise (e.g., the accounting major presents the financial analysis, the management major presents the strategic analysis, and the marketing major presents the discussion of marketing alternatives). One good alternative is to have the most articulate student present the introduction and conclusions, with other group members presenting the intervening content. This forms a sort of "presentation sandwich," with first and last impressions similar and as good as your group can make them.

Whatever division you decide to follow, remember that you are all being graded for the group effort, and you may be graded individually as well. Accordingly, try to divide the presentation in such a way as to allow all members equal time to "do their stuff."

Practice Setting Up and Using the Equipment

Even something as simple as an overhead projector can seem baffling when you are facing an audience. The more familiar you are with the equipment and its operation, the less likely you are to fumble. One thing that frequently escapes students is the reality that you only get one chance to deliver your presentation. Any error is permanent and irreversible. We do not mean that you will flunk the assignment if you make several small mistakes, or even a large blunder, but you must realize that to achieve excellence requires a flawless presentation. Unlike a written work, where you have as much time as you need to review and rework before turning the document in for a grade, your presentation will be created in "real-time" with absolutely no grace period. Learning to use your equipment removes just one more potential source of embarrassment.

As in most things human, a heirarchy of difficulty exists in presentation equipment. Written media such as flip-charts are the least difficult, especially if you prepare them in advance so that all you have to do is flip the next one over. Chalk and white boards are next. These media require that you write during your presentation, which is a new skill for everyone who has never done this. A good idea is to write something during a practice session, then move into the rear of the room and critically view your work. Is it too small, crooked, out of alignment? Practice is the only way to prevent such errors during your presentation.

Moving up the hierarchy of difficulty is the overhead projector. This little device offers lots of error potential. Consider the rules for using the overhead projector listed below as you practice.

- While you are delivering the oral presentation, let someone else in your group operate the overhead projector, including turning it on and off, adjusting the focus, and changing slides. If you must, you can manage the overhead projector while you also deliver the oral presentation, but if you are a novice, you should use an assistant to operate the equipment if allowed by your professor. You will find you have plenty to occupy your mind just trying to deliver an effective presentation.

- Make sure your slides cover the entire surface of the projector platform. Light that escapes around the edges of your slide will detract from your presentation.

- Turn the projector light off when changing slides. Simply jerking a slide off the platform with the light still on hits the audience with a blinding flare of light. This can be very unsettling (and will not get you any brownie points with your professor either!).

- Make sure that the part of the image you are discussing is actually visible on the screen. Always look at your projected image as soon as it is up so you can be sure the placement is correct.

- While you are looking at the projected image, be sure to refocus as needed and straighten the slide. One guaranteed way to sink your otherwise stellar presentation is to have your slide crooked. This drives some people right up the wall, leaving them little attention for what you are saying.

- Do not stand between your audience and the slide. One good tipoff that you are in the way is the bobbing and weaving that your audience engages in as they try to see over or around you.

- When a slide includes several points on which you intend to elaborate, cover all of them and reveal them only when you are ready to discuss each. If you reveal all at once, you may lose much of your audience's attention. They will focus on reading ahead and may even drift off entirely, having already drawn their own conclusions (right or wrong) about what you are going to say.

- Turn off the slide projector whenever you want the audience to attend to you. As long as that slide is projected on the screen, you will have to compete with it for attention, so when you are finished using it, even for a moment, turn it off!

• Finally, get all of your slides organized and keep them that way during your presentation. Put all of your slides into slide holders that are designed to fit into a ring binder. Have a printed copy of each slide with the projector version. This will make the slide easier to identify and can be carried around or referred back to readily. As you take slides off the projector (with the light off, please!), put them back into the ring binder. This will just take a second and will help you find the slide later if needed.

Still more difficult is the electronic presentation. All of the same rules just presented for using an overhead projector apply to electronic presentations. Using a computer, though, requires a bit of additional skill. To begin with, you should have at least two separate copies of your presentation on disk. Your presentation should be delivered from the hard disk, as floppy drives are too slow and may cause unwanted delays while the next slide comes up. If you have failed to follow our advice and have not practiced presenting your electronic slides, you are almost certainly in for an unpleasant shock. You will be amazed how long 30 seconds can be when you are waiting for a crucial slide to show up after you have clicked where you were supposed to click.

Another unpleasant problem may arise when you try to go back or go forward to find a particular slide you need to answer a question from the audience. To help you with this problem, print out a set of miniature or "thumbnail" slides. All mainstream electronic presentation programs allow you to print thumbnail pictures of your slides, all grouped on a page or two, depending on the number of slides and the thumbnail size you choose. These thumbnails can be a real life-saver during your presentation as you try to find quickly the slide you need to answer a question from the audience or from your professor.

Electronic presentations call for the use of either an LCD projection panel or a video projector. Neither of these pieces of equipment is simple nor user friendly. Be sure you get thoroughly checked out on the equipment well before the time of your presentation. Failure to do so usually means no presentation at all. These devices, especially the LCD display panels, also need a fairly dark room for an effective presentation. Before you begin, get the room suitably dark or your audience will not be able to see the information on your slides.

The last point we need to make about electronic presentations concerns the use of a pointing device. If you are fortunate enough to have a professional presentation system in your classroom, great! You probably also will have an appropriate platform on which to operate your mouse without leaning over to operate the mouse on a desk-height table. Better yet, you may even have a wireless pointing device that allows you to point a laser dot at the presentation screen and click to actuate the program.

But if your school is like most, you will be fortunate indeed even to be able to deliver your presentation in electronic form. Under these rather primitive circumstances, we suggest that you find a podium with as flat a surface as possible. Locate the podium near the computer so that you can place the keyboard and the mouse on the podium, allowing you still to see the computer screen and the projection screen (and, of course, the audience). Using this setup, when your computer locks up in the middle of your presentation (there is a [previously] unwritten rule that this absolutely will happen during every important electronic presentation), you can retain an elegant posture as you pound your keyboard and wiggle your mouse in a hopeless effort to resuscitate your dead presentation.

Yes, you are correct. We do strongly suggest that if your grade depends in any meaningful way on the presentation you are about to give, and if you have any choice in the matter, do not use an electronic presentation. Transfer your slides to print or film and use the simplest presentation media you can get by with and still make the impression you are aiming for. Never use an electronic presentation unless you have good reason to do so.

Rehearse the Presentation

In the preceding sections of this discussion we have repeatedly suggested that you should carefully prepare each element of your presentation. You should study the speaker's script or notes, and you should set up and try out the equipment you plan to use. Beyond just becoming familiar with the materials and equipment, though, you should conduct at least one full rehearsal. Each participant should fulfill his or her role; someone should time the presentation and help the presenter with pacing, delivery, and cuing difficulties. Additional notes can be scribbled in the margins to help solve particularly difficult spots, and sometimes you may even wish to call in the group who created the presentation plan in the first place for a consultation.

Usually, though, one rehearsal session should be enough to prepare for a class presentation, provided all group members have adequately prepared before the rehearsal. Anyone who attends the rehearsal cold will certainly slow everything down by attempting to play catch-up with better-prepared peers. Be responsible. Remember, this is the key to really effective group projects: everyone pulls his own weight.

If, during rehearsal, you decide to make any substantive changes in the presentation, be sure to give a revised copy of the presentation plan to your professor before you deliver the presentation. Your revisions should be plainly evident, so that your professor can properly allocate credit for the work done by your group as different from that done by the planning group.

Dress the Part

Students, including business students, tend to dress like students. Enjoy the privilege! Soon enough you will be forced into the uniforms of business professionals, which, to be kind, are not nearly as comfortable as the non-uniforms most students choose. However, for purposes of your business class oral presentations, pretend you are a mid-level management team making your presentation to the corporate board of directors. Suitable attire includes suit coat, slacks, dress shirt, tie, and dress shoes for men, and the equivalent for women. Make sure you are clean, your hair is neatly combed, and you smell good. If you are not familiar with appropriate business attire, check out the books *John T. Molloy's New Dress for Success* (for men) and *The Woman's Dress for Success Book*, both by John T. Molloy.

If the very idea of getting dressed up for a business class tends to stick in your craw, we suggest that you consider this a familiarization exercise for the interviews that will come shortly. The more you wear a set of clothing, the more comfortable you become in it and the more natural you begin to act when wearing the clothes. If you are uncomfortable in your new suit, you will tend to be doubly uncomfortable in an interview in that suit. If you are comfortable wearing that suit, then you will be a little less uncomfortable in the interview. Since you must do it, you will feel better about dressing up if you can find additional personal gain somewhere in the exercise to boot.

CHAPTER 10

The Internet and the World Wide Web

10.1 WHAT'S ALL THE HYPE?

Unless you have been living on Mars or in a remote African village, you already know something about the Internet and the World Wide Web (WWW). For the business student, the WWW is a magical place where informational treasures abound. In this chapter we will provide specific instructions for gaining access to these resources, for employing e-mail, and for using the Internet to complete your business class assignments. But, first, let us present a brief description of the Internet and the World Wide Web.

The Internet

To understand the Internet and how to use it, we need to begin with the basics. Let's let this symbol ⌨ represent a computer. Two or more computers linked together by a telephone line, fiber optic line, radio wave, or satellite beam compose a network:

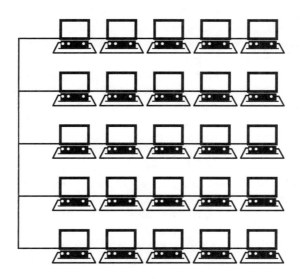

Let's call this dot [.] a symbol for a network of computers and place a dot on a map of the world for every network. Some of these networks have just a few personal computers. Others may include thousands of computers. The map would probably look like this:

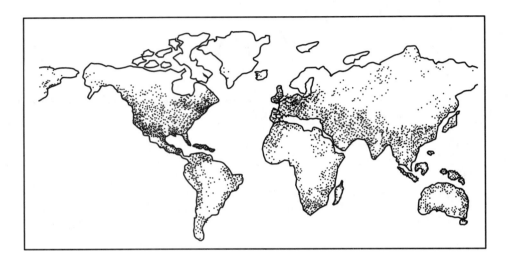

This map represents the Internet, a network of millions of computer networks linked together by communications lines and using a common computer language to communicate with each other. The Internet was conceived in the late 1960s when the Advanced Research Projects Agency of the U.S. Department of Defense, working to develop military communications systems capable of surviving a nuclear war, produced ARPANET, a network of computers which at first linked military research labs and universities but later added many more computer systems.

Two decades later the National Science Foundation initiated a project called NSFNET, the purpose of which was to connect American supercomputer centers. Throughout the world similar networks were being established, and by the late 1980s connections among these networks came to be known as the Internet, which is now growing at a phenomenal rate. In 1991 there were about 700,000 people using the Internet. By 1997 that number was approaching 40 million, with 160,000 new users each month.

Prior to the development of the World Wide Web, the Internet was used mainly by scientists and educators to communicate via e-mail and to provide and explore vast repositories of information. The primary tools by which early Internet users actually obtained the information they sought from the Internet included such programs as FTP (file transfer protocol), Usenet (an Internet-wide newsgroup system), Gopher (a command line file transfer system), Listserve (an automatic e-mail remailer used for on-line discussions), and various kinds of e-mail programs. Today, however, all of these early tools have been replaced by the modern Web browser—that is, in modern systems. Some university computer systems are not yet capable of providing access to a Web browser, and students using these systems are still required to use some of these older Internet tools. We will discuss older tools as well as current ones.

The World Wide Web

The World Wide Web (WWW or Web) is an organized system for accessing the information on the Internet. Tim Berners-Lee of CERN, the European Laboratory for Particle Physics in Geneva, Switzerland, launched the WWW when he successfully created a method for using a single means of access to the networks on the Internet. The Web is now the primary system for accessing information on the Internet.

For your purposes, differentiating between the Internet and the Web is not really necessary. Once your PC (personal computer) is connected to an ISP (Internet service provider) via a modem and telephone line, you are plugged in. Using your Web browser software, you can then "navigate" the Web, collecting information as you go.

For those of you who are not satisfied with the plug-it-in-and-turn-it-on approach to learning, here is a more comprehensive explanation of the relationship between the Internet and the World Wide Web. Think of the Web/Internet relationship as analogous to the U.S. system of roads. The Internet is the highway on which communications occur. A message or request for information on the Internet is a package to be delivered to another address somewhere on the Internet. The vehicle carrying our package starts from a particular address on a city block. The package travels the neighborhood streets that feed into major thoroughfares, which in turn feed into state and interstate highways. At the other end of the trip, the vehicle carrying our package exits the highway onto major streets, then it turns off on a side street leading ultimately to the particular destination.

Traveling this Internet of communications highways are the "trucks" and "buses" of the Internet—Unix® command line programs such as FTP, Gopher, Archie, Veronica, and Kermit. These vehicles require users to be experts, just as real trucks and buses on the highway require professional drivers. With the introduction of Web browser programs (the "cars" in our analogy) to the Internet, virtually everyone can easily travel the information highways and obtain ready access to the information resources of the Internet with almost no training. Before the development of the Web only trucks and buses were able to use the Internet, and many experts now bemoan the loss of their exclusive domain! The Web lets amateurs make the trip along with the professionals. The modern Web browser handles the arcane task of communicating on the Internet automatically. Almost all you have to do to access information on the Web is point and click your mouse.

So in reality the Web is simply a subset of all computers connected to the Internet. To be a part of the Web, each computer or network agrees to employ a set of standard communication protocols used by all the other computers comprising the Web.

NOTE: Web documents are interconnected through the use of *links*. A link is a specially coded piece of text or a graphic image that, when clicked with a mouse, will cause a new document to be displayed in your Web browser program.

10.2 USING THE TOOLS OF ELECTRONIC COMMUNICATION

In the sections that follow we present specific instructions for using some of the basic tools of the Internet and the Web. Parts of this chapter will not apply to your circumstances. We have attempted to cover the systems we believe exist in most university schools of business across the United States. Since your professor has probably required that you buy this book, you can be pretty sure that your situation is also covered in this chapter. If not, you may need to seek additional support elsewhere.

One of the greatest resources you can find to help you survive your battles with technology is a knowledgeable person (KP) you can go to for help with those niggling little problems that always seem to hang you up for hours. A colleague of ours once spent three hours trying to figure out how to underline a blank space in his word processing program! A friend, our KP, answered the question in a 30-second phone call. We too have spent hundreds of hours fighting our computers. You are not alone. We trust this chapter will help you win some of your little battles.

E-mail

E-mail, short for "electronic mail," is simply a system for receiving and delivering written messages on computer. For students and faculty today, e-mail comes in two basic types: SMTP and POP. SMTP (Simple Mail Transfer Protocol) is the type you can use in a shell account session (see the section "Steps in Logging On" later in this chapter). The most common SMTP program in use today is Pine®, running on a Unix® platform. (Unix® is the mainframe version of DOS®, that is, the operating system most commonly used on mainframe computers.) POP (Post Office Protocol) is a modern e-mail system that supports the graphical e-mail facilities available as an integral part of Web browsers such as Netscape® and Internet Explorer®, or in stand-alone (single computer) programs such as Eudora® or Pegasus Mail®. In other words, POP allows you to see and to make graphics (drawings, photographs, graphs, etc.) as you use e-mail. Such SMTP programs as Pine® do not have this capability. If you have any choice in the matter, choose the POP server connection, and not just because of POP's graphics capabilities: the POP e-mail systems are also a great deal easier to use than SMTP e-mail systems, which will soon be as archaic as the punch-card input devices of just a few years ago. You have plenty to learn without committing to memory a bunch of procedures you will never again use after leaving school.

In the following section we discuss how to perform e-mail functions using the SMTP program Pine®, and also using the POP program Eudora®. (We will use a Unix® system to demonstrate Pine® and a PC to demonstrate Eudora®.) These two options cover most business student circumstances. If, however, you are using the Mail program on Unix® or some other e-mail program on your PC, you will need to obtain additional information on your system. We suggest you contact your KP or computer center for more specific information.

Pine®

A software program common to the central mainframe computer in many university computer systems, Pine® may be the most often-used e-mail program for students and faculty alike. To use Pine®, you must first log-in (or log-on; same thing, different terms) to the mainframe. This procedure is accomplished in one of two ways. You can go to your computer lab where your school maintains dedicated terminals, or terminals connected to a mainframe computer. These keyboards and screens allow you to log into the mainframe to conduct your business. Most schools also allow students to dial in using a modem connected to a PC, either on or off campus. Once you have dialed up the mainframe computer and logged in, the rest of the procedure is nearly the same as that used when you are working from a dedicated terminal on campus.

To begin, then, you must first initiate a shell account session, i.e., get to a starting point called a command prompt on the mainframe. Instructions for getting to this point are presented below for both a dedicated terminal and for a PC using a dial-up facility.

STEPS IN LOGGING ON FROM A DEDICATED TERMINAL

1. Turn on the terminal if it is off.

2. Press "Enter" (or "Return") to activate the screen if it is blank.

3. The first screen you should see is a log-in screen with one or more numbered choices and some instructions for moving among the choices and selecting your option. Select your option and press "Enter." Ask the lab assistant or your professor which option to choose. This will be school specific.

4. The next screen you should see will prompt you for your log-in name, or username. Be sure to type your log-in name correctly, including all special characters, numbers, and upper/lower case. Unix® is very sensitive to case. While you are typing in your user identification information, the system may not let you make any corrections. If you do make an error, simply press "Enter" until you are prompted to enter your username again, then start over—carefully.

5. Next, you will be prompted for a password. Again, type your password in carefully, being sure your "Caps Lock" key has not been activated. Do not use the keypad numbers on your keyboard. Instead, use the line of number keys above the letters. The keypad may sometimes work, but the overhead keys will always work. (You can experiment later, but let's just get you logged in for now.)

6. Once successfully logged in, you will have to contend with a little (or a lot) of administrative "stuff," such as warnings to unauthorized users, information about your last log-in (provided to help you spot unauthorized use of your account), or system operator messages, that shows up on the screen. You may have to repeatedly press "Enter" or the space bar to get past this material. Eventually you will see a basic command prompt—probably a "$". If your system does present such messages, you will quickly learn to clear the initial screens so that you can proceed to Pine®!

STEPS IN LOGGING ON FROM A PC

Depending on the programs available on the PC you are using, you may choose to connect to the school's mainframe computer using a variety of software. If you have a communications program such as Crosstalk, Qmodem, or Commworks, refer to the documentation that is provided with the software. These books will provide detailed instructions. For our purposes, we will assume you have nothing except the basic communication program that came with Windows®. That program is called Terminal® (for Windows® 3.x) or HyperTerminal® (for Windows® 95).

1. Open the Terminal® program. You may have to look for it. If no icon labeled "Terminal" or "Log-in" (to your mainframe computer) is present on your computer desktop, you can launch Terminal® by using the Windows File Manager®. Open File Manager®, and look under the Windows® directory for the file named "terminal.exe." When you find it, double-click the file name. This should launch the program. If it does nothing, try double-clicking faster.

2. Once the Terminal® program is running, click "Phone" on the menu bar, then "Dial." If nothing happens, this means the computer's default ".trm" file does not contain the proper settings to allow your PC and the mainframe computer to talk to each other.

   a. Before you change the Terminal® settings, look for a setup file (.trm) that someone else (or you in an earlier session) may already have created that will suit your purpose. Click "File," then "Open." In the dialog box that opens, see if you can find a likely looking file ending in ".trm." The first part of the file's name—the part before the dot—may suggest what system that file is set up for. For example, the file set up to connect to the University of Central Oklahoma may be named "uco.trm." If such a file does exist, choose it in the dialog box and click "OK." Then try step 2 again.

   If no such file exists, then you may wish to create one as follows:

   b. Click "Settings," then each of the following in turn: "Phone Number," "Terminal Emulation," and "Communications." In each dialog box, enter the information or choose the options shown below, then click "OK":

Phone Number	Enter the dial-up number for the mainframe computer.
Terminal Emulation	Select VT-100, unless told otherwise by a KP.
Terminal Preferences	Uncheck the box (by clicking it once) that says "Use Function, Arrow and Ctrl Keys for Windows." If you do not do this, your arrow keys may not work when you try to move around in your shell account session on the mainframe (bummer!). If you wish, you can also choose a different typeface or font size from the options presented here. Leave everything else alone, unless you want to experiment or already know what you are doing.
Communications	*Baud rate*—Choose the speed (or the next higher number) of which your modem is capable.
	Data bits, Stop bits, Parity, and *Flow control* should be left alone, unless a KP tells you to change them.
	Connector—Choose the COM port your modem is attached to. If you do not know, first try COM3, then COM2, then COM1. If none of these works, you will probably need that KP to help you.

   c. Click "File" then "Save As." Type in the file name, which must end in ".trm." Next time you start Terminal®, you can just look under File for your new .trm file and change all the settings at once by double-clicking that file.

3. Once Terminal® is properly set, choosing "Phone" then "Dial" should cause your computer to dial the correct number and make a connection to the mainframe computer, starting what is called a shell account session. The screen you see inside the Terminal® program should be the first log-in screen. All you now need to do is log into the mainframe by following the steps presented for connecting using a dedicated terminal.

There are some drawbacks to operating e-mail through the Terminal® program. For example, you cannot use your mouse to manipulate the text inside the Terminal®

(or HyperTerminal®) box on your computer screen. You must use the arrow keys to move the cursor. You can make a rough copy of the text in HyperTerminal® only by clicking and dragging your mouse across the text you want to capture, but you cannot do this in Terminal®.

You can see more of the shell account session if you maximize the Terminal® box on your screen. Just click the little up arrow in the upper right corner of the Terminal® box (if you are using Windows® 3.x), or the middle icon in the same location (for Windows® 95).

Running Pine®

Now that you are connected, type "pine" and press "Enter" to launch the Unix® e-mail program called Pine®. Pine® will then open to the main menu screen.

In Pine®, you choose the option you want by "arrowing" around until the item you want is highlighted, then pressing "Enter." Alternatively, you can usually type the letter next to your menu choice. If you are in an editing session in Pine® while you are composing a new message or revising one before forwarding it, you will need to use a two-key combination to execute a menu command, for example, "ctrl-o" to save the current message but not send it now.

To read your mail, choose "L" from the menu list. Then select INBOX from the choices of mail folders shown on the screen. Of course, INBOX is probably the only mail folder you have at first. We will discuss additional mail folders later under the heading "Managing Your Mail." Choosing INBOX opens this mail folder and lists its contents.

Messages that you have not yet read have an "N" ("New") to the far left of the message listing. Those you have already read have nothing in that space; those you have replied to have an "A" ("Answered"); and those you have selected for deletion have a "D" ("Delete") next to them.

To read a message, arrow to the message you want and press "Enter." You can then scroll up or down by repeatedly pressing the up or down arrow key to move a line at a time or by pressing either the space bar to move down a page at a time, or the minus key to move up a page at a time. To return to the listing of messages in your currently open mail folder (INBOX in our discussion), press "i" to access the Index of the open folder.

To mark a highlighted message for deletion, type "d." To undelete a message marked for deletion, type "u." Messages that have been marked with a "d" are not actually deleted until you exit the Pine® program. You can also cause messages marked for deletion to be deleted from the folder index by typing "x." You will be asked to confirm the deletion, and if you type "y," the marked messages will disappear immediately—forever.

Composing a New E-Mail Message in Pine®

To send mail, you first must compose a new message or choose a message from an open mail folder to which you want to reply. First, let's discuss creating a new message. Type "c" from nearly any screen in Pine® and you will be presented with a blank e-mail form to be filled in. Of course, if you are *already* composing a new message in an editing session, typing a "c" will simply cause a "c" to appear at the location of the cursor. And if you have saved an unsent message earlier, or if your shell account session was interrupted in the middle of an editing session, typing "c" will result in a question as to whether or not you wish to see your uncompleted message. To make this annoying question stop appearing every time you try to compose a new message, you will have to answer "y," sooner or later. You can then type "ctrl-c" to delete the incomplete message, and it will go away.

Once in the blank new-message form, type in the "To:" e-mail address—carefully. Press "Enter" to move to the "Cc:" block. Fill in an address if you wish to send a copy of the message you are about to compose. We suggest that you always send a copy to yourself. This is the only means you have of making a copy of your outgoing e-mail messages in Pine® without asking the recipient of your message to e-mail it back to you. Press "Enter" once or twice to move to the "Subject:" line. (We will discuss the use of the "Attachmnt:" block in the section on File Transfers.) Type in a short description of the subject of the message you are going to compose, such as "Meeting postponed to 4:00" or "Help!" We suggest that you always include a subject line on your messages. Busy people who get lots of e-mail (your professor, for instance) may skip over your message if the subject line is blank or if the message looks like it will keep for a while. To get attention immediately, use an appropriate subject descriptor (*but remember the boy who cried "Wolf!"*).

Once the "header" information has been typed, press "Enter" to move the cursor to the body of the form, then type your message. The editor in Pine® is not mouse-friendly, nor does it offer much in the way of bells and whistles, but it is serviceable (and a real improvement over the miserable editor used in the old Unix® mail program). The commands you can use to spell-check, justify text, cut and paste, and so on, are listed at the bottom of the screen when you are using the editor to compose an e-mail message. Remember that the menu options shown at the bottom of the screen change depending on exactly where in Pine® you are, so when you get stuck, remember to carefully examine all of the menu options then available.

Once you are satisfied with your newly composed message and all of the header information has been properly entered (and rechecked for accuracy), type "ctrl-x" to send the message. Before you send your message, *be careful*: stop and think if you are really ready to send that blistering attack piece or that outpouring of affection for the classmate who sits next to you in accounting. When you respond to the question "Send mail?" by typing "y," your choice is irretrievable. The recipient already has it, and you can't get it back.

Replying to or Forwarding a Message in Pine®

Most of the time you will not start an e-mail message from scratch. Instead, you will be responding to a message in one of your e-mail folders or forwarding a message you have received to another person. There are several differences in replying and forwarding that merit discussion, but first the similarities.

Choosing either "Reply" or "Forward" while viewing a message you have received will launch the e-mail editor in Pine®. From the editor you will then be able to revise the existing message, add to it, delete portions, revise the address and subject blocks—all just as if you were working on a newly composed message of your own. The benefit of both reply and forward is that you are not starting with a blank form, and often much of the information (especially those complicated e-mail addresses) is already filled in! Pine® also automatically sends along your address in the "From:" box that appears in each message that you send, no matter how you composed it.

Both "Reply" and "Forward" screens retain the original subject line, but with small modifications. "Reply" adds "re:" before the previous message, and "Forward" appends "(fwd)" on the end of the subject line. If you want to modify the subject line to remove these indicators, you certainly can.

"Reply" also fills in the "To:" block with the sender's address. When you choose "Reply" from the menu at the bottom of the screen while you are viewing a received message, Pine® will ask you up to three questions, depending on the nature of the message to which you are replying. First, it will ask if you want to include the original message in your reply. Second, it will ask if you want to send your response to the "Reply to:" address instead of to the "From:" address. Third, Pine® asks if you want to send your reply to all recipients of the original e-mail message. (The sender may have sent the message to several recipients.) Depending on your responses to Pine®'s questions, the program will then fill in the "To:" block, the "Cc:" block, modify the subject line, and insert a ">" character at the left end of every line in the original message (if you responded "y" to the question above) in order to differentiate that message from your response.

"Forward" opens a new message that includes all the incoming header message information within the body of the message you are about to forward. Pine® modifies the subject line and places the cursor in the "To:" block, prompting you to type in the address of the person to whom you plan to forward the message. Pine® does not ask you any questions, but you are free to modify the forwarded message before sending it on.

Use "Reply" when you wish to respond to the content of the message you have received. There is no accepted convention as to where your comments should be placed in relation to the body of the message you are responding to. Some put their comments before the earlier message, some place their comments after the other message, and some even insert their responses within the earlier message, immediately following the part to which they are responding.

We suggest that you adopt the approach needed in that situation to provide readers of your message the kind of support they may need to interpret your message accurately. Placing your response above the message may lead to misunderstandings about the part of the original message to which you are responding. Putting your response after the message instead of before it might encourage readers to review the earlier message as they scroll to the bottom looking for your comments. This can be especially helpful when your "Reply" will be sent to people other than the original sender. If you decide to intersperse your comments within the message, insert several blank lines before and after each of your comments to draw attention to them as separate from the original message. In all cases, consider deleting as much of the original message as you can while still retaining the meaning. Messages can get quite lengthy, convoluted, and hard to follow when you are responding to comments that are themselves a response to a still earlier message. We have seen as many as a dozen iterations of a single message.

When you mean for the original message to stand unchanged, consider "Forwarding" the e-mail message instead of "Replying." When forwarding an e-mail message, Pine® does not put in the ">" characters on each line, so the message can be more easily read and handled by the new recipient.

The foregoing discussion has indicated only a few of the capabilities of Pine®, but it should assist you in getting logged in, starting Pine®, reading your e-mail, and sending responses and new messages. These are the rudiments of e-mail. Learn how to perform these steps, and you will very probably be able to complete any business class assignment requiring the use of e-mail.

More of the capabilities of Pine® will be discussed in later sections of this chapter as we discuss e-mail management and file transfer.

POP Server Access Programs

This section is for those of you fortunate enough to have access to a graphical Internet connection, also known as an SLIP, PPP, or TCP/IP connection. But how do you know if you have one of those things, you may ask. The short answer is that if you have a dial-up account into any computer that lets you browse the World Wide Web using any browser except Lynx®, you have what you need. All of these advanced Internet connection protocols allow an e-mail program that runs on your PC to handle the sending, receiving, and management of e-mail messages, instead of your having to log into a mainframe computer.

The most common e-mail protocol your PC will use to communicate with the mainframe computer about your e-mail is called Post Office Protocol (POP). With a POP server connection, your e-mail program will allow you to use a mouse. You can easily cut and paste text into and out of e-mail messages you send and receive. Saving messages is as simple as choosing the message, then clicking "File" and "Save As," just as you would in any ordinary Windows® program.

With a POP server connection, you can choose to use any one of a hundred e-mail programs—or, since virtually all of the Web browsers contain pretty good programs, you can simply use Netscape® or Internet Explorer® as your e-mail program. You can download, for free, a copy of Eudora®, a very good e-mail program. Another is Pegasus Mail®. Any of these will serve your purposes as a student. We suggest that you start by using the e-mail programs that are free and change to the more powerful programs only when you see a need for something the freeware will not do.

Although connecting to your e-mail account is much simpler if you are connected to a POP server, some discussion is warranted. Please note that we cannot anticipate which program you might choose to adopt, so we have opted to present the procedures for the most popular freeware e-mail program in circulation: Eudora®.

Using Eudora®

Before you can send or receive e-mail using Eudora®, you must first establish an Internet "TCP/IP Socket." This connection requires the use of Winsock®, Windows® 95, or other proprietary software. If you are connected via an Internet Service Provider from your home or office, your provider will have already provided you with the software you need. (And you probably already know how to use e-mail, so why are you reading this? Go study.) If you are connected through your school lab, you can readily ask your lab assistants how to establish the connection you need. Usually your e-mail is effectively connected any time you have established a connection to the World Wide Web. Once that connection is open, all you do to use e-mail is launch your e-mail program and go to work.

Launch Eudora® by double-clicking the Eudora® icon (it may look like a post office letter and be labeled "E-Mail"). If you do not find an icon, you can start Eudora® by double-clicking the file name "eudora.exe" from File Manager® (Windows® 3.x) or Windows Explorer® (Windows® 95). Either action will launch the Eudora® e-mail program.

Once you have launched Eudora®, maximize the Eudora® screen that opens by clicking the appropriate icon in the upper right corner of the Eudora® box (the up arrow in Windows® 3.x and the middle icon in Windows® 95). This will increase the area in which you can work with your e-mail.

Creating a New E-mail Message in Eudora®

To create a new message, click "Message," then "New Message." This will open the Eudora® message editor with a blank e-mail form and the cursor in the "To:" box. The "From:" box will also be filled in with your name and e-mail address. If your name and/or e-mail address are missing or wrong, click "Special," then "Configuration" to open a dialog box where you can correct your "Real Name" and/or "Return Address" as needed. If you do make corrections, you will need to close the currently open message editor box and once again choose "Message," then "New Message."

Fill in the header information as needed for your purposes. At a minimum, we suggest that you include the "To:" (How else would the computer know where to send your message?), "From:" (if it is not filled in correctly already), and "Subject:." Next, fill in the body of the message. If you like, you can use the Windows® clipboard to move existing text from a Web page, a word processor, nearly any Windows® program, or even from another e-mail message in Eudora® into your new message.

To use the clipboard, minimize Eudora® by clicking the down arrow icon in the upper right corner of Eudora®'s main box. If you choose to minimize the open e-mail editor session, Eudora® will remain open and an icon will appear near the bottom of the open Eudora® box. Once Eudora® is minimized, open the application you plan to copy text from. Open the document within the application, select the text you want by clicking and dragging with your mouse. Once the text is highlighted, choose "Edit," then "Copy" from the menu bar. This action will place the selected text into the clipboard. Nothing will appear to have happened, but, trust us, the text should now be ready to place into your message.

Now minimize the application from which you are copying text, then maximize Eudora® by double clicking the Eudora® icon. You should now see Eudora® open back up, with your e-mail message under construction just as you left it. Click in the new message box wherever you want to place the copied text and choose "Edit," then "Paste." The copied block of text should now appear where your cursor was located in the new message.

To copy the contents of another message already in Eudora® into your new message, minimize your message under construction, open the message you need, select the text you want, choose "Edit," then "Copy," close that message, maximize your new message, click where you want the new text, and finally choose "Edit," then "Paste" to finish the procedure. There are faster ways to move text around among Windows® applications. If you know them, by all means use them. If you don't, ask your KP for a little tutoring on the finer points of Windows® basics.

To send the new message—when you are sure you are ready—click the "Send" button *once*. Do not double-click it! That may cause two copies of the same message to be sent. Remember that once your message is sent, you cannot get it back. Be careful. Think before you click!

Sending a Message Using Reply, Forward, Redirect, or Send Again in Eudora®
"Reply" is meant for use when you want to respond directly to the comments in an e-mail you have received. "Forward" should be used to send a copy of an e-mail message you have received to someone else while identifying you as the intermediary. Use "Redirect" to send mail to another addressee when you really are not the proper recipient. "Send Again" will simply try again to send a message if, for some reason, your attempt to send a message was not successful on the first try.

To "Reply" to a message in Eudora®, choose "Message," then "Reply." Eudora® will then open the message editor and insert the e-mail address of the original message sender into the "To:" line and your address in the "From:" line. Eudora® will also append "Re:" to the original contents of the subject line and place this new subject into the "Subject:" line of the new message, appending ">" characters to each line of the original message, which will be placed in the body of the new message. Finally Eudora® will place the cursor at the beginning of the first line so all you have to do is begin typing to add your additional comments to the original message before clicking the "Send" button to transmit your reply.

To "Forward" a message you have received, choose "Message," then "Forward." Eudora® will open the message editor; place your e-mail address in the "From:" line; place the previous subject line with "(fwd)" appended into the "Subject:" line; put the original message; with ">" characters added to each line, into the body of the new message; and place the cursor at the beginning of the "To:" line. All you have to do is type the address of the person you want to forward the message to before clicking the "Send" button to complete the process.

To "Redirect" a message, choose "Message," then "Redirect." Eudora® will then open the message editor and duplicate the entire body and header information with no changes except to leave the "To:" line blank and place the cursor at the beginning of that line. All you need do then is type the new address and click the "Send" button. The new recipient will never know the message passed through your "hands."

At this point a couple of examples might help you better understand how to use these three options. Suppose you have received a message such as the following:

> Dear [your name]
>   At our meeting last Wednesday you suggested that we consider a new marketing strategy involving Cyber the Clown. Upon reflection, some members of the executive committee feel that you may have been suggesting more than just a new marketing strategy. Before this matter is turned over to your supervisor for further investigation, would you care to offer an explanation? Today would be nice.
> Bob—

Clearly, such a message calls for a response. Use "Reply" to answer. This function will automatically address your response to the sender and include the original message so the recipient will see immediately just what you are writing about.

Now, suppose you have received this message:

A Guide To Understanding Work Reviews

Says: "Maintains a high degree of participation."
Means: "Comes to work on time."

Says: "Excels in the effective application of skills."
Means: "Makes a good cup of coffee."

Says: "Displays excellent intuitive judgment."
Means: "Knows when to disappear."

Says: "Displays great dexterity and agility."
Means: "Dodges and evades superiors well."

Says: "Demonstrates imaginative leadership."
Means: "Imagines self to be Ivan the Terrible."

Says: "Inspires cooperation of others."
Means: "Gets everyone else to do the work."

Says: "Excels in sustaining concentration while avoiding confrontations."
Means: "Ignores everyone."

Says: "Is willing to take calculated risks."
Means: "Doesn't mind spending someone else's money."

Says: "Identifies major management problems."
Means: "Complains a lot."

Says: "Keeps well informed on business, political, and social issues."
Means: "Subscribes to the *National Enquirer*."

Says: "Is exceptionally well informed."
Means: "Knows where all the skeletons are kept."

Says: "Delegates responsibility effectively."
Means: "Passes the buck well."

Says: "Accepts new job assignments willingly."
Means: "Never finishes a job."

Says: "Optimizes the use of available resources."
Means: "Conserves supplies and funds by never doing anything."

You might want to thank the sender for the message. If so, you should use "Reply." If you really like the joke, you may decide to send it on to someone else—Bob, for instance, who could use a little humor. Using "Forward" will identify you as the sender so Bob will know what a great sense of humor you have, and it will also make a copy of the message ready to send.

But what if you receive the following message?

Dear Adrian [not-you-but-someone-you-know], Love of My Life—
Won't you please run away with me this weekend? I long for your touch. I have such a great time planned for just the two of us. As soon as we are alone, I plan to . . .

Several possibilities exist here. If you wish to let the sender know of the mistake, you could use "Reply." If you want to let "Dear Adrian" know that you know about this message, you could use "Forward." Finally, if you choose to be discreet and stay out of it but still get the message to Adrian, you could use "Redirect."

E-Mail Management

Whenever you use your telephone to call someone, you have a high degree of confidence that your call will go through directly to the person you are calling. If you get a wrong number, you also fully expect to find out right away that you have made an error, and you know just how to correct the error. Despite such minor inconveniences, today's phone system is a model of efficiency and convenience compared to the phone systems of the past.

Remember those old black and white re-runs of *Lassie*? The mother would always use the phone to call for help locating Timmy. She would lift the earpiece and crank the handle like mad. That cranking would ring a bell at the location of the operator, who might or might not answer, depending on where she was at the time. Telephone traffic was very light in those days, so the operator worked part-time and ran her home in between calls. If the operator was not paying close attention, she might well plug your call into the wrong line, giving you a false "no answer" response.

The e-mail system of today is at the "hand-crank" stage of reliability. Each time you send an e-mail message, you embark on a small adventure. You might well experience a 20 percent failure rate in your attempts to send and receive e-mail. Why so high? When you execute a "Send" command in Eudora® or a "ctrl-x" command in Pine®, you must already have entered a complex string of characters with *absolutely no errors of any kind*. Then a whole bunch of independent, roughly interconnected systems must all perform flawlessly (or nearly so) for your message to get through the Internet. Finally, at the other end, the recipient must execute a fairly complex set of key strokes to find, open, and read your message. While most people of college age have at least 15 years of telephone experience, few have as many as two years of e-mail experience, and most students can measure their experience, if any, in weeks or months.

Of course, as you and those with whom you communicate via e-mail gain experience, the process will become nearly automatic. Sending and receiving e-mail really is not as difficult as you may currently believe it to be. (Remember learning to drive a car? Talk about complicated!) Even when you do become proficient, though, the Internet will still lose, misdirect, and mangle your messages. A message sent via the Internet from your home or school computer may be broken into 500 distinct "packets" and travel 30,000 miles, through 20 different computers operated by a dozen different companies located in a half-dozen states and a couple of different countries, before being reassembled in the mail server on which your Internet mailbox resides. If everything goes as it is supposed to, your PC will let out a small "cry" to let you know a new message has arrived, and you will read it. If everything does not go as it is supposed to, you may spend a week trying to send or receive a single e-mail message.

If it were not quite so frustrating, we might find it funny when students make four or five phone calls to an intended recipient, trying to work out the problems of sending a simple e-mail message they could easily have delivered by phone in a single conversation! Remember, this is all about learning how. Do not let it get to you.

Here are some suggestions for managing your e-mail.

Always keep a copy of every e-mail message you send. Yes, even your casual notes. Why? While you are composing an e-mail message, you may believe that your computer connection to the Internet is waiting patiently there for you to finish your task so that it can silently and efficiently whisk your message away to be delivered to the addressee. Nothing could be farther from the truth. Your computer is busy, all right—busy plotting how it can most effectively thwart your puny attempt at communication. Will it simply lose your entire message today, or will it chop off only the last paragraph? Perhaps it will convert your words into binary code so that no one will ever be able to decipher it!

If you have kept a copy, all you then have to do is re-send your message. If you did not keep a copy, you will have to rewrite the message. If it was just a little note, you may decide you do not have time, and the note simply will not get sent. But if the message is your Business Law homework assignment, you may well have to spend another hour trying to recall your brilliant wording—perhaps to have the computer lose it again, only differently this time.

If you are using Eudora®, your outgoing messages are automatically saved in your "Out Box" and your incoming messages in your "In Box." If you are using Pine®, however, your outgoing messages are not automatically saved. In fact, the only practical way to save outgoing messages is to send yourself a copy. To do so, type your e-mail address in the "Cc:" box. That way, you (probably) will receive a copy of the message, even when the computer decides to mangle your message before sending it on to the "To:" address.

Always send a copy of important messages to yourself by including your own e-mail address on the "Cc:" line or box. You may not be able to e-mail a homework assignment to your teacher successfully, but by sending yourself a copy, you can prove you tried. Because we are all quite young in our experience with e-mail, and because the systems are not yet reliable, instructors are often liberal in accepting an "attempted" date as an acceptable excuse for a late assignment sent via e-mail. To document your attempts to send assignments via e-mail, always send a copy to your own address and save the incoming message when it arrives. Then when your professor tells you she did not receive your assignment, you can "Forward" the copy you have saved. This will send her the original message, including all the header information with the date you received the copy, thus offering evidence that you did attempt to send the assignment on time.

Such messages can, of course, be faked. Your instructor knows this and will apply judgment in accepting such "late" assignments. Until everyone gets fairly comfortable with e-mail, though, we suggest that this alternative to a hard and fast time rule is a reasonable accommodation.

Check your e-mail regularly. No matter what system your Internet mailbox resides on, the space allocated to your mail is limited. If your mailbox gets full, the mail server will refuse to accept any more incoming messages to your mailbox—*without telling you!* This means the critical announcement sent out by your professor will be rejected and you will not be told that it happened. No one we know will make any allowances for this sort of error. Do not get caught in this trap. *Check your mail at least once every day.*

Simply checking your mail in Eudora® will download all of the incoming messages from your Internet mailbox. This action will clear your e-mail space for more mail. Simply checking your mail in Pine®, however, will not remove messages from your Internet mailbox. To remove messages from your mailbox using Pine®, you must delete each message. If you wish to keep messages for documentation purposes, you must explicitly save each message before you delete it from your INBOX folder — your Internet mailbox — in Pine®. To save a message, first view the message (or just highlight the message in the index of the INBOX folder), then type "s." A prompt will appear at the bottom of the screen: "SAVE to folder [saved-messages]:" followed by a block with a flashing cursor. What Pine® is asking in its own inscrutable way is, "Where do you want to save this message?" Further, Pine® is also telling you that if you simply press "Enter," it will append this message to the folder named "saved-messages." Pine® will not write over the previously saved messages. It will add this message onto the end of the file.

If you press "Enter," the message will be saved to the "saved-messages" folder and the message will be marked for deletion in the currently open folder (INBOX, in this case). The messages marked for deletion will then be deleted when you exit Pine®, close the open folder, or type "x" in the index view.

You can type in the name of additional folders if you wish to separate your saved messages by course, by month, or by some other category. This will make your task of finding a particular saved message much easier.

Periodically transfer your saved messages into an archive file for long-term storage. Depending on what assignments your professor gives you, you may collect from a few dozen to hundreds of messages during the course of a single semester. Saving all of these messages can unnecessarily clutter your PC or gobble up your limited space on the mainframe. Accordingly, you should get into the habit of cleaning house at the end of each semester. Each of the mail folders (in Pine®) or mailboxes (in Eudora®) is really a text file with a structure that the mail programs can easily read. Fortunately, any modern word processor can also read these e-mail files once they are on your PC. This makes saving your accumulated e-mail files simple. All you have to do is give the archive mail file a name that is useful and save it to a floppy disk. You should put some thought into naming an archive mail file. For example, "SBM05107.txt" could be a coded name meaning "Small Business Management messages through May 10, 1997." Remember, you are allowed only 8 characters to the left of the "." unless you are using Windows® 95. Even then, you should still use the 8-character limit for your archive files for a variety of reasons we will not go into here. The ".txt" filename extension identifies the file as a plain text file. Now all you have to do is label the disk and delete the original file from your hard disk, and you have successfully archived your mail messages.

If you are using Eudora®, the foregoing procedure is really simple because your mailbox files exist *only* on your PC, so all you need do is copy the files, renamed if needed, onto a floppy disk, and delete the file from the hard disk to complete the process. If you are using Pine®, you must first get the folder from the mainframe to the PC. That is accomplished using either WSFTP, if you have it, or a command line file transfer protocol via Terminal® (HyperTerminal® in Windows® 95). File transfers and all the related programs and protocols will be discussed in the next section. To retrieve your saved messages, you need to know where in your directory they are located and what they are called. You can find out what e-mail folders you have by opening Pine®, then typing "l" (that is a lower case L, not a number one) to show a list of your folders. They will usually be located in your home directory under a subdirectory named "mail." This directory should not be confused with another subdirectory you may have, called "Mail." In the world of Unix®, file, folder, and directory names are case sensitive, so Mail and mail refer to different subdirectories on the mainframe.

File Transfer

We assume you already know how to move files on your PC from a floppy disk onto the hard drive or from one directory to another. What you may not yet know is how to move files from your PC to the mainframe and back. If you are blessed with a POP server installation, you may well never have to learn this skill. If you or your professor is using Pine® to handle e-mail, however, you will need to learn how to move files between the mainframe, where all your e-mail files are stored, and your PC, where most of your reports and messages will be created and/or stored.

So those of you who use Eudora®—meaning those of you who do indeed have a POP server connection—can skip the next section. All of your e-mail and attachments will be managed entirely from your PC, without your ever having to interact directly with the mainframe. (Eudora® will handle this task in the background, well out of sight.)

Sending and Receiving Files with X-Modem and Kermit

To execute file transfers between a PC and a mainframe, you must first enter into a shell account session by logging onto the mainframe computer. This is accomplished by using a communications software program such as CrossTalk®, Qmodem®, or Terminal®. Nearly every communications software program is better in many ways than Terminal®, but we have already given step-by-step instructions for Terminal® because all of you except for the Mac users out there (who will have to see their KP for help) have that program; it is included in each copy of Windows®. Windows® 95-97 includes HyperTerminal®, an updated version of the same program. See "Steps in logging on from a PC" earlier in this chapter.

NOTE: You cannot transfer files to and from a dedicated terminal, because terminals usually provide no means for copying files to or from a floppy disk.

Before presenting the steps in connecting and transferring files, we need to tell you that you will actually be operating the mainframe computer from a command line (like the familiar "c:\" DOS prompt). To move files around on the mainframe, you will need to know the basic Unix® commands, described as follows.

Basic Unix® Commands

Each of the commands listed below is case sensitive. Each should be typed at the command prompt, which is usually a "$" though it may also be any of a number of alternative configurations. When you first log onto the mainframe, the command prompt will appear right after the message telling you that you have succeeded in logging on.

pwd Displays the present working directory. This command is useful in helping you find yourself when you have been trying to move among your mainframe directories and subdirectories. It will tell you exactly where you are.

ls Lists the contents of the present working directory (pwd). This is analogous to the DOS "dir" command. Use this command to determine what files exist on the mainframe in the directory you are currently using.

cd [another directory name] Change the present working directory (pwd) to another directory you specify. This command is useful for looking for a file on the mainframe, or for changing the pwd to the directory in which you want to put a file you are transferring from your PC to the mainframe, which you plan to attach to an e-mail message later on. Typing "cd" without a specified directory name will change the pwd back to your home directory on the mainframe.

cp [existing filename in the pwd] [new filename] Make a duplicate of the existing file and rename it "new filename." This renaming method leaves the original file intact.

mv [existing filename in the pwd] [new filename] This command just renames the existing file without making a duplicate copy.

rm [existing filename in the pwd] This command erases the existing filename. Be careful! Once erased on the mainframe in Unix®, there is no way to recover your files. Furthermore, you can use wildcards to erase a whole bunch of files at once. For example, typing "rm *" *will erase every file in the pwd.* Worst of all, Unix® will not warn you when you are about to erase files. It will simply assume you know what you are doing.

cat [existing filename in the pwd], more [existing filename in the pwd], less [existing filename in the pwd] These commands will let you view the contents of a file. The first, "cat" (short for catenate), will type out the contents of a file to the screen. Use cat when you want to view a very small file to see what is in it before transferring it to your PC. Use "more" if the file is larger than a couple of screens long. This program will let you view a screen at a time and scroll through the file (forward only) by repeatedly pressing the space bar. Use "less" as an alternative to "more." This program will allow you to move both forward and backward in a file. Usually "more" is available when "less" is not. You will need to try out these commands on your mainframe to find out which are available to you.

Viewing files on the mainframe can be a real time saver. Some file transfers will take a good while, so it is best to use "cat" or "more" or "less" to view a part of your file to make sure you have the right one before going to the trouble of downloading it to your PC.

xmodem [existing filename in the pwd] -sb This command tells the mainframe to send the existing filename to your PC using the Xmodem protocol and to treat the file as a binary file. We recommend that you always transfer files as binary. It takes a little longer, but it is less likely to generate errors than transferring files in text format (the only other alternative).

kermit This command launches the Unix® program Kermit (it has nothing at all to do with a frog) and then lets you transfer files as follows:

At the Kermit command prompt, ">" or "C-Kermit>," type the commands below to send and receive files as described.

help This command displays a list of commands you can use to run Kermit. Most of them you will never need.

set file type binary This string of commands sets the type of file to binary. Kermit usually starts in text mode. Always type in this string before attempting to send or receive files using the Kermit program.

send [existing filename in the pwd] This command generates the following message: "Return to your local Kermit and give a RECEIVE command . . ." We will discuss this more later in this chapter.

man [Unix® command] This command, which stands for "manual," looks for help. You can get much more information than you are likely ever to want to know by typing "man" before any of the commands in this list.

ctrl-c Do not type this. Instead, hold down your "Ctrl" key, then press the "c" key. This command will interrupt most Unix® processes, including all of the commands listed here. If you cannot get a command prompt to show up, before you bother your KP *again*, try typing "ctrl-c" or "ctrl-x" or "ctrl-z." If none of these commands will stop a runaway Unix® process, you can just skip right over your KP and call the computer center for help. Workers there will have super-user privileges (that is what they call them!), which are usually required to go in and stop your whacked-out account. Do not be reluctant to call; your computer center personnel are used to fielding cries for help. It is their job. Unless you already know whom to ask for, call the computer center and ask for the machine room.

Now that you are logged onto the mainframe and looking at the Unix® command prompt "$," the next step is to decide which program you plan to use to transfer files. We suggest you try Xmodem first. Xmodem requires only a "one-sided" set of command entries, while Kermit requires that you enter commands on both ends to effect a single file transfer. So let's walk through the steps in sending and receiving a file using Xmodem.

Sending a File Using Xmodem

1. Launch the Terminal® program and log onto the mainframe. (See "Steps in logging on from a PC" earlier in this chapter for specific instructions.)

2. In the Terminal® box, click "Transfers," then "Send Binary file . . ." A dialog box will then open.

3. Select the drive, then the directory, then the filename you wish to transfer, then click "OK." If everything works correctly, a message will appear at the bottom of the Terminal® box that indicates "Sending: [filename]." A progress indicator will also appear showing a bar that gets longer as the file transfer progresses.

4. If the "Retries: 1" indicator moves to "2," you have a problem. Click the "Stop" button. (One time will do it, but you may feel free to click Stop as many times as needed to help you vent your frustration.) Then get on with changing your settings. The most likely cause of trouble is the protocol setting. Click "Settings," then "Binary Transfers . . .," then make sure the circle is darkened beside "Xmodem/CRC," and, finally, click "OK." Now go back to step 2 and try again.

   If you have tried this and it did not work, don't be discouraged. With our computer setup we cannot use Xmodem. This may be your situation as well, in which case, read the section below on using Kermit.

Receiving a File Using Xmodem

When we use the terms "sending" and "receiving," we mean sending to the mainframe and receiving from the mainframe.

1. Launch the Terminal® program and log onto the mainframe. (See "Steps in logging on from a PC" earlier in this chapter for specific instructions.)

2. At the Unix® command prompt "$," type the following command:
   xmodem [existing filename in the pwd] -sb

      The "-sb" that follows the file name means "send binary." You can also use "-st" for "send text" but, as suggested earlier, if you want to retain formatting and/or the native file format of the file you are transferring, you should always use a binary transfer method. Except for the fact that transfers are a little faster, there is no good reason to use a text transfer method. Text transfer mode is just a leftover artifact from the days of slower, 1200 baud modems.

3. If everything works correctly, when you press return you will see a message appear at the bottom of the Terminal® box that indicates "Receiving: [filename]." A progress indicator will also appear, showing a bar that gets longer as the file transfer progresses. If everything does not work and you get an error message, try changing your file transfer protocol as described in step 4 above. If this does not fix your problem, try using Kermit as described in the next section.

Sending a File Using Kermit

Remember, you are sending a file from your PC. Kermit, on the mainframe, will be receiving the file. This is a two-sided command system. You will alternately issue commands to the mainframe, then to the PC, then to the mainframe again.

1. Launch the Terminal® program and log onto the mainframe. (See "Steps in logging on from a PC" earlier in this chapter for specific instructions.)

2. Once you are successfully logged in, find the directory in which you want to place the file you are about to transfer. To find out where you are now, type "pwd." The path you will then see on your screen is your present location and the ending location for the file to be transferred. To move to another directory, use the Unix® commands described earlier in this chapter.

3. At the Unix® command prompt "$," type "kermit" and press "Return." This will launch the Unix® program Kermit which will talk to Terminal® during the file transfer. You will tell both programs what to do.

4. At the Kermit command prompt, "C-Kermit>," type "set file type binary." This will insure that the Kermit program is configured to receive the file you are about to send as a binary file using Terminal®.

5. Type "receive [new filename]" and press "Return." If you do not wish to change the name of the file you are about to transfer, you do not need to specify a new file name. Kermit will print a message on your screen as follows:

      "Return to your local Kermit and give a SEND command . . ."
      "KERMIT READY TO RECEIVE . . ."

6. In the menu bar at the top of the Terminal® box, click "Transfers," then "Send Binary file . . . ." A dialog box will open. Choose the drive, then the directory, then the file to be sent. Click "OK" to execute the send command. While you are looking around for the file you want to send, Kermit is waiting not-so-patiently on the mainframe. You have

about 15 to 30 seconds to begin sending a file, or Kermit will time out, and you will need to type "receive" at the Kermit command prompt to restart Kermit in order to try again.

Because of this time limitation, you should locate the file you want to transfer before firing up Kermit. This will greatly reduce your frustration. Trust us on this.

Once you click "OK" to begin sending, if everything works correctly you will see a message appear at the bottom of the Terminal® box that indicates "Sending: [filename]." A progress indicator will also appear showing a bar that gets longer as the file transfer progresses.

7. If the "Retries: 1" indicator moves to "2," you have a problem. Click the "Stop" button, then change your Terminal® settings. The most likely source of trouble is the protocol setting. Click "Settings," then "Binary Transfers . . .," then make sure the circle is darkened beside "Kermit" and, finally, click "OK." Now go back to step 4 and try again. If Kermit is stuck, type "ctrl-c" to interrupt the Kermit program, then restart it and begin again with step 3.

If you have tried this and it did not work, it is time to be discouraged. Call in your KP.

8. When finished, at the Kermit command prompt, type "q" (for quit), then press "Return." This should bring you back to the Unix® prompt from which you can log-out, log-off, quit, or do whatever your system demands of you. Ask a KP if you still do not know how to log-off. Sometimes you can simply type "exit."

Receiving a File Using Kermit

1. Launch the Terminal® program and log onto the mainframe. (See "Steps in logging on from a PC" earlier in this chapter for specific instructions.)

2. Once you are successfully logged in, find the directory in which the file you want to transfer is located. To see a list of files in the current directory, type "ls." To find out where you are now, type "pwd." To change to another directory, type "cd [existing directory name]". (See also the Unix® commands described earlier in this chapter.)

3. Once you are in the directory containing the file to be received by your PC, at the Unix® command prompt "$," type "kermit" and press "Return." This will launch the Unix® program Kermit, which will talk to Terminal® during the file transfer. You will tell both programs what to do.

4. At the Kermit command prompt, "C-Kermit>," type "set file type binary" to insure that the Kermit program is configured to send the file you are about to receive as a binary file using Terminal®.

5. Next, type "send [existing filename] [new filename]" and press "Return." If you do not wish to change the name of the file you are about to transfer, you do not need to specify a new file name. Kermit will print a message on your screen as follows:

"Return to your local Kermit and give a RECEIVE command . . ."
"KERMIT READY TO SEND . . ."

6. In the menu bar at the top of the Terminal® box, click "Transfers," then "Receive Binary File . . . ." A dialog box will open. Choose the drive, then the directory where you want the file to be sent. Click "OK" to execute the receive command. While you are looking around for the directory in which you want your file to be saved, Kermit is waiting impatiently on the mainframe. You have about 15 to 30 seconds to begin receiving a file before Kermit will time out and you will need to start over at step 5.

Once you click "OK" to begin receiving, if everything works correctly you will see a message at the bottom of the Terminal® box that indicates "Receiving: [filename]." A progress indicator will also appear showing a bar that gets longer as the file transfer progresses.

7. If the "Retries: 1" indicator moves to "2," you have a problem. Click the "Stop" button, then change your Terminal® settings. The most likely source of trouble is the protocol setting. Click "Settings," then "Binary Transfers . . . ," then make sure the circle is darkened beside "Kermit" and, finally, click "OK." Now go back to step 5 and try again. If Kermit is stuck, type "ctrl-c" to interrupt the Kermit program, then restart Kermit and begin again with step 3.

8. When you are finished with Kermit, type "q" to quit, then exit your shell account session, unless you plan to do more work.

Sending and Receiving Files Using WS_FTP

You can only use WS_FTP if you have a PPP or SLIP connection, so you cannot use this program to transfer files in a shell account session. In some cases you may be able to use a PPP connection from the library or labs on campus, but you have to use a shell account session when you dial up the mainframe from home. In this situation, you can greatly speed the process of file transfer by choosing to transfer files using the on-campus lab computers, then continuing to manage your e-mail using Pine® in your usual manner.

You may also find yourself moving files around for a variety of other reasons when you do have a graphical connection to the Internet. In these cases, you should become acquainted with the freeware program called WS_FTP. Once installed, this single-purpose program lets you move files between two Internet-connected computers with just a mouse click. To transfer files using WS_FTP, proceed as follows:

1. Open the program WS_FTP by double-clicking its icon from the desktop, or the name of the file from File Manager® (Windows® 3.x) or Microsoft Explorer® (Windows® 95).

2. The first WS_FTP screen will contain the Session Profile information. Your local system profile may already be entered. Click the "Profile Name" box to see a list of names. Click the one you want, then click "OK." If you must, type in the "Host Name:" and your "User Id:"; then type in a new name for your session profile in the top box and click the "Save" button to save your profile. You can also enter other information, but you must at least enter the host name. Otherwise, the program will not know where you want to connect to.

3. When prompted, enter your password and click "OK."

4. Two lists of directories and files will appear, either one above the other (in Windows® 3.x) or side-by-side (in Windows® 95). One of these lists represents the directory and file structure of your space on the remote computer; the other represents the directory and file structure on your PC's hard drive. You can move up in a directory by double-clicking the two dots that appear at the top of the list of directories. You can go down to a lower subdirectory by double clicking the name of a subdirectory. Move around in the local and remote directories until you are where you need to be on both ends.

5. Select the files you wish to transfer. You can transfer either from the remote computer to the local computer or in the reverse direction. To select a single file to transfer, click that filename once. *Do not double-click the filename* because this will immediately start the transfer of that file—whether you are ready or not. Always select the file first, *then* click the "Send" or "Receive" buttons, depending on what you want to do. If you are using

Windows® 95, you may have a later version of WS_FTP in which file transfer is accomplished by clicking an arrow button. If this is the case, click the arrow that points to the destination window.

6. Several warnings are in order here. First, you are probably working in Unix® when you use WS_FTP. (The interface may not look like Unix®, but it is there nonetheless.) This means that if you send to the mainframe (the remote computer) a file with the same name as another existing file, Unix® will simply replace the old with the new, and you will lose the older file. Unix® will not warn you.

Second, you should always double-check your current directories in both windows to make sure you are transferring the files you mean to move and that these files will end up in the correct directories on the mainframe. The rule is to *double-check before you click*. Remember, Unix® will not warn you when you are about to make a mistake.

Third, WS_FTP provides two additional features you may want to use, but be very careful. WS_FTP lets you rename a file on either the local or remote system. This facility is fairly user-friendly, but again, Unix® will not warn you if your new file name is about to destroy another file by the same name, so be careful. The other facility is "view file." We suggest you not use this facility. The problem with viewing a file using WS_FTP is that it cannot actually display a file at all. Instead, WS_FTP launches another program— Microsoft Notepad®—by default, then prompts that program to open the file. If you choose to view a file on your local computer, that is not much of a problem. However, if you attempt to view a file on the remote system, WS_FTP automatically downloads the file, writing over any file by the same name on your local computer, then opens Notepad® and displays the contents of the file. This is a great way to lose an updated file you are about to upload to the mainframe. We suggest that you use WS_FTP to transfer files, but view them with another program.

Sending and Receiving Files Using E-Mail

One of the most useful capabilities of modern e-mail programs, including Pine®, is the ability to "Attach" files to an e-mail message. When a file is attached, it is automatically sent along with the e-mail. Unfortunately, as you might expect by now, problems still exist in using the file transfer capabilities of e-mail.

Before we get to those problems, a brief explanation of how file attachment works will help you solve most of the difficulties you can expect to encounter. When you tell your e-mail program to attach a file, it first locates the file, then compresses it in order to minimize the time it takes to transmit the file via the Internet. The file is then transmitted in its binary form. Transmitting the file in binary form allows it to retain its bit-by-bit identity. This means a successfully transmitted file can be a text file, a word processor file, a picture file, or even a program file. The e-mail programs do not care. All they are doing is moving bits from one place to another.

When an e-mail program receives the incoming attached file, the receiving e-mail program uncompresses the attachment and alerts the e-mail recipient that it has a file to deliver. PC e-mail programs such as Eudora® even ask where you would like to put the file. The problems start with the fact that two different e-mail programs (Eudora® and Pine®, for instance) on one of three major platforms (Unix®, Windows®/Dos®, and Macintosh®) must agree on the standards by which the files are compressed and uncompressed in order for the transmission to occur without damage to the attached file. Even when two different versions of Pine® or Eudora® are "talking" to each other, various options in the programs may be set differently, causing communication errors that damage or destroy attached files.

The biggest problems we have seen appear to be related to attempts to send attached files from Pine® to Eudora® or vice versa. Usually, when attached files are sent from Eudora® to Eudora® or from Pine® to Pine®, the attached files come through fine. Pine® supports several Internet Protocols automatically. MIME (Multipurpose Internet Mail Extensions) is the most likely one to be available to you in Eudora® or in other PC-based e-mail programs. The Internet protocol chosen must match on both ends of the transmission. If it does not, you will not be successful in getting your file from one place to another in a useable form. If your attached files do not arrive intact, and you think it might have to do with an incompatible Internet Protocol, change (or have changed) the options in Eudora®. These options are apparently automatic in Pine®, so it is up to the Eudora® end to try and fix it.

To change the Internet Protocol settings in Eudora®, click "Special," then "Switches." In this dialog box, be sure the box is checked next to the line that reads "Always as Attachment" and that the circle next to "MIME" is blackened. If these settings are already there, but you are still seeing your attached files turned to garbage, it is time to call in your KP. Your problem is beyond the help we can offer here—almost.

As a last resort, you can usually send a report inside an e-mail message even when you cannot successfully send the same report as an attachment. Of course, there is a trade-off. The e-mail programs usually contain message editors that allow inclusion of plain text only. This means that once you incorporate your report within the body of an e-mail message, the formatting—all your settings for tabs, alignment, bold, alternative font sizes, and typeface—will turn into jibberish, serving only to confuse the reader. If you can find a way to send your files as attachments, you will rapidly come to appreciate the increased freedom this new capability will give you.

Attaching a File in Pine®

To attach a file to a message in Pine® you should be in the message editor, "composing" a new message or "replying" to or "forwarding" an existing message.

1. Make sure the file you wish to attach is located on the mainframe computer. If it is not, refer to the appropriate preceding section for detailed instructions for transferring your file from a PC to your space on the mainframe.

2. Type the name of the file you wish to attach into the "Attchmnt:" box. You must include the *relative* path as well, or Pine® will not be able to find your file. When you first log on to the mainframe, you will be in your "home" directory. All relative paths you use will begin there. Let us illustrate:

   Suppose you log in and type "pwd" to see where you are. Unix® may print your *absolute* path as follows:

   /users/local/etc/business/students/your_login_name

   This is the absolute path to your home directory. Suppose further that the file you want is in your home directory. You can find this out by typing "ls" to list the contents of the "pwd" when you first log in. If this is the case, to attach the file that is located in your home directory, you need only enter Pine®, compose a message, and type the file name into the "Attchmnt:" box.

   However, suppose the file you want to transfer is located in one of your subdirectories rather than in your home directory. You can discover whether the file you wish to transfer is located in the "mail/" directory by typing "cd mail," then "ls" when you first log in. These commands change the present working directory to "mail/" and show a list of all the files that directory contains. To attach this file—let's call it "filetobeattached"—you will need to enter Pine®, compose a message, and type into the "Attchmnt:" box the relative path and the filename: "mail/filetobeattached." Notice that you do not need to type in the absolute path of the "mail/" directory which is:

/users/local/etc/business/students/your_login_name/mail

You can omit the part of the absolute path that points to your home directory, and use only the relative path, or "mail/". To attach files located in other subdirectories, proceed as above, except substitute the other subdirectory name for "mail."

3. If you wish to attach additional files, you can do so by typing the appropriate relative path/filename for each, separated by a comma, into the "Attchmnt:" box.

4. To determine whether you have properly typed in the path and name of the file(s) to be attached, all you have to do is move your cursor out of the "Attchmnt:" box or press "Return." Doing so will cause Pine® to go looking for the file(s) you have named. If it cannot find the file(s), Pine® will print an error message near the bottom of the Pine® screen saying "File [absolute path/filename] not found." If, however, Pine® does find the file(s), it will add the absolute path and the file size to the file designation.

5. When you are sure the message is ready to be sent, together with the attachment(s), type "ctrl-x" just as you would to send any e-mail from Pine®.

6. If you have trouble getting your attached file to arrive intact, refer to the above discussion on sending e-mail with Pine®.

Attaching a File in Eudora®

If you are a Pine® user, and you have no choice about that, we suggest you skip this section.

1. Compose a message to which you wish to attach a file located anywhere on your PC or on a floppy disk.

2. Choose "Message," then "Attach document . . . ." This will open a dialog box.

3. Choose the drive, then the directory, then the file you want to transfer. Click "OK."

4. The file, with the proper path, will be added to the "Attachments:" line. To add additional files as attachments, repeat steps 2 and 3.

5. When finished, click "Send" to e-mail the message with all attachments.

Using the World Wide Web for Course Work

If you have not yet been "surfing" on the Web, you are really in for a treat! In fact, the biggest problem you will have as you go surfing will probably be keeping your focus. There is so much amazing stuff on the Web that nearly all websurfers find themselves, sooner or later, wandering around, looking at something really neat instead of staying on track and digging out those bits of data they went looking for in the first place. Our students routinely come back saying they couldn't find anything on the subject. In most cases, we find on further questioning that they did indeed spend several hours on the Web, but only a few minutes actually digging for the target information. The rest of their time they spent surfing.

We will offer some very specific advice about how to find information, but first we present a very brief discussion of Web browsers and a couple of tips for their effective use.

Lynx®

If you are fortunate enough to have Internet access via TCP/IP protocol (also referred to as a PPP or SLIP connection), you can use any of a dozen or so modern Web browsers (HTML 2.0 or greater compliant). In a moment we will discuss two: Netscape® and Internet Explorer®. But if you do not yet have this type of connection, the odds are good that you have an Internet connection through your school and access to an old program called Lynx®. A text-based Web browser, Lynx® lets you move easily among Web pages by simply "tabbing" from one link within the open document to the next, then pressing "Return" to quickly move to the new Web page.

Lynx® is a very basic program; it does not display pictures, tables, or frames, and it may not exist on your mainframe at all. However, if it is there, you can use it to move among Web pages at lightning speed compared to the speed of modern Web browsers that require extra time in order to display pictures.

Since your goal as a student is mainly to find information, try using Lynx®. You may actually find it better than the flashier Netscape® or Internet Explorer® for your purposes. To use Lynx®, start a shell account session. (See the earlier sections for specific instructions for logging onto your mainframe.) At the Unix® command prompt "$," type "lynx" and press "Return" to start the program. If you want to learn more about using Lynx®, you may do so by typing "man lynx" at the Unix® prompt. This should produce a help file you can read on screen telling you everything you need to know about operating Lynx®. Happy surfing.

Netscape® and Microsoft Internet Explorer®

Most of you already have access to the Web via a graphical connection (PPP or SLIP). This type of connection enables you to use one of the increasing number of excellent Web browsers. With just a few differences, all Web browsers work the same way. To "go to" a location, you type in the URL (uniform resource locator, or Web address). Then, once you are viewing a Web page, you click your mouse on a bit of text or a graphic to go to another site or page. There is a lot more to it than that, of course, but the power of the World Wide Web lies mainly in that nearly anyone can navigate the Web effectively with just a brief explanation.

Naturally, we want you to do more, so in the next two sections we present some additional information that will supercharge your Web surfing skills and help you to really mine the Web for the nuggets of gold that reside there. Read on.

Constructing Effective Searches on the Web and Capturing Data

The first insight we want to offer you is this: every time you are faced with a research question, think of the Web first! During the past several years, researchers have begun to consider the electronic resources of the library (CD-ROM indexes and on-line databases) as a place to start research rather than as just another resource. Today, we routinely begin with these electronic resources, moving to the less friendly paper and microfilm sources only when necessary to develop the full detail needed by the current research project. With the advent of the World Wide Web, we have begun to think of the Web first. In this regard, many of our students are ahead of us. They (maybe you) have already adapted to this new medium, preferring to begin their research projects by browsing. If you have not yet discovered this new gold mine of information, now is the time.

Estimates of the size of the Web range upwards of 50,000,000 separate pages and over a million separate Web sites. A *Web page* is one file, containing text and embedded commands, that is formatted in HTML (Hyper Text Markup Language). A collection of related Web pages, all managed by one entity, is usually referred to as a *Web site*. Finding the bit of data you need in this virtual mountain of information is a daunting task at best, and impossible without the right approach. Researchers have developed three basic approaches to help you find just what you are looking for: specialized Web sites, Web indexes, and search engines.

Specialized Web sites are collections of Web sites and pages that are all related. For example, if you are looking for a site where you can buy products, you can find collections of Web sites with items for sale. These are usually called "on-line malls," and as part of their services, they allow you to search the whole site for just the products you may be looking for, and/or categories of goods through which you can readily browse. Other specialized Web sites may focus on a set of related information. One example of such a site is the "International Franchise Internet Service" <http://www.ifis.com/> Web site. This site provides lots of information on franchising, plus lots of links to other Web sites that offer information on the same subject.

A major drawback of specialized Web sites is that they contain only the information possessed by the owner of that site. The Web changes constantly, and keeping up with even the narrowest of specialized topics is an intimidating challenge, one that no single organization has yet been able to meet.

Web indexes are collections of links to anything and everything. These sites offer a brief description of the Web site and a categorization system. The most famous of the Web indexes is Yahoo!. A quick visit to Yahoo! will usually yield a well-organized listing of Web sites that deal with your specific need. Even if Yahoo! does not contain exactly the topic you need, you can almost certainly find a lead to a site that might provide you with a new search term that will lead you to the nugget you are seeking. The primary difficulty with Web index sites is that they contain only Web sites (not newsgroup discussions) and they only contain those sites that the owners of other Web sites have chosen to submit for inclusion in the index. Millions of Web sites are not in anyone's Web index.

Search engines such as Alta Vista and Web Crawler are collections of links with associated descriptive blurbs. Search engines systematically "travel" the Internet looking for new Web sites and Web sites that have changed since last visited. When the search engine finds a new or revised site, its URL is added to the database in the form of a link to the site, along with a brief description of the site. Search engines do not categorize the Web sites they find; rather, they simply store them all in a gigantic database which they enable browsers to search through using a data entry form. These sites usually contain the most data—even newsgroup archive files and Gopher sites. The problem with search engine databases is that you really need to know what search terms to use or the results will almost certainly be of little use to you.

Developing a Search Strategy

An effective search strategy begins before you turn on your Web browser. We suggest that as you explore the net you keep notes in a word processing file, preferably Microsoft Notepad®, since that simple word processor is included with Windows® 3.x and Windows® 95. Having your search terms, category descriptors, and URLs in electronic form will allow you to copy helpful words and phrases from your Notepad® document to your browser, saving you the need to retype the information. Here is a step-by-step procedure for developing a search strategy:

1. Write down your research question, then list the kinds of data you think you might need in order to answer the research question. Add new data targets that may occur to you during your research.

2. Write down a list of all the search terms you can think of that might relate to any of your target information. During the remainder of your search, add any new terms that occur to you.

3. Write down a list of all the categories in which you think your data might be included. During the remainder of your search, add any new categories you may come across. There is no such thing as a standard classification scheme on the Web, so you are nearly certain to find your data targets in lots of strange categories.

4. Write down a list of all the specialized Web site URLs you know. Include all of the sites that might deal with your topic. During the remainder of your search, add those new ones you find. All modern browsers allow you to save the URL (Uniform Resource Locator, or Internet address) of a Web page you are viewing. Usually all you do is click a button near the top of the screen, or select a menu option. In Netscape®, click "Bookmarks," then "Add Bookmark" to add the URL of the Web page currently being viewed to the bookmark file that is currently open. Unless you have told Netscape® to open another bookmark file, the program opens the file named "bookmark.htm" by default. Any URLs you may have already saved will be in this file. If no one using your computer has saved bookmarks, your "bookmark.htm" file will be empty.

You are now almost ready to turn on your browser and go looking for the data targets you have identified. Before you begin, however, we have a couple of suggestions. First, create a new bookmark file just for this project. This will organize all of your project-related bookmarks separately from your other bookmarks. In Netscape®, to create a bookmark file, click "Bookmarks," then "Go to Bookmarks . . . ," then "File," then "Save As . . . ." Now type in the name of your new bookmark file and click "OK." These steps have resulted in your making a copy of the existing bookmark file. You can now delete any of the bookmarks present in your new bookmark file and save it. Before adding bookmarks in the steps that follow, make sure you have the correct bookmark file open.

Our second suggestion is to get an overview of your research project before you begin capturing data about it. As you first review a site, collect bookmarks, new data targets, category names, and search terms. Capture the URL of each site of interest to you, in the form of a bookmark so that you may return to the site easily. Also, make notes about the contents of each site of interest in a Notepad® file which you should keep open throughout your search. To move back and forth between your browser and Notepad® , hold down the "alt" key and repeatedly press the "tab" key. Release the "alt" key when you see the name of the target program appear in the center of your screen. This is called "cool switching," and it works with any Windows® programs that are open. It is much faster than closing and reopening application programs each time you change from one to the other. It is also faster than minimizing one program before maximizing another.

If you prefer, you can also use note cards to describe each site you plan to use later. Even so, we highly recommend that you always capture the URL as a bookmark as well. Trying to write down the URLs is nearly certain to cause lots of problems due to errors in the addresses.

After thoroughly reviewing all of the sites you find (or as many as you think you need), dig into the data, capturing the details. A note of warning is in order here. The Web is highly unstable. The perfect mother lode of information you find today may become inaccessible an hour from now, and without warning of any kind. If you do find the perfect information and you do not know where else in the world you could ever come across that data again, print it out. This will greatly slow you down, but more than once we have seen great sources simply disappear. Even better, just save the Web pages you need into a file, if you can. Sometimes Web page files are too big to fit on a floppy, and you may not have access to the hard drive on your school computer from which you are surfing. Create a new directory for this project, and when you come to a page you want to be certain you have captured, click "File," then "Save As . . . ." Type in a name that means something to you, retaining the ".htm" extension, and click "OK." To view that file later, click "File," then "Open File . . ."; then select the drive, directory, and file you want to view and click "OK."

Finally, we suggest you first try using Lynx®, the Unix®-based text browser. As we said earlier, Lynx® is very fast compared to other graphical browsers and will help you speed through your first review of Web sites. If you do not wish to use Lynx® but would still like to speed up your overview of sites, turn off the feature of your browser that automatically loads pictures into Web pages as you browse. In Netscape®, click "Options," then "Auto Load Images" to remove the checkmark next to the phrase. This is a "toggle" switch, so you can turn the feature off or on by simply repeating the procedure. With this feature turned off, you can view pages as much as ten times faster than when all those pictures are loading. If you do wish to see the pictures on a particular page, you can simply click the "Images" button near the top of the browser box.

5. Now you are ready to begin using your browser. Start by looking at all the specialized sites you know of (if any). If you do not know of any specialized sites, skip to step 7 and return here after you have found some.

    Review each site, looking for the data you need. During your search, re-read frequently the data targets you wrote down in step 1. This will help you to stay on track. Remember, the biggest problem you are likely to face when browsing the Web is keeping your focus.

6. Once you have reviewed all the sites, all of these Web page files are stored in the "web cache" file on your hard drive. This means that you can quickly return to any of these pages in the cache. (*Note*: A Web page is only saved into the cache if it is completely loaded during viewing. If you interrupt the loading of a page, that page will have to be reloaded before you can view it again.)

    Systematically return to each page in some order (so that you don't get lost in hyperspace) and visit each link from that page that is of potential interest. Bookmark any of these second-level pages/sites you find useful. Follow any second-level links as well, capturing descriptions and links as you go. The biggest danger at this point is that you will get really lost in all the links. Keep careful notes and capture those URLs into your Notepad® file. The chances of your ever finding your way back to a particular page decline to nearly zero as you navigate your way from one site to another, then to another and still another. Drop those breadcrumbs!

7. Explore the Web indexes, looking for the proper category(ies) in which sites of interest to you are located. Once you find the proper category, explore the sites listed therein, using

the strategies suggested in steps 5 and 6 above. At any time, if the search terms and categories you are using produce nothing of value, revise your search until you begin to find what you need. This is very much a repetitive process. As soon as you identify a path as nonproductive, drop it and try another path.

In the following list we have included the URLs of several popular Web indexes. You should explore all of them before you quit — unless, of course, you satisfactorily answer your research question sooner.

WORLD WIDE WEB SITE INDEXES:

One reality about the World Wide Web is that it changes constantly. Accordingly, the following list most likely contains at least one or two erroneous addresses. Some may even be extinct by the time you are reading this. If a URL is in print, you can safely bet that the information it offers is stale, if still useful at all. We have included the specific addresses because many will still be useable, and others will point to forwarding sites.

We suggest that early in your search you look for a specialized Web site that contains links to several Web indexes and search engine sites, then use those links, rather than entering all these URLs. These are only meant to offer a variety of starting places.

Yahoo!
http://www.yahoo.com/
Clearinghouse for Subject-Oriented Internet Resources Guides
http://www.clearinghouse.net/
WWW Virtual Library
http://www.w3.org/pub/DataSources/bySubject/Overview.html
Internet Scout Report
http://wwwscout.cs.wisc.edu/scout/
LookSmart
http://www.looksmart.com/
Magellan
http://www.mckinley.com/
NetLink Server
http://netlink.wlu.edu:1020/-su
Planet Earth Home Page
http://www.nosc.mil/planet_earth/info.html
TradeWave Galaxy
http://galaxy.einet.net/
World Wide Web Yellow Pages
http://www.mcp.com/nrp/wwwyp/

8. Once you have exhausted the specialized Web sites you have been able to find by looking in other specialized Web sites and the Web indexes, your next stop should be the search engines. Here you want to sniff out those hidden articles, discussions, and references that have not made it into anybody's Web site. Alta Vista, the largest database on the Web, contains lots of these gems. The trouble is constructing a search that will call up just the

documents you want. Since you have already conducted a respectable search of the Web, you might limit your search to just the newsgroup archive files (Usenet). During your completed survey of Web sites, you should also have a pretty good list of descriptive terms you can now exploit in constructing your search of the search engine databases. Below is a list containing the URLs of several top-notch search engines. Conduct a thorough search of all of these and few stones will remain unturned.

WORLD WIDE WEB SEARCH ENGINE SITES:

Alta Vista

    http://altavista.digital.com/

Excite

    http://www.excite.com/

Lycos

    http://www.lycos.com/

webCrawler

    http://www.webcrawler.com/

InfoSeek

    http://www2.infoseek.com/

Find-it

    http://www.iTools.com/find-it/find-it.html

All-In_One Internet Search

    http://www.albany.net/allinone/

The Inquirer

    http://www.mcs.net/~bratton/www/search.html

The Internet Sleuth

    http://www.isleuth.com/

search.com

    http://www.search.com/

webtaxi

    http://www.webtaxi.com/

a2z

    http://a2z.lycos.com/

Open Text Index

    http://index.opentext.net/

What's New Too

    http://newtoo.manifest.com/WhatsNewToo/

Savvy Search

    http://savvy.cs.colostate.edu:2000/

MetaCrawler

    http://metacrawler.cs.washington.edu:8080/

HotBot

    http://www.hotbot.com/

10.3 STEPS IN PREPARING AN INTERNET-RESEARCHED, PAPERLESS REPORT

Now that we have covered the various skills you will need to research and write a paperless Internet-researched report, you are ready to complete the assignment. Each step in the process is discussed in the sections that follow. Except for two unusual elements (finding data on the Internet only, and never printing the document on paper), this assignment should be approached just as you would any other written report. Do not forget your writing skills just because you are not rendering your ideas on paper.

Identify a Suitable Topic

There is hardly anything in the world that is not discussed on the Web today, and every day the available information expands rapidly. Using the search techniques described earlier in this chapter, you can find plenty of information about nearly everything.

Accordingly, choose your topic just as you would in preparing any business research project. Refer to Chapter 1 for specific suggestions for identifying and narrowing your topic. Be sure to gain your professor's approval of the topic you select before you spend a lot of time gathering data.

Plan Your Search Strategy

In this project, you are to use sources available only through the Web or the Internet. Before you turn on your browser, however, develop a pencil-and-paper plan for your Web search. As discussed in the earlier section on executing a Web search, this step will help keep you on track in your search for relevant information. The planning document may even be a part of the materials your professor asks you to submit.

Whether or not you are required to turn in your search plan, planning is a fundamental business activity. Do it. You really will end up with a better report than if you decide to "wing-it."

Conduct a Search for Relevant Sites and Pages

Follow the search procedure presented earlier in this chapter. Begin by reviewing all the sites you can find that may bear on your project. Capture the URL of each site in the form of a bookmark to facilitate your return later. Do not get bogged down at this point: go for the overview. While you are reviewing sites, make notes, preferably in electronic form, to remind yourself what gems are in each site or page. Be sure to capture the URL along with the notes pertaining to each page. You will need the URL later when you construct the references page for your report.

Continue this procedure until you have exhausted all the leads you have developed during this exercise. When finished reviewing sites, you should have a pretty good idea of the depth and breadth of the available information on your topic.

Collect the Data

Having now obtained a clearer picture of the structure of your report, the data you need, and the location of each bit, return to the relevant pages and capture the information you will use in your report. Be sure also to grab all the information you will need for the bibliography. See Chapter 6 for information about how to cite electronic sources.

At this point, you can simply copy text from the Web pages where you find it and paste it into your word processing document wherever you plan to use the data. But beware of a potential trap: any use of someone else's words or ideas without giving proper credit is *plagiarism.* Chapter 3 discusses plagiarism and answers such questions as when to quote from a source directly and when to paraphrase. If after reviewing this passage you still have any questions about plagiarism, it is vital that you ask your professor. *Do not take chances.* In the world of academia, where our ideas are all we have to sell, stealing someone's words or ideas is a serious crime.

Ponder the Data

Once you have carefully collected all the data you feel is relevant to your research question, take some time to reconsider your original research question. Think carefully about all the information you have found, especially the unexpected ideas and facts you may have tripped over. New relationships among your ideas may have been formed. You must not allow any preconceived notions you had to force an awkward interpretation on your data, when a new, simpler, and more probable interpretation may be at hand. Research should be informed by our early questions, but the conclusions we present should flow easily from the data, even when those conclusions are contrary to our beginning expectations.

Construct the Report

Having carefully considered the data within the context of your research question, you are now ready to develop a final structure for the report. With outline and notes in hand, write your report. You must use a word processor for this assignment because you will be submitting the report in electronic form. This project is meant to give you an opportunity to learn about the technology as well as the content of the business course in which you are enrolled.

Once you are finished writing the report, put it aside for a day or two, then revise it as needed, and, finally, edit it and proofread for spelling errors and other format problems. See Chapter 1 for more information on the mechanics of report writing. Put some effort into this report. Even though it will be submitted in electronic form, you will still be held accountable for the quality of your work, both in form and in content. If there is a word length, check the work count in your word processor. Be assured that your professor will check it.

Submit the Report

Consult with your professor as to his or her preference for the method of transfer. Your choices are generally the following. This chapter gives instructions for each choice.

- Transfer as an attachment, using Eudora® or a similar e-mail program. This method, if available to you, is preferred.
- Transfer as an attachment, using Pine®.
- Transfer via WS_FTP.

CHAPTER 11

Survey Reports

11.1 GETTING STARTED

On any given day *The Wall Street Journal,* arguably the world's premier business news source, will report the results of one or more significant business surveys. Sometimes these surveys are used to estimate figures of various types, such as the number of job openings over a period of time or the number of cars sold in a particular market. This type of survey is based on the responses of a sample population (of employers, car dealers, and so on) to a carefully designed series of questions. The result is then used to compute an estimate of the numbers for the whole population of interest (all employers or all car dealers). This kind of survey is fairly straightforward. The surveyor identifies the people who have the information, writes the list of questions to be asked, chooses an appropriate sample of those people, then analyzes the reported numbers. Very little in the way of subjectivity enters into such survey projects.

Another kind of survey often used in the business world involves considerably more complexity. Instead of measuring numbers, this type of survey, illustrated in the news story below, attempts to measure the attitudes and opinions of people.

Manufacturers Expect Slower Growth to Continue,
But Builders Are Upbeat

Construction executives say they expect moderate growth through February while manufacturing executives expect continued slower growth, according to Dun & Bradstreet Corp.'s monthly survey.

"Although growth probably won't match the strong pace of 1996, builders expect a combination of very low interest rates and high general employment to help sustain the industry's expansion through the coming months," said Joseph W. Duncan, Dun & Bradstreet's chief economic adviser.

The Murray Hill, NJ, information-services company surveys 200 construction executives and 1,000 manufacturing executives. (1997, A2, col. 3)

Virtually every day surveys are conducted to find out what business people plan to do about a range of challenges. Store owners are asked about their plans to hire additional employees or to invest in additional equipment. Salespeople are asked about their expectations for sales levels in the coming months and the likelihood of an increase or decrease in interest rates. In the world of finance, money managers are frequently surveyed because their opinions and plans are of considerable interest to all who stand to make or lose money when the financial markets move. Similarly, in the world of labor, human resource managers are often subjects of survey because their opinions and plans are crucially important to people who are looking either for work or for workers.

Information is the lifeblood of the business world. It would be wonderful if every day we could ask all the people involved in a particular business what they plan to do, then feed that information back to everyone else in business. Since such a system is impossible, the approach we use to gather information is to survey a representative sample of business personnel. Note that in the *Wall Street Journal* article, just 1,200 people are surveyed. How can so few accurately represent the views of the millions of their peers? The answer lies in applying the science of statistics to the responses from carefully prepared survey questionnaires.

Surveys do a number of different jobs. Marketers, faced with the challenge of predicting the tastes of millions of consumers, are constantly surveying potential and current customers for their preferences in a range of products. (Should a shampoo company add avocado to its product? Ask the people who might—or might not—buy it.) Proper use of expertly prepared survey instruments and analysis of their results can help virtually any company become or remain a leader in its chosen marketplace. The flip-side of that argument is that failure to accurately predict the changing tastes of customers will inevitably doom the best companies to oblivion. If you need an example, consider the waning fortunes of former computer great IBM, which has seen a tremendous decline in its business because of its failure to predict accurately the demand for personal computers and local area networks as replacements for centralized computing systems.

Surveys are also of great value in measuring internal environmental factors, which are key to establishing and maintaining a smooth, reliable system of operation from raw materials through the delivery of the finished products or services. If employees are dissatisfied, no amount of accurate economic, financial, or marketing information will enable a company to succeed. After all, the employees' attitudes are vital to an efficient operation. Inefficient operations mean higher costs and poorer quality products and services than those offered by the competition. The challenge for the human resources department manager is to make sure the attitude of employees remains consistent with that required for smooth, efficient operations. For this business professional, the employee attitude survey is an important tool.

In the sections that follow, we will first discuss two kinds of survey reports you may be called upon as a student to prepare: a marketing survey report and an employee attitude survey report. Following these discussions, we present the basics of writing the survey questionnaire and analyzing the results. Finally, we show you how to assemble all of the parts of a survey report.

Please note that this chapter does not include a detailed discussion of surveys used to estimate objective data, such as the number of available job openings or the amount of available office space for lease. Such surveys call for objective, numerical answers or simple yes/no responses, and analysis consists mainly of a pro-rata scaling up of the totals reported by the sample, or computing a percentage of yes/no responses. The survey type included here calls for a considerably more complex form of analysis.

Do not be intimated by the rigor of the analysis section. Your professor may allow you to use a computer program to perform the statistical analysis or may even allow you to omit parts of the analysis entirely. We have attempted to provide you with all of the tools needed to help you to perform a professional quality analysis of the data you collect, and even if you are not specifically required to do so, you will gain much by the experience of completing the exercise.

11.2 THE SCOPE AND PURPOSE OF TWO KINDS OF BUSINESS SURVEY REPORTS

Although there are nearly as many different applications for a survey approach to data collection as there are business disciplines, we will limit our discussion to two student projects: *a marketing survey report* and an *employee attitude survey report*. These two projects will cover the basics of conducting a survey that deals with internal environmental variables as well as one that addresses external environmental variables. Internal environment variables are those elements under the control of management, such as pay rates, lighting, and work rules. External environmental variables, that is, those not under the control of management, include such factors as interest rates, the pool of available prospective employees, the number of potential customers who live within the local trading area, and the amount of discretionary spending in which customers may engage.

A Marketing Survey Report

Marketing surveys are sets of questions designed to answer research questions of interest to professional marketers. Remember that marketing deals with a broad range of items and activities, including the product itself, the pricing of that product, the distribution of the product, and finally the promotion of the product. About the only two business functions that are not directly of interest to the marketer are operations and finance. Accordingly, marketing surveys can be used to collect information on a broad range of topics. As a consumer, you may have been asked at one time or another to answer a survey pertaining to your buying behaviors. If not, you almost certainly will be.

The data collected from marketing surveys are used to direct management's strategic and tactical decisions, and they frequently make the difference between a failed company and a highly successful one. Without such information, businesses must rely only on customer feedback for their decisions, and though feedback is vitally important for many reasons, in marketing, a "try it and see what happens" approach is a recipe for financial disaster.

As a student of business, you will benefit in at least two ways from constructing a marketing survey report. First, you will learn the rudiments of designing a survey questionnaire, administering the survey, and analyzing the data you collect. Second, you will get to see first hand many of the things that can happen to cause a survey project to produce erroneous data. You will also get to feel the power that advance knowledge can offer you as you contemplate important marketing decisions. (Exactly what vegetable should we put into our shampoo?)

An Employee Attitude Survey Report

Surveys of employee attitudes are problematic for a variety of reasons. The people asking and the people answering the survey questions usually have a lot of history in common. This means that no question is ever *just* a question. Employees will naturally read into each question some underlying meaning derived from the whole context of their working environment. For example, a simple question—"How long do you expect to continue working for this company?"—asked as a measure of employee satisfaction might well be interpreted by employees as a warning that the plant may be about to close! Survey questions must be carefully chosen and worded to minimize unintentional communications.

Another problem with employee attitudes is that many factors not under the control of management may have a profound effect on employee attitudes. The nature of the job, the general economic conditions in which the employees live, and the level of industry competitiveness all tend to affect employee attitudes. Workers subjected to the vagaries of weather probably tend to have a poorer attitude during a cold spell than they do during balmy weather. Workers who work in hostile environments (those containing dirt, loud background noise, extremes of heat and cold, danger, psychological pressure, and so on) probably tend to express poorer attitudes than do their peers who work in more benign environments.

When general economic conditions are bad, employees bring some of their personal problems to work in the form of grouchiness, substance abuse, absenteeism, and work errors due to preoccupation with personal problems. Even the competitiveness of an industry may adversely affect workers' attitudes. When the company teeters on the verge of bankruptcy or when workers see competing companies fail, the general level of anxiety increases. The company itself may be forced to maintain downward pressure on pay and benefits as a result of competition, while pushing for more output from workers.

For these reasons, employee attitude surveys are best used as normative rather than as objective measurement tools. That is, the current survey results should be interpreted only as compared to previous attitude surveys conducted in that firm in that location. Other uses of employee attitude surveys should be made with extreme caution.

While a student, you will gain valuable experience in designing a survey questionnaire, in administering the survey, in analyzing the data collected, and in delivering the results to the business owner and discussing your findings with that client. During this project you will have the opportunity to learn first hand many of the frustrations a manager must deal with as you question workers and discuss with them the emotional dimensions of their jobs. The insights you gain from such real-world experience will help you decide what kind of a job you want to pursue when you graduate in the coming year or two and help you to understand better what you might be getting into when you arrive on the job as a newly hired graduate.

11.3 STEPS IN WRITING A MARKETING SURVEY REPORT AND AN EMPLOYEE ATTITUDE SURVEY REPORT

We suggest that both of the survey projects discussed here be assigned as group projects; three to five students per group is optimal. Properly conducting a survey and writing the subsequent survey report are big jobs with many opportunities for individual growth through group problem solving. The more "real-world" the project, the more opportunity for increased complexity to enter the equation. We also suggest strongly that the group perform as a prerequisite task the group administration project described in Chapter 8.

Identify the Research Question

All survey projects are designed to answer a specific research question. As any experienced survey writer will tell you, failure to carefully consider the purpose of the survey will invariably end in frustration. Some survey questions you should have asked will be omitted, some of the questions asked will turn out to be irrelevant, and the form of other questions will turn out not to provide useful information when with just a small change they could have provided valuable insight.

In designing the research question, begin with a clear statement of the problem to be addressed. Pay attention to the kinds of marketing problems listed in the scenario below. Several of them that might be addressed by an employee attitude survey are discussed later in this section.

Marketing problems can take many forms, and not all problems call for a survey. Which of these marketing problems do you think can best be answered by using a survey of potential or existing customers?

Marketing Problems — To Survey or Not To Survey:
That Is the Question!

Sheila Montrose, Vice President of the Western division of Juce-Pak, Inc., just met with Saba Rath, the company's marketing manager. Sheila was not happy. She has given Saba one week to come up with a plan to address all of the problems discussed in the meeting. Saba must now decide on a plan for solving each of the five problems listed below or face Sheila's wrath, which he is certain he would rather not do!

1. Spruce-Juce, the newly introduced product line, has not moved off the store shelves the way the marketing department projected it would.

2. Jucey-Juce, the mainstay of the product line, has shown declining sales ever since the introduction of Nu-Juice, a competing product. Both products enjoy similar distribution advantages and advertising efforts, and the prices are virtually the same.

3. Promotional costs for the company are running 20 percent over budget.

4. The Juce-Pak, Inc., system includes around 1,500 distributors, and the declining level of their requests for product marketing literature suggests they may not be putting as much effort into promoting the Juce-Pak line as they have in the past.

5. Increasing fruit juice prices have put pressure on profit margins, leading management to push marketing to increase prices. Saba is concerned that the requested price increases may lead to further profit declines rather than increases.

Before jumping to the conclusion that a survey is warranted, remember that a survey is a very large and expensive job. Make sure there is not a cheaper, faster alternative. Use a survey only as a last resort.

Consider the possible reasons for Saba Rath's first problem in the list above. Failure to meet sales projections might be caused by a whole range of things. The new product may not have adequate shelf space in the stores. The planned advertising schedule may not have been properly executed. The introduction of the new product may have been poorly timed, or production problems may have led to delays in shipment. Until a thorough investigation of all these and any other related difficulties has been completed, it is too early to conduct a survey.

In the second problem, however, all of the other factors seem to have been addressed. The product is on the shelf, and the promotional and distribution systems are in order. That leaves customer preference as the most likely factor to produce an explanation for the decline in sales. Here a survey can provide useful information.

The third problem is purely administrative. If costs are out of line, then somebody goofed. Either the projections were wrong, or the activities being carried out are. Either way, no survey can provide the information needed to resolve this problem.

Problem number four may well call for a survey, not of customers but of distributors. In a sense, the distributors are a customer group: they must choose to promote the company's products. If instead they choose to promote the competitors' products, we can fully expect the observed result, declining sales. The relevant question is, "Why are distributors choosing not to promote our products as they have in the past?"

Finally, in problem number five, a survey could be used to test consumer price sensitivity, but responses to questions about price are notoriously inaccurate. Those being surveyed want to please the surveyor, or else they are irritated at the interruption. The pleasers try to guess what you want to hear so they can tell you that. The grouches try to guess what you want to hear so they can mislead you. Neither group will tell you the objective truth even if they know it, which they often do not. A far better approach to answering pricing questions is to use test markets. Change the price in a limited area then measure the effects on profits. If the price change results in a profit increase, implement the change in other areas.

As for marketing surveys, the first step in conducting an employee attitude survey is to identify the problem to be addressed. Again, the survey is a powerful tool, and an expensive one. If you can find an answer to your research question another way, you will probably save money in so doing. For this project, your professor will assist you in identifying a suitable problem.

An employee attitude survey, as a normative tool, is commonly administered annually, at the same time each year. In this way the tool can help management identify emerging problems as well as give insight into how best to resolve ongoing employee-related difficulties. When unusual problems arise, the employee attitude survey can be used to help uncover the cause and facilitate corrective measures. Special circumstances that might warrant a survey of employee attitudes include the following:

Excessive employee turnover

A general rise in the number of disciplinary incidents

A general increase in the number of job-related accidents

More than the usual number of rumors of a union organization effort

An unusual number of requests for transfer out of a particular location

In most of these cases the underlying problem might be discovered without using a survey. In fact, sometimes a survey cannot identify the problem because that knowledge is not possessed by the workers being surveyed. For instance, an excessive turnover rate might simply be due to changing economic conditions that make more jobs available to workers. With more options available, greater turnover is to be expected. Similarly, bad things happening at home frequently translate into discipline problems at work. People tend to believe that getting a house repossessed or going through a divorce is a unique misfortune, while in reality the same kind of thing may be happening to many workers due to a general decline in the economic fortunes of the whole community.

Many employee-related problems may have causes that can be determined by means other than conducting an attitude survey. Be sure you investigate these possibilities as best you can before dragging out your big gun—the survey.

When you conclude that the problem you are facing clearly calls for a survey, write as clear a statement of the overall research question to be answered by the survey as you can. The purpose of your survey, then, is to answer this research question. Stating the research question will help guide your efforts to design a survey that will gather all the data that might bear on your task, while helping you resist becoming distracted by irrelevant issues.

Working with some of the problems on Saba Rath's list, we might design the following research:

1. What product attributes account for the reduction in sales of Jucey-Juce beginning in July 1996 and relative to sales during the same period in the previous year?

2. Why have the Juce-Pak, Inc., system distributors failed to promote the Juce-Pak line as effectively as they did in the preceding year?

3. Why has the Monroe, Oklahoma, division of Excelsior Company experienced significantly higher employee turnover in the past year than in previous years?

4. What factors account for the general rise in the number of disciplinary incidents reported by the Johnson Arts, Inc., California plant, as compared to the incidences experienced by the St. Louis and Myrtle Beach facilities?

Develop the Research Hypotheses

As you can see, business surveys rarely deal with simple issues. All business systems are inherently complex because they involve people as integral parts of the system. In marketing, people are customers, and their individual tastes must be investigated. In operations, people are employees, and their perceptions and emotional responses must be considered. As a result, in virtually every case the business survey will need to investigate a number of possible factors.

Once the research question has been formulated, the next step is to identify all of the factors that might help to answer the question. The implied hypothesis for each factor is that each factor identified has an impact on the research question. The results of the survey may either support or fail to support these hypotheses.

Identifying the Factors in a Marketing Problem

Saba Rath considered the first marketing problem he planned to address with a marketing survey: Spruce-Juce, the newly introduced product line, has not moved off the store shelves the way the marketing department projected it would. After some deliberation, Saba developed the following research question and identified the list of relevant factors to be addressed by the survey.

The Research Question: What product attributes account for the reduction in sales of Jucey-Juce beginning in July 1996 and relative to sales during the same period in the previous year?

Factors Potentially Related to the Problem: The declining sales are assumed to be occurring due to some customer-perceived difference(s) between Spruce-Juce and competing products. So the questions Saba needs to ask on a survey might include those designed to identify customer perceptions of such factors as these:

    Packaging
        Name
        Color
        Design
        Information provided
        Size
        Quantity (singles, 6-pak, case)
        Physical construction
            Materials
            Shape
            Opening/serving mechanism
    Contents
        Formula
            Juice concentration
            Nutritional value
            Texture
            Taste
        Variety of flavors/textures

Identifying the Factors in an Employee Attitude Problem

Bobby Smith, Saba Rath's counterpart in the Excelsior Company's Human Resources Department, has been assigned the task of preparing a new employee attitude survey for the Monroe plant. Bobby began to list all the factors that might bear on the high turnover that management has told him to investigate with this survey. But first things first. Bobby recalled from his college courses in Human Resources that he should first formulate a research question to help keep his investigation focused.

Research Question: Why has the Monroe, Oklahoma, division of Excelsior Company experienced significantly higher employee turnover in the past year than in previous years?

Factors Potentially Related to the Problem:

Pay
  Base rate
  Premiums for overtime
  Timing of raises
  How widely pay varies within the company

Physical conditions
  Temperature
  Lighting
  Seating
  Desk space
  Level of isolation
  Noise levels
  Air quality
  Parking
  Barriers to movement

Psychological conditions
  Nature of the work
  Working hours
  Manager-employee relations
  Peer relations
  Company reputation
  Departmental reputation

As an inherently practical science, business research of the sort you are undertaking usually omits the step of constructing a formal hypothesis and the complementary null hypotheses required in other academic disciplines. Business practitioners are ordinarily interested in answering their own research questions rather than in advancing the knowledge of the business theorists. In keeping with this practical perspective, the current project will not include a formal hypothesis.

Once the problem has been identified and the factors to be investigated have been determined, the next step is to identify the group to be surveyed.

Select Your Sample

In a small company, an employee attitude survey might well be administered to everyone on the payroll. In a large company, however, getting everyone to participate would probably be too costly. So, too, in the case of most marketing surveys, the total number of potential or existing customers makes 100 percent coverage impractical. Most surveys, therefore, question a small but representative *sample* of the total group that is being studied. The entities being surveyed are sometimes referred to as the *elements* of the survey. Elements can be workers, managers, customers, or even other kinds of entities such as corporations, distribution companies, or governmental agencies. The *population* is the total number of elements covered by the research question. If the research question is "Why has the employee turnover in the Greenville plant increased over the past year?" then the population is all of the employees (current and former) of the Greenville plant. The *sample* is the part of the population that is selected to respond to the survey.

All samples are drawn from a *sampling frame*, which is the part of the total population being surveyed. *Representative samples* include numbers of elements in the same proportions as they occur in the population. In other words, if the total population of the Greenville plant is 14 percent Hispanic and 52 percent female, a representative sample will also be 14 percent Hispanic and 52 percent female. *Nonrepresentative* samples do not include elements in the same proportions as they occur in the population. In general, any attributes on which individual elements may differ can lead to errors in data analysis, so the more representative the sample can be made to be, the better will generally be the outcome.

Of course, in the case of an attitude survey including everyone, the sample is equal to the population, so the whole sampling issue is irrelevant. By contrast, when sampling potential customers who number in the tens of thousands, or when conducting an attitude survey for a multinational corporation, the surveyor must be very careful to design the sampling frame so as to obtain as representative a sample as is practical.

Here is an example of a typical survey project design:

Survey Question: "Why are customers choosing Better-Boy Bananas in preference to Checotah Bananas?"

Population: Grocery store shoppers in the Southwest U.S.

Sampling Frame: A total of 500 shoppers selected at random upon leaving a store. Twenty-five shoppers will be selected from each of 20 stores. The stores will be selected at random from the *Official Register of Grocery Outlets and Stores.*

Sample: The first 500 shoppers selected who answer the survey questions when requested in person by the surveyor to do so.

NOTE: The *sampling frame* defines the parameters that will control the selection of the sample. The *sample* is a unique set of shoppers chosen in accordance with the frame parameters.

In order to represent the population accurately, a sampling frame should include all types of elements (elderly, women, Hispanics) of interest to the research question. In the case of the banana study above, random selection of shoppers should offer all elements of the population an opportunity to be included. Of course, with any sample that possibility might not work out the way it is planned. But if the methods of selection are truly random, the sample will usually be fairly representative of the population.

Strata are groups of similar individuals within a population. Strata of the grocery shoppers of the Southwest may include shoppers over 60, women, college graduates, and Hispanics. *Stratified samples* include numbers of respondents in different strata of the population that are not in proportion to the population. For example, a stratified sample of the population of shoppers might purposely include only Hispanic women if the purpose of the survey is to determine the buying propensities of this group.

How large must a sample be in order to accurately represent the population? This question is difficult to answer, but two general principles apply. The first is that a large sample is more likely, simply by chance, to be more representative of a population than a small sample. The second is that the goal of a representative sample is to include within it representatives of all of the strata that are included in the whole population.

Suppose, for example, that you find a bolt of cloth at the store. You want to make curtains for your room but you are not sure your roommate will like the cloth you have selected. You decide to buy a sample of the bolt to take to your roommate for approval. Your objective is to buy as small a piece of cloth as possible that will still reveal the entire pattern of the cloth. In this example, all the bolts of cloth of the design you have chosen make up the population, the sampling frame is the particular bolt of cloth you have found at the store, and the sample is the piece of cloth that you cut from the bolt to take back to your roommate.

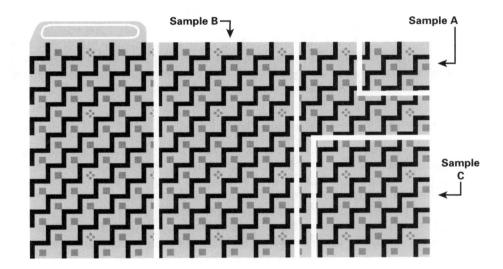

Assume that the cloth you have selected has the pattern pictured here. Notice that three possible samples are indicated. **Sample A** is not representative because it does not contain all of the types of objects (strata) included in the pattern. **Sample B** is representative, but is unnecessarily large. **Sample C** is representative and of adequate size.

For the projects under discussion, the primary objective of the exercise is to learn the procedures. Accordingly, you need not worry overly much about the representativeness of your survey sample. Be sure to address this issue in your survey report, however, and be wary of making unwarranted conclusions based on nonrepresentative sample responses. If the final report is to be delivered to a business professional, be sure that you obtain the permission of your professor before delivering the report.

If allowed by your professor, you should consider conducting your employee attitude survey using your school as the employer and the employees of the school as your respondents. This has several advantages. These employees are readily available, permission from the school administration should be easily obtained, and most colleges and universities offer a genuinely complex set of strata which will offer you a meaningful challenge in designing a suitable sampling frame. Each group of students could be assigned to study a separate college, department, or other suitable division of the school.

If your project is a marketing survey, numerous opportunities exist to conduct surveys of your fellow students. Again, the most convenient samples (whole classes) are rarely representative of the population of potential customers you wish to study. If your professor does allow you simply to administer your survey to whole classes, be sure to include a discussion of this important limitation of your study in the survey report.

NOTE: Business surveys ask people for their opinions. The people whose opinions are sought are known as human subjects of the research. Most colleges and universities have policies concerning research with human subjects. Sometimes administrative offices known as *institutional review boards* are established to review proposals for research in order to ensure that the rights of human subjects are protected. It may be necessary for you to obtain permission from such a board or your college to conduct your survey. *Be sure to comply with all policies of your college and university with respect to research with human subjects.*

Construct the Survey Questionnaire

Your research question and the factors you have identified as potentially important in answering that question are the primary guides for constructing your survey questions. As you begin to write your questions, ask yourself what it is that you really want to know about each factor. For example, assume you are conducting the banana study, and you are interested in price as a potentially important factor. You could simply ask, "Is the price of Checotah bananas too high, in your opinion?" If the responses were predominantly "yes," you would have some information, but you would need to ask more questions to determine what you needed to do about it. A simple "yes" response is therefore insufficient. You need to know more, and you can get much more by redesigning your question.

Two ways to ask about price include asking for the respondent's opinion on a range of prices: "Which of the following prices is most appropriate for bananas, in your opinion?" Then offer several alternatives to choose from. The second way of asking about price is to ask, "What is the amount you usually pay for bananas?" This question should be accompanied by the same alternatives offered for the previous question. By comparing the responses to these two questions and the prices usually charged for Checotah bananas and for the competitors' products, not only can we determine whether we are charging too much for our product, but also we can answer several additional questions, including the following:

Is our price too low; if so, by how much?

Is our price perceived as too high; by how much?

Do customers seem to be sensitive to the price of bananas?

Similarly, when we ask questions about preference, we need to find out both the *direction* and *magnitude* of the feeling reflected by the answers. For example, if we asked about taste—"Do you prefer the taste of Checotah bananas over the taste of other bananas?"—with "yes" and "no" offered as responses, we would find out only the direction of the feeling. By asking for a *graduated response*, we can find out not only the *direction* (yes or no), but we can find out the magnitude of the response as well—

"How much do you prefer the taste of Checotah bananas over the taste of other bananas?"—with "prefer Checotah very much," "prefer Checotah somewhat," "no preference," "prefer others somewhat," "prefer others very much" offered as responses.

The number of questions to include in your questionnaire is a matter to be carefully considered. The first general rule, as mentioned above, is to ask a sufficient number of questions to find out precisely what it is you want to know. A second principle, however, conflicts with this first rule. The second principle, which may be less of a problem if you survey students or school employees, is that people in general do not like to fill out surveys. Survey information can be very valuable, and surveyors are found on street corners, in shopping malls, in airports, and on the telephone. Short surveys with a small number of questions are more likely to be answered completely than are long questionnaires. The questionnaire for your survey report should normally contain between ten and twenty-five questions, in addition to questions aimed at eliciting *qualifying* information. Qualifying questions reveal the attributes of the individuals and/or their positions in the organization. This information is required so that you can demonstrate that you have adhered to the sampling frame and so that you can determine how representative your final sample is.

Surveys consist of two types of questions, closed and open. Closed questions restrict the response of the respondent to a specific set of answers. The advantage of using closed questions is that the data are much easier to analyze. Of course, as with most human endeavors, there is a significant trade-off. Respondents may wish to answer something that is not present among the choices you provide. Let us say, for example, that the questions on price is "What do you normally pay for bananas?" The responses you offer are "$.10-.20 per lb., $.21-.30 per lb., $.31-.40 per lb., $.41-.50 per lb., over $.50 per lb." If, instead, you asked an open question, respondents could tell you about their $.09 purchases and explain that they usually do not buy by the pound, but instead by the price per banana.

In the world of the professional business person, a good first step would be to ask several targeted individuals a series of open-ended questions to help you get a fix on what sort of responses to expect. Then, after you are sure you understand your respondents, construct a survey questionnaire that will provide data you can analyze. As a student, however, you will be best served by selecting a topic about which you and your group members know enough to anticipate what choices are appropriate to offer your respondents.

Do's and Don'ts on Multiple Response Questions

In general, the rule on constructing multiple response questions is to provide an option that covers every possible response, while insuring that no responses overlap. Consider the following:

INEFFECTIVE

1. How many times do you normally buy bananas in a typical month?
   a) 1–2 times
   b) 3–4 times
   c) 4–5 times
   d) 5 or more times

Can you spot three errors in the responses?

How would a respondent answer if she wished to tell you that she never buys bananas? Failure to provide an option for a *null response* ("0," "never," "none," etc.) forces the respondent to either give no response or lie.

The second kind of error included in the illustration is overlapping response choices. Which answer would a respondent choose in order to tell you "4 times," or "5 times"? In both cases two of the options provided will be correct. This mistake in question structure automatically introduces error and should be avoided in all cases.

The third kind of error is a bit more subtle. How would a respondent tell you that he buys bananas once a year? or once every 5 years? Of course, as the question is written, he could not. Again, the respondent would have no choice but to either omit the question or lie. Both alternatives would reduce the usefulness of your data.

The next choice for an answer, following the null response, should be worded to include all possibilities from the null response through the end of the first range of responses; the choice after that one should begin with the next possible option, and so on. The final choice should be worded to include all possibilities greater than the previous option. Consider this revision of the previous question:

BETTER

1. How often do you normally buy bananas?
   a) never
   b) sometimes, but less often than once a month
   c) 1–2 times per month
   d) 3–4 times a month
   e) 5 or more times a month

Now the question offers every possible choice from none through an infinite number in a single day (or even more). To test your survey questions, try answering this question with extreme responses ("How often do you eat out?—14 times a day," "How frequently do you buy from our competitors?—always," "How often do you buy clothing?—never," "If you found the perfect product, how much would you be willing to pay for it?—nothing"). If there is no choice that fits the extreme response, you need to rewrite the question so that a correct choice is offered.

How Many Response Choices Are Too Many?

The general rule on the number of response choices to offer is: *enough to capture the important variation in the opinions or behaviors being measured, while keeping the number of responses as small as possible to minimize the chance of aggravating the respondent.*

Apply reason to your choices, too. If you know that the price of gasoline moves in one-penny increments, you need not ask about intervals of a half penny. Similarly, since virtually everyone eats one lunch each day, you need not ask about fractions of a lunch. Consider the following illustration:

INEFFECTIVE

1. In considering the difficulty you may experience in using your health insurance benefits here at Linterhoop, Inc., how many hours do you usually spend preparing a single health insurance claim?
   a) 0–.9 hours per claim
   b) 1–4.9 hours per claim
   c) 5–9.9 hours per claim
   d) 10 or more hours per claim

This question offers virtually every option (in 1/10 hour increments), but can you imagine anyone "usually" spending more than 5 hours filling out one claim form? The odds are that answer a will be the choice of virtually everyone. How useful would that information be? Reason would serve nearly as well in this case, so the question becomes an expensive waste of time. To really capture the variance that exists in this issue, the question might be better written as follows:

BETTER

1. In considering the difficulty you may experience in using your health insurance benefits here at Linterhoop, Inc., how long do you usually spend preparing a single health insurance claim?
   a) None (my health care providers or others prepare my claims)
   b) 1–3 minutes per claim
   c) 4–10 minutes per claim
   d) 11–20 minutes per claim
   e) 21 or more minutes per claim

This rewritten question may still generate clustered responses, but using more reasonable ranges greatly increases the chance that we will capture more of the variability that exists in the population's behavior we seek to measure.

How to Ask Qualifying Questions

Virtually all qualifying questions are personal, and many potential respondents will object to answering them. Even so, as a marketer or attitude surveyor you must have the personal information as well as the opinions of your respondents in order to interpret the data. How then can you get the personal data?

The first rule for collecting data of a personal nature, usually referred to as *demographics*, is to ask the most sensitive questions last. After investing time in answering the impersonal questions—most people enjoy expressing their opinions—respondents are much more likely to answer questions about themselves. Also, placing the sensitive questions last reassures the respondents that the survey is not some sort of trick, since they will already have seen the whole survey.

The second rule is to be as nonspecific as possible and still obtain the data your analysis requires. For example, marital status is quite sensitive. Asking for excessive details ("married," "never married," "divorced," "shacking up, but no intentions to wed," and so on) will often anger a respondent and will certainly not help you to achieve your objective of answering the research question. If all you really need to know is whether the individual is married or not, simply offer the two relevant choices—"married" and "single."

Questions about income and age are also important but very sensitive questions you will frequently need to ask. Here again, consider just what you really need to know. If your purpose is to identify age so that you can later plan a more narrowly targeted advertising campaign, remember that people in their 20s are very much alike, as are those in their 30s, 40s, and so on. This means that instead of asking respondents to pinpoint their age exactly, you can ask them to place themselves within an age bracket. This is a much less personal question, but it still provides you with the information you need. Treat family or household income in the same way, as illustrated in the following examples. Note that the responses you provide must adhere to the rules discussed previously: all possible responses must be covered, and no responses should overlap.

23. Choose the range that best describes your annual household income.
    a) 0–$9,999
    b) $10,000–$19,999
    c) $20,000–$29,999
    d) $30,000–$40,000
    e) Over $40,000

24. Choose the option that best describes your current marital status.
    a) Married
    b) Single

25. How many children live in your home?
    a) none
    b) 1
    c) 2
    d) 3 or more

The multiple-choice questions discussed so far are of a type best used to gather numerical data (prices paid, number of purchases, number of absences from work, hours spent on a task, and so on) and objective, descriptive data (age, gender, marital status). Often, however, multiple choice questions are constructed for the purpose of identifying the respondents' positions in a range of attitudes. A *Likert scale multiple-choice question* measures a respondent's "magnitude of agreement" with a statement. Likert questions can be phrased as statements with which the respondent is asked to agree or disagree as in the examples shown below:

For Each of the Statements Below, Circle the Number that Best Indicates Your Agreement or Disagreement with That Statement.	*Strongly Agree* 1	2	3	4	*Strongly Disagree* 5
1. "My supervisor treats me and all of the other workers in our department equally."	1	2	3	4	5
2. "My plant manager treats me and all of the other workers in our plant equally."	1	2	3	4	5
3. "My company-provided benefits are as good as I would expect for my position."	1	2	3	4	5
4. "My working environment is comfortable."	1	2	3	4	5

When constructed as statements, Likert scale questions can be used to measure very subtle differences of opinion as well as to check for consistency in response. Consistency can be checked by presenting logical opposites of opinion and then observing whether respondents who disagree strongly with one statement agree strongly with its logical opposite. Such capabilities help to explain why this form of survey question is so popular.

Another way to construct Likert scale questions is to phrase them as questions calling for an indication of attitude or behavior probability. The examples that follow illustrate several such questions.

For Each of the Statements Below, Circle the Number that Best Indicates Your Answer to that Question   *Note: N/A means, "Does not apply to me."*

1. "When shopping for groceries, how likely are you to purchase real ice cream?"		Very Likely					Very Unlikely
	N/A	1	2	3	4	5	
2. "As compared to others in your household, how frequently do you do the grocery shopping?"		Very Frequently					Very Infrequently
	N/A	1	2	3	4	5	
3. "How important to you are all-natural ingredients in the foods you buy?"		Very Important					Very Unimportant
	N/A	1	2	3	4	5	
4. "How satisfied are you with the range of ice cream products available at your local grocery store?"		Very Satisfied					Very Dissatisfied
	N/A	1	2	3	4	5	

Likert scale questions offer the survey writer a powerful attitude-measuring device. There are points to consider when designing Likert scales, however. For one thing, the *anchor statements*—the rating scales to the right in the list of questions above—should be identically worded except for the negative prefix (or suffix): *satisfied* versus *dissatisfied*. Any intensity modifiers, such as *very, extremely, tremendously,* and so on, must be used at both ends. Violating this rule of construction has been shown to skew the responses in an unpredictable direction. The idea is to measure a single dimension (importance, likelihood, satisfaction, and so on) insofar as is possible. Different wording on the anchor points or use of different intensity modifiers will interfere with your survey's ability to measure a single dimension.

Two other issues generate a great deal of debate among professional assessment scholars: the number of response choices to offer and the question of whether to offer an odd or even number of responses. Our suggestion is to use five response choices, though research suggests that up to 15 responses can still capture meaningful differences. Logic suggests, however, that for practical purposes the number of gradations allowed in the responses will not make much of a difference in the recommendations we base on our analysis of the data collected.

Whether to offer an odd or even number of choices depends on whether or not you think the respondents could hold a legitimately neutral position on the question. If so, then you should offer an exact middle response, which an odd number of responses does. If, however, you believe it is appropriate that you force respondents to answer with a positive or with a negative choice, you must offer an even number of choices. Most business survey questions call for a middle position. Lots of people have never formed opinions on the questions you are asking, and all you accomplish by forcing a positive or negative response is to introduce error into your data.

Finally, we suggest that you offer a null response on most of your Likert questions to allow respondents as much freedom to answer truthfully as possible. Respondents tend to get anxious and upset when they are forced to tell lies or skip questions. People really do try to tell the truth, and they try to follow directions. Anything you do to interfere with these inclinations will invariably introduce error into your data. Notice in the illustrations that a null response has been provided to give respondents a "way out" if they choose to take it. In the case of the agree/disagree format, the middle response serves a similar purpose.

We certainly have not exhausted the topic of question formats, but the three types discussed will provide you with more than enough options to complete your current assignment. If you need more options, we suggest that you ask your professor for assistance or refer to an assessment professional's handbook which you can find in your school library.

Once you have written the survey questionnaire, you need to conduct the survey. You will need to distribute it to the class or other group of respondents. Be sure to provide on the survey form clear directions for answering each kind of question. You should also repeat the instructions on every page, or at least at the top of the section. The idea is to make filling out the questionnaire as simple as possible. If students are to fill out the survey in class, read the directions out loud to the class and ask if there are any questions before the students begin.

You can choose to conduct the survey in one of two ways: in writing, by delivering a printed form to be filled out by respondents; or in person, either face-to-face or by telephone, reading the questions and response options, then marking the answers as the respondent speaks them into the phone. Written surveys are usually the easiest to conduct, but they are the most likely to produce erroneous data due to omitted questions or errors in understanding the questions, since you are not there to explain when needed. Oral responses are more likely to be complete and accurate, and the chances that a potential respondent will answer the questionnaire are greatly increased when you ask the questions in person. Of course, administering 30 to 100 questionnaires can be rather time consuming. Your professor will help you to decide on the approach you should use as well as the number of questionnaires you need to administer.

Data Collection and *Scantron* Sheets

If your sample is only the size of a small business class you will be able to tabulate the answers to the questions directly from the survey form. If you have a larger sample, however, you may want to use data collection forms such as those available from the Scantron Corporation. You may be using Scantron forms in some of your classes now when you take multiple-choice tests. On Scantron forms, which are separate from your survey form, respondents use a number 2 pencil to mark multiple-choice answers. The advantage of Scantron forms is that they are processed through computers that tabulate the results and sometimes provide some statistical measurements. If you use Scantron sheets you will need access to computers that can process the results, and you may need someone to program the computer to provide the specific statistical measurements that you need. Again, ask your professor for assistance if you think the survey calls for the use of Scantron forms and/or electronic data analysis.

Data Analysis

Once you have collected the completed survey forms, you will need to analyze the data that the forms provide. Statistics help with three basic tasks:

1. Describing the data
2. Comparing components of the data
3. Evaluating the data

This chapter provides examples for only a few of the many statistical procedures designed for these three tasks. Consult your professor or a survey research methods textbook in order to learn about other types of statistical measurement tools.

Statistics designed to *describe* data may be very simple. We shall start our discussion with two example questions, both employing the Likert scale:

QUESTION 1:

"The benefits I receive are fair considering the position I hold in the company."

Strongly Agree   Agree   Not Sure   Disagree   Strongly Disagree

QUESTION 2:

"The pay I receive for the work I do is reasonable."

Strongly Agree   Agree   Not Sure   Disagree   Strongly Disagree."

Our objective in describing the data is to see how our respondent sample, as a group, answered these questions. The first step is to assign a numerical value to each answer, as follows:

Answer	Points
Strongly Agree	1
Agree	2
Not Sure	3
Disagree	4
Strongly Disagree	5

Our next step is to count our survey totals to see how many respondents in our sample marked each answer to each question. The following results are from a hypothetical sample of 42 respondents:

Answer	Points	Q1 Responses	Q2 Responses
Strongly Agree	1	8	13
Agree	2	16	10
Not Sure	3	12	1
Disagree	4	4	12
Strongly Disagree	5	2	6

We may now calculate the mean (numerical average) responses by performing the following operations for *each* question.

1. Multiply the point value by the number of responses to determine the number of value points.
2. Add the total value points for each answer.
3. Divide the total value points by the number of respondents (42 in this case).

To see how this procedure is done, examine the chart below, which analyzes the responses to Question 1. Notice that Column 1 contains the answer choices provided to the respondents; that Column 2 contains the point value assigned to each choice; that Column 3 contains the number of respondents who selected each answer; and that Column 4 contains the value points assigned for each answer choice, multiplied by the number of responses.

Column 1	Column 2	Column 3	Column 4
Answer	Points (Value Assigned)	Q1 Responses (Frequency)	Q1 "Value Points" (Q1 Values × Frequency)
Strongly Agree	1	8	8
Agree	2	16	32
Not Sure	3	12	36
Disagree	4	4	16
Strongly Disagree	5	2	10
Total		42	102
Mean			2.43

We can see that there are 42 total responses and 102 total value points. Dividing the number of value points (102) by the total number of responses (42), we get a mean of 2.43.

If we conduct the same operation for the responses to Question 2 in our survey, we get the following results:

Answer	Points (Value Assigned)	Q2 Responses (Frequency)	Q2 "Value Points" (Q2 Values × Frequency)
Strongly Agree	1	13	13
Agree	2	10	20
Not Sure	3	1	3
Disagree	4	12	48
Strongly Disagree	5	6	30
Total		42	114
Mean		2.71	

We see from the table above that the mean of the responses for Question 2 is 2.71. Comparing the means of the two questions, we find that the mean for Question 1 (2.48) is lower than the mean for Question 2. Since the lowest value (1 point) is assigned for a response of "strongly agree," and the highest value (5 points) is assigned for a response of "strongly disagree," we know that a high mean score indicates that the sample surveyed tends to disagree with the statement made in the survey question. It is possible to conclude, therefore, that there is slightly more agreement with the statement in Question 1 than with the statement in Question 2. Comparing the mean values in this fashion allows us to compare easily the amount of agreement and disagreement on different questions among the people surveyed.

Another frequently used statistical measure is the *standard deviation*, which provides a single number that indicates how dispersed the responses to the question are. It tells you, in other words, the extent to which the answers are grouped together at the middle ("Agree," "Disagree," "Not sure") or are dispersed to the extreme answers ("Strongly agree," " Strongly disagree"). In order to calculate the standard deviation (S) for Question 1 , we will follow these steps:

Step 1: Assign a value to each response and the frequency of each response.

Step 2: Find the mean for the question.

Step 3: Subtract the value from the mean.

Step 4: Square the results of step 3.

Step 5: Multiply the results of step 4 by the frequency of each value.

Step 6: Sum the values in step 5.

Step 7: Divide the values in step 6 by the number of respondents.

Step 8: Find the square root of the value in step 7, which is the standard deviation.

Our calculation of the standard deviation of Question 1, therefore, looks like this:

Step 1	*Step 2*	*Step 3*	*Step 4*	*Step 5*	*Step 6*	*Step 7*	*Step 8*
Value (V) & Frequency (F)	*Mean*	*Mean Minus Value*	*Step 3 Squared*	*Step 4 Times the Frequency*	*Sum of Values in Step 5*	*Step 6 Divided By # of Respondents (42)*	*Square Root of Step 7: Standard Deviation*
V=1, F=8	2.43	1.43	2.04	16.32			
V=2, F=16	2.43	.43	.18	2.88			
V=3, F=12	2.43	−.57	.32	3.84			
V=4, F=4	2.43	−1.57	2.46	9.84			
V=5, F=2	2.43	−2.57	6.6	13.25			
					46.08	1.10	1.05

The standard deviation of Question 1 is 1.05. To understand its significance, we need to know that survey samples usually correspond to what is known as a *normal distribution*. In a normal distribution, 68.26 percent of the responses will fall between the mean minus one standard deviation (2.43 − 1.05, or 1.38 in Question 1), and the mean *plus* one standard deviation (2.43 + 1.05, or 3.48 in Question 1). In other words, in a normal distribution, about two-thirds of the respondents to Question 1 will express an opinion that is between 1.38 and 3.48. Another one-third of the respondents will score less than 1.38 or more than 3.48.

For convenience, we shall call the responses "Strongly agree" and "Strongly disagree" *extreme responses*, and we shall designate "Agree," "Not sure," and "Disagree" as *moderate responses*. We see that a score of 1.38 is closest to our first extreme, "Strongly agree." A score of 3.48 inclines to "Disagree" but is closer to "Not sure." We may conclude that a substantial portion of the respondents (about one-third) tend to give extreme answers to Question 1. We may also notice that the score 1.38, which indicates strong agreement, is closer to its absolute extreme (1.38 is only .38 away from its absolute extreme of 1.0) than is the score 3.48 (which is 1.52 points from its absolute extreme of 5). This means that the responses are slightly more tightly packed towards the extreme of strong agreement. We may conclude that extreme respondents are more likely to strongly agree with the statement in Question 1. We can now see more completely the degree of extremism in the population of respondents. Standard deviations become more helpful as the number of the questions in a survey increases, because they allow us to compare quickly and easily the extent of extremism in answers. You will find other measures of dispersion in addition to the standard deviation in your statistical methods textbooks.

After finding the amount of dispersion in responses to a question, you may want to see if different types of respondents answered your question in different ways; that is, you want to measure *relationships* in the data. For example, from examining our demographics questions, we find among our respondents to Question 1 15 Omaha plant workers, 14 workers from the Springfield plant, and 13 from the Cedar Rapids plant. To compare their responses, we need to construct a *correlation matrix* that groups responses by identifier:

Answer	Omaha Responses	Springfield Responses	Cedar Rapids Responses	Total (Frequency)
Strongly Agree	4	2	2	8
Agree	8	4	4	16
Not Sure	3	5	4	12
Disagree	0	2	2	4
Strongly Disagree	0	1	1	2

Each number of responses in the matrix are found in locations known as a *response cell*. The numbers in the Total (frequency) column are known as *response total cells*. From this matrix, it appears that Omaha plant workers are more likely to agree with the Question 1 statement than are either Springfield or Cedar Rapids workers. If this is true for the sample population, there is a *correlation* between the plant where they work and their opinion on the issue. How strong, however, is this correlation? How does this relationship compare to others in your survey? The answers to these questions may be gained by using a correlation measure, such as a *Kendall's Tau c*, which is calculated by identifying pairs of responses and matching the pairs of responses according to a set formula. A Tau c is used when the number of rows is not the same as the number of columns. Use a Tau b or other statistical measure provided by your statistics text or instructor if the number of columns and rows is identical.

To calculate a Tau c for the responses in the correlation matrix above, the first step is to find the number of *concordant pairs* of responses by multiplying the number of responses in each cell in the correlation matrix by the numbers in the cells below and to the right. For example, we would multiply the number of "Strongly agree" responses from Omaha plant workers (4) by the sum of the numbers in response cells (not response total cells) below and to the right. Our calculation for this procedure would be as follows:

$$4(4 + 4 + 5 + 4 + 2 + 2 + 1 + 1)$$

We then repeat this procedure for every response in the response cells. When we have completed all possible operations of this type in the matrix, we add them together to obtain the number of concordant pairs (P):

$$4(4 + 4 + 5 + 4 + 2 + 2 + 1 + 1) + 2(4 + 4 + 2 + 1) + 8(5 + 4 + 2 + 2 + 1 + 1) +$$
$$4(4 + 2 + 1) + 3(2 + 2 + 1 + 1) + 5(2 + 1) + 0(1 + 1) + 2(1) = 297 = P$$

Our next task is to calculate the number of *discordant pairs* (Q), which equals the total of the numbers in the cells above and to the right of each response. In our matrix above, there are no numbers above and to the right of the first number in the matrix (4), so we begin by multiplying the number 8 by the number in response cells (not response total cells) above and to the right. Our calculation would be as follows:

$$8(2 + 2) + 4(2) + 3(2 + 2 + 4 + 4) + 5(2 + 4) + 0(2 + 2 + 4 + 4 + 5 + 4) +$$
$$+ 2(2 + 4 + 4) + 0(2 + 2 + 4 + 4 + 5 + 4) + 1(2 + 4 + 4 + 2) = 138 = Q$$

Using the numbers we have obtained, we will now calculate the following formula:

$$\frac{P - Q}{\frac{1}{2}(N)^2[(m - 1) / m]}$$

where N = number of cases and m = the smaller number of rows or columns. The numbers for this formula that our example as yielded are as follows:

$$\frac{297 - 138}{\frac{1}{2}(42)^2[(3 - 1)/3]}$$

To complete our calculation:

$$\frac{159}{588} = .27$$

Our Tau c value is therefore **.27**. This value may now be interpreted. Tau c values range from +1.0, a number indicating a perfectly positive correlation between the variables tested (in our example, response to Question 1 and the worker's location), to −1.0, a perfectly negative correlation between the two variables. A value of 0 would indicate no correlation at all. A positive correlation is a relationship in which one value is found when another is present. If, for example, flowers bloom after it rains, then there is a positive correlation between rainfall and the blooming of flowers. A negative correlation indicates the presence of one factor when another factor is absent. If flowers fail to bloom when it snows, there is a negative correlation between flowers blooming and snow. Strong positive correlations have scores close to 1.0 (.8 or .9, for example). Strong negative correlations have scores close to −1.0 (−.8 or −.9, for example). Weak correlations have scores close to 0 (−.2, or .1, for example). In our example, the correlation between the plant where one works and having a particular view on employee benefits is positive: .27. This is a relatively weak positive correlation. That is, workers from the Omaha plant (and workers from Springfield and from Cedar Rapids) *tend* to have a particular view (in the case of Omaha workers, they tend to agree that their employee benefits are fair), but not all Omaha workers will share the same view. If you calculate the Tau c values for a number of different relationships among your questions and your identifiers, you will be able to evaluate the strength of relationships among many factors.

The third type of statistical procedure that should be performed in analyzing opinion survey data is a measure of *statistical significance*. In the Tau c that we have just calculated, we found a .27 correlation between plant location and agreement that benefits are fair. How do we know if the results of our sample accurately represent the population from which they are drawn? The answer is that we must test the statistical significance of the data. The purpose of testing statistical significance is to determine the likelihood that our findings are not representative, but merely the result of chance.

A *Chi-square* (χ^2) is one commonly used measure of statistical significance. It may be calculated as follows, using our Question 1 example:

Answer	Omaha Responses	Springfield Responses	Cedar Rapids Responses	Total (Frequency)
Strongly Agree	4	2	2	8
Agree	8	4	4	16
Not Sure	3	5	4	12
Disagree	0	2	2	4
Strongly Disagree	0	1	1	2
Totals	15	14	13	42

Notice the totals for each row and column. In order to calculate χ^2, we must first determine *expected* values for each category of response. This means that we must find out what values would occur in each cell if all responses were exactly proportional to the totals. We shall make up a new matrix, starting with the column and row totals, but filled in not with the actual responses, but with expected values instead.

To find the expected values, we multiply the row total by the column total and divide by the matrix total (the total number of responses in our example is 42). The expected values may be rounded to the closest whole number. To find the expected value for the cell for Omaha workers who strongly agree, therefore, we multiply row total (8) by the column total (15) divided by the matrix total (42), which yields the result (3). We now continue the same process, filling in the expected values for each cell to arrive at the following matrix of expected values:

Answer	Omaha Responses	Springfield Responses	Cedar Rapids Responses	Total (Frequency)
Strongly Agree	3	3	2	8
Agree	6	5	5	16
Not Sure	4	4	4	12
Disagree	1	1	1	4
Strongly Disagree	1	1	1	2
Totals	15	14	13	42

The next step is to find the differences of expected and actual values. Within each cell, subtract the expected value from the actual value. In the cell for Omaha workers who strongly agree, therefore, we subtract the expected value (3) from the actual number of responses for that cell (4), and our result is 1. Completing this calculation for each cell, we have the following table of the differences among expected and actual cell values:

Answer	Omaha Responses	Springfield Responses	Cedar Rapids Responses	Total (Frequency)
Strongly Agree	4 − 3 = 1	2 − 3 = −1	2 − 2 = 0	8
Agree	8 − 6 = 2	4 − 5 = −1	4 − 5 = −1	16
Not Sure	3 − 4 = −1	5 − 4 = 1	4 − 4 = 0	12
Disagree	0 − 1 = −1	2 − 1 = 1	2 − 1 = 1	4
Strongly Disagree	0 − 1 = −1	1 − 1 = 0	1 − 1 = 0	2

Our next step is to square the differences within each cell, which yields the results shown below:

Answer	Omaha Responses	Springfield Responses	Cedar Rapids Responses	Total (Frequency)
Strongly Agree	$(1 \times 1 =)1$	1	0	8
Agree	4	1	1	16
Not Sure	1	1	0	12
Disagree	1	1	1	4
Strongly Disagree	1	0	0	2
Totals	16	14	12	42

Next, for each cell, divide the squared difference values in the above matrix by the expected values, as shown below:

Answer	Omaha Responses	Springfield Responses	Cedar Rapids Responses	Total (Frequency)
Strongly Agree	1/3 = .33	1/3 = .33	0/2 = .00	8
Agree	4/6 = .67	1/5 = .20	1/5 = .20	16
Not Sure	1/4 = .25	1/4 = .25	0/4 = .00	12
Disagree	1/1 = 1.00	1/1 = 1.00	1/1 = 1.00	4
Strongly Disagree	1/1 = 1.00	0/1 = .00	0/1 = .00	2

We next add the values in the above matrix for a total of 6.23, which is the χ^2 value for Question 1. To use the value, however, we need two more pieces of information. First, we must determine the matrix's *degrees of freedom*, which are a statistical device that relates the number of response choices to the results of the survey. To find the degrees of freedom in a matrix:

1. Count the number of data (not total) columns in the matrix (in our case there are 3), and subtract 1. The result for our example is 2.
2. Count the number of data (not total) rows in the matrix (in our case there are 5), and subtract 1. The result for our example is 4.
3. Multiply these two numbers to obtain the degrees of freedom. The result for our example is 8.

Using the following table, find the value corresponding to the degree of freedom for your matrix. If your X^2 value exceeds the value in the table, then your result is statistically significant at the .05 level. This means that there are only 5 chances in 100 that the results of your survey are not statistically significant.

Degree of Freedom	χ^2 Value	Degree of Freedom	χ^2 Value	Degree of Freedom	χ^2 Value
1	3.8	11	19.7	21	32.7
2	6.0	12	21.0	22	33.9
3	7.8	13	22.4	23	35.2
4	9.5	14	23.7	24	36.4
5	11.1	15	25.0	25	37.7
6	12.6	16	26.3	30	43.8
7	14.1	17	27.6	40	55.8
8	15.5	18	28.9	50	67.5
9	16.2	19	30.1	60	79.1
10	18.3	20	31.4	70	90.5

Our results for Question 1 show a χ^2 of 6.23 with 8 degrees of freedom. Our chart shows that we need a value of at least 15.51 for our data to be significant at the .05 level. Any value for our data higher than 15.51 would indicate that our results are significant, but our total is only 6.23. According to our χ^2 test, therefore, our data are not statistically significant. This is probably because our sample size is too small. You may well have the same result with your own survey if you use your business class as your sample. We have used as an example a sample that is not statistically significant, and we encourage the use of classroom samples that may also not be statistically significant, for two reasons. First, the convenience and educational potential of using the classroom sample are substantial. Second, the purpose of writing your report is to learn how to conduct and analyze a business survey; it is not necessary for your sample to be significant for you to gain this knowledge. It is perfectly acceptable, of course, to use a sample of sufficient size to secure statistical significance.

11.4 ELEMENTS OF A BUSINESS SURVEY REPORT

Both kinds of business survey reports discussed in this chapter (marketing and employee attitude surveys) are composed of five essential parts:

1. Title Page
2. Abstract
3. Text
4. Reference Page
5. Appendices

Title Page

The title page should follow the directions in Chapter 5. The title of your survey report should provide the reader with two types of information: the subject matter of the survey and the population being polled. Examples of titles for papers based on in-class surveys might be "University of South Carolina Student Text Book Buying Behaviors"; "ABM Corp. Hourly Employees' Attitudes About Sexual Harassment"; or "Small Business Employees' Reactions to a Proposed New Cambodian Restaurant."

Abstract

Abstracts for your survey report should follow the directions in Chapter 5. In approximately one hundred words, the abstract should summarize the subject, methodology, and results of the survey. An abstract for the example used in this chapter might appear something like this:

Sample Abstract

A survey was taken of attitudes of factory workers at the Linterhoop Corporation. The sample was comprised of forty-two workers selected from the three U.S. plants operated by the corporation. The purpose of the survey was to determine the extent to which workers are satisfied with their benefits and pay. The results indicate a weak correlation (Tau c value = .27) between the workers' locations and their attitude toward benefits, with workers at the Omaha plant being more satisfied with benefits than their peers at the other two plants. A χ^2 analysis, however, indicates that the results of the survey are not statistically significant at the .05 level.

Text

The text of the paper should include five sections:

1. Introduction
2. Literature Review
3. Methodology
4. Results
5. Discussion

Introduction

The introduction to your paper should explain the purpose of the paper, define the research question, and describe the circumstances under which the research was conducted. Your purpose statement will normally be a paragraph in which you explain your reasons for conducting your research. You may want to say something like the following:

> The purpose of this paper is to define Howard University student attitudes towards the campus bookstore. In particular, this study seeks to understand how students view the selections of textbooks offered, the prices charged, and the return policies of the bookstore. Further, the survey is expected to indicate the amount of business the bookstore may be losing due to failure to effectively meet the needs of students. The primary reason for conducting this study is provide information that can be used by

the bookstore's management to improve the store's operations, thereby better serving the student population.

Next, the introduction should state the research question and identify all of the related factors to be studied in the survey. The research question might be "In what ways do the current offerings of the bookstore fail to meet the needs of its student customers?" A list of factors to be examined might include the following:

Merchandise
  Textbooks
    Pricing
    Quantity
    Condition (used/new)
    Special order policies
    Buyback policies
    Return policies
  Other merchandise
    Pricing
    Selection
    Special order policies

Hours of operation

Staffing

Communications with student customers

Literature Review

You write a literature review to demonstrate that you are familiar with the professional literature that is relevant to the survey and to summarize the content of that literature for the reader. Your literature review for a business survey report should address two types of information, the subject and methodology of the survey.

The subject matter of the survey of the example above is the operation of the local bookstore. In this case, the purpose of the "subject matter" section of your literature review would be to briefly inform your readers about (1) the environment in which the bookstore must operate and compete, and (2) the relevant operational characteristics of similar bookstores at other schools. In providing this information you will cite appropriate documents, such as articles you have found in business periodicals such as *The Wall Street Journal*, and trade periodicals such as *The Bookstore Review*. In such marketing surveys you should always endeavor to present sufficient background on the relevant industry to allow the reader to interpret your conclusions properly.

The purpose of the methodology section of your literature review is to cite the literature that supports the methodology of your study. If you follow the directions in this manual or your course textbook to write this paper, briefly state the procedures and statistical calculations you use in the study (Tau c, χ^2, Likert scale, and others) and the source of your information (this manual or your text) about these procedures.

Methodology

The methodology section of your paper describes how you conducted your study. It should first briefly describe the format and content of the questionnaire. For example, how many questions were asked? What kinds of questions (open, closed, Likert scale) were asked, and why were these formats selected? What demographics were selected? Why? What factors related to the research question were studied? Why?

The methodology section should also briefly address the statistical procedures used in data analysis. What statistical methods were used (Tau c, χ^2, Likert scale, and so on)? Why were they selected? What information are they intended to provide?

Results

The results section of your paper should list the findings of your study. Here you report the results of your statistical calculations. You may want to construct a table that summarizes the numbers of responses to each question on the questionnaire. Next, using your statistical results, answer your research question. That is, tell your reader if your research question was answered by your results, and, if so, what the answers are.

Discussion

In your discussion section, draw out the implications of your findings. What is the meaning of the results of your study? What conclusions can you draw? What questions remain unanswered? At the end of this section, provide the reader suggestions for further research that are derived from your research findings. Usually you will find during your analysis that respondents generally misunderstood one or more of your questions. This conclusion may be the result of conflicting and inconsistent data on related questions, or on logical opposites. Such data that simply "do not make sense" should be interpreted as the result of measurement error. Include frank acknowledgment of the errors you identify, and provide suggestions for how such errors might be avoided in a repeat of the same project. Trying to pretend that each project we complete is perfect only proves our naiveté, not our professionalism. Do not hesitate to discuss your errors. Only through fully acknowledging our errors do we grow.

Reference Page

Your reference page and source citations in the text should be completed according to the directions in Chapter 5 of this manual.

Appendices

See Chapter 5 of this manual for further directions on placing appendices at the end of your text. Appendices for a business survey report should include:

- A copy of the questionnaire used in the study
- Tables of survey data not sufficiently important to be included in the text but helpful for reference
- Summaries of survey data from other sources, if such data are available and discussed in your text.
- For marketing surveys, maps of trading areas or product pictures that may help the reader better visualize factors important to interpreting the survey data.

- For employee attitude surveys, background information on the company and its leaders, including excerpts from the annual report or clipped articles from business periodicals that profile the company.

NOTE: Students and instructors should note that the applications of the mean and standard deviation suggested in this chapter are controversial because they are applied to ordinal data. In practice, however, such applications are common.

CHAPTER 12

Business Plans

12.1 THE PURPOSES OF A BUSINESS PLAN

Outside the university, fledgling entrepreneurs usually first encounter the business plan when they arrive at the bank, hat in hand, looking for a loan to start their first business. Almost immediately upon hearing the request for a loan, the loan officer asks, "Do you have a business plan?" At this point the aspiring entrepreneurs commonly respond in a way that usually destroys their chance to obtain a loan from that particular loan officer: "What's a business plan?"

The business plan is the foundation document for virtually every sound business venture. People who do not know to prepare a business plan in advance of making an application for a loan, or requesting a start-up investment, brand themselves as novices. To become an experienced business professional, you must understand the business planning process, the outcome of which is a comprehensive business plan.

Purposes of a Business Plan

- To demonstrate viability of the business, given a set of strategies presented in the plan
- To provide supporting rationale for an application for a loan or investment
- To provide evidence the business will succeed to help persuade key personnel to come on board prior to start-up
- To provide a plan of action and a financial budget for the first years of operation

12.2 THE BUSINESS PLANNING PROCESS

The business plan as a document has considerable value, but an even greater value is derived from the *business planning process* that underlies every competently prepared business plan. During this process you must develop a set of strategies or guiding principles. The overall design of your business will take shape as you try out variations in strategy. You will evaluate each alternative set of strategies for profitability, and each set will be revised and retested until satisfactory. If you reach the point where you can devise no further improvements in your plan and the business still looks as though it will not make sufficient profits, you will have to abandon your project, and it's back to the drawing board. If the business looks promising, though, it's off to the bank!

By far the most likely result of the business planning process is the projection of a failed enterprise. This often comes as a shock to novice entrepreneurs, but experienced business professionals expect this outcome. After all, if it was easy, anybody could do it! Of all the purposes of a business plan, this is the most important: identification of nonviable businesses. Although this may seem at first glance to be nonsense, consider the alternative. If the only means of testing a set of business strategies were to construct a building, buy the equipment, hire the people, run the advertisements, and wait to see if anybody came to buy your products, the risk of business creation would be dramatically increased. Paper plans are cheap and easy to revise compared to the cost of changing a business once it has been created.

The next few paragraphs provide you with an outline of the process of designing and writing a business plan. Following this brief overview is a detailed discussion of each element of the plan.

Developing a Business Plan: From Choosing a Frame of Reference to Writing the Draft

The first decision you must make when beginning a business plan concerns your frame of reference. In other words, which of the plan's three basic elements will serve as the initial focus of your plan: the product, the market, or the trading area? For this discussion, *product* should be taken to mean a product, a service, or some combination of both, as in the case of a restaurant meal. A *market* means a group of people (or organizations) who exhibit similar buying behaviors. A *trading area* is the geographical region or stream of traffic (as in the case of a business that taps into the rush hour traffic on a major thoroughfare) from which a particular business draws most of its customers.

When you choose the product as your frame of reference, your first job as a business planner is to determine the kind of business you want to open. Then you analyze one or more selected trading areas to find a suitable location for the business. Your analysis will focus on the task of identifying the size of the target market within the trading area and the available market share, given the existing and anticipated levels of competition.

Starting with a target market is similar to starting with a product, except when you start with a market, you may choose a potentially wide range of products to serve the same market. If, instead, you start your business plan by considering a specific trading area, you may begin by looking for underserved markets that offer new business opportunities.

Whatever the beginning frame of reference, all business planning processes proceed along similar lines from this point forward. First, the planner performs a marketing analysis. The primary output from this analysis is a sales forecast. Once the planner has a sales forecast, the next step is to develop supporting strategies for marketing, operations, and the overall structure of the business. Supporting strategies for marketing include developing a pricing policy, finding a specific location for the business, choosing a distribution system, and developing a promotional plan. Depending on the type of business, supporting strategies for operations may include a facilities plan, a human resources plan, a production plan, and a plan for managing inventories. Supporting strategies for the organizational structure of the business must take into account such issues as risk management and capitalization.

As each section of the business plan is completed, the relevant costs are determined. Once all the costs have been determined, the planner generates *pro forma* financial statements which show how much profit will be forthcoming (if any!) for a given sales forecast. If the results are not satisfactory, the planner revises various strategies until the financial picture is acceptable.

With projected finances in satisfactory condition, the planner then writes a presentable draft of the plan. (See Chapter 1 for general instructions on revision and editing.) If the plan is to be used to support a loan or investment request, the planner adds three sections to the beginning: a synopsis of the proposal, an executive summary, and a description of the business. Now the plan is complete.

The remaining sections of this chapter provide guidance in the preparation of each part of the business plan.

12.3 THE STEPS IN WRITING A BUSINESS PLAN

Most novices approach the writing of a business plan as an exercise in persuasion. They see their task as convincing the lender to loan them the required money to establish their enterprise. Unfortunately, this perspective gets in the way of the business planning process and results in far more failed ventures than there need be.

The first and most important person to convince of the viability of your business is not the lender. It is you. You must take the business planning process seriously. Be skeptical. Think every strategic decision through. Gather data to support every important projection. Once you are solid in your understanding of the business and its prospects for profit, the time for writing your business plan is at hand. Your job now becomes that of communicating your vision in such a manner that the experienced business people who will review it will easily and naturally reach the same conclusion you do.

So far in this chapter we have presented a conceptual structure for the business plan. Actually, many different business plan outlines are perfectly acceptable, and your instructor may have a specific outline for you to follow. The outline below is a good starting place, but you should feel free to add, rename, and even reorder sections to fit your own purposes and those of your instructor. As you will also note, we have presented the business plan outline in two orders. First, we present the plan in its formal, completed order: the synopsis first, the summary next, then the body of the plan, and finally the supporting documents and detailed computations and schedules. Second, we present the business plan in the order in which you should write the plan. This second presentation should allow you to produce a better flow of information, making the plan more powerful and effective. Note that you will write the bibliography as the plan progresses, and you will develop and collect the supporting schedules and attachments as they are needed to support each section. Similarly, as you determine the revenues, expenses, and costs for each section of the plan you will insert them into your financial spreadsheets to support the *pro forma* financial statements that you will need.

Business Plan Outline

Written Document Order	Writing Order	
Synopsis of the Proposal	Description of the Business	
Executive Summary	Marketing Analysis	→ Bibliography
Description of the Business	Marketing Strategy	→ Appendices and Attachments
Marketing Analysis	Operations Plan	→ Financial Plan
Marketing Strategy	Administrative Plan	
Operations Plan	Financial Plan	
Financial Plan	Executive Summary	
Bibliography	Synopsis of the Proposal	
Appendices and Attachments		

References and Appendices

Document Sources of Information

An amazing number of business plans do not provide bibliographic information regarding the sources of the information presented in the plan. This lapse on the part of other writers presents you with an opportunity to shine. Bankers and investors view their job as investing in people, rather than in projects, and they are very impressed by preparation and attention to detail. The logical questions "What makes you think that?" and "Where did you get that information?" should always be answered clearly for every important piece of information in the plan. The preferred method of citing sources in the business plan is to use superscripted numbers to refer to a set of end notes containing the bibliographic information. This method works well for plans which cite only numerical information. In the odd case where you need to use quotes from cited works, the parenthetical author-date method is preferable.

Style Tips

Plan conservatively.   For each variable considered in the plan, a range of values is possible. Choose the value that is least flattering to your business (the highest cost, the fewest potential customers, the lowest price). This makes the business even more appealing if it projects a profit even under these adverse conditions.

Write conservatively.   Avoid advertising hype; don't use phrases like *very, extremely, extraordinary, super, outstanding, superb, one-of-a-kind, nothing like it, new and improved!* Let the numbers do the shouting. Efforts to make the numbers appear better than they really are will have a negative effect, making the writer appear naive and disingenuous. Which of the following statements do you find most appealing?

We project extremely high profits of 18 percent.

We project profits of 36 percent.

Write concisely.   The body of the business plan should read like a very short book (10–30 pages). There should be a single "stream of consciousness" from beginning to end, but the business professionals who read the plan also require lots of detail. This presents a challenge which is best met by liberal use of appendices. The general rule is to include the summary numbers (total sales, total payroll costs, number of potential customers in the trading area) in the body, with a reference to a detailed schedule in an appendix showing how the summary numbers were obtained. This allows the reader to read through the plan quickly, stopping only where and when she wants more detail.

Avoid jargon—mostly.   This advice applies mainly to the technical, that is, the nonbusiness aspects of your proposal, for example, the details of the manufacturing operations or the technical specifications of the equipment to be purchased. These should not be omitted. Instead, they should be included in a technical discussion, included in an appendix. Here, you should include all relevant terms appropriate to use with a technical expert. This section will usually be reviewed by a technical expert engaged for that task by the lender or investor. Throughout the body of the business plan, use common business terms. You are writing to a business professional. Just be careful that you use the terms correctly, and when in doubt, restate your meaning using nonbusiness terms.

Marketing Analysis

Let us examine the second step of your business plan in a little greater detail. As you might expect, the organization of your marketing analysis will be determined to some extent by the frame of reference you selected at the beginning of the planning process. Let us illustrate with the following example:

Students in a Small Business Management class were assigned the project of writing a business plan.

- Sam Elliot chose to begin his analysis with a sporting goods store (a product frame of reference).
- Margaret Smith began by choosing to find a product to sell to working mothers (market frame of reference).
- Fannie Wu selected the city of Casper, Wyoming, as the location of her new business (trading area frame of reference.)

Sam Elliot, who chose a product frame of reference, would continue his planning by examining one or more selected trading areas until he found one that would allow the sporting goods store he has in mind to succeed. Margaret Smith, who started with a market in mind, would study the needs of working mothers in a particular trading area, and proceed with the business plan once she identified a need which would allow the proposed business to prosper. Fannie Wu would begin by studying the area around Casper, Wyoming, looking for indications of underserved markets within the city.

The hallmark of the marketing analysis is reliance on hard data. Most novice business people falter at this point because they do not know where to get information. You have two types of data from which to choose: primary data and secondary data. *Primary data* includes information that may be obtained through interviews you can conduct yourself or surveys which you can either conduct yourself or pay someone else to conduct for you. (See Chapter 11 for detailed instructions for conducting a survey.) *Secondary data* consists of information already collected by someone else. Many useful sources of secondary data are listed and described in Chapter 4. In addition, you may choose to purchase industry-specific reports which may be available through industry trade groups, depending on the particular business at hand.

Most quality business plans use a combination of interview data and secondary data. The important point here is that *the sales forecast must be based on facts,* not on opinions and wishful thinking. In the marketing analysis section, you have two goals. First, you need to compute a sales forecast, both in units and in dollars. Second, you need to develop as complete a "picture" of the economic environment (the competitive situation and the customer potential) as possible. From this snapshot of the business environment will emerge the marketing strategies necessary to support the sales forecast computed from the available data.

Working from the general to the specific, the marketing analysis section might be broken into four sections:

- General Economic Conditions
- Customers
- Competitors
- Sales Forecast

This arrangement assumes that sufficient data are available to allow you as the planner to compute a sales forecast directly. Unfortunately, such data are not always available on a particular trading area. Instead planners often use a comparative sales forecasting method which compares the target trading area to a different trading area containing a successful business similar to the one being planned. The assumption in the comparative approach is that if the business works elsewhere, and if the conditions are similar in the target area, the new business will work too. This alternative forecasting approach calls for organizing the marketing analysis section differently. For example, the following arrangement might be adopted:

- The Existing Business
  - General Economic Conditions
  - Customers
  - Competitors
- The Proposed Business
  - General Economic Conditions
  - Customers
  - Competitors
- Sales Forecast

The main determinant of the approach to be used is the amount and quality of data available. Accordingly, the business planner must first gather data, then, after studying the available information, devise a strategy for calculating a sales forecast, then, finally, select an organizational plan for the marketing analysis section.

The Shape of a Marketing Analysis

Bobbie Heart is planning a daycare service to be located in Phoenix, Arizona. She has found lots of information about the city and about her market there. Specifically, Bobbie knows the following:

Phoenix has about 72,000 children needing day care.

About one-half of these children are cared for while attending a preschool.

Of the remaining 36,000 children, about 60 percent are cared for in licensed centers. (The remainder are cared for in private, unlicensed homes, by relatives, or others.) This yields a total of 21,600 customers.

There are presently 240 day care centers with a total capacity of 28,800 children.

Based on this information, Bobbie has computed her sales forecast by assuming that she will start an average-sized center (120-child capacity) and that she will obtain enough customers to reach the average percentage of utilization as other centers in the trading area. This would yield 90 customers, based on a capacity of 120 and a utilization rate of 75 percent (21,600/28,800 = 75%). These 90 customers would then represent a total annual sales level of $304,200, assuming $65 per week per child for 52 weeks per year (90 × $65 × 52 = $304,200).

Given the information she has obtained and the sales forecasting approach she has chosen, Bobbie has decided to present the relevant information she has found in the order she used it in developing her sales forecast. Her marketing analysis was presented in the following order:

- Economic Conditions in Phoenix, Arizona
- Customers
- Competitors
- Sales Forecast

Sam Tillman is planning an automotive repair shop to be located in Boulder, Colorado. Sam's proposed business will use a new set of business strategies patterned after *Le Garage, Inc.,* a highly successful business located in Garden Springs, California. Sam has studied the existing business carefully, as well as its environs. He has completed his examination of the target area, Boulder, Colorado, and has collected the following information:

Garden Springs has a population of 74,500, who own a total of 22,450 automobiles.

The average income of the households in Garden Springs is $34,000.

Each of Garden Springs' households contain an average of 4.3 people.

Garden Springs has 36 auto repair businesses employing 206 auto mechanics.

The total annual sales of the existing repair business located in Garden Springs is $546,000, earned on 1,290 repairs, each costing the customer an average of about $423.

Boulder has a population of 123,600, who own a total of 31,180 automobiles.

The average income of a household in Boulder is $45,600.

The average Boulder Household has 4.1 people.

Boulder has 249 auto mechanics working in 49 businesses.

Based on the foregoing information, Sam has developed a sales forecast by starting with the known sales level of the Garden Springs business and then adjusting that number for the observed differences in the two trading areas. Sam has decided to include a chart to help clarify the comparison as follows:

Variable	Garden Springs	Boulder	Adjustment Factor
Number of vehicles	22,450	31,180	1.4 (31,180/22,450) More cars means more repairs.
Average income	$45,600	$34,000	.75 (34,000/45,600) Less income means less expensive cars and repairs more likely to be left undone when optional.
People per household	4.3	4.1	1.05 (4.3/4.1) Fewer people supported by the income frees more money for buying repairs.
Number of mechanics per vehicle	109 (22,450/206)	125 (31,180/249)	1.15 (125/109) More vehicles per mechanic means the competition will be less. With fewer mechanics, they stay busier and spend less time and money on marketing. Also means more dissatisfied customers due to longer waiting times.
Total adjustment			1.27 (1.4 × .75 × 1.05 × 1.15) The compound effects of the four factors considered are computed by multiplying all factors together.
Sales forecast			$693,420 ($546,000 × 1.27) 1683 unit sales (1290 × 1.27) One unit sale is one repair bill—average, $423.

Having worked out his sales forecasting strategy, Sam has also decided to present his data in the order he used it in his analysis. Sam adopted the following order for presenting his marketing analysis:

- Garden Springs and *Le Garage, Inc.*
  - General Economic Conditions
  - Customers
  - Competitors
- Boulder Colorado
  - General Economic Conditions
  - Customers
  - Competitors
- Sales Forecast

As you can see from the foregoing examples, the marketing analysis can be approached in a variety of ways, each calling for its own presentation format. The keys to a successful marketing analysis, one that effectively communicates the relevant facts and conclusions to the reader, are a thorough analysis and a carefully thought out order of presentation that leads the reader step by step to the same conclusions you have reached.

In presenting your analysis, be careful not to leave out steps in your thinking process. Readers may not be able to make the same leaps of logic that you do, so take them by the hand and lead them carefully through your thought process. This is vital. Unless your readers agree with your sales forecast, they almost certainly will reject your proposal, no matter how well the remainder of the business plan is written.

For the remainder of this section of the chapter we will develop a more involved illustration than those above and present it from a product frame of reference. Our goal will be to ascertain whether a proposed business idea, a lawn maintenance company we will call Lawn Pro, Inc., would be workable in the Edmond, Oklahoma, area. (Assuming the business does prove feasible and we were not simply conducting an academic exercise, we would polish the plan and begin our efforts to implement it. If Lawn Pro proves unworkable in our chosen market, we might choose to look for an acceptable location rather than abandon the project.)

Lawn Pro Marketing Analysis

Our Lawn Pro, Inc., planners have completed their marketing research and collected the following information pertinent to the sales forecasting strategy adopted:

- Edmond, Oklahoma (the target trading area), contains 31,400 single-family homes.

- A survey of homeowners shows that 11 percent of them pay someone to mow and trim their lawns and that they pay an average of $40 per mowing.

- Analysis of the survey further finds that 60 percent of those who pay for mowing services are dissatisfied in some way with their past service provider and 45 percent say they would be willing to try out a new service if the opportunity presented itself.

- From discussions with area horticultural experts concerning the rate of growth of lawn grasses in the Edmond area, the planners have estimated that each customer will require about 12 mowings per season.

- From surveying homeowners and reviewing classified ads in local newspapers, the planners have identified over 50 individuals and small companies who offer mowing services, none of whom operate more than two crews. The planners believe that many more such small service providers exist, but no dominant firms were found in the trading area.

- Homeowners surveyed also indicated that, if approached, they would consider buying chemical lawn services from a company other than the one they currently or formerly used.

- Telephone surveys of chemical service providers suggest that each contract is worth an average of $540. A strategic alliance with Weeds-R-Gone, a local firm with 150 current customers, will enable Lawn Pro, Inc., to offer chemical services under contract at competitive rates and earn a 30 percent profit on these services, will be performed entirely by Weeds-R-Gone.

Based on the foregoing information, the planners have forecast mowing/trimming sales by using a simple estimate of the market share attainable, beginning with a 10 percent market share and increasing to a 30 percent share over a three-year period. This sales forecasting strategy then results in a forecast of 345 customers in year one, each requiring 12 mowings at $40 each for a total of 4,140 mowings in year one, worth $165,600; growing to 1,035 customers, 12,420 mowings, and $496,800 by year three.

Chemical services are forecast at 20 percent of Lawn Pro customers, or 69 contracts in year one, growing to 207 by year three. Each contract is worth $162 per year to Lawn Pro ($540 × .30), so revenue from chemical services is projected at $11,178 for year one, growing to 33,534 by year three.

Given this sales forecasting strategy, the planners proceeded to develop and write the following marketing analysis section.

LAWN PRO
MARKETING ANALYSIS

THE EDMOND, OKLAHOMA, MARKETPLACE

Located just north of Oklahoma City, Edmond is an affluent bedroom community of approximately 60,000 residents, over 90 percent of whom occupy their own single-family homes. Edmond residents enjoy the highest average household income in the state of Oklahoma at $52,941. Edmond now contains approximately 30,000 residences. The city is growing rapidly, with no end in sight. During the past five years, the population has increased by 7,000, and numerous new businesses have entered the market, suggesting that additional growth is expected. Further evidence of growth is provided by the recent explosive growth in the restaurant sector. Edmond saw 25 new restaurants either started or completed during 1995, including a number of national chain restaurants (Denny's, Perkin's, El Chico, Logan's Roadhouse, Appleby's, and Chili's), all of which target rapidly growing trading areas as their primary strategies.

In the Edmond area, several strong lawncare companies compete vigorously for commercial lawncare business, but there is little evidence that any of these businesses have chosen to pursue the residential market. Interviews with several commercial lawncare companies revealed that they find homeowners difficult to deal with. Their strategies are focused on commercial customers, a fact which allows them to contract for large amounts of business through a single entity. These companies use advertisements in the local yellow pages and personal selling as their primary promotional strategies. Two such companies are Greener Pastures and Turf King. These two companies employ 45 and 28 people, respectively. Based on interviews with the owners of these two companies, we estimate their annual sales at $1,300,000 and $875,000. Although these two companies do not strategically pursue the residential market, we consider them to be our greatest threat. They have the capital, the operational expertise, and access to our trading area should they decide to address this market. Our marketing strategy, presented in the next section, is designed to defend against this threat.

In addition to these two leading firms, there are another 12 firms listed in the local yellow pages offering lawn services. Four appear to offer full services similar to those to be offered by Lawn Pro, with the remainder offering only chemical services. Based on our interviews with 25 competitors (see details in Appendix C), those who serve the homeowner are primarily either small, one-crew, part-time individuals who work mainly on weekends, or the teenagers in the neighborhoods. We do not consider these individuals and small companies to pose a significant threat. Although they already address our target market, they have yet to grow, suggesting flaws in their strategies.

To determine why such a potentially lucrative opportunity has not yet suc-ceeded, we developed and executed a survey of potential customers (see Appendix D for detailed information on the survey). Our survey suggests that the primary perception homeowners have of lawncare workers is that they are un-reliable, ill-mannered, and sloppy. The risk of hiring someone even worse seems to be the primary reason for keeping the service currently at hand, rather than any high level of satisfaction with workmanship. Virtually none of the residen-tial lawn services operate on a contract basis, preferring instead to collect in per-son following each job performed.

The survey further suggests that, unlike the mowing and trimming ser-vices, the chemical lawn maintenance sector is well organized in addressing our target market of homeowners. Area firms are aggressive in obtaining annual contracts for these services, and customer loyalty is quite high.

Our survey also suggests that 11 percent of Edmond homeowners (11 per-cent of 31,400 = 3,454) comprise the market, with 60 percent expressing dissatis-faction with current and past lawncare service providers. As of 1995, the total size of the market for residential mowing and trimming services was estimated at 41,448 mowings for 3,454 customers, worth $1,657,920 at an average of $40 per mowing. The market for lawn chemicals was estimated at 4,300 annual con-tracts, worth $2,322,000 at an average of $540 per year.

Based on the foregoing information, we have forecast mowing/trimming sales by using a simple estimate of the market share attainable, beginning with a 10 percent market share and increasing to a 30 percent share over a three-year period. This sales forecasting strategy results in a forecast of 345 customers in year one, each requiring 12 mowings at $40 each for a total of 4,140 mowings in year one, worth $165,600; growing to 1,035 customers, 12,420 mowings, and $496,800 by year three.

Chemical services are forecast at 20 percent of Lawn Pro customers, or 69 contracts in year one, growing to 207 by year three. Each contract is worth $162 per year to Lawn Pro ($540 x .30), so revenue from chemical services is pro-jected at $11,178 for year one, growing to $33,534 by year three.

The marketing analysis section yields the sales forecast. Note that there is as yet no effort to determine whether this sales forecast will produce a profit, whether we can mount a sufficient effort to produce enough customers to meet these sales projections, or what other costs will be incurred in the process of meeting this level of demand. The subsequent sections of the business plan address these questions, beginning with the marketing strategy, which will reveal how much it will cost to produce the demand predicted in the marketing analysis section just completed.

In the foregoing discussion of the sales forecasting procedure, we have assumed that you are writing a business plan for a new start-up business. If you are developing a business plan for an existing business, refer to the discussion on marketing plans in Chapter 13.

Marketing Strategy

This section of the plan identifies the marketing strategies that the business will use. Components of the marketing strategy to be discussed include the *product* (what will be sold to whom), the *price* (how much will be charged), the *place* (where it will be sold), and the *promotion* (how it will be delivered). In addition to the strategies to be adopted, the specific policies and marketing tactics need to be detailed in this section as well.

Key Terms in the Marketing Strategy

Strategy *Strategy* is a term business has borrowed from military science, where it is used to refer to the overall plan for a military action. In business, strategy refers to the fundamental perspective, i.e., the "big picture." Two parts of a business strategy are the goal and the plan of action to be used to attain that goal.

> *Example:* In opening an ice cream store, Mary Jones has adopted the promotional strategy of becoming so well known in her community that the townspeople at least consider going to her store whenever they think about purchasing ice cream. She plans to accomplish this goal by using a number of *tactics* (see below), including advertising, publicity, and sales promotional activities.

> *Example:* Roberta Juarez has as her operational strategy to operate her drycleaners at the highest level of efficiency of all her local competitors by using the latest equipment and establishing a training regimen for all of her employees.

> *Example:* For his hardware store Sammy Jordan has chosen a pricing strategy of always offering his lawn and garden equipment at less than that available from the highest priced competitor, but higher than that offered by all other local competitors.

Policy A *policy* is a statement that offers guidance to management and employees in the decisions they must make on a daily basis. A policy may state the standards by which a situation is to be evaluated, the timing or frequency for such evaluations, and the actions to be taken as a result of the evaluation. The policy helps management achieve their chosen strategies without having always to consider each decision in light of its potential impact on the strategy.

> *Example:* Mary Jones has established a policy regarding placing advertisements for her ice cream store in available publications as follows: The publication must offer

general interest content or family-oriented information. The publication must be issued at least once a month (no one-time, quarterly, or annual publications), and the cost must be less than $.30 per thousand impressions.

Example: Roberta Juarez has established a policy that each employee will be required to attend no fewer than 24 clock hours of industry-specific training each year. She has also established a policy of upgrading each piece of equipment in the plant as a newly improved model is introduced and becomes available.

Example: Sammy Jordan's policy on pricing requires that he check his competitors' prices on each model once each month to determine what their prices are. Sammy then revises his prices as needed to place his prices 1-3 percent below those of the highest priced competitor and above that charged by the rest.

Tactic Another military science term, *tactic,* or *stratagem,* is a component of a *strategy*. Several tactics can work together to form a strategy.

Example: Mary Jones has chosen to advertise each week in her home town newspaper. This tactic supports her promotional strategy described above.

Example: Roberta Juarez has joined the Drycleaners of America (DOA), because as a member her business will receive a 35 percent discount on training courses offered by the DOA. This tactic supports her above-described operations strategy by alerting Roberta of upcoming training opportunities while also minimizing the cost.

Example: Sammy Jordan is planning to subscribe to the *Garden Tractor Gazette,* a regional publication that focuses on his industry. One feature is a regular pricing survey of area dealers. This tactic reduces the cost of implementing Sammy's strategy.

The marketing strategy section of your business plan is the first to address the cost issues, so in addition to determining here just what marketing actions you will follow, you must also determine as accurately as possible how much such actions will cost. In the preceding marketing analysis section you have identified your offerings in a general form. Now, in presenting the product portion of the marketing strategy, you should precisely identify what you intend to offer your customers.

Product

In discussing your product, be specific. Up to this point the reader has a general idea only as to just what you will offer your customers. Now is the time to answer all those unasked questions—before they can trip up your chances for the loan or investment you are proposing. If you are offering a product rather than a service, be specific as to the nature of the product. This includes a complete description of all relevant attributes: range of sizes, colors, quantities, packaging, and warranties offered. In many cases, and especially if the product is proprietary (i.e., available only from you) you may also need to include pictures and technical specifications as attachments. If your differentiation strategy is to offer a product that is technologically superior to that of your competitors' products, then you should also include a detailed "technical discussion" section in which you explain just exactly how and why your technical approach is better. In this section use jargon freely. Write as though you are presenting this to the leading technical expert in your field. Since few bankers and investors are comfortable judging such matters, they will almost certainly have this section reviewed by a technical expert.

If your product is a service, or if it includes a service component (as in the case of a restaurant), you will need to describe fully the services you will perform. Perhaps the best way to present a service is to write a set of *protocols* (step-by-step procedures) which you will then use as a basis for directing your staff in the actual delivery of services during operations. Presenting such detail accomplishes two goals: it shows exactly what you intend to offer your customers, and it shows that you are well prepared. Failing to provide such detail leaves your reader with far too many questions.

For both products and services you should explicitly present a plan for managing *customer service*. This ubiquitous term is a catch-all for the things you do that result in good feelings for you in your customers. Included in this category are such tactics as sending birthday cards to your customers, calling customers by name when they enter the store, and handling inquiries and complaints politely and efficiently. Since we generally all agree that customer service is important in businesses today, this too should not be left to chance. Develop a plan for customer service and present it in this section. Here the best approach is to break customer service into specific, manageable, component parts, and then show how you will manage each customer service component to insure your customers continue to have good thoughts about your business.

The Dimensions of Customer Service
Those dimensions of customer service which you decide are important should be explicitly controlled. Control can be effected in a number of ways, but always you must first set standards. Once you have established standards, usually all you have to do is train employees in their tasks, monitor their performance, and correct as needed.

Finally, no matter what you offer, you must present a plan for *quality control*.

In his laundromat Jeffrey McDonald has decided to include standards for customer waiting time, recognition, inquiries and complaints, and ancillary services. Jeffrey's business plan includes the following sections on customer service.

Customer Waiting Time
Because we recognize that having to wait to use a dryer following the completion of the washing cycle is a major irritant to our customers, we will implement three policies: (1) Those using our washers will receive first priority over customers using only dryers and over our drop-off loads (loads we are running for customers). (2) We will install 10 percent more dryers than called for by the manufacturer's recommendations. We consider the additional investment in equipment a cost-effective investment in better customer service. (3) In the event all dryers are full at the time a washer customer needs to use them, we will offer to finish the load(s) at no additional charge and let the customer pick the dry laundry up later.

Recognition
The sound of our own name is sweet music to nearly all of us. Our attendants will, therefore, be encouraged to learn the names of all who patronize our

business. All adults will be addressed by their titles and surnames, not by their first names, unless invited to do so by the customer. The goal is for every customer to be named by their fourth visit. Management will monitor this policy to insure it is adhered to by all attendants. As a means of acquiring this information, we will offer a free wash for each 20 washes and issue customers a check-off card bearing their name.

Inquiry Handling

An attendant will be on premises at all times during operating hours. This individual will carry a wireless telephone to be able to answer all calls by the second ring, no matter where the attendant is at the time. Every attendant will be trained in the proper response to all normal inquiries, and calls will be monitored on a random basis to insure that appropriate responses are being given by all attendants.

Complaint Handling

Complaints will be handled according to the following policy: every time a customer registers a complaint with an attendant, the attendant will attempt to address the complaint. Attendants will have discretionary authority to give free washer and dryer time, using a stock of tokens. The attendant will also complete an incident report which will be reviewed by management within 2 days. Management will personally contact the customer to insure the customer was satisfied by the attendant's response. If the customer was not satisfied, the manager will attempt to address the complaint as he or she deems appropriate, up to and including a reasonable reimbursement for damaged clothing. Any injury to customers will be reported to our insurance carrier for disposition.

Ancillary Services

Requests for ancillary services by customers will be handled by attendants as a priority above routine activities such as cleaning, restocking vending machines, and running drop-off loads. Ancillary services include assistance with loading and unloading customers' cars, moving loads to dryers during customers' absence, helping remove spots for customers, and other such small, short-duration services as may be requested by customers. Any perception that regular customers are taking advantage of these additional services to the detriment of the attendants' abilities to complete their assigned duties will be reported to management.

Key Terms

One of the most misunderstood terms in the business vocabulary is *quality*.

Quality Definition 1: Quality is the sum of all attributes of a product or service that together make up that product's or service's ability to solve the customer's problem. Under this definition, the better the thing is, the better is its quality.

Example: A one-third pound, hand-formed, cooked-to-order hamburger costing $3.78 is a higher quality product than a one-quarter pound MacDonald's hamburger costing $1.65. This is true because the bigger burger is more likely to satisfy the individual needs of the customers being served, since the burger is larger and it is cooked to order.

Quality Definition 2: Quality is a measure of the consistency with which a product or service item meets the standards by which the item is measured. By this definition, the more consistently the item meets its specifications, the higher is its quality.

Example: A one-quarter pound MacDonald's hamburger costing $1.65 is a higher quality product than a one-third pound, hand-formed, cooked-to-order hamburger costing $3.78. The reason, under this definition of quality, is that the fast-food burger is carefully controlled and all of them are the same (or very nearly the same), while the greater variability of the hand-made burger is almost assured by the process used.

Do not become confused as to which definition of quality you are using. When presenting a plan to control quality, the second definition of quality is the only relevant definition: *Quality is the degree to which your offering meets your standards.*

Continuing our example of Lawn Pro, Inc., we begin the marketing strategy section with a discussion of the product dimension, including a detailed description of our offering and our customer service policies and, finally, presenting our plan for managing quality.

LAWN PRO, INC.
MARKETING STRATEGY

PRODUCT

Mowing/Trimming. Lawn Pro will offer residential lawn care services directly to homeowners. We will offer mowing/trimming services on a seasonal contract basis or on an as-called basis. Lawn Pro crews will mow, edge, and clean up after each job, carrying away all waste. Contract customers will be automatically scheduled for mowings. As-called customers will be scheduled on a first-come-first-served basis, with the goal to serve all these customers within a maximum of three days of their request. (A detailed service protocol is presented in Appendix M.)

Chemical Maintenance. In addition to mowing/trimming, we will also offer chemical maintenance via annual contract or on an as-called basis. Chemical services include liquid fertilizer applications, weed prevention, and weed grasses management. All chemical applications will be accompanied by literature explaining exactly what chemicals were applied, what precautions the homeowner should take, and the reasons for each chemical. A schedule of all chemical applications will be delivered to the homeowner annually and revised as needed to meet the local conditions of that lawn. (A detailed service protocol is presented in Appendix M.)

Customer Service. Three dimensions of customer service will be explicitly managed: intrusiveness, recognition, and ancillary services.

Mowing a lawn is necessarily a very intrusive activity. Pets must be put away, the lawn toys must be cleared, children and adults need to be kept out of the mowing area, and the noise level is quite high, potentially disturbing resting babies and others. Accordingly, we will take a three-step approach in scheduling services. First, during the initial contract signing or phone scheduling session, we will obtain a preferred time of day for services to be performed. Second, the day before the mowing is scheduled, we will call to verify the time we will be there to alert the homeowners and to give them and us time to reschedule if our planned time is not convenient. Third, when we arrive, the crew leader will announce the crew's arrival to the home occupants and verify that now is a convenient time to mow. Our policy is that all preferred times of service will be honored insofar as is possible. If a conflict arises, the field rep will be called immediately and he/she will resolve the conflict.

Most people like the sound of their own name. Our policy will be for our field reps to "make a friend of every customer." All field reps will be responsible for the initial sale of each contract in their area and for the subsequent monitoring of the contracts. Each rep will be expected to learn the names of all customers, as well as a bit about them personally, such as children's and pet's names, etc. Time will be allotted for short visits with customers to allow ample opportunity for the customers to become comfortable enough to freely discuss any problems they may have with the services of Lawn Pro. Of course, any problems which surface will be dealt with expeditiously by the field rep or the general manager.

Small, short-duration, ancillary services that are not covered by contract, such as carrying home trash to the curb, tossing the newspaper onto the porch, trimming off a broken limb, removing toys and furniture from the yard and returning them after mowing, and other such small services as may be requested will be budgeted for in the time estimates for the jobs scheduled. Such services offer Lawn Pro an opportunity to improve the customer's perception of value. We will always willingly, cheerfully perform such ancillary services insofar as we can possibly accommodate our customers' requests. No charge will ever be levied for such minor additional services. Should any customer abuse the privilege, the field rep will be called in to handle the potential problem.

Quality Control. Lawn Pro will adopt a total quality control perspective concerning all aspects of operations. Each procedure will be subjected to careful scrutiny in order to set appropriate standards for its performance. Every employee will be held personally responsible for the proper completion of work assigned in accordance with the work standards applicable. Any deviation from acceptable standards will be called immediately to the attention of the next supervisory level. Crew chiefs will be responsible for carefully checking all aspects of each service event against a specification sheet that will be maintained for each customer. Any deviation will be carefully investigated by the field rep and a full report made to the general manager as to the cause of the deviation. Corrections will be made at the systems level wherever possible to prevent reoccurrence of the problem.

Price

In the price portion of the marketing strategy section, you should clearly state what your pricing strategy is and then exactly what your pricing policy will be to effect that strategy. Elements of your pricing policy may include quantity discounts, sales events (fourth annual going-out-of-business sale!), loading tactics (methods used to get customers to stock up on your products), and premiums for special services.

LAWN PRO, INC.
MARKETING STRATEGY (continued)

PRICE

Lawn Pro will adopt the strategy of being recognized as the high quality lawn-care service in our trading area. Consistent with that image, we will charge prices that are equivalent to those charged by our highest priced significant local competitor (currently Greener Pastures, Inc.).

The methods for establishing a price for each customer are subject to the following pricing policy.

1. All mowing prices will be based on a time estimate for the job. This time estimate will be made by the field rep at the time of contract signing. The rate to be used for such a quote is currently $40 per estimated hour of service.

2. Seasonal contract customers will receive a 5 percent discount from the straight time estimate.

3. As-called customers will be charged the straight time estimated.

4. As-called customers requiring less than a 24-hour response time guarantee will be charged double the straight time estimated.

5. Chemical lawn maintenance contracts and as-called applications will be charged the current rates in effect by Weeds-R-Gone, our strategic ally.

6. Twice each year, the general manager will survey the competitors in the trading area to determine if any changes in the hourly rate is warranted.

Place

The place, or distribution, element of the marketing strategy calls for identification of the limits of your trading area, the exact address where your business will be located, and the methods you will use to deliver your offerings to your customers. In service businesses, especially, the timing of service delivery can often have important marketing implications.

As you devise your distribution strategy, be sure that you do not become *too* creative. Put your retail store in a retail location, not in a warehouse district. Plan to deliver meals at meal time. Plan to operate your business service company during hours that are normal for the type of service you provide. Creativity can be a gamble;

any deviation from the professional norm may either wreck your chances for success or give your new business just the right advantage to let you succeed beyond your wildest dreams. (We have never met an entrepreneur whose wildest dreams ever could be exceeded!) The rule for presenting any strategy that deviates from the norm is to present a thorough rationale for your creative new approach. Without compelling evidence or argument, the reader will seriously question any expectations of success you may present.

LAWN PRO, INC.
MARKETING STRATEGY (continued)

DISTRIBUTION STRATEGY (PLACE)

Lawn Pro, Inc., will be located in a warehouse or industrial area of Edmond, Oklahoma. The business needs a repair shop, a secure, sheltered equipment storage area, a sales office, and at least three additional offices to accommodate the managerial and support staff. A suitable location has been identified at 1024 S. Yukon Drive. This site is available at a price of $650 per month under a 5-year lease.

Lawn Pro will serve the retail trading area of Edmond, Oklahoma. (See map of geographic limits of the trading area in Appendix R.) Customers will not be sought outside this geographic area, but referred customers will be served outside this area if practical. Each such situation will be evaluated on an individual basis.

Service hours for Lawn Pro will be 6:30 A.M. to 3:00 P.M. Monday through Friday. During crunch times, additional crews will work from 3:30 P.M. to 9:00 P.M. as needed to meet the temporary demand necessitated by weather conditions. Emergency and as-called services may be performed during nonstandard service hours as needed to meet the needs of our customers.

Promotion

Finally, the promotion section of the marketing strategy presents your detailed plans for letting the world know who you are, what you offer, where you are, and why they should buy from you.

The promotional strategy is the portion of the marketing strategy in which cost is most crucial. The best means of estimating the cost of the promotional strategy is to develop a preliminary promotional plan. This promotional plan then guides the advertising activities to be performed upon launching the business and provides a budget for promotional expenditures. Although a comprehensive promotional plan can be quite complex, most small start-up businesses do not need such a plan. Just a few simple and effective promotional tactics are preferable.

As you devise your promotional plan, keep in mind the limitations of each promotional tactic.

The Power of Promotion

Advertising	**What It Is . . .**
	Any paid message carried by a communication medium, including newspaper, billboard, park bench, football stadium marquee, television, restaurant place mat, or radio
	What It Can Do . . .
	Increase name recognition
	Help potential customers find you
	Cause potential customers to call for more information
	Cause potential customers to visit your store
	Make customers feel good about their purchases
	. . . And What It Cannot Do
	Cause potential customers to buy (with a few exceptions)
	Deliver your message to those not looking for your offering
Sales Promotion	**What It Is . . .**
	Any paid promotional method that is not included as advertising or personal selling, such as coupons (which may be carried by an advertisement), dancing bears on a street corner carrying signs promoting your restaurant, pens with your business name on them, seminars used to promote consulting services, skywriting, search lights, in-store displays, red tag specials, and sales
	What It Can Do . . .
	Increase name recognition and reputation
	Help potential customers find you
	Cause potential customers to call for more information
	Cause potential customers to visit your store
	Cause potential customers to buy (and even buy more than they intended)
	Make customers feel good about their purchases
	Deliver your message to those not looking for your offering
	. . . And What It Cannot Do
	Limited only by your imagination
Personal Selling	**What It Is . . .**
	Any use of a paid person whose job it is to interact directly with potential customers. This category includes active telemarketing (you call prospects), passive telemarketing (potential customers responding to advertising call you for information), in-store sales ("May I help you, ma'am?"), door-to-door sales (*ding-dong.* "Howdy sir! May I take just a minute of your time . . ."), party plan sales, and counter sales ("Would you like fries with that?")
	What It Can Do . . .
	Increase name recognition and reputation
	Cause potential customers to visit your store
	Cause potential customers to let you visit their home or office
	Cause potential customers to buy (and even buy more than they intended)
	Make customers feel good about their purchases
	Deliver your message to those not looking for your offering
	. . . And What It Cannot Do
	Deliver your message to a widely dispersed market
Publicity	**What It Is . . .**
	Any voluntary mention made of your business in any medium, at no cost to you; examples include announcements of employee hirings, stories in the local newspaper concerning your company's sponsorship of a

drug awareness program, and articles on some innovative aspect of
your business
What It Can Do . . .
Increase name recognition and increase reputation
Increase name recognition and *decrease* reputation
Cause potential customers to visit your store
Cause potential customers to buy
Make customers feel good about their purchases
. . . And What It Cannot Do
Deliver *your* message precisely
Target your message to your market
Deliver your message precisely when you want

The promotional plan should include an array of tactics that take customers "by the hand" and leading them step by step to the actual purchase of your product, and then even farther. After the customer has made a purchase, promotional tactics should be used that will insure customers will feel good about their purchase. This last step, so often omitted by novice business planners, can make all the difference in your profit levels. Happy customers come back for more, and just as important, they refer their friends.

Unless you have good reason to believe otherwise, you should assume you are starting with complete strangers. Your first "sale" in most retail businesses will be to get potential customers to visit (or let you visit them.) Usually the tactic of choice is advertising or active telemarketing. If advertising is used to generate telephone inquiries, the next logical tactic is passive telemarketing. This means the person who answers the phone must be trained to sell callers on making the visit. Once the visit occurs, you may use a range of tactics to make the sale, including displays of products (as in a grocery store), counter sales people (as in an auto parts or fast-food store), or direct sales contacts (as in an auto dealership or clothing store).

In other kinds of businesses such as manufacturing, wholesale, or business services, the first "sale" will typically be to let your sales person call on the prospect. Once the appointment has been generated, the sales professional is dispatched to execute the sales process appropriate to the offering.

Lawn Pro's product offering is a seasonal mowing/trimming contract and a separate contract for chemical maintenance. These are large sales, so they can bear the high cost of a personal selling effort. To get the opportunity to make the pitch to the homeowner, Lawn Pro will need to set appointments. This is a separate "sale" that must be made first. To support both the first "sale" (an appointment for a sales call) and the sale of the contracts for services, Lawn Pro must provide skeptical homeowners with evidence of the firm's integrity, honesty, and professionalism. Once the sale of the contracts for service has been made, Lawn Pro must continue to communicate with customers to insure their continued satisfaction with the services performed.

Merely possessing the vision of the plan in your head is not sufficient. You must also present your vision clearly so that no part of it is left unseen by the reader. As previously stated, a common failing we all have is to assume our readers are capable of the same leaps of logic we have performed during the development of our plan. Remember to include all of the steps necessary to lead the reader to the same conclusion you have so painstakingly reached.

LAWN PRO, INC.
MARKETING STRATEGY (continued)

PROMOTION

The promotional strategy of Lawn Pro is to focus on our market within strategi- cally chosen, small geographic areas (1–3 subdivisions), one at a time, to insure adequate density of customers, thereby increasing our productivity by minimiz- ing travel time between customers.

Accordingly, we will use a combination of promotional brochures distrib- uted door-to-door with follow-up active telemarketing, using a *Criss Cross Di- rectory* to set appointments for a field rep to make home visits. Field reps will then use personal selling tactics to secure the sale of seasonal contracts, or, fail- ing that, to leave promotional literature encouraging the use of our as-called services. In order to control the geographic distribution of our customers as much as possible, we will not advertise.

As an inducement to sign a seasonal contract, we will offer an initial scalp- ing for the same price as a regular mowing (usually three times the cost) and a performance guarantee stating that the seasonal contract can be canceled at any time should the homeowner become dissatisfied for any reason.

Our selling efforts will begin during the first week of January and will con- tinue until we have secured a sufficient number of seasonal contracts to meet our sales objective, or until the end of May. The normal attrition of customers will be made up by customer referrals and, where necessary, additional sales ef- forts by field reps who will approach the neighbors as the opportunities arise.

In addition to the seasonal sales period, field reps will continue to offer our chemical maintenance services as the opportunity arises during their regu- lar contacts with customers.

A complete promotional plan is shown in Appendix N. The projected cost of the plan is $15,460. This includes the commissions paid to field reps for secur- ing contracts, commissions paid to telemarketers for setting appointments, and the cost of brochures and other promotional literature.

Operations Plan

Conceptually, at least, the operations plan is the easiest part of the business plan for most people to create. Here you will develop your plans for managing most of the costs in your business. Generally you will need to include a human resources plan, an inventory plan, and a set of procedures to be followed by employees. This section also includes the specific design and layout of facilities; a comprehensive list of equipment, furniture, fixtures, and refurbishments needed for the building identified as the home of the proposed business; and plans for a management information system. Your man- agement information system should include procedures for bookkeeping, billing and collections, cash management procedures, monthly financial statements and budget reports preparation, customer account records management, sales statistics genera- tion and analysis, employee training management, and annual strategic plan review.

This sounds like a plate full of work, but lots of help is readily available for every item on the list. As the business plan writer, you do not have to become an expert in facilities design, equipment selection, redecorating, accounting, and training, as the above list might suggest. All you have to do is marshal the resources to do the job. The first job is to be sure you have addressed all the relevant areas of your business. This is the assurance the business plan reader will require: that you have demonstrated your competence to manage the business by identifying all of the critical areas that must be addressed, then by addressing each in a reasonably competent manner.

The key to showing your competence as a manager is to acknowledge your weaknesses by incorporating the expertise of others where you do not know enough to go it alone. As you read through the Lawn Pro, Inc., operations plan, notice how much of the information has been generated by outside consultants. The integration of the reports obtained from outside experts requires mainly common sense rather than any special expertise.

LAWN PRO, INC.
OPERATIONS PLAN

Lawn Pro operations will consist of three distinctly different phases throughout the year. During the off-season, from mid-October through mid-March, we will have no regular crews. What little mowing/trimming we may need to do will be handled by one part-time crew, which we will maintain on an as-needed basis. During the first portion of the off-season, from October through November, we will maintain a minimum staff, including the office personnel and the field reps. Activities will be limited mainly to training, analysis, and planning for the next year. The offices will be closed during the month of December.

During the second half of the off-season, activities will consist mainly of sales and sales support efforts. Field reps will distribute brochures, a temporary telemarketing crew will set sales appointments, and the field rep(s) will call on potential customers to secure sales. The office staff will be engaged mainly in fielding telephone inquiries. They will use passive telemarketing techniques to set sales appointments from these calls.

About two weeks earlier than the grass begins to grow (to allow time for scalping operations), mowing/trimming crews will begin their work. We will staff all crews by the first week in March. All employees who regularly make contact with customers will be outfitted with uniforms and trained prior to the beginning of the season.

We will schedule all seasonal contract customers into a regular sequence. Weather conditions will determine when the sequence needs to begin, and at that time our customers will receive mowing/trimming services in turn. If we place those who water regularly in a sequence separate from those who rely on rainfall, each customer should experience very nearly the same time period between mowings. Our standards for mowing height will be set at the time the con tract is signed, and we will normally cut the lawn when it has grown from 1'' to 2'' above the desired height.

Crews consisting of one crew leader and either one or two assistants will be organized into teams of three crews. Each team will be dispatched and managed by a field rep. Each team is expected to handle 240 customers on contract. This assumes a 10-day mowing cycle and 8 jobs per day per crew. During year one operations, the general manager will perform the role of field rep, with approximately one field rep added each year through year three. Two field reps will be added in year two to allow the general manager to move out of the field rep position.

Field reps will organize the work of all team members each day, then handle problems as they come up during the work day. The field rep will make routine follow-up calls to all customers to insure satisfaction with the crews' service performance. As time permits, the field rep will pay short visits to customers to reinforce a personalized service image and visit with their neighbors, as the opportunities present themselves, for the purpose of gaining additional business.

Chemical maintenance services will be handled entirely by the Weeds-R-Gone organization; however, each chemical application will be authorized by the field rep prior to application, and the field rep will call on the customer following the application to insure satisfactory service and adherence to established protocols (see Appendix O for chemical application protocols.)

All services will be billed monthly, with payment due to us within 10 days of billing date. All employees will be paid weekly, and billings from Weeds-R-Gone will be paid by us monthly, with 30 days credit.

Human Resources. Lawn Pro, Inc., will employee 14 people during the first year of operations: 1 general manager/marketing director, 1 operations manager, 1 office manager, 5 crew chiefs, and 6 crew assistants. In year two we will add 2 field reps, 3 crew chiefs, and 5 crew assistants. In year three we will add one more office assistant and two additional teams consisting of 1 field rep, 3 crew chiefs, and 4 crew assistants each. By the end of year three we will have a total of 40 employees. See Appendix S for detailed job descriptions and for employee specifications.

To reinforce the total quality concept, every Lawn Pro employee, from general manager through the office assistant will be required to obtain field experience, working as a crew member for at least one day. This experience will help employees to visualize the work we do for our customers and the conditions under which our teams must do their work. Such a perspective will help insure good decisions throughout the Lawn Pro organization, and help us to remain focused on the needs of our customers.

Team members will each receive at least three days of training each year, just prior to the start of the season, or as needed for new hires during the season. The field reps will be responsible for the delivery of training under the supervision of the operations manager.

Pay for team members will be incentive-based to allow each member the maximum income economic conditions will allow. A significant portion of the team members' pay will be awarded in the form of a seasonal bonus. All seasonal bonuses will be forfeited by employees who do not complete the season for any reason other than a work-related injury. Pay will be based entirely on production, with extra pay for work exceeding a standard day.

Field reps will receive a base salary with additional compensation opportunities in the form of sales commissions and a percentage of all work done by their team members. All nonoperations personnel will be placed on a salary, with compensation for overtime when required.

The total cost of labor is projected to be $209,000 in year one, increasing to $342,500 in year two, and $446,000 in year three. See detailed computations in Appendix T.

Equipment. Our operations plans have been reviewed with Johnson Industrial Supply of Oklahoma City, an old-line supplier of commercial lawn mowing equipment. We have adopted their recommendations with few modifications.

Each field rep will be equipped with a pickup, notebook computer, and cellular telephone, at a cost of $22,000. Each crew will be fully equipped with all of the tools required to do the work assigned. The basic equipment for each crew will include a ½ ton pickup with a trailer, 48" and 24" commercial self-propelled walk-behind mowers, gasoline-powered edgers and string trimmers, power blowers and vacuums, and miscellaneous other tools as may be deemed necessary by operations management. The cost of the equipment recommended by Johnson Industrial Supply will be $25,100 per crew. All of this equipment is expected to have a useful life of three years. See complete list of equipment in Appendix U.

One duplicate set of equipment, including a truck and trailer, will be obtained to help minimize downtime. All equipment maintenance will be performed under contracts for outside services with local shops. The cost of maintenance has been estimated at $23,600 per team per year. See detailed computations of maintenance costs in Appendix U.

Office equipment, including three networked computers, office furniture, telephones, a copier, fax, and cellular phones will cost an additional $31,400. Our choices of equipment and furniture were informed by Smith and Smith, Ltd., a full-line office supply company. In reviewing our operations plans, Smith recommended the office equipment listed above. This equipment is expected to have a useful life of 5 years. See detailed list of office equipment in Appendix U.

Organizational Structure

In this section the business planner presents the legal structure, rather than the administrative or functional structure of the firm. There are three general choices of legal form. If the firm is to be owned by a single individual, the firm will become a *sole proprietorship* by default, unless the owner formally chooses another alternative. If the firm is to be owned by more than a single individual, the firm will become a *partnership* by default, unless the owners formally choose to constitute the firm as a *corporation*. Many business authors present the alternative forms of ownership dispassionately, discussing the pros and cons of each, leaving the decision entirely up to the owner. Even though these authors are theoretically correct—there are pros and cons to each form of ownership—the important thing to know is that both default forms of ownership are flawed and should be avoided in every case possible. The critical flaw is that all of the owners' personal possessions are jeopardized by possible business losses in sole proprietorships as well as in partnerships. This weakness is sufficient reason to always select the corporate form. Sophisticated business professionals know this, so business planners should always choose to form a corporation in order to impress the reader of the plan with their foresight and business acumen.

Risk Management

This section of your plan is an excellent place to address the issue of risk management. All businesses are subject to a variety of risks, which must be managed if the business is to earn the trust of lenders and investors. Be sure to tell the reader exactly how you will address this important issue. Risk can be managed in three distinct ways, as follows:

Loss prevention strategies consist of those actions which prevent a deleterious event from occurring.

Examples:
— Shirley Jones has decided to install nonflammable materials throughout her day care center to prevent fires from occurring.
— Bob Lawrence will subject every employee in his furniture moving business to training in proper lifting techniques to help prevent back injuries to employees while on the job.

Loss reduction strategies mitigate the amount of the loss, though they do nothing to prevent the loss from occurring.

Examples:
— Sammie Brennan will install sprinklers in her tee shirt manufacturing facility to reduce the damage that a fire may cause.
— Fred Willis has installed an emergency eye-wash system in his auto shop and trained employees to use it if they should get acid in their eyes during battery recharging operations. This procedure should minimize the severity of injuries that might occur.

Loss sharing strategies consist mainly of buying insurance coverage. Insurance companies charge premiums that are sufficient to reimburse them for all losses they cover for their customers, plus a premium to cover their administrative overhead and a profit. The effect of this strategy is that losses by an individual firm are shared by all of the firms covered by a class of policy.

Examples:

—Rico Hernandez plans to buy a $1 million liability policy to cover damages to customers' persons and property. This policy will pay for all losses Rico incurs beyond the $5,000 deductible stipulated in the policy.

—Sheila Perot will buy a casualty policy to cover all of her clothing store inventory, equipment, and fixtures for losses due to *fire, storm, and theft.*

In the Lawn Pro, Inc., business plan section that follows, can you identify the three kinds of risk management strategies?

LAWN PRO, INC.
ORGANIZATIONAL PLAN

Lawn Pro will be constituted as an Oklahoma Limited Liability Company. This is a special form of corporation that automatically offers limited liability of all stockholders, the same tax treatment as offered under the S Corporation provisions of the IRS tax code, while eliminating the limitations on the number of stockholders that are allowed. The cost of forming the corporation will be $750, and annual costs related to the corporation filings and taxes are estimated to be $250, according to Jones & Adamack, our chosen legal firm. See Appendix V for articles of incorporation and bylaws.

RISK MANAGEMENT

The primary risk events to be addressed in the Lawn Pro, Inc., organization are injuries to employees and customers, damage to customers' property, damage to Lawn Pro's property, and lost income due to business interruptions.

Employee and customer injuries, as well as damage to customers' property and damage/loss of Lawn Pro equipment, will be managed through a combination of training, operational rules enforcement, equipment maintenance, and insurance coverage. Insurance is expected to cost a total of $4,863 per year. See Appendix X for details of the insurance coverage. See Appendix T for rules of operation included in the service protocols that are designed to insure safe operations.

Income loss due to business interruptions will be addressed through maintenance of sufficient reserves (equal to 10 percent of annual operating cash requirements). These will be accumulated as soon as is practical in order to provide capital that may be needed to purchase replacement equipment as required. This will enable Lawn Pro to continue operations while insurance claims are being processed.

We will also obtain a business interruption policy at a cost of $860 per year. Details of this policy are included in Appendix X.

Financial Statements for the Business Plan

Of all the parts of the business plan, financial statements seem to cause students the greatest grief. The difficulty lies with the student's lack of knowledge of accounting procedures and a seemingly general aversion to numbers. Like it or not, though, you have been assigned a business plan, and no business plan is complete without a set of pro forma financial statements. In this section, we will attempt to show how the different kinds of financial statements interrelate and give some tips for succeeding at building the financial statements you need. If you know nothing about accounting, you may need some outside assistance (say, from your professor) in completing this portion of the business plan. The good news for your future life as a business professional is that outside assistance is readily available from your local CPA or even from the local Small Business Development Center, a program run by the Small Business Administration offering free services. The bad news is that as a student you will probably be required to build the financial statements yourself.

All business plans should include income statements, cashflow statements, and balance sheets.

- *Income statements* (also known as *profit and loss statements or P & Ls*) show how much *revenue* or income the business receives and how much *expense* the business incurs during the accounting period (month, quarter, or year). The statement is set up so that expenses are subtracted from revenues to produce the amount of *profit*. Income statements show the amount of all sales, even if the customer has not yet paid for his purchases. Income statements also show the amount of all expenses, even if the expense item (such as inventory) has not yet been paid for.

- *Cashflow statements* show the actual amount of cash that the company receives and the actual amount of cash that the company pays out during the accounting period (month, quarter, or year).

- *Balance sheets* show the value of the things the company owns, the amounts the company owes, and the difference between them, which is referred to as *equity*.

Financial statements must be prepared in a specific order; first the income statement, next the cashflow statement, and finally the balance sheet. Information on the cashflow statement comes from the income statement, and information on the balance sheet comes from the other two statements. The diagram on p. 255 shows these relationships.

In the business plan, you need to include projected financial statements for the first, second, and third years, as a minimum. Some professors may even ask for the first five years, but three years is more common. Since these financial statements are predictions of the future, they are of necessity based on numerous guesses—informed guesses (we hope!), but guesses nonetheless. Accordingly, a common practice is to provide more detail for the first year than for the last. Using this approach, then (unless otherwise instructed), you should provide income and cashflow statements for every month of the first year, then quarterly statements for year two, and just annual statements for year three. Add to these statements four balance sheets—one for the point in time at which you first begin operations (that is, just before your first sale), then one for the end of each of the first three years of operations—and you are almost finished.

		LAWN PRO, INC. PRO FORMA INCOME STATEMENT			
	1997				
	Jan	*Feb*	*Mar*	*Apr*	*May*
Income					
1 Mowing/Trimming	0	0	32,430	48,645	48,645
2 Chemical Services	0	0	966	966	966
3 **Total Sales**	0	0	33,396	49,611	49,611
4 **Expenses**					
5 Administrative Salaries	6,667	6,667	6,667	6,667	6,667
6 Labor	0	0	6,900	10,350	10,350
7 Seasonal Bonuses	0	0	2,760	4,140	4,140
8 Sales Commissions	2,095	2,095	2,416	826	826
9 Payroll Tax & Insurance	2,190	2,190	4,686	5,496	5,496
10 Fuel	0	0	1,380	2,070	2,070
11 Equipment Maint.	1,000	1,000	1,000	1,000	1,000
12 Supplies	0	0	690	1,035	1,035
13 Rent and Utilities	850	850	850	850	850
14 Insurance	117	117	117	117	117
15 Office Supplies	50	50	50	50	50
16 Depreciation	4,969	4,969	4,969	4,969	4,969
17 Interest	2,965	2,881	2,796	2,711	2,626
18 **Total Expenses**	20,904	20,819	35,281	40,281	40,196
19 **Net Income Before Tax**	−20,904	−20,819	−1,885	9,330	9,415

FOR THE YEAR ENDED 12/31/1997

Jun	July	Aug	Sep	Oct	Nov	Dec	Total
48,645	48,645	32,430	32,430	16,215	16,215	0	324,300
966	966	966	966	966	966	966	9,660
49,611	49,611	33,396	33,396	17,181	17,181	966	333,960
6,667	6,667	6,667	6,667	6,667	6,667	6,667	80,000
10,350	10,350	6,900	6,900	3,450	3,450	0	69,000
4,140	4,140	2,760	2,760	1,380	1,380	0	27,600
826	826	583	583	340	340	97	11,854
5,496	5,496	4,227	4,227	2,959	2,959	1,691	47,114
2,070	2,070	1,380	1,380	690	690	0	13,800
1,000	1,000	1,000	1,000	1,000	1,000	1,000	12,000
1,035	1,035	690	690	345	345	0	6,900
850	850	850	850	850	850	850	10,200
117	117	117	117	117	117	117	1,400
50	50	50	50	50	50	50	600
4,969	4,969	4,969	4,969	4,969	4,969	4,969	59,633
2,542	2,457	2,372	2,288	2,203	2,118	2,033	29,992
40,111	40,027	32,565	32,481	25,020	24,935	17,474	370,093
9,500	9,584	831	915	−7,839	−7,754	−16,508	−36,133

		LAWN PRO, INC. PRO FORMA CASHFLOW STATEMENT				
		1997				
		Jan	Feb	Mar	Apr	May
Sources of Cash						
20 Loans	280,000					
21 Owner's Investment						
22 Collections of A/R—Mowing		0	0	0	32,430	48,645
23 Collections of A/R—Chem			0	0	966	966
24 **Total Sources of Cash**	280,000	0	0	0	33,396	49,611
Uses of Cash						
Start-Up Costs:						
25 Crew Equipment	125,500					
26 Field Rep Equipment	22,000					
27 Office Equipment	31,400					
28 Leasehold & Utility Deposits	850					
29 Printing	650					
On-Going Costs:						
30 Monthly Operating Expenses	0	15,934	15,850	30,311	35,311	35,227
31 Loan Principal Repayment		7,778	7,778	7,778	7,778	7,778
32 **Total Uses of Cash**	180,400	23,712	23,627	38,089	43,089	43,005
33 Net Cashflow This Period	99,600	−23,712	−23,627	−38,089	−9,693	6,606
34 Cumulative Cash Position	99,600	75,888	52,261	14,172	4,478	11,085

FOR THE YEAR ENDED 12/31/1997

Jun	July	Aug	Sep	Oct	Nov	Dec	Total
							280,000
							0
48,645	48,645	48,645	32,430	32,430	16,215	16,215	324,300
966	966	966	966	966	966	966	8,894
49,611	49,611	49,611	33,396	33,396	17,181	17,181	612,994
							125,500
							22,000
							31,400
							850
							650
35,142	35,057	27,596	27,511	20,050	19,965	12,504	310,459
7,778	7,778	7,778	7,778	7,778	7,778	7,778	93,333
42,920	43,835	35,374	35,289	27,828	27,743	20,282	584,193
6,691	6,776	14,237	−1,893	5,568	−10,562	−3,101	28,801
17,776	24,552	38,789	36,896	42,464	31,902	28,801	

LAWN PRO, INC.
PRO FORMA INCOME STATEMENT
FOR THE YEARS ENDED 12/31/1998, 1999

	1998					1999
	Jan-Mar	Apr-Jun	Jul-Sep	Oct-Dec	Total	Jan-Dec
Income						
1 Mowing/Trimming	64,860	291,870	259,440	32,430	648,600	972,900
2 Chemical Services	5,796	5,796	5,796	5,796	23,184	34,776
3 **Total Sales**	70,656	297,666	265,236	38,226	671,784	1,007,676
4 **Expenses**						
5 Administrative Salaries	33,750	33,750	33,750	33,750	135,000	155,000
6 Labor	13,800	62,100	55,200	6,900	138,000	207,000
7 Seasonal Bonuses	5,520	24,840	22,080	2,760	55,200	82,800
8 Sales Commissions	3,105	9,915	8,942	2,132	24,095	36,142
9 Payroll Tax & Insurance	14,044	32,651	29,993	11,386	88,074	120,236
10 Fuel	2,760	12,420	11,040	1,380	27,600	41,400
11 Equipment Maint.	6,000	6,000	6,000	6,000	24,000	36,000
12 Supplies	1,380	6,210	5,520	690	13,800	13,800
13 Rent and Utilities	850	850	850	850	3,400	3,400
14 Insurance	550	550	550	550	2,200	2,800
15 Office Supplies	200	200	200	200	800	1,200
16 Depreciation	27,200	27,200	27,200	27,200	108,800	157,967
17 Interest	10,755	9,500	8,245	6,990	35,490	24,960
18 **Total Expenses**	119,914	226,187	209,571	100,788	656,459	882,704
19 **Net Income Before Tax**	−49,258	71,479	55,666	−62,562	15,326	124,972

As you prepare the financial statements, you must also write a set of *line explanations* for the income and cashflow statements. Line explanations are just what you might expect from the title: explanations of exactly how you arrived at the numbers appearing on that line in the financial statements. A common mistake is to provide incomplete explanations for how you computed the numbers in the financial statements, or worse, to provide no explanations at all. Experienced business professionals often read the financial statements right after they read the executive summary. These folks do not have a full understanding of your plan in all of its glory, so you must help them understand exactly where you came up with each and every number. Failing to answer all of the likely questions will leave your reader unsatisfied. If the level of dissatisfaction is too great, you

	1998					1999
	Jan-Mar	*Apr-Jun*	*Jul-Sep*	*Oct-Dec*	*Total*	*Jan-Dec*

LAWN PRO, INC.
PRO FORMA CASHFLOW STATEMENT
FOR THE YEARS ENDED 12/31/1998, 1999

Sources of Cash

	Jan-Mar	Apr-Jun	Jul-Sep	Oct-Dec	Total	Jan-Dec
20 Loans	197,000				197,000	
21 Owner's Investment						
22 Collections of A/R—Mowing	64,860	291,870	259,440	32,430	648,600	972,900
23 Collections of A/R—Chem	5,796	5,796	5,796	5,796	23,184	34,776
24 **Total Sources of Cash**	267,656	297,666	265,236	38,226	868,784	1,007,676

Uses of Cash

	Jan-Mar	Apr-Jun	Jul-Sep	Oct-Dec	Total	Jan-Dec
Start-Up Costs:						
25 Crew Equipment	125,500				125,500	125,500
26 Field Rep Equipment	22,000				22,000	22,000
27 Office Equipment						
28 Leasehold & Utility Deposits						
29 Printing						
On-Going Costs:						
30 Monthly Operating Expenses	92,714	198,987	182,371	73,588	547,659	724,738
31 Loan Principal Repayment	39,750	39,750	39,750	39,750	159,000	93,333
32 **Total Uses of Cash**	279,964	238,737	222,121	113,338	854,159	965,571
33 Net Cashflow This Period	−12,308	58,929	43,116	−75,112	14,626	42,105
34 Cumulative Cash Position	16,494	75,423	118,538	43,427		85,532

LAWN PRO, INC.
PRO FORMA BALANCE SHEETS

	Pre-Startup	Dec 31, 1997	Dec 31, 1998	Dec 31, 1999
Assets				
Cash	99,600	28,801	43,427	85,532
Accounts Receivable		966	966	966
Equipment	178,900	178,900	326,400	473,900
Accumulated Depreciaton		−59,633	−168,433	−326,400
Deposits	1,500	1,500	1,500	1,500
Total Assets	280,000	150,534	203,859	235,498
Liabilities and Equity				
Loan 1	180,000	120,000	191,333	131,333
Loan 2	100,000	66,667	33,333	0
Retained Earnings		−36,133	−20,807	104,164
Total Liabilites and Equity	280,000	150,534	203,859	235,498

LAWN PRO, INC.
FINANCIAL STATEMENTS LINE EXPLANATIONS

1. Mowing/trimming revenue is computed from the sales forecast presented in the Marketing Analysis section of this plan. Detailed computations are based on the number of mowings typical of each month, the number of contracts in force, and a price of $47 per hour per crew. See detailed computations in Appendix A.

2 Chemical services revenue consists entirely of a 30% commission paid to Lawn Pro by Weeds-R-Gone under an agreement (see discussion in the description of Business section). The number of contracts is estimated at 20% of the mowing/trimming contracts obtained. Chemical services revenue is computed as all chemical contracts in force at $14 per application, yielding $966 per month in year one, beginning in month three, to allow time for initial sales of contracts (69 contracts x $14 = 966). For year two the assumption is $5,796 per quarter (138 contracts × $14 × 3 months). The year three statement shows a total of $34,776 (207 contracts × $14 × 12 months).

3. Total Sales = line 1 + line 2.

4. Heading only.

5. Administrative salaries includes salaries for management and office employees as shown in the table below:

Employee Title (No. of Empl.)	Pay Rate	Expense Amount
Year 1		
General Mgr (1)	$ 40,000	40,000
Operations Mgr (1)	40,000	40,000
Total	**80,000**	
Year 2		
General Mgr (1)	40,000	40,000
Operations Mgr (1)	40,000	40,000
Office Mgr (1)	15,000	15,000
Field Rep (2)	40,000	40,000
Total	**$135,000**	
Year 3		
General Mgr (1)	40,000	40,000
Operations Mgr (1)	40,000	40,000
Office Mgr (1)	15,000	15,000
Field Rep (3)	20,000	60,000
Total	**$150,000**	

6. Labor expense is computed at the rate of $10 per hour of service. The distribution is $5.50 per crew chief and $4.50 per crew assistant.

7. Seasonal bonuses are additional payments to crew members for a total of $4 per hour of service, distributed at $2.50 per hour to the crew chief and $1.50 per hour to the crew assistant. These bonuses will be paid in a lump sum to employees during November only if the employees qualify by completing the season and not missing work more than a specified number of days.

8. Sales commissions are paid to temporary telemarketers and to field reps at a total rate of 3% of the value of the seasonal contract, ½ on signing of the seasonal contract and the balance on delivery of the services. The commission structure is the same for chemical contracts, except the rate is 20%.

9. Payroll tax and insurance includes FICA (7.65%), FUTA/SUTA (5.9%), and Workers' Compensation Insurance (11.45%). The total, 25.00%, is applied to the sum of administrative salary, labor, bonuses, and commissions.

10. Fuel is estimated at $2 per hour. An average mowing is assumed to take one hour for a crew.

11. Equipment maintenance is estimated at $12,000 per year per team. We plan to have one team in year one and add one team per year through year three.

12. Supplies are estimated at $1 per mowing.

13. Rent and utilities are expected to be an average of $850 per month, $600 per month rent plus an estimated $250 per month in utilities.

14. Insurance, per quote (see Appendix J), will grow from $1,400 in year one to $2,800 in year three.

15. Office supplies are estimated at $600 in year one, growing to $1,200 by year three.

(continued)

16. Depreciation is calculated straight-line, based on a 3-year life with no residual value.

17. Interest is computed at 12% on loan 1, which is a straight bank loan for the purchase of equipment. Interest on loan 2 includes 12% payable to the bank, plus 3% payable to the guarantor. Interest is computed monthly on the principal outstanding.

18. Total expenses are equal to lines 5 through 17.

19. Net income before tax is equal to line 3 minus line 18.

20. Loans indicate the amount borrowed (as a source of cash); initial loans total $280,000, and an additional loan is required during the first quarter of year two in the amount of $197,000. It should be noted that during year 1, principal of $93,333 will have been repaid.

21. Owner's investment is zero. The business will be fully funded through loans. See the Synopsis of the Proposal for details.

22 & 23. Collections of accounts receivable assume that all payments for services will be fully collected within 30 days of the date of service.

24. Total sources of cash is equal to the sum of lines 20 through 23.

25. Crew equipment is $125,500 per team. Beginning with one team in year one, one additional team each is added in years two and three.

26. Equipment for each field rep will cost $22,000. Beginning with one field rep in year one (position to be filled temporarily by the operations manager), we will have three field reps by year three, in addition to the general manager.

27. Office equipment sufficient to support operations through year three will cost $31,400.

28. Lease and utility deposits will cost $850.

29. Printing includes developing the needed promotional and administrative materials at a cost estimated at $650.

30. Monthly operating expenses are equal to just the cash portion of expenses; line 18 minus line 16.

31. Loan principal repayment is calculated at $\frac{1}{36}$th of the initial loan amount (per month).

32. Total uses of cash is equal to the sum of lines 25 through 31.

33. Net cashflow this period is equal to line 24 minus line 32.

34. Cumulative cash position is equal to the prior period cumulative cash position (line 34) plus the current period net cashflow (line 33). This represents the period's ending bank balance.

may receive a simple and abrupt rejection (or in class, a poor grade!), not because your plan is flawed, but tragically, because you failed to clearly present all your thinking so that potential investors or lenders could examine it to satisfy themselves that the plan has an acceptable level of risk.

The financial statements for our continuing Lawn Pro illustration include income and cashflow statements by month for year one, by quarter for year two, and by a simple total for year three. Balance sheets are presented for the day we open for

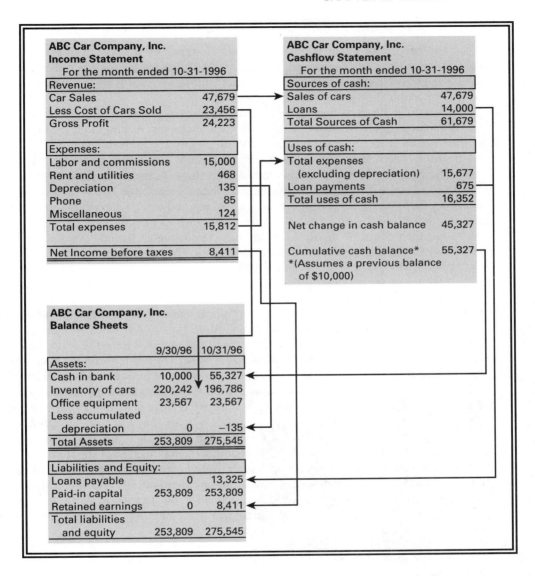

business, then for the end of each of the first three years of operations. Following the statements are the line explanations for the income and cashflow statements. The balance sheets do not get line explanations. The assumption is that the reader understands what a balance sheet is and so will know where all the numbers on your balance sheets came from. Of course, you must also know where all the numbers in the balance sheets come from, or it will not balance! In the next section, we will review the composition of the balance sheet.

To help you learn to write good line explanations, we have included with the complete set of financial statements, all of the proper line explanations for Lawn Pro. The words we used are not important; the concept of full and complete explanation of every number is.

The Three Types of Businesses

The preceding Lawn Pro, Inc., financial statements are fairly representative of service businesses. *Service businesses* offer to do things for customers rather than deliver things to customers. Examples besides our Lawn Pro business include barber shops, car repair shops, and consulting services.

Two other types of businesses are common among small businesses: merchandise and manufacturing. *Merchandise businesses* offer to customers things that the business itself buys elsewhere. Examples include dress shops, grocery stores, gas stations, and hardware stores. Merchandise businesses are broken down into two types: retail and wholesale. *Retail businesses* sell their merchandise to those (either individual businesses or other organizations) who plan to consume the items themselves rather than resell them to others. Examples include shoe stores, gas stations, and office supply businesses. *Wholesale* businesses sell their merchandise to businesses which plan to resell the items to others rather than consume the items themselves. This category includes shoe distributors, gasoline jobbers, and paper distribution companies. The latter three, all *wholesalers*, sell their products to the first three *retailers* who, in turn, sell to the end users: customers.

Manufacturing businesses create the items they sell, beginning with component parts or raw materials. Manufacturers may then sell their items directly to those who will consume the items (retail) or to other businesses which will then resell the items (wholesale.)

The most important difference in the three types of businesses (service, merchandise, and manufacturing) lies in the income statement. Where the service business simply shows the total revenue (broken down by separate categories such as mowing and chemical services as needed), the other two types of business must also show the related costs of the items sold. This cost is then subtracted from the sales revenue to arrive at a gross profit. Expenses are then subtracted from this gross profit to arrive at the income before taxes. This accounting process helps the reader to see quickly how potentially profitable each sale of a product can be. In merchandise businesses the item cost is called *cost of goods sold*. In manufacturing businesses the item cost is referred to as either the *manufacturing cost* or *manufacturing cost of goods sold* and includes both the cost of component parts and/or raw materials and the cost of labor that goes into the making of the items. Except for the treatment of the cost of the items offered for sale, the financial statements are essentially the same for all three kinds of businesses.

Balance Sheet Items

Using the Lawn Pro, Inc., illustration, we will explain some of the finer points of each line on the balance sheets in this section.

Cash

Information about cash comes from the cashflow statements you have already prepared. The pre-startup cash amount can be found on line 34 in the pre-startup column. Subsequent year-end cash amounts can be found in the last period column, on line 34.

Accounts Receivable

Accounts receivable is the amount of product or service you have sold but not yet collected. This must be zero in the pre-startup balance sheet, of course, and subsequently is equal to the difference between the amount collected (lines 22 + 23, total column) and the amount sold (line 3, total column). Accounts receivable accumulate from year to year, so if there is a difference between the amounts sold and collected in a given year, this difference is added to (or subtracted from, if negative) the accounts receivable amount in the previous year.

In the case of Lawn Pro, Inc., we have only a $966 accounts receivable balance because we have time after the close of the season to collect for all services performed except for the chemical services sold during the last month of the year. We used a simplifying assumption that this amount will not change during years two and three. As our number of chemical services increases to triple the initial amount, the accounts receivable will increase, too (to about $2,484). Since this is a minor amount, we decided not to make the statements any more complicated than they have to be; thus the assumption of static accounts receivable.

Philosophically, you need to understand that you are ultimately guessing about what will happen in the future. We hope our guesses are accurate, of course, but they are still guesses, so do not get overly concerned about precision. In our balance sheet we have $233,000 worth of assets. Changing the accounts receivable amount from $966 to $2,484 would make no appreciable difference.

Equipment

Equipment, and all other assets for that matter, are carried at historical cost (what you initially paid for the asset) on the balance sheet. The only time this amount will change is either when you get rid of a piece of equipment or when you buy some additional equipment, as we did in Lawn Pro, Inc.

Accumulated Depreciation

The sad fact is that all tangible assets decrease in value (that is, excluding land, which according to Will Rogers increases in value because "they aren't making any more"). To protect the integrity of the historical cost number, a contra-account called *accumulated depreciation* is established. The term contra means that the account's normal balance is the opposite of other accounts in the same classification. In this case, asset accounts usually have a positive balance, while the accummulated depreciation account (a *contra-account*) usually has a negative balance. The accumulated depreciation account contains the total depreciation expense that has accumulated over time since the assets were first purchased. When an asset is disposed of, its historical cost is removed from the asset account and its accumulated depreciation is removed from the accumulated depreciation account. In this way the net book value of tangible assets (excluding land) can be ascertained at any time by simply subtracting accumulated depreciation from the related asset account balances.

The keys to the accumulated depreciation entry in the balance sheet are the facts that (1) the amount is always negative, and (2) the amount accumulates over time. Each subsequent period's amount is based on the amount in the prior period to which is added the current period's depreciation expense (line 16 of the income statements.)

Deposits

Deposits are normally a static amount equal to the initial deposits required by the utility companies and the landlord. Unless deposits are refunded or additional deposits are required, as when you obtain additional phone services or open a new location, there should be no change in the deposits amount.

Loans

The loan balance shows how much the business owes at any time. Unlike the asset accounts, there is no effort to retain the integrity of the initial loan balances. (Plenty of paperwork exists to support that number if needed.) Accordingly, the loan balances fall as the loans are repaid and grow as new loans are obtained. The current period loan balance is determined by beginning with the prior period's amount and subtracting the principal repaid in the current period (line 31 on the cashflow statements).

If the business will use *trade credit,* that is, credit granted directly by vendors, then the balance sheet will also contain an item called *accounts payable.* A good conservative assumption is that you will not use trade credit. That way, if you should get into a tight cashflow period due to unanticipated events after you implement the business plan, you will be better able to survive the problem because you will not have already used this valuable source of credit.

Retained Earnings

Business plan writers often are confused by retained earnings, mainly because they do not grasp just what this account is. *Retained earnings* represents the sum total of all profits and losses made by the company from its date of inception through the date of the balance sheet, reduced by the amount of dividends (which are the earnings *not* retained). Since you will very likely retain all of your earnings during the business planning period (there will very probably be no dividends), you can readily compute retained earnings by taking the prior period amount and adding current period net income before tax (line 19 of the income statements) to it (or subtracting the loss).

One you have finished your balance sheets, you have completed the business plan. Congratulations!

Presentation of the Business Plan

Now you must complete your presentation of the plan by writing the three components which will be inserted in the front of all the sections just prepared: the synopsis of the proposal, the executive summary, and the description of the business. These three sections summarize what you have created—your business plan.

Synopsis of the Proposal

The *synopsis of the proposal* is a one-page summary of the important financial elements of the business plan, along with a statement of the capitalization strategy and the amount and terms of the investment and/or loan(s) being sought. This document, of necessity, is prepared after the other parts of the business plan are complete. How could it be otherwise? Because of the dual nature of the business planning process—part document preparation and part strategy development—the planner cannot even know how much money will be required until the planning process is complete.

The primary rules that govern this section are brevity, clarity, and flexibility. The synopsis should rarely be more than a single page, and it should contain a clear statement of the amount of funds being sought, their purpose, collateral and/or ownership offered, and the desired repayment terms. Here is the synopsis of the proposal for the Lawn Pro business plan:

LAWN PRO, INC.
PROPOSAL

Lawn Pro is a start-up company providing residential lawncare and lawn chemical maintenance services in the Edmond, Oklahoma, trading area. In its first full year of operations, to begin January 1, 1997, Lawn Pro is expected to generate $333,960 in first-year sales revenues, with a net loss of $39,083. By year three, the new company is expected to earn $127,372 net profit on sales of $1,007,676 for a 12.7% return on investment.

We require an initial capitalization of $280,000, of which $178,900 will be used to purchase vehicles and equipment. The balance of $101,100 will be used to cover working capital needs during the first six months of operations.

The principals will contribute real estate valued at $24,000 as collateral for a requested $180,000 loan, in addition to the collateral value of the vehicles and equipment purchased with the loan proceeds. Repayment over a five-year term, with monthly payments beginning three months after the date of the loan, are desired, but the attached business plan assumes a three-year payback, beginning immediately.

Co-signers are being sought to secure a second loan in the amount of $100,000. Co-signers will receive the following benefits:

- All loan payments will be made by Lawn Pro.
- Co-signers will receive interest on the outstanding loan balance each month at an annual rate of 3%.
- Co-signers will receive 40% of the net earnings of Lawn Pro, to be distributed annually in September, as long as any part of their co-signed loan remains un-paid.
- Co-signers will receive an option to purchase 10% ownership at the par value of the stock, and a first right of refusal on any offer to sell additional stock in Lawn Pro.

A Brief Note On Raising Money

The question often arises as to just exactly how a new business person can raise the money needed to begin a business. Those who ask this question do not understand the value of the business plan. Raising the money to capitalize a new business is actually quite simple. Once a *competently prepared* business plan has been developed, all the new business person has to do is to ask everyone who might have money to loan or to invest. Ask the family doctor, dentist, or tax preparer. Ask the banker, the CPA, the attorney, the neighbor, the professor at school, the potential vendors of the proposed business, the potential customers of the business. *Do not ask your relatives,* at least not those with whom you would like to remain friendly. If the proposed business is a good idea as for-mulated in the business plan, savvy investors will eagerly support it. If it is not a good idea, do you really want to involve your family?

If the new entrepreneur will follow this strategy, and if the business plan legitimately indicates a viable business opportunity, the money required will be quickly forthcoming. If, however, the business plan is flawed, either in form or substance, only a fool (or someone who loves you) would choose freely to invest, and the reality is that very few fools have any money to invest!

Executive Summary

The *executive summary* is not so much a summary as it is a complete mini-business plan. It must include all of the parts of the business plan, but in summary form. As in the case for the synopsis of the proposal, the executive summary should be brief, concise, and to the point. Leave elaboration to the body of the business plan, where readers can find it if they desire, but where it is out of the way of their obtaining a clear overview of the business plan.

In the example that follows, we have identified each part of the business plan in brackets as an aid to understanding. These notations should not be included in an actual executive summary. They are included here only as a reminder that you must include each part.

LAWN PRO, INC.
EXECUTIVE SUMMARY

[Description of the business]
Lawn Pro will provide mowing/trimming and chemical maintenance lawn-care services to residential homeowners in the Edmond, Oklahoma, trading area. We will offer annual "as-needed" contracts with monthly billing, or "when-called" services, on a space available basis.

[Marketing analysis]
Edmond is an affluent bedroom community of approximately 60,000 residents, over 90 percent of whom occupy their own single-family homes. Edmond now contains approximately 30,000 residences. The city is growing rapidly, with no end in sight. During the past five years, the population has increased by 7,000, and numerous new businesses have entered the market, suggesting that additional growth is expected.

In the Edmond area, several strong lawncare companies compete vigorously for commercial lawncare business, but there is little evidence that any of these businesses have chosen to pursue the residential market. Those who serve the homeowner are primarily small, one-crew, part-time individuals who work mainly on weekends, plus, of course, the teenagers in the neighborhoods. The primary customer perception of lawncare workers is that they are unreliable, ill-mannered, and sloppy. The risk of getting someone even worse seems to be the primary reason for keeping the service currently at hand, rather than any high level of satisfaction with workmanship.

Unlike the mowing and trimming services, the chemical lawn maintenance sector is well organized in addressing our target market of homeowners. Area firms are aggressive in obtaining annual contracts for these services, and customer loyalty is quite high.

As of 1995, the total size of the market for residential mowing and trimming services was estimated at 60,000 mowings for 3,000 customers, worth $3,000,000 at an average of $50 per mowing. The market for lawn chemicals was estimated at 1,500 annual contracts, worth $810,000 at an average of $540 per year.

Based on the strategies developed for Lawn Pro, our market share is projected to grow from a first year base of 11.5% to a maximum of 34.5% of the market by the end of our third year in business. These projections yield a sales forecast of $333,960 for year one, increasing to $1,007,676 by the end of year three.

[Marketing strategy]

Lawn Pro will present a professional alternative to the traditional sources of lawncare services. All Lawn Pro employees will wear uniforms identifying them as Lawn Pro team members. We will offer a full, no-questions-asked, money-back guarantee for all services performed. By using a field rep system of quality control and customer follow-up, we will insure that customers' expectations are always met or exceeded.

The possibility exists that one or more of the commercial enterprises might choose to compete with Lawn Pro once our success becomes evident. Our best defense will be strong customer satisfaction, and so this will be a crucial part of our marketing strategy.

Lawn Pro will form a strategic alliance with Weeds-R-Gone, Inc., a local firm, to provide fertilizing and weed control services under our lawncare contracts, while enabling Weeds-R-Gone to offer trimming services under their contracts, with Lawn Pro performing these services. We have negotiated a contract which will allow both companies to realize a 30% gross profit margin on the work performed by the ally company, while remaining competitive in pricing.

Lawncare, though quite fragmented, is a mature industry. Because of this, we conform to local competitive pricing, which we have determined to be about $40–60 per hour, depending on the service being performed.

Lawn Pro will use direct mail and personal selling promotional tactics to gain and to keep contract customers. These tactics will enable Lawn Pro to maintain an efficient operations strategy by enabling us to control the geographic limits of our expansion as well as our rate of growth. Most sales efforts will be focused on the decision period for our customers, that is, February through May.

(continued)

[Operations plans]

Work will be performed by fully-equipped, autonomous crews of two or three workers, loosely supervised by one field rep per team. Each team will consist of three to five crews. The field rep will perform dispatching, management, and quality control functions. Direct supervision will be provided by the crew leader. Year one sales projections will require one team made up of five crews. By the end of year three, four teams with a total of 14 crews will be required. All chemical maintenance services will be performed by Weeds-R-Gone under a reciprocal agreement discussed above.

Employee development will be encouraged through a set of policies that strongly reward initiative. Seasonal incentive bonuses will be used to reduce turnover during the critical growing season.

[Organization and risk management plans]

Lawn Pro will be constituted as an Oklahoma corporation. Standard insurance coverage will be obtained for ordinary casualty and liability losses. All employees will be covered by workers' compensation insurance, and all applicable OSHA regulation will be enforced as a means of protecting employees from job hazards. Equipment will be routinely maintained and inspected daily. Spare equipment will be made available to prevent the need to use equipment not in full working order.

[Financial projections and capitalization plan]

The projected third year profits of $127,372 justify the investment risk. Our strategy is to obtain all of the required capital in the form of two loans, one secured by equipment purchased plus the owner's real estate equity, the second secured by co-signature of one or more investor(s). Investors will receive a share of the business, a larger share of the profits during the period of loan repayment, and a risk premium interest payment.

The importance of this part of the business plan is often overlooked by novices. To see what the purpose of the executive summary is, you need to understand the order in which readers characteristically examine a business plan.

Unlike documents which may be read for enjoyment, business documents usually have as their primary purpose to deliver information and often, as in the case of the business plan, to elicit a desired response, such as a loan approval or a contribution of a requested investment amount. Accordingly, readers of a business plan, always busy people with no time to waste, usually begin by reading the synopsis of the proposal. This clearly tells the readers what you want of them. Next, if they are still interested, they may read the executive summary. Here they will be looking for the big picture: the overview of the proposed business. If your readers are still interested after reading your summary, their next stop may be any section of the plan, depending on their personal dispositions: marketing, financial statements, operations, or even the appendices. Numbers-oriented readers might go to the financial statements, where they are most comfortable, while marketing professionals might prefer to examine the details of the marketing strategies presented in the relevant sections of the business plan.

Only if the reader's questions are adequately addressed at each step in their reading will your plan continue to hold her attention. Once that attention is lost, so too is the possibility of a positive response to the proposal.

Although always important, accuracy — in spelling, grammar, and punctuation — is critical in the executive summary. The time you spend writing, revising, editing, and proofreading the executive summary will be time well spent. Any error, no matter how small, in this early contact point of the business plan can critically injure your chance to obtain the funding you seek. This may seem petty, but the competition for investors' attention is fierce, and these business professionals' time is too valuable to be spent trying to figure out a vague pronoun reference or an ambiguously spelled word. These professionals have learned from experience that if accuracy is absent in form, all too often it is also absent in substance.

To make sure your great ideas are not dismissed without a hearing, spend the time required to get them right. Do not quit writing until you have produced the best document of which you are capable. Remember, this document has to convey your ideas into the minds of people who must be persuaded to part with their money so that your financial dreams can be realized.

Description of the Business

For an existing business, this section provides an opportunity to present the history and the current status of the business. For both the existing business and the new start-up, this section is the place to describe just what the business does (or will do) for a living. In addition, the description of the business should include the mission statement and objectives of the business and present the management team.

LAWN PRO, INC.
DESCRIPTION OF THE BUSINESS

SERVICES

Lawn Pro will begin operations in January, 1997, providing mowing and trimming services, plus chemical lawn services to the residential homeowners in the Edmond, Oklahoma, trading area. Our services will be offered under seasonal contracts at competitive prices. Seasonal contracts will allow us to plan accurately for the efficient use of all crews and equipment.

Lawn Pro will develop and maintain a professional image as a dependable, skilled lawncare service. This image will be supported throughout all elements of the business. Trucks and equipment will bear the corporate trademarks, as will workers' uniforms, all advertising messages, and correspondence media.

Rather than attempting to become expert in both mowing/trimming and chemical applications, Lawn Pro will enter into a strategic alliance with Weeds-

R-Gone, a local lawn chemical service firm (see Appendix R for full description of Weeds-R-Gone), under which Weeds-R-Gone will perform all chemical services called for in our contracts with customers and Lawn Pro will perform all mowing/trimming services called for under their customer contracts. A formula for profit sharing at 50%–50% has been settled. The strategic alliance contract has been approved by the principals of both firms, pending successful capitalization of Lawn Pro, Inc.

MISSION STATEMENT AND OBJECTIVES

As members of the Lawn Pro team, we offer our customer, the homeowner, the freedom to enjoy a beautiful lawn without the sacrifice of precious leisure time to maintain it. Through a customer-oriented professionalism we offer complete peace of mind that every job we do will be done right, done on time, and done according to the wishes of our customer.

Our marketing objective is to obtain a 10% market share by the end of our first year in business and grow that percentage to our expected maximum of 30% by the end of year three. In support of the marketing objective, we will develop autonomous and highly motivated work teams made up of well-trained, energetic individuals from whose ranks we will promote all managerial personnel.

Lawn Pro team members will enjoy above average incomes, which are fully justified by their high levels of productivity, made possible by an efficient organizational structure; the use of state-of-the-art equipment; efficient work routing and scheduling systems; and a well-balanced, autonomous work team system.

Lawn Pro, Inc., will earn a minimum of 30% return on the initial investment of $112,000 as a result of meeting the preceding objectives and by remaining true to the mission of the firm.

MANAGEMENT

Lawn Pro operations will be headed by Mr. John Conway, who currently holds the position of superintendent of operations for a landscape company. In this position Mr. Conway manages 48 employees comprising 12 crews and is responsible for the hiring, training, and work scheduling of all crew members. Mr. Conway practices the autonomous work team approach that will be used in Lawn Pro.

Prior to his current position, Mr. Conway's professional experiences have included over 20 years in supervisory positions, most dealing with some aspect of landscaping or construction. See Mr. Conway's résumé in Appendix L.

The general management position will be held by Ms. Stephanie White. In this position Ms. White will be responsible for marketing and administrative functions. Currently employed as administrative vice-president in a small local manufacturing company (60 employees), Ms. White was formerly a manufacturer's representative for an industrial supply company. She has also held positions as an accountant and secretary. Ms. White's résumé is also included in Appendix L.

All other managerial personnel will be selected and trained by one or both of these top management people.

Three additional professionals will be retained on a consulting basis. Dr. Thomas P. Bergman, Marketing Professor, will be engaged to assist in the development and periodic reevaluation of a comprehensive promotional plan for Lawn Pro. Mr. Kenneth Lyle, Attorney, will be engaged as general counsel, and Dr. Mary Sheets, CPA, will be engaged for the initial design of the management information system, including the development of appropriate internal controls as well as billing and accounting systems. Dr. Sheets will also be consulted quarterly for tax planning advice and for other financial matters as needed.

CHAPTER 13

Marketing Plans

13.1 WHAT IS A MARKETING PLAN?

At its most basic, a marketing plan is a document that identifies who the customers are, how you will serve them, and how much profit you expect to receive from your efforts. A marketing plan is very similar to a business plan (see Chapter 12 for a full discussion of business plans):

- Both contain a well-supported sales forecast.
- Both contain a thorough description of the business proposition.
- Both contain a financial analysis that yields a projection of the profits expected.

However, business plans and marketing plans also have several key differences:

- While a marketing plan assumes the money required for implementation is available, a business plan usually includes strategies for raising capital.
- Unlike a business plan, which includes detailed plans for operations, a marketing plan incorporates only the cost estimates that flow from the operations plans.
- A marketing plan includes a more in-depth analysis of the market conditions, leading to a sales forecast, than normally found in the typical business plan.

As a business student asked to prepare a marketing plan, you will face a task that varies widely in scope from course to course and school to school. Your professor may give you guidance in the specific outline to follow as well as in the specific elements and analyses to include in your plan, or she may leave you with the additional task of discovering just what a marketing plan is supposed to look like. If left to your own devices, just follow the outline provided in this chapter. If your professor does provide you with an outline, use the contents of this chapter to help you complete each section as needed.

Because marketing plans share so many attributes with business plans, we have not repeated the instructions for completing the common sections. Instead, we refer you to the business planning chapter for detailed instructions wherever appropriate.

13.2 THE PURPOSES OF A MARKETING PLAN

Like the business plan, the marketing plan has two distinct but interlocking phases. First, you will conduct the marketing planning *process,* then you will prepare the marketing plan *report.* The report is simply the document that conveys the ideas and conclusions you developed through the planning process. As you begin to analyze a market, you will discover data that will guide your analysis and strategic decisions. For example, if you discover that the market is growing at a rapid rate and supply shortages are common, you will probably conclude that customers are not especially sensitive to pricing. This discovery will then lead you to establish higher prices than you would otherwise.

In most of the strategic decisions you make concerning your marketing plan you will probably be following the lead of established marketing leaders. Any time you choose to adopt a different approach, you will need to explain why. Ordinarily, the reason existing market leaders *are* the market leaders is that they have found a formula that works. Emulation is usually a better idea than reinventing the wheel. Believe us, everything that you will think of (well, almost everything) has already been tried. If it is not in practice, the reason is nearly always because it did not work as well as the established procedure.

The method you must use to evaluate the effectiveness of your tactics is financial analysis. Each alternative product/service variation (package size or design, length of service, product mix, and so on), each promotional tactic (advertising, sales promotion, personal selling, publicity, and so on), each pricing policy (penetration, skimming, and others), each distribution choice (direct to consumer or via standard wholesale system, and so on), and each location decision (to lease space in a regional mall or in a strip center, build a stand-alone facility, and the like) carries with it cost implications. Each decision will also affect your sales volume. For example, if you locate in a regional mall, you will probably not need to advertise to obtain the same volume of sales you might get in a strip center with lots of advertising. The regional mall location, however, will cost a lot more to rent.

If this sounds complicated, that is because it is. (If it was simple, you would not need a college education to become a well-paid marketing professional.) Your job in planning the marketing function of a business is to address all of these issues systematically and contrive a set of tactics that will be likely to yield an acceptable *profit*. (Business professionals do not really care what the sales forecast is, directly. They only use the sales forecast as an indicator of profit.)

The financial analysis is performed *iteratively,* or recurrently. This means that you choose a strategy (a set of tactics), enter the relevant costs into your *pro forma* financial statements (including income statements, cashflow statements, and balance sheets), then observe the effects of your decisions on profit. You will revise your strategy and repeat until you have found the set of tactics that maximizes your profits while minimizing your risk. Sounds simple, doesn't it? Once you have devised a successful strategy, you can finish writing the report we call the marketing plan.

You can readily see that a marketing plan can be a valuable resource. Marketing plans are helpful in all the following activities:

- Selling a strategy to the owners/managers of the firm
- Providing a plan of action for implementation of the marketing strategy
- Providing a budget for inclusion in the overall financial strategy of the firm and for control of spending by the marketing department
- Providing standards against which to compare performance of the firm's sales and marketing staff

13.3 THE PARTS OF A MARKETING PLAN

Executive Summary

In a marketing plan, just as in business plans, you use the *executive summary* to describe all of the plan's parts. Do not just repeat your conclusions but take the reader step by step through the highlights of your whole analysis, leading with your conclusions. Remember, in business you should avoid the inductive writing structure, in which you make the reader wait until the last page to find out your conclusions. Tell your readers right up front what they will find when they get to the summary of your report. Review the executive summary section of Chapter 12 for detailed instructions for preparing an executive summary.

Situation Analysis

In the *situation analysis* you will examine all the relevant factors that may affect the marketing decisions which you will present later in the report. Such factors will include the size of the market and the intensity of the competition. For convenience you should divide these factors into discrete categories. Unless your professor asks you to employ a particular structure for this section, we suggest that you choose a set of headings that seems to you to organize your data effectively into a meaningful structure. Remember that your goal here is to cover *every* important factor, so that when you eventually present your chosen strategic decisions you can also explain how your decisions fit into the big picture.

A Two-Category Approach

One common heading scheme uses just two categories:

External Environmental Factors
In this section you will discuss conditions over which the company CEO (Chief Executive Officer) has little or no control. Examples of *external environmental factors* include the cost of raw materials, changes in law relating to the industry, and the level of competition. These and other factors are considered as external because one CEO acting alone cannot change them.

Internal Environmental Factors
This section deals with environmental factors which the CEO can manipulate directly. Examples of *internal environmental factors* include employee morale, degree of automation relative to the rest of the industry, relative pay rates, and production efficiency relative to other firms in the industry.

A Four-Category Approach

Another heading scheme uses four categories. The first three are subgroups of external factors; the fourth section is dedicated to discussion of internal factors.

Industry-Specific Factors
In this section you should present and discuss the factors that you believe to be especially relevant to marketing efforts in your industry. For example, in the computer software security industry the federal government has passed laws prohibiting the export of advanced encryption software for fear of our enemies using it to our political and economic

disadvantage. In the agricultural industries, genetic engineering has recently become an explosively controversial issue. If your segment of the industry plans to utilize such new technologies, you would be well advised to carefully consider the industry experts' predictions for passage of new industry-specific legislation, as well as the drift in public opinion.

General Environmental Factors

General environmental factors are those that tend to affect all businesses across many industries. This section of your report ought to include a discussion of such issues as the "hard" (or "soft"?) dollar and its impact on imports or exports relevant to your case at hand. Other factors might include the aging of the baby boomers, the increased commuter traffic congestion in the relevant trading area, or the remarkable rate at which people are entering the world of the Internet.

To decide whether a particular factor belongs in this section, think of two very different industries, for example, the ostrich industry and the automobile industry. Ask yourself, "Would the factor I am thinking of affect both industries?" If the answer is yes, you probably are thinking about a general environmental factor.

Competitive Factors

Competitive factors include the rate at which competitors are entering and leaving your industry and your trading area(s). This section should include a discussion of the potential responses your competitors might make to your actions. When you enter the market with a lower price, will competitors lower theirs? Usually they will, but not always. You need to present a pretty good set of reasonings, built on a solid basis of factual data if you plan to count on a nonresponsive reaction.

How rapidly do prices change in the market? Are they trending up or down, or are they fluctuating wildly? If price fluctuations are the norm, price changes may not be the result of competitive actions, but rather the result of weather effects on the raw materials that go into the products. If price fluctuations result from a highly competitive marketplace, discussion of price fluctuations should be included in this section. But if the prices vary due to highly variable raw materials prices, the discussion would be better included in the section on industry-specific environmental factors.

"But, where do I discuss that factor?"

You may notice that the classification of factors gets a bit fuzzy around the edges. Not to worry. Your goal in reporting the situation analysis is to present all the data you have found to be relevant, organized in a manner that helps the reader of your marketing plan understand why you chose the particular set of strategies and tactics you will present later in the plan. Do not get overly concerned with categories. Just be sure your final product—the written plan—clearly presents your case and its foundations.

Company-Specific Environmental Factors

Finally, in this section address the constraints under which your firm must operate. Here you should address budgetary limitations. If your professor asks you to prepare a marketing plan for an existing company, you will be provided with data you need to identify your internal constraints. In addition to money limitations, you may also be missing key expertise or access to particular markets due to management decisions over which you have no power. If the CEO could fix it, you probably should include that part of the discussion in this section.

Many of the factors you may consider important and difficult to change, such as an outmoded facility, are still ultimately under internal control. Discuss all of these here. Of course, if you have reason to think it unlikely that the needed changes will be forthcoming, you probably ought to offer alternative solutions rather than presenting one take-it-or-leave-it solution. Be creative. After all, this is a marketing class!

The Target Market

A *market* is loosely defined as a group of potential buyers who exhibit similar buying behaviors. All of the people who buy hot dogs for home consumption comprise the hot dog market. Those who choose low fat hot dogs comprise a *segment* of the hot dog market. A *market niche* is a very small market segment. Usually this term is used to refer to a segment so small that major players in the industry choose to ignore these customers, viewing them as an unprofitably small segment. Although sometimes you will be asked to develop a marketing plan for an undifferentiated market, ordinarily you will develop marketing plans for one or just a few market segments. The market or segment you choose to serve with your product or service is referred to as your *target market.*

In this section you need to identify the potential buyers who comprise your target market as thoroughly as you can. Identify their demographic and psychographic profiles to the maximum extent that information is available to you. *Demographics* are personal attributes, such as marital status, gender, age, ethnic origin, religion, number of children, health, home ownership, number of cars owned, and so forth. *Psychographics* are attitudes and beliefs: sense of self-worth, beliefs about the viability of social security, sense of security from crime, attitudes about obligations to society, and so on. The better you can define your target market, the more likely you will be able to construct a set of strategies and tactics that precisely meets its needs.

The Trading Area or Service Area

Businesses frequently need to identify their *trading area,* that is, the geographic area from which most of their customers will be derived. For resellers and service providers, the trading area concept is usually very helpful. Resellers are businesses that do not change the form of the products they sell. They usually just buy in large quantities and then sell in smaller quantities. Resellers frequently offer their products at a central location and attract their customers to the store.

For manufacturing, import/export, or specialty services the trading area concept may be less useful. These three kinds of firms usually arrange for delivery of their offerings directly to customers, allowing these businesses to define their service area almost arbitrarily. So, a *service area* is the geographic area within which a business chooses to market and deliver products or services.

If you notice the spacing of stores and other businesses, you will realize that some competing businesses cluster in a central location ("the magnificent mile of cars," "fast food row," "furniture alley," "stripper city," and so on). Such *shopping goods businesses* benefit from proximity to other competing businesses because they all must tolerate the need of their customers to shop several places before buying. (Of course, sometimes businesses are clustered together because that is the only place in the area citizens will tolerate their presence.) In the case of shopping goods resellers, the trading area is usually very large, covering several counties or even parts of several states.

Other times stores are sprinkled across the landscape, all spaced with amazingly constant distance between competitors. As a superb example, use your phone book's Yellow Pages® to plot the locations of metropolitan-area retail liquor stores on a city map. These stores are good examples of *convenience goods*. For such products, each store monopolizes and must defend its natural trading area. Customers usually patronize the store that is most convenient to them, since all of these stores carry much the same items. In such businesses, differentiation is tough. Usually the best way to differentiate your convenience business is through the quality of customer service you offer. If you try to carry a large selection of one product line at the expense of another (for example, lots of variety in beers of the world and fewer options in whiskies), you risk losing the market segment in your trading area that prefers the displaced merchandise. All other things being equal between you and your competitors, simply calling all your customers by name can help you build an appreciative list of loyal patrons.

We have presented a brief discussion of types of goods to illustrate some of their effects on trading area. For a thorough discussion of all the categories of goods and the implications for an appropriate trading area analysis, refer to your marketing text.

Two General Rules Regarding Trading Area Size

> **Rule 1:** *All other things being equal, the larger the purchase, the larger the trading area.*

For example, car dealers, mobile home dealers, and major appliance centers have large trading areas. Shoe stores, linen shops, and garden centers usually have smaller trading areas.

> **Rule 2:** *With all other things equal, the less frequent the purchase, the larger the trading area.*

For example, appliance parts stores, wig shops, and medical specialty centers all have large trading areas, even though the money spent on the average purchase may not be large at all. Customers put up with the inconvenience of the long trip because they have to make the trip infrequently. By contrast, grocery stores, auto parts stores, and barber shops have small trading areas because customers demand the convenience of a nearby store due to the necessity of frequent visits.

The most important point to make in your discussion of trading area, if you decide you need such a discussion at all, is to identify the dimensions of your trading area in support of the distribution and promotional tactics you propose later. Your trading area dimensions also will have an impact on your analysis of competitors. Once you identify a competitor as residing within your trading area or one that overlaps yours, you should pay special attention to that particular business and its perceived and expected strategies as you enter or revise your presence in the same markets.

Be sure all your tactics are consistent with your analysis. If you plan to roll out a product line nationally, you should match the reach of your distribution and promotional tactics to the dimensions of a national trading area. Similarly, if you are preparing a marketing plan for a local grocery store, you must limit the reach of your promotional tactics to just your trading area, which may be as small as five miles across. Advertising for grocery store customers 50 miles from your store is usually a waste of money. Grocery customers need close proximity to their homes.

Problems and Opportunities

Problems? Everybody has problems! We could fill up the rest of this book just by listing the problems possible in any marketing case you choose. In this section of your marketing report, however, the problems you should address are those difficulties and circumstances which you have decided will lead you to adopt strategies and tactics you would not otherwise choose. Such relevant problems may include general factors, industry-specific factors, or company-specific factors. These problems should be presented so the reader can share in the reasoning behind your choice of tactics.

For your purposes, an opportunity is usually the flip side of a competitor's problem or weakness. For example, if all your competitors have shabby, run-down facilities, you may have an opportunity to gain an advantage in image by choosing to construct a new building to differentiate your business as clean and new.

Opportunities should also be selectively presented in your plan. Do not present every possible opportunity, just the ones you plan to address in your strategic and tactical plans. You should also include a discussion of opportunities suggested in materials provided to you by your professor and logical opportunities that "everyone" will know about. Other than these opportunities, just be sure you include a full discussion of the opportunities (in other words, competitor weaknesses) you plan to take advantage of in your plans.

Marketing Objectives

Goals or *objectives*? Is there a difference in the two terms? We suggest that here is a distinction without a difference—at least, without a meaningful difference. Some business professionals use the terms interchangeably, as we do. Others use *goals* to describe a higher-order intention and *objectives* to describe a lower-order, more practical intention. Thus a CEO might state that the goal of her company is to increase profits by 25 percent over the next year and that to achieve this goal each department must formulate a set of objectives that will enable the company to meet its goal. As we stated earlier: a distinction without a difference. Unless your professor instructs you otherwise, we suggest you do not even introduce goals. Just refer to all of your intentions as objectives. This is the conservative approach and is less likely to be misunderstood by your reader.

Three Attributes of a Useful Objective

Whether you discuss goals or objectives, both have the same three required attributes:

1. Objectives must be *measurable*. If you simply aim for "improvement in customer relations" or "increased sales," there is little reason to continuing striving for more once the

previous benchmark has been passed. Some may even ask, "improvement compared to what?" or "increased relative to when?" If, however, you have a measurable objective, such as "a reduction of 50 percent in customer complaints as compared to 1996" or "a 15 percent increase in sales over the prior year," say so in your written objectives. Such specific statements leave no doubt as to just what you mean and allow everyone to be clear as to whether and when the objective is met (or missed).

2. The objective must be *time specific.* Any time you are called to task for not having reached an objective such as "a 43 percent improvement in defect rates as compared to 1997," you can always respond with, "Well, not yet!" Without a specific time frame, even measurable objectives are worthless. How can you pin anyone down if you did not say when the job was to be completed? You may have experience in using that dodge, "Bobby, did you take out the trash like I asked you?" "Not yet, Ma!"

3. The objective must be *achievable.* Objectives that cannot be reached are worse than no objectives at all. Such objectives lead to frustration and unnecessary stress in any organization. Of course, if the objective is too easy to reach, potential profits will be missed. Make sure the objectives you set for each marketing function are realistic, but just a bit stretching. Everyone benefits from meeting such objectives. The company maximizes its profits, and employees gain a sense of accomplishment.

Before you develop your marketing objectives, you must remember that your primary objective in the business is to maximize profit. Yes, your primary objective is the same as the primary objective of the accounting manager and that of the production superintendent, and that of just about every other employee. Maximizing profits should be the primary objective of every employee, and in your business courses you can make that assumption. As a business professional you will be expected to lead your employees to acceptance of maximum profit as everyone's primary objective.

Developing Marketing Objectives

To develop a set of marketing objectives, you should work backwards. Start with the profit objective. We do not mean some vague objective such as "maximize profits," but a specific objective such as "increase profits by 24 percent this year as compared to profits last year." You may have such an objective given you by your professor or by the case from which your marketing plan is being developed. If so, accept the stated objective and continue. If no such objective has been imposed, choose one for yourself. Do not tell anyone (such as your professor) what you have chosen just yet. You may decide, after a little more thought or legwork, that the objective you chose arbitrarily is not achievable. If so, change it.

Once you have set your primary objective, you must identify objectives for every marketing function you assume control over in your marketing plan. This process can get a little tricky. You really cannot set these detailed objectives completely until you have some sort of strategy in mind, and that fact leads you to the next section on strategy, and even beyond, into the tactics section as well. *Tactics* are the specific, practical activities you will use to reach your strategic objectives, which will, in turn, lead to your primary objective of reaching a profit target.

Do not get discouraged. Remember you are completing a process, the marketing planning process. Once your plan is complete, you will begin to write, and your writing is designed simply to communicate your ideas, not to represent the order in which you arrived at them. Keep this sequence in mind—first the process, then the writing—and you will be less likely to get tangled up in your marketing plan structure.

The Four Ps

Marketing professionals by convention divide the marketing function into the Four Ps: product, price, place (or more accurately, distribution, but that doesn't begin with a p), and promotion. Your marketing plan should include objectives for all four marketing functions and for every tactic within each function. The power of the business system lies in that it is a system. The outcome produced by the firm is not random. The profits show up because sales occurred. Sales happened because the right *product* at the right *price* arrived at the *place* where buyers were told, via *promotion,* that they would find what they were looking for. Each step in the process, beginning with the first contact with customers, must be designed to support the next. Advertising causes people to become aware of your products and come to the store for a visit. Signs help folks find you when they set out looking for your store. Once in the store, static displays or salespeople help customers find the products they are seeking.

Each part of the business system must work with other parts to achieve the primary objective. Each part of the system needs specific objectives to keep that part on track. A business is too complicated for every employee to keep the big picture in mind all the time. Your job as a marketing planner is to identify just exactly what objectives must be met within each marketing function for that part of the system to produce the output needed to support the primary objective. Got it? Here is an example.

Auto Ozone, Inc., 1997 Marketing Objectives

In support of our corporate goal of 5 percent increase in profits next year, the marketing department has set objectives for each function as presented below. To achieve this profit objective, we plan to reach a sales objective of $4,500,000, an increase of 12 percent over the prior year's companywide sales level. Based on an average of $25 per sales transaction, we anticipate delivery of 180,000 units in the coming year.

PRODUCT

Six new products will be introduced by May 1997. These products will fill the current void in our price line and are expected to yield a 10 percent increase in sales by the third month following their introduction.

Five existing products will be phased out by September. A sales reduction of 1.5 percent is expected immediately upon removing these products from all 30 company stores.

PRICE

All prices will be re-examined in light of recent price reduction announcements by our direct competitors. The objective of each store manager is to revise prices at the store level such that no product of ours is more than 2 percent higher in price than similar competing products in the local market. This revision is to be completed by June 30, 1997, and is to be incorporated into store policy immediately. To prevent price disparities from developing in the future, each store will implement quarterly price reviews beginning immediately following June 30, and continuing indefinitely.

PLACE

Six new stores will open during the coming nine months. Once in operation, these new stores will add 3 percent to the total sales of the company. All are expected to achieve a profit level of 15 percent within 60 days of opening.

PROMOTION

A new advertising campaign has been commissioned to begin January 31 and run through April 30. Results expected are 12 percent sales increases in all markets, with a retention of 6 percent (one-half the increase) through the end of the year.

Notice that the marketing objectives begin with a statement of the primary objective—ordinarily a profit objective, but sometimes stated as a sales objective, or less often as a gross profit objective. Whatever the primary objective you begin with, the next step is to develop a sales objective. The sales objective then becomes the sales forecast for the planning period, the same sales forecast used in the financial analysis discussed under "implementation" later in this chapter. *This sales objective is also used to derive all other marketing objectives.* Be sure to state your sales objective in both monetary terms and units.

Keeping the Trees and the Forest in Perspective
(or "What is it that I am supposed to be doing, again?")

Let us review. As you perform your marketing analysis, you begin formulating your marketing plan by first identifying the primary objective, then establishing a sales objective that will produce the profits you need. Next, you choose a strategy that will yield those sales, and finally you choose an array of tactics that, taken together, will produce the sales you need. During the planning *process,* these choices are not linear. They are iterative (meaning you do it, test it, change it, test it, and repeat). You begin by setting up the financial statements, then try different combinations of strategy and tactics that might meet your sales and profit objectives. If your efforts do not produce the numbers you need, given the results and costs your data lead you to expect, you revise your plans and test for improved results. Repeat this process until your plan works.

In the report you will write once you have your plan, the presentation should *appear* linear to the reader, each subsequent section flowing naturally from the preceding section, and all sections remaining consistent with the data and discussions presented in the situation analysis.

In most cases, you will be asked to prepare a sales forecast that is a modification of a firm's past performance. This greatly simplifies the sales forecasting problem. Sometimes, though, especially in the case of business plan writing assignments, you must develop a sales forecast for a new operation or business. In this case, refer to the marketing analysis section of Chapter 12 for a full discussion of sales forecasting for a new business.

Marketing Strategy

The marketing *strategy* is usually thought of as a sort of conceptual battle plan, with competitors being the enemy forces. The strategy may be as simple as developing "the lowest prices in the state" or announcing that "We want our customers to think of us first when they want an ice cream treat." The strategy may be primarily distributional: "We will control the market with our stores by buying every key location as it comes available." The strategy can also be multidimensional, and frequently is. You might, for example, claim "the lowest prices and the fastest service." Whatever your strategy, you should be able to capture its essence in just a phrase or at most a sentence or two. If you can't clearly present your strategy in very brief statements, you probably do not yet have it defined precisely enough. Too complex a strategy will cause you to dilute your message, making your marketing efforts less effective.

Marketing Tactics

Once you have developed a strategy, the strategy then provides you with guidance in developing a complete set of *tactics,* or specific action items. Each tactic must be developed in a manner that will further the strategy, and both tactics and strategy must lead toward the achievement of the primary objective. If, for example, you plan to position your grocery store as "Omaha's source for organically grown vegetables" (a strategy), you might choose to place stores in all major trading areas to capture the market segment seeking such products (a distribution tactic). In order to determine if this tactic is appropriate, you would first need information suggesting that such a market, once captured, would enable you to achieve the sales objectives established elsewhere in the marketing plan.

Other tactics you might employ to further the organic veggie strategy include hiring a known environmentalist as spokesperson for the grocery chain, redecorating the stores to emphasize the all-natural theme, or moving the produce aisle into the front-center section of the store to display the specialty items more prominently. For each such tactic (or group of tactics) specific objectives should be established. For the ones just mentioned, you might use a customer survey to measure the effectiveness of the campaign in obtaining new customers, with a goal of a 2 percent increase in customers per month for a year at each remodeled store, or an increased awareness factor of 15 percent following airing of TV spots featuring the new message and spokesperson.

Present in your marketing plan all the tactics you need in order to support your strategy and achieve the primary objective. *Include a cost for every tactic* and an objective for each as well. (Remember, each objective must be measurable, time specific, and achievable). Be sure to explain how each tactic fits into your overall strategy, referring to the situation analysis to help explain what opportunities you are pursuing and/or problems you are attempting to address.

Implementation and Control Plans

Here is where you place a complete financial analysis of your marketing plan. This analysis includes a set of income statements for the planning period, by month in year one, by quarter for year two, and just annual summaries for years beyond year two. Include cashflow statements for the same periods as for income statements. Include a beginning balance sheet (before plan implementation) and another for each subsequent year end. See Chapter 12 for complete instructions for preparing these financial statements. *Note:* You cannot complete these statements until you know how much each of the tactics you plan to implement costs.

You will also need the costs of production/operations, including direct costs and overhead. Sometimes you will be given these costs. Other times you will have to develop them yourself. If you must develop all the costs yourself, you can take two different approaches. As described in the appropriate sections in Chapter 12, you can develop the costs of facilities, personnel, and so on, and build up the complete cost picture you require. Alternatively, you can use industry averages to estimate the costs you need. Several sources of average industry costs are readily available in your school library. One common source is *Key Business Ratios,* published by Standard & Poors. This comprehensive report shows, for most industries, each ordinary expense item as a percentage of sales, for both profitable and unprofitable firms. (We suggest you use the numbers for profitable firms.) Since you will have already developed your sales forecast, in both dollars and in units, you can simply multiply by the relevant percentages to obtain an estimate of each cost item. Be sure to clear with your professor the approach you intend to use in preparing your marketing plan report.

Summary and Appendices

In the summary, reiterate your strategy and give a quick overview of the tactics you plan to use. Emphasize the manner in which all of the parts of your plan implicitly coordinate with the situation analysis you presented at the beginning of your report. Also, be sure to tie your strategy and tactics back to the primary objective so the reader can see that you have your feet planted firmly on the ground, even if your plans may seem to put your head in the clouds.

Persuasive, data-driven discussion of each tactic, presentation of well-documented costs for each tactic, and a comprehensive set of pro forma financial statements will win the day. Study this chapter and the relevant parts of Chapter 12 several times as you work through the rather challenging task before you. If you keep in mind your dual roles (planner and writer) and allow adequate time to put in the effort required to address all the issues presented by your assignment, you will produce a report you can be proud of.

Include all the exhibits you need to illustrate the points you are trying to make in your report. Put everything that could interrupt the flow of your narrative into an appendix. Appendices should be attached to the marketing plan following the summary, with each document clearly labeled. If you are using copies or originals of other materials (brochures, maps, and the like), you should insert divider pages labeled with an appendix letter, and if the document is very thick at all, use labeled tabs to divide appendix sections even more clearly. Remember the *marketing concept.* Your job as always is to meet the needs of your customers. For the marketing plan you are preparing, your customer is your professor. Make life simple for him, and he will be more likely to "buy" your "product."

CHAPTER 14

Case Analyses

14.1 THE PURPOSES OF A CASE ANALYSIS

Until this century the world of business operated from a very different perspective than the one we now have. Business used the *journeyman/apprentice* system of education to develop future leaders. Under this antiquated system, future leaders of a firm worked under the direction of their manager. The apprentice learned by observing the boss and by trial and error, with a dash of explanation thrown in for good measure. In this system, management was art. Each individual eventually acquired his own unique set of procedures and competencies. Each manager did things pretty much as he chose, with heavy influence from the mentor. One difficulty with this method was that it took a long time; typical apprenticeships lasted 10 to 15 years! Since the student could only learn when the opportunities to encounter a particular situation came up, learning was almost entirely dependent on the environment.

Around the turn of the twentieth century, Frederick Winslow Taylor and others ushered in the approach to management we now use, an approach called *scientific management*. From this modern perspective has evolved the educational approach in which you are now engaged. Instead of each student learning at the feet of a master, now every student is exposed to a common body of knowledge we refer to as *theories, principles,* and *procedures*. The theories help you to understand why the principles exist and enable you to develop new principles beyond those you have been explicitly taught. You learn procedures that have become routine for performing tasks in all of the circumstances we can teach you, because greater efficiency is realized by getting everyone in business to perform such tasks in the same manner.

Our problem is that we have far too few procedures to give you. For all the problem situations you must face that call for solutions beyond the procedures we can specify, the best we can do is to help you learn the principles and the theories on which the procedures are based, then assist you in learning to apply these principles. Educational critics often suggest that we should send our business students into the "real world" where they can learn how business "really works" and in this way receive a more useful education. The problem with this approach is that it is grossly inefficient. The student who spends a year in such an environment might get the opportunity to participate in two marketing campaigns from beginning to end, learning whatever lessons there might be in those two situations. A management intern might see one firing, three hirings, and one strategic planning session. Another student might get the opportunity to see a business law case unfold from beginning to end, though few important cases are resolved within a single year. In all three of these examples, the learning opportunities are embedded in real situations and are almost certainly more motivating and more effective, for being "real," in helping the student learn the available lessons. The trouble is that the lessons are not learned very efficiently. How would you like to wait ten years for your first real job?

Enter the *case analysis* approach to business education. Especially in management, marketing, and business law, decisions must be made and problems solved that frequently involve complex situations and/or the feelings and attitudes of people. Cases are presentations of a company and its environs that can be used as substitutes for real experience. Students can consider all the information presented as though they had been assigned the real task of managing that particular situation. Working under the guidance of their professor, students attempt to develop an appropriate response given the details of that particular situation and drawing on what they have learned in the way of theories, principles, and procedures. Such case studies allow the professor to create or select situations in which students can obtain virtually any imaginable set of "experiences" in order to practice the skills required to run a business or resolve subtle applications of business or tax law.

Case analyses are assigned to students as a compromise. We would very much like to give each of you all the experiences needed to learn your business skills in a completely real environment, but we do not have the time. We use case analyses to condense the real world and let you develop and practice your skills on realistic situations.

Although there is no "typical" case study, most case studies have at least three attributes in common. Cases usually deal with real companies and real situations, cases rarely have a "solution," and finally cases generally contain lots of information that is of little or no value, intermixed with data of critical importance.

Beyond these similarities, case studies may be as short as a single page or as long as a hundred pages, though most are in the range of 5 to 25 pages. Cases may present tons of detailed financial data or none at all. Cases may be written in a very cryptic style ("Just the facts, Ma'am.") or in a very *qualitative* style, with lots of information about the feelings and attitudes of the characters in the case. You may be given a rich history of the company and its leaders or no information at all about their background. And, always, most of the information is superfluous—just as it is in the real world.

A case analysis requires that you choose from the babble of information those facts that are relevant to your assigned perspective. A marketing assignment, for example, will call for analysis from a different perspective than that used for a human resources assignment. Cases usually present you with situations that call for decisions of great importance. These decisions call for careful consideration of all the relevant environmental factors, both internal and external, as well as the goals of the company.

Your mission in a case study is to extract all the relevant data (including *hard data,* such as numbers, and *soft data,* such as facts about attitudes and feelings) from the case study, apply appropriate procedures to the data provided—in other words, turn *data* into *information*—organize that information into some meaningful order, and, while remaining true to the theories of your discipline, apply the relevant principles to arrive at a solution to the problem or to arrive at a recommendation of action to address the needs of the firm as you determine them to be. Sound simple?

14.2 THE PARTS OF A CASE ANALYSIS

The case analysis assignment has two parts. The first part is your analysis of the data presented in the case study. The second part is the presentation of your findings and the rationale for them.

Analyzing the Case Study

Just as case studies presented for your analysis may differ, so too will the analyses you are asked to perform. Some assignments will call for narrowly focused analysis and a brief, oral report. Others will call for a more comprehensive analysis and a lengthy, formal, written report, and each of these possibilities may call for one of many different perspectives.

What's Your Perspective?

The same case may be analyzed from a variety of perspectives. From whatever perspective you approach the case, what is generally required is that you adopt a strategic level perspective, that is, a fundamental and long-term view.

Assignment	*Response*
In a finance course Bobby Jones was asked to analyze the financial condition of Superior Savings Centers, Inc., and make recommendations as to what actions management should take to improve the company's financial picture.	Bobby decided to try to determine an appropriate debt to equity ratio, given the goals the company had for expansion in order to gain market share. His recommendations included likely sources of additional loans and a strategy for acquiring additional assets that would further support the financial strategy proposed.
In a business law class Sheri Airen's assignment was to determine the applicable law and to recommend what, if any, legal remedies Superior Savings Centers, Inc., should pursue for two suits brought against the company by customers claiming that one of Superior's tellers mishandled deposits.	Sheri chose to recommend a new set of operating policies for Superior Savings Centers, Inc., that she designed to address the weaknesses in legal compliance which she deduced from the case study. She also suggested that the currently pending cases be settled out of court since the applicable law appears to support the plaintiffs' positions against the company.
In a marketing management course Steven Smythe's assignment was to develop a comprehensive marketing plan as a means to achieve the perceived goals of Superior Savings Centers, Inc.	Steven considered the image problems Superior Savings Centers, Inc., was experiencing and their financial condition, and he concluded that the company should create a new subsidiary with an entirely new identity. This new subsidiary could then be used to develop a network of franchises as the basic strategy for market expansion.
In a strategic management course Teri Eustice was simply asked to analyze the Superior Savings Centers, Inc., case.	Teri concluded that the goals of the company were incompatible with current market conditions and that unless the company

Assignment	*Response*
	was willing to invest heavily in new equipment and to fundamentally revise current marketing strategies, as well as to cure glaring weaknesses in managerial practices, the assets of the firm should be sold, since its net book value is much higher than the total value of the stock at current prices.

Business enterprises are complex organizations. As you can readily see, there are many ways to look at a single case. Your professor will ordinarily provide you with guidance as to just which perspective she wishes you to take in analyzing the case study. In the absence of such guidance, simply consider the business from the owner's perspective. If you owned this business, what, if anything, would you like to see changed, and why?

Once you have adopted a particular perspective, the next task is to perform your analysis. The analysis of the case should be completed before you begin to write the case analysis report. Too often students lack an understanding of exactly what is meant by this ubiquitous word, *analysis.*

> **A-nal'y-sis:** "a breaking up of a whole into its parts to find out their nature, etc." (Guralnik)

The three primary tools of analysis are *comparison, contrast,* and *synthesis. Comparison* means looking for then pointing out the similarities between or among elements of the case study being analyzed.

> Judy Blevins noted that debt-to-equity ratio of Gerbils, Inc., *was very much in line with* the ratios of other pet breeders in the industry.

> The proposed marketing plan for the new line of golf pants to be offered by Shirts, Pants & All, Inc., *looked to George Wan as though it had been developed by the same person* who had created the recently failed leisure shirt marketing approach.

Contrast means looking for then pointing out the differences between or among elements of the case study.

> Sheila Rodriguez observed that the CEO of Weird Things, Inc., had established a set of import contacts that gave the firm its distinctive assortment of products. *This strategy was very different from the usual practice* in the industry of buying from a single import house.

> Harold Carney was the first in his group to notice that, *unlike the previous operations manager* in the LTV, Inc., Omaha plastic molding plant, Jenny Link was well educated, but not in the technical aspects of the job.

Synthesis means integrating facts, comparisons, contrasts, principles, and outcomes of procedures and/or other interpretations already arrived at into a consistent interpretation of the elements of the case study. This interpretation of the situation can then yield a reasonable and supportable conclusion.

> Julie Sharpe decided that even though he was the owner's son, the manager must be fired. Her conclusion was based on his performance during the past six months (fact), which was very poor by industry standards (contrast), and the chief stockholder's actions (fact), which Julie *interpreted* as being more focused on profit than on kinship— even though the stockholder was the manager's grandmother!

The key to performing a case analysis is to use your tools methodically. Carefully compare and contrast all of the facts in the case that may be relevant to your analytical perspective. Draw in the theories and principles of your discipline. What would the theories suggest about the elements of the case? What principles apply and which principles have been violated? Apply the procedures you have learned which allow you to obtain additional second-order facts for consideration as you synthesize all the disparate elements of the case. Such derived data often illuminate and clarify a course of action in cases where the raw data are so confusing and contradictory as to seemingly preclude every possible course of action.

Most cases are, in fact, chosen so as to preclude an obvious answer. The challenge of the case study lies not in finding the correct answer, but rather in learning to apply what you have learned in realistic situations in a competent, considered manner as a means of reaching a reasonable and supportable conclusion. Accordingly, most of the work of the case analysis should be completed before you ever begin to write. The following procedure will help to ensure that you cover all the bases in your analysis and help you achieve the highest quality recommendations.

> **TIP**
> If you would really like to impress your professor, bring into each of your analyses a theory, principle, and procedure learned in some other course, one not covered in the current course. Every professor wishes for you to learn in such a way that you can apply what you have learned outside the present course assignments. Demonstrating your ability to do so will warm the heart of the crustiest old prof—guaranteed!

THE TEN COMMANDMENTS OF CASE ANALYSIS
1. Read the case twice, once for an overview and once to gain full command of the facts; then take care to explore every one of the exhibits.
2. Make a list of the problems and issues that have to be confronted.
3. Do enough number crunching to discover the story told by the data presented in the case.
4. Look for opportunities to use the analytical tools: *comparison, contrast,* and *synthesis.*
5. Be thorough in your diagnosis of the situation, and make at least a one- or two-page outline of your assessment.
6. Support any and all opinions with well-reasoned arguments and numerical evidence; do not stop until you can purge "I think" and "I feel" from your assessment and, instead, are able to rely completely on the phrase "My analysis shows."
7. Develop charts, tables, and graphs to expose more clearly the main points of your analysis.
8. Prioritize your recommendations and make sure they can be carried out in an acceptable time frame with the available skills and financial resources.

9. Review your recommended action plan to see if it addresses all of the problems and issues you identified.

10. Avoid recommending any course of action that could have disastrous consequences if it does not work out as planned; in other words, be as alert to the downside risks of your recommendations as you are to their upside potential and appeal. (adapted from Strickland and Thompson 1995, 12)

Ratio Analysis

If synthesis is the engine of your case analysis, financial ratio analysis is the suspension system. All business analyses must ultimately examine the effects of each factor on profitability, since profit is the most important criterion for success in business. However, simply observing that profits are less than satisfactory or that a recommended decision may impact profits in a particular direction is not sufficient. The modern management tool of ratio analysis provides far more detailed guidance for effective strategic decision-making. Many variables may affect profits: sales may go up or down, expenses may go up or down, inventories may be too large or too small, receivables may be too large or too small, and so forth. Many financial ratios have been developed to help the analyst better understand the subtleties of various strategic decisions and their potential impact on the firm's profits.

Every case in which financial data has been provided should be subjected to a thorough financial analysis. Such an analysis includes the computation of all relevant ratios for which the required numbers are provided. Ratio analysis requires comparison data to be very useful. In one industry a quick ratio of 1.6 may be excellent, while in another industry, the same ratio may indicate real financial problems. Accordingly, not only do you have to compute the ratios, but frequently you will be expected to locate the appropriate standards for the immediate industry as well. Fortunately industry ratios are commonly available in virtually every school and public library; ratio analysis is such a fundamental financial analysis tool that there is lots of demand for the information. Some common financial ratios, a method for computing them, and a brief description of what the ratios indicate are presented on pp. 284–86.

Where to Find Standard Financial Ratios

Once you know what industry you are working in, you should check several of the sources listed below to be sure you are getting the ratios most appropriate to your industry. Several of these sources provide ratios for profitable firms as well as a second set of ratio values for *unprofitable* firms in each industry, thus adding another interesting dimension to ratio analysis

Almanac of Business and Industrial Financial Ratios. Prentice Hall.

Industry Norms and Key Business Ratios. Dun and Bradstreet.

Robert Morris Associates' Annual Statement Studies. Robert Morris Associates.

Financial Studies of the Small Business. Financial Research Associates.

Modern Industry. Dun and Bradstreet.

Dunn's Reviews. Dun and Bradstreet.

Your library is sure to carry one or more of these citations.

TABLE I

Ratio	How to Compute	What it Indicates
Profitability Ratios		
1. Gross Profit Margin	$\dfrac{\text{Sales} - \text{Cost of Goods Sold}}{\text{Sales}}$	Indicates the portion of revenue available to cover overhead and to provide profit (contribution margin).
2. Operating Profit Margin	$\dfrac{\text{Net Profit Before Taxes and Interest}}{\text{Sales}}$	Indicates the firm's profitability from operations. Factors out the effects of debt on profitability.
3. Net Profit Margin	$\dfrac{\text{Net Profit}}{\text{Sales}}$	Shows the percentage of sales revenue that gets to the bottom line. A rough measure only. May result from margins too low, expenses too high or both.
4. Basic Earning Power	$\dfrac{\text{Net Profit Before Taxes and Interest}}{\text{Assets}}$	Measures the degree to which assets have been profitably deployed.
5. Return on Total Assets	$\dfrac{\text{Net Profit}}{\text{Total Assets}}$	Measures the efficiency with which assets are employed. Adding interest to the profit helps the lender assess the true risk of their loan to the company where the loan is secured by the firm's balance sheet.
6. Return on Stockholder's Equity	$\dfrac{\text{Net Profit}}{\text{Total Stockholders' Equity}}$	Provides a strong indication of the profitability of the firm to its investors.
7. Return on Common Equity	$\dfrac{\text{Net Profit} - \text{Preferred Stock Dividends}}{\text{Total Stockholders' Equity} - \text{Par Value of Pref. Stock}}$	Measures the actual return on investment that is allocated to the holders of common stock.
8. Earning per Share	$\dfrac{\text{Net Profit} - \text{Preferred Stock Dividends}}{\text{Number of Shares of Common Stock Outstanding}}$	Shows the dollar amount of profits that would theoretically be allocated to each share of stock. This ratio can help explain swings in stock price.

Liquidity Ratios

Ratio	Formula	Description
9. Current Ratio	$$\frac{\text{Current Assets}}{\text{Current Liabilities}}$$	Suggest the firm's ability to cover short term obligations using only expected short term income streams.
10. Quick Ratio (Acid Test Ratio)	$$\frac{\text{Current Assets} - \text{Inventories}}{\text{Current Liabilities}}$$	Measures the firm's ability to cover short term obligations without making any additional sales of inventory.
11. Inventory to Net Working Capital	$$\frac{\text{Inventory}}{\text{Current Assets} - \text{Current Liabilities}}$$	Measures the degree to which working capital is tied up in inventory.

Leverage Ratios

Ratio	Formula	Description
12. Debt to Assets Ratio	$$\frac{\text{Total Debt}}{\text{Total Assets}}$$	Shows how much of the assets of the firm have been purchased with debt rather than equity.
13. Debt to Equity Ratio	$$\frac{\text{Total Debt}}{\text{Total Stockholders' Equity}}$$	Shows the portion of the funds obtained by the firm that came from debt vs. stockholders' investments.
14. Long-term Debt to Equity Ratio	$$\frac{\text{Long-term Debt}}{\text{Total Shareholders' Equity}}$$	Indicates the degree to which a firm has relied on credit in its capital structure. Suggests how much borrowing capacity the firm might have available for emergencies and planned expansions.
15. Times Interest Earned	$$\frac{\text{Profits before Interest and Taxes}}{\text{Total Interest Charges}}$$	Measure the ability of the firm to meet its interest obligations should profits decline.
16. Fixed Charge Coverage	$$\frac{\text{Profits before Taxes \& Interest} + \text{Lease Obligations}}{\text{Total Interest Charges} + \text{Lease Obligations}}$$	Measure the firm's ability to meet all of its long-term fixed costs should profits decline.

Activity Ratios

Ratio	Formula	Description
17. Inventory Turnover (Merchandise Reseller)	$$\frac{\text{Total Annual Cost of Goods Sold}}{\text{Average Inventory}}$$	Measures the adequacy of inventory levels. Should not be too high or too low as compared to that of successful competitors.
18. Inventory Turnover (Manufacturer)	$$\frac{\text{Annual Sales}}{\text{Average Inventory of Finished Goods}}$$	Measures the adequacy of inventory levels. Should not be too high or too low as compared to that of successful competitors.

(Continued)

TABLE 1 (cont.)

Ratio	How to Compute	What it Indicates
19. Fixed Assets Turnover	$$\frac{\text{Sales}}{\text{Fixed Assets}}$$	Measures the efficiency of the firm's use of plant and equipment.
20. Total Assets Turnover	$$\frac{\text{Sales}}{\text{Total Assets}}$$	Measures the efficiency of the firm's use of all assets.
21. Accounts Receivable Turnover	$$\frac{\text{Annual Credit Sales}}{\text{Average Accounts Receivable}}$$	Measures the effectiveness of the firm's collection efforts. This number, when divided into 365, gives the average number of days the firm takes to collect accounts receivable.
Other Ratios		
22. Dividend Yield on Common Stock	$$\frac{\text{Annual Dividends per Share}}{\text{Current Market Price per Share}}$$	Measures the return on investment stockholders receive in the form of dividends.
23. Price-Earnings Ratio	$$\frac{\text{Current Market Price per Share}}{\text{After Tax Earnings per Share}}$$	Measures the relationship between the market valuation of the firm's stock and the earnings of the firm.
24. Dividend Payout Ratio	$$\frac{\text{Annual Dividends per Share}}{\text{After Tax Earnings per Share}}$$	Shows the portion of the firm's earnings that are distributed as dividends to the stockholders.
25. Book Value per Share	$$\frac{\text{Tangible Net Worth}}{\text{Number of Common Shares Outstanding}}$$	Measures the underlying tangible value of stock.
26. Market to Book Value Ratio	$$\frac{\text{Market Value of Outstanding Stock}}{\text{Book Value of Outstanding Stock}}$$	Measures the degree to which the market values the firm above or below its tangible worth.
27. Cash Flow per Share	$$\frac{\text{After Tax Profits} + \text{Depreciation}}{\text{Number of Common Shares Outstanding}}$$	Measures the cashflow received by the firm that is available for uses other than paying for operating costs.

Presenting Your Findings

The level of formality in your report, as noted earlier, is highly variable. The outline below is a formal, comprehensive one. Some or even many of the parts of this formal case analysis report may be omitted or condensed into other sections as needed to meet the specific requirements of your assignment.

Executive Summary

Unlike a mystery novel, which uses an inductive technique, building components of the story carefully before reaching the surprise conclusion, business writing calls for a *deductive* presentation approach. In other words, business writers should nearly always reveal the ending right at the beginning. The reader first sees the overall situation, including the outcome of the analysis, in generalities. Then, after the big picture has been painted, the writer fills in the details so that the reader will see clearly where each detail in the analysis fits.

See if you can spot the structural strengths and weaknesses of the following two presentations:

Presentation Order

The primary reason why business writing usually calls for a deductive presentation order is that deduction is more effective as a tool of persuasion in business situations. Shu-Wan Lee presented her case analysis using the other approach: induction. Excerpts from the case follow:

The Johnson Company Case Analysis

- Profits in the industry have been. . . .
- Last year Johnson Company's profits were. . . . This year they were. . . .
- Johnson Company has been having a hard time financially. . . .
- Sheri Jones, the operations manager did . . . and she was also observed to. . . .
- Sheri Jones seems, therefore, to be incompetent.
- In May raw materials prices were . . . while in September they had already increased to . . . and by the end of the year they were back down to. . . .
- Raw materials prices have been especially volatile over the past several months.

. . . Therefore it is our conclusion that Sheri Jones should be replaced and Johnson Company should establish a trading desk to invest in commodity futures contracts to counteract the effects of raw material price swings.

By contrast, Jenny Hernandez took a *deductive* approach to her presentation as follows:

The Johnson Company Case Analysis

The Johnson Company should address its inadequate profit levels by taking two separate actions: it should train or replace the operations manager and it should establish a trading desk to invest in commodity futures to offset the volatility in its raw materials markets. These conclusions are based on the following evidence:

- Sheri Jones, the operations manager seems to be incompetent, as shown by her decisions to. . . .
- She also did . . . and was observed to. . . .
- Raw materials prices have been highly volatile over the past several months. In May prices were. . . . In September they had increased to . . . and by year end they were back down to. . . .

Notice in the preceding illustration how the deductive approach helps to clarify the presentation immediately by showing the reader why each fact is presented. By revealing your conclusions in the beginning, you show your readers the purpose of each fact as it is presented, without allowing them to become distracted by their curiosity about the inclusion of any part of the presentation.

It is a good idea to use the deductive structure at each level of the document. The first section should reveal the ending, the first paragraph in each section should reveal the conclusion reached in that section, and each paragraph (or segment) of the section should begin with a statement of the conclusion reached in the paragraph, with the remainder of the paragraph's sentences giving details that support that conclusion.

An executive summary is not often included in a case analysis presentation, but it provides an excellent way to present an overview of the analysis results. This section should begin with a one- or two-paragraph statement of the important factors in the case: who the case is about, what their problems are, and what your recommendations are. The executive summary should rarely be longer than a single double-spaced page.

Background

The case study will virtually always contain a lot more information than you need to complete your assigned analysis. In presenting background information, your task is to choose carefully and present only the information that bears on your analysis and your interpretations of the data.

Company History

We spend a great deal of time in business courses dealing with the "culture" of a firm, meaning the general opinions, the work ethic, the sense of taste, and any other factors which unite the members of a firm in a collective sense of identity. Research has taught us that often the culture of the company is a more powerful factor in its success or failure than are other, more objective elements, such as the level of competition for market share or the prices of raw materials. The history of the firm often provides the only evidence of the firm's culture, always an important element in your analysis.

Remember to use a deductive approach in this section as well as throughout the report. Begin with a statement that clarifies the reasons you have for presenting the history that follows. For example, you might open with a statement such as the following:

> The problems Excel Graphics, Inc., is suffering today stem from over 20 years of ironfisted management by Bob Jeffries and his wife Arlene.

After an opening like that, you would then lay out the pertinent facts of the company's history that led you to this conclusion.

For completeness you should always include a history section if the case provides the information. If the history does not bear on the analysis, you might begin this section with a statement such as the following:

> Historically the Marcor Companies have operated as smoothly as could be asked by any business owner. Only in the past six months have conditions deteriorated to the point where strategic change has become necessary.

You might then follow this opening with a couple of paragraphs detailing your evidence of the historical stability, then review the events of the recent history in greater detail to show the validity of your second claim.

In preparing the background, your biggest problem will be to choose the information that is important from the piles of data you are usually given. Choose well. Select just the parts of the history that are clearly pertinent to your analysis. Your professor is much more likely to appreciate a concise, clear presentation than a fuzzy one fluffed up with a lot of irrelevant information.

Mission and Objectives

The mission statement is a concise expression of the role a firm has chosen to fill in society. In many case studies where a mission statement is presented, the facts may suggest that the company has strayed from their stated mission, and the strategic choice in question may be simply resolved by referring back to the question, "What business are we in, Bob?" This is the power of the mission statement: to offer guidance in making the hard, daily decisions required of every manager.

In far more case studies, as in the real business world, there will be no mission statement. We suggest that you attempt to dream one up, that is, construct one from the facts of the case. Often by carefully considering the role of the business at its most fundamental level you will be able to clarify and illuminate the present situation in such a manner that the best decision becomes obvious.

Inventing a Mission Statement

Shirley McGinty and her group members were reviewing the facts of a case history of IBSCO Enterprises:

BOB: The sales manager had always refused to go along with Harry's attempts to get IBSCO into the furniture business.

SALLY: That's right, and the one time IBSCO tried the trucking business, they quickly got out of it. Harry said it 'just didn't feel right' to them.

SHIRLEY: So, guys, what can we say about IBSCO's mission? How about this: 'IBSCO is in the ice cream store equipment business'?

BOB: Not bad. How about 'IBSCO is in business to help ice cream store owners by providing the equipment they need when and where they need it'?

Objectives

As with the mission statement, your case study may or may not include objectives. Whether they are explicitly presented or not, you need to include a set of relevant objectives in this section of your report. The number and specificity of the objectives will depend on your perspective. Again, the rule is to present only relevant information. In a marketing case analysis, for example, the objective of eliminating in-plant injuries within six months may be irrelevant, while an objective to obtain a 5 percent increase in market share in each of the next 5 years should obviously be included.

Environmental Analysis

Just as "No man is an island," so too no business operates in a vacuum. Evaluating any course of action, including a choice of inaction, requires an understanding of the environment both inside and outside the company. As a rule, any factors over which the company cannot exert significant control belongs in the *external* environment section. Factors which are amenable to control by the firm's owners should be included in the *internal* environment section. Be warned: classifying factors as internal vs. external frequently gives students a great deal of trouble. See how you fare on the quiz that follows.

A Short Quiz   Classify each of the factors below as internal or external:

Factor	Internal	External
1. Personnel	___	___
2. Installed equipment	___	___
3. Available equipment	___	___
4. Market size	___	___
5. Market share	___	___
6. Market growth rate	___	___
7. Compensation	___	___
8. Organizational resistance to change	___	___
9. Corporate culture	___	___
10. Rate of technological advancement	___	___

Answers: 1-I, 2-I, 3-E, 4-E, 5-I and E, 6-E, 7-E, 8-I, 9-I, 10-E

External Environment

Here you should address the world at large and how it impacts the company under examination. To reiterate the rule: factors that cannot be controlled by management should be addressed as *external* environmental factors. Be sure to address all of the relevant factors—and none of the irrelevant ones—from the list below. If your presentation will require more than a paragraph or two to cover some of the factors, use subheadings to identify each factor under discussion. If all of the relevant external factors can be covered in just a few paragraphs, subheadings are probably unnecessary.

Some External Factors

The following list of factors, most of which are *external factors* (those beyond the control of management), is not comprehensive. We present this list as a catalyst for your thinking about your case under consideration. Choose all that apply—and *only* those that apply—to your case analysis.

PRODUCTION

Raw materials (availability, quality, pricing)

Labor (availability, skills of applicants, amenability to change/training, cost)

Equipment (productive life, technological life, cost)

Facilities (availability, cost)

MARKETING

Product life cycle stage of a given product (introduction, growth, maturity, or decline)

Market dimensions (size, growth rate history, growth projections)

Customers (demographics, overall satisfaction levels, buying motivations)

Competitors (number, strength, differentiation strategies)

Pricing (price ranges, variation across targeted territories)

Distribution (industry norms, alternatives available)

REGULATORY

O.S.H.A. (general and industry-specific rules)

Federal regulations (ICC, FCC, FTC, EPA, FAA, etc.)

State regulations (specifics of those in the targeted territory, implications for expansions considered)

History and prospects for future rules changes

TECHNOLOGICAL

Availability of tools to improve productivity

Rate at which new tools and/or competing products enter the marketplace

Internal Environment

By contrast, *internal factors,* such as most of those in the following list, are controlled primarily by the owners and/or the managers of the firm. This list, like the one preceding, is not homogeneous; in other words, not all the factors in it are solely internal ones. We have included these lists to aid your thinking about items to address. Choose all the factors in the lists that apply to your case analysis.

PRODUCTION

Quality (number of defects, amount of rework, employees' attitudes toward quality)

Labor (productivity, turnover, unions, skill levels in the workforce, attitudes, injury rates)

Equipment (breakdown frequencies, degree of obsolescence)

Facilities (level of repair, effective utilization)

MARKETING

Our mix of products in the various life cycle stages (introduction, growth, maturity, or decline)

Our trading area dimensions (local, regional, national, or international)

Our customers (satisfaction levels with our products, loyalty)

Our market share

Our pricing (where we set prices within the acceptable range)

Our distribution choices from the alternatives available

REGULATORY

Compliance levels

Leadership role we choose to play in our industry

CORPORATE CULTURE

Sense of community

Manager/worker differences

Gender differences

Ethnic differences

Employee loyalty

Leadership style

TECHNOLOGICAL

Rate at which we adopt new technology

Level of training provided to employees

Rate of our product development

Note that the proper order in which to present these factors is, first, the external factors, then the internal factors. In this manner you can lay out for the reader the big picture constraints which will clarify the reasons for many of your decisions and observations about the internal dimensions of your analysis. Remember, external factors are a given: you cannot change these. Internal factors are those you can control. *The Serenity Prayer* can help you keep these two sets of factors clearly separated:

Give me the strength to accept the things I cannot change, the courage to change the things I can, and the wisdom to know the difference.

Special Tools for Business Analysis

While there are a number of specialized analytical tools that can help you with your case analysis, three tools are especially useful: a SWOT analysis, Michael Porter's Industry Competition Model, and the BCG Portfolio Mix Matrix. Learning how to use these analytical techniques now will make later work easier. You may even impress your professor by demonstrating knowledge of them, even when not directly instructed to use them.

SWOT Analysis

SWOT stands for strengths, weaknesses, opportunities, and threats. This analytical tool is also referred to as *situational analysis.* In performing a SWOT analysis, you must identify the appropriate market niche for your firm in relation to the opportunities and threats posed by the environment (external factors) and the strengths and weaknesses of the firm (internal factors). Ideally you should find the perfect match of opportunities and capabilities, but this rarely occurs in the complex world of business. This tool will provide you with a useful framework for your analytical work.

Michael Porter's Model

Porter's model, shown graphically below, provides a convenient, detailed checklist of items to consider in evaluating the external environmental factors that might affect the firm (Porter 1980.) For a thorough explanation of the model, refer to the original book by Porter.

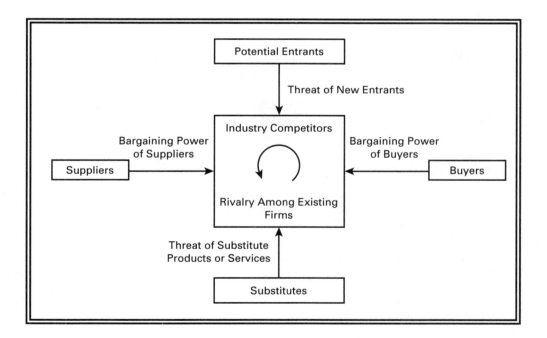

BCG Matrix

Another commonly used analytical tool is the Boston Consulting Group's BCG Portfolio Mix Matrix (Henderson 1973.) This tool is primarily aimed at market positioning. The analyst can place each segment of the business in the BCG Matrix as an aid to deciding what to do with that segment and which segments to concentrate on developing.

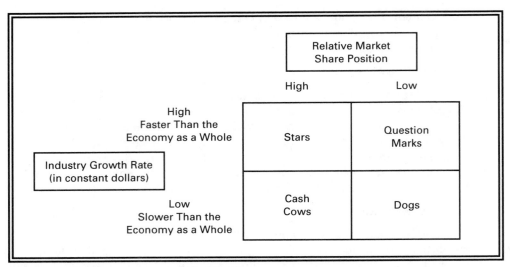

The Boston Consulting Group Portfolio Mix Matrix

The model classifies a business unit as a star (high market share, high market growth rate), a question mark (low share, high growth), a dog (low share, low growth), or a cash cow (high share, low growth). The objective of the firm should be to create cash cows while avoiding creating dogs. This may be done through converting question marks into stars and then feeding and nurturing the stars until the market begins to slow its growth, at which time the star becomes a cash cow.

Conclusions

In the concluding portion of the report, you are to clarify the outcomes of your analysis. Much of the analysis actually occurs in the mind of the analyst. A common mistake we all make is to abbreviate our findings to such a degree that the reader cannot follow our rationale. By breaking your findings into the following parts, you should be able to avoid that trap, and as a result, get your conclusions across so that everyone clearly understands your recommendations and your reasons for making them.

Assumptions

Inherent in every conclusion we draw is a set of assumptions. Many are *implicit,* or unexpressed assumptions. These are very dangerous in that their absence from your report often leads the reader to question the quality of your analytical conclusion and therefore of your ability to think clearly. Consider the following illustration.

Assumptions? What Assumptions?

The case concerned the Nissen Company, makers of a line of personal sized microwaveable soups. Bobbie Johnson completed her analysis of the company and concluded that the firm should sell off their noodle division and instead buy from outside vendors. Her explanation for the recommendation was that this action would reduce Nissen's risk and position the company to compete better in their newly opened territories in the Western Hemisphere.

During her analysis, Bobbie considered a number of factors and made these *assumptions:*

1. The noodle division has been problematic since its inception over 10 years earlier.
2. The noodle division demanded greater capital investment than all the rest of the company put together.
3. The expertise of the management was not in manufacturing but in marketing and distribution.
4. Bobbie believed that in the current investment markets Nissen could not obtain additional financing at acceptable rates.
5. Bobbie also assumed that without additional investment to support expansion, Nissen could not serve the expected increase in demand from the newly opened markets.

Without a careful explanation of the last two assumptions, Bobbie's conclusion raises more questions than it answers. Be sure you clearly state *all* of your relevant assumptions before presenting your recommendations.

Your goal when handling assumptions, then, is to turn implicit ones into explicit ones, meaning assumptions which are clearly stated. Throughout all of human discourse are scattered the inefficiencies of communication caused mainly by failure to express assumptions explicitly. Once the underlying assumptions in your analysis have been clearly identified, your recommendations become far more logical and meaningful, the focus of your analysis becomes sharper, and the persuasive power of your presentation increases to its maximum.

Problem Definition

In a manner similar to the one at work with assumptions, the *explicit problem definition* helps the reader accept your recommendations as reasonable and prudent. Presenting a recommendation without first explaining just why change is needed causes confusion and leads to more questions than commendations for an analysis well done.

A favorite sort of case that professors assign is one with seemingly no problems. This sort of case presents most students with a great deal more difficulty than do cases in which many problems are evident. Nevertheless, *all case analyses must produce a problem definition statement.*

Problem? What Problem?

When confronted with a case analysis of a company enjoying success in all of the dimensions measured, student analysts frequently labor to find something wrong, only to conclude with trivial recommendations that they realize would get them laughed out of the board room should they be called upon to present their findings to the company's directors. In each case you analyze, consider your findings in this light: how would the directorate of the firm probably react to your recommendations?

In handling this sort of case, rely on your assumptions to bail you out! When you read a case study that presents everything with a rosy tint, what are the *implicit assumptions*? By *explicitly* stating these, you may find much to recommend. Take the following case summary, for example:

Summa Cum Loudly

This upstart stereo speaker manufacturer targeting students as its customers has seen nothing but success. All of the original management team are still in place and now earning six figure salaries. Sales have been climbing at a rate of 20 percent per year for the past 10 years, with no end in sight. Production is well under control, as the company has contracted for 100 percent of their production with five established speaker producers located in the U.S.

Stuart Hayes got a long face as he finished reading the case. "Where can I find a problem in this information?" he thought to himself. "Aha! I will list the *implicit assumptions* on which rest the glowing projections presented in the case."

ASSUMPTIONS

1. Student populations will not shrink.
2. Students will continue to have sufficient disposable income to be able to afford such luxuries as stereo speakers.
3. No direct competitors will successfully attack Summa Cum Loudly's market.
4. Summa's sources of supply will continue without interruption.
5. Summa's management will continue to function effectively as in the past.

Based on these assumptions, there appears to be no problem to identify. However, when Stuart examined assumptions 1 and 2 in light of current and predicted developments, Stuart deduced the following problem statement:

> Summa Cum Loudly faces a potential flattening and/or decline in demand through the foreseeable future due to a dramatic increase in college tuitions predicted for the coming years. This will act to reduce student populations and reduce the discretionary income of those who do attend college.
> Given these problems several courses of action are possible. . . .

Whatever the case you are assigned to analyze, identify a *meaningful* problem to address. Take it on faith that such a problem does exist. Your job is to find it. By considering the implicit assumptions, you may readily find the meaningful problem in even the most positive of business case studies.

Of course, you will also be assigned case studies that contain many problems. Finding a fundamental problem may solve many of the more superficial ones. For example, a firm having difficulties in many areas may simply have the wrong corporate culture, and solving that problem may make the other troubles disappear. The best approach is to find the most fundamental problem(s) and then discuss its (or their) relationship with the other problems you identify. Look for the pressure points where change will do the most good.

Alternative Courses of Action

A hallmark of promotable employees is that they always offer a solution whenever they report a problem. The employee takes a "hit" right in the reputation whenever he cannot answer the expected question, "Well, what do you think we should do about that?" when reporting a problem.

No one is under more pressure to offer solutions to problems than the analyst who defines the problem in the first place. It is vital for the analyst to consider all practical options (and sometimes the impractical ones) before making a final recommendation. Here is your opportunity to apply all of the creative talent you possess. If you are working in a team, even better. Too often students spend all of their efforts drudging through the data presented in the case study, only to present some pedestrian solution that weakly addresses the problem. This is not the place to let down your efforts. Spend time thinking about the problem. Consider every angle. Use brainstorming sessions to develop as many possible alternative solutions as you can. You are the analyst! Your job is to identify *all* of the feasible options. When you present your analysis, *your readers should not be able to come up with any alternative you have not already listed.* If they can, you have not completed your job—or else the reader is a lot more creative or experienced than you are!

Student analysts frequently miss some alternative. Do not be disheartened if this happens to you. Over time and with experience you will get better at identifying the universe of alternatives in most of the business cases you are presented. This should be your goal: no reader will identify any meaningful alternative I did not present. By striving toward this objective you will improve your skills, focus your analyses, and make your recommendations more useful and persuasive.

Recommended Course of Action

As you present your choice of the alternatives developed in the last section, you also need to present your rationale. A bare statement that "our recommendation is as follows . . ." will naturally draw the question, "Why?" As an analyst, you should try to explain your recommendations in sufficient detail so that the reader clearly understands two things: (1) why you chose the alternative you did, and (2) why you did not choose any of the other alternatives listed.

Summary of Analysis

This section is optional and should be included in only the most complex of cases. If you have taken the readers on a trip through the jungle and feel you may have lost them along the way, consider sending back a search party in the form of this section. In this section you should review the salient points in the data, your assumptions, the relationship of the fundamental problem to all the other little problems, your key alternatives, your choice recommendation, and your rationale. This section may be used in place of or in addition to the executive summary, depending on your preference. The three keys to making this section useful to the reader are as follows:

1. *Redundancy.* Do not introduce anything new here. Only summarize what has already been presented elsewhere.

2. *Focus.* Leave out everything that is not critical in your review of what has come before. This will help the reader to see clearly what is obscured by the immaterial clutter of the case.

3. *Brevity.* You have already elaborated on the themes of the case. Here you need to be as concise as possible without leaving out important elements.

References and Appendices

Usually you will not need to include references; however, if you do need to seek outside information sources or employ formal analytical tools, by all means cite your sources. See Chapter 6 for the preferred methods for citing sources and presenting bibliographic citations. If you are called upon to analyze cases involving real-world clients, you should attach as appendices any and all exhibits needed to give the reader a full understanding of the inputs on which your analysis rests. Such exhibits might include financial statements, job descriptions and résumés, maps, product literature, and corporate annual reports. This certainly is not an exhaustive list. Use your own judgment. Include everything your readers need in order to understand your presentation and nothing they do not need. Do not use attachments to fatten up your report. Take the high road. Perform a detailed, complete, sophisticated analysis, and you will have a work you can be proud of. Even better, you will have an improved *you* to be proud of as well!

CHAPTER 15

The Written Requirements of Financial Statements

15.1 INTRODUCTION

Students of accounting and finance are usually focused so finely on the difficulties of learning the highly complex procedural skills required by these disciplines that they have little time to work on improving their writing skills. This chapter is designed to assist professors of accounting and finance and their students by providing a supplementary source of guidance for the written elements of those courses, leaving everyone free to focus on the tougher elements of the disciplines during course time.

Writing well in the fields of accounting and finance offers special problems. The inherent difficulty of the material forces students and professionals alike to concentrate on the procedural skills required by their discipline. Numbers experts often find that while they are able to understand and use complicated formulas, explaining them in writing to someone else is another matter. It requires, in effect, the merging of two languages, the reliably systematic language of numbers and the not-quite-so reliably systematic language of written words. The problem is made worse by the fact that the reader for whom the financial expert writes is often no expert in math and needs things explained very simply in coherent and confident prose. Another problem is that there is zero tolerance for error. (All of us are sensitive about money!) This means that in your writing the two languages have to work together seamlessly.

You are certainly capable of improving the writing you do in your discipline. Real improvement, however, takes commitment. And that commitment can come only from you. You must look within yourself for the energy and the resolve to strive for excellence.

Now let's discuss the details of financial statement writing.

15.2 LINE EXPLANATIONS

Business professionals rely heavily on financial statements and reports for the information they need to make strategic and tactical decisions. Many times, therefore, they will skip over the written report that often accompanies the financial statements. Notice the order: nonbusiness people would say that financial statements accompany the written report rather than the other way around. Because the financial information is so information rich, though, the savvy business professional will frequently start with the numbers, only reading the accompanying text if time permits or if additional information is desired.

Because of this reality, financial statements for your plan should be constructed to stand alone insofar as is possible. Unfortunately, numbers cannot explain very well. They cannot direct the reader's attention to another part of the statement, nor can they point out erroneous assumptions on the part of the reader. The mechanisms of choice to accomplish these essential tasks are the *line explanation* in the case of the *pro forma* (projected) statements, and the *variance report* in the case of historical financial statements.

Line explanations are concise reports of relevant information needed by the reader of a financial statement to interpret properly the numbers contained in the statement. These explanations can contain just a textual explanation or the detailed computations used to formulate the financial statement number referred to, along with a textual explanation or even a reference to additional information that exists elsewhere. The objective is to provide a full explanation in a manner that is most useful for the reader.

In general, the rules for writing line explanations are as follows:

1. Write clearly, concisely, briefly, and conservatively. Conservative writing means using common words—unusual words add charm and depth to prose, but information transmission is the goal here. Use your creativity in verbal pyrotechnics elsewhere. (Even accountants must take humanities courses.) Conservative writing also means not using contractions (*don't, won't, didn't,* and so on), since contractions can be misconstrued more easily than fully written words. Use complete sentences. Incomplete sentences can sometimes make for ambiguity of reference or meaning. If there is ever a place where effective communication is mandatory, it is in communicating financial information.

2. Present enough information and explanation to answer fully the question the reader may logically ask: "How did you get that number?"

3. When the answer is especially complex and cannot be answered with a brief explanation, refer the reader to a full explanation elsewhere. Such explanations are usually placed in an accompanying business plan, variance report, or other formal report.

4. Explain every number in the financial statement—even numbers that seem to need no explanation, such as the difference between numbers on two different lines (an example: "Gross profit on sales is equal to gross sales minus cost of goods sold."). The reason for these simple explanations is that they provide continuity for the reader and preempt the aggravation caused by missing information, which can cause readers to wonder about the thoroughness of the entire report.

5. Number all line explanations sequentially, with no gaps in the sequence. Unless you are using pre-printed forms which have every line numbered or you have been instructed by your professor to do otherwise, number only the lines of the financial statement which contain numbers. That way, your line explanations will be numbered sequentially, with no annoying gaps in the sequence, and without the rather silly-looking explanation otherwise required, "This line left blank intentionally."

6. Attach the line explanations page(s) to the back of the financial statement to which they refer. If the report contains a table of contents, be sure to include the line expla-

nations in the table. This will alert the reader to the presence of the explanations which may otherwise be overlooked.

The first two figures following illustrate the proper use of line explanations for an income statement. The next two figures illustrate the proper use of line explanations for a cashflow statement. Because the formula for computing each number in a balance sheet is fixed and known to the business professional reader, line explanations are not needed for pro forma balance sheets.

Using Line Explanations in an Income Statement

	JERRI'S FLOWER EMPORIUM					
	PRO FORMA INCOME STATEMENTS					
	FOR THE QUARTERS ENDED 3-31, 6-30, 9-30, AND 12-31, 1998					
		Jan-Mar	*Apr-Jun*	*Jul-Sep*	*Oct-Dec*	*Total*
	Income:					
1	Flower and Gift Sales	45,450	49,995	54,995	60,494	210,933
2	Service Sales	12,500	13,750	15,125	16,638	58,013
3	Total Sales	57,950	63,745	70,120	77,131	268,946
4	Cost of Goods Sold	22,725	24,998	27,497	30,247	105,467
5	Gross Profit	35,225	38,748	42,622	46,884	163,479
	Expenses:					
6	Management Salaries	10,000	10,000	10,000	10,000	40,000
7	Labor	18,000	18,000	18,000	18,000	72,000
8	Sales Commissions	625	688	756	832	2,901
9	Rent	2,100	2,100	2,100	2,100	8,400
10	Utilities	750	750	750	750	3,000
11	Advertising	4,057	4,462	4,908	5,399	18,826
12	Office Supplies	250	250	250	250	1,000
13	Phone	610	360	360	360	1,690
14	E-mail and Internet	150	150	150	150	600
15	Travel and Entertainment	100	100	100	100	400
16	Depreciation	2,583	2,583	2,583	2583	10,332
17	Interest	367	342	315	296	1,320
18	Total expenses	39,592	39,785	40,273	40,820	160,469
19	Net Income Before Income Tax	−4,367	−1,037	2,350	6,064	3,010

Pro Forma Income Statements

JERRI'S FLOWER EMPORIUM
PRO FORMA INCOME STATEMENTS
FOR THE QUARTERS ENDED 3-31, 6-30, 9-30, AND 12-31, 1998
LINE EXPLANATIONS

1. In the first quarter, flower and gift sales are projected at 5% of the total projected market sales of $909,000, or $45,450, then growing by 10% per quarter through the remainder of the year. See page 6 of the accompanying business plan for additional information on the sales forecast.

2. Service sales include project planning and design fees and are expected to include five major projects at $2,500 each, for a total of $12,500 in the first quarter, increasing by 10% per quarter through the remainder of the year. See page 8 of the accompanying business plan for additional information on the service sales forecast.

3. Total sales is equal to the sum of flower and gift sales plus service sales (line 1 plus line 2.)

4. Cost of goods sold is computed at 50% of flower and gift sales (line 1 × .50).

5. Gross profit is equal to the total sales less cost of goods sold (line 3 − line 4).

6. Management salaries includes the owner's salary of $32,000 per year plus related payroll taxes and insurance equal to 25% of the salary, or $8,000, for a total of $10,000 per quarter.

7. Labor is estimated based on four full-time employees each earning $15,000 per year, plus 20% of wages for payroll taxes and insurance, for a total of $18,000 per quarter.

8. Sales commissions will be paid on service sales only, at a rate of 5% of total service sales (line 2 × .05).

9. Rent is projected to be $7 per square foot per year. At 1,200 square feet needed, rent will be $2,100 per quarter (1,200 × $7 divided by 4 = $2,100).

10. Utilities are estimated to average $250 per month or $750 per quarter.

11. Advertising is planned at 7% of projected sales (line 3 × .07).

12. Office supplies are estimated at $250 per quarter.

13. Phone expense includes an estimate of $120 per month, or $360 per quarter, plus an initial installation fee of $250 shown in the first quarter.

14. E-mail and Internet fees are projected at $50 per month, or $150 per quarter.

15. Travel and entertainment is budgeted at $100 per quarter.

16. Depreciation expense is based on the straight-line method. Computer equipment and the delivery van are set at a three-year life. All other assets are set at a five-year life as shown in the table below.

Asset	Historical Cost	Life	Depreciation Expense per Month
Delivery van	$18,000	36	500
Computer system	4,000	36	111
Furniture and fixtures	15,000	60	250
Total Depreciation Expense per month			861
			×4
Total Depreciation Expense per quarter			2,583

17. Interest is derived from the amortization schedule shown in Appendix L.
18. Total expenses are equal to the sum of lines 6 through 17.
19. Net income before income tax is the difference between gross profit and total expenses (line 5 − line 18).

Using Line Explanations in a Cashflow Statement

1	JERRI'S FLOWER EMPORIUM					
2	PRO FORMA CASHFLOW STATEMENTS					
3	FOR THE QUARTERS ENDED 3-31, 6-30, 9-30, AND 12-31, 1998					
4						
5		Jan-Mar	Apr-Jun	Jul-Sep	Oct-Dec	Total
6						
7	*Sources of Cash:*					
8	Cash Sales	57,950	63,745	70,120	77,131	163,479
9	Loans	37,000				37,000
10	Owner's Equity Contributions	10,000				10,000
11	Total Sources of Cash	104,950	63,745	70,120	77,131	315,946
12						
13	*Uses of Cash:*					
14	Cash Expenses	37,009	37,202	37,690	38,237	150,137
15	Inventory Purchases	22,725	24,998	27,497	30,247	105,467
16	Principal Portion of Loan Payments	833	858	885	904	3,480
17	Computer System	4,000				
18	Delivery Van	18,000				
19	Furniture and Fixtures	15,000				
10	Deposits	1,200				
21						
22	Total Uses of Cash	98,767	63,057	66,072	69,388	297,284
23						
24	Current Period Cashflow	6,184	688	4,048	7,743	18,662
25	Cumulative Cash Position	6,184	6,871	10,919	18,662	

Pro Forma Cashflow Statements

JERRI'S FLOWER EMPORIUM
PRO FORMA CASHFLOW STATEMENTS
FOR THE QUARTERS ENDED 3-31, 6-30, 9-30, AND 12-31, 1998
LINE EXPLANATIONS

1–7. Used for headings only.

8. Cash sales includes all sales revenue. This amount comes from line 3 of the income statements.

9. Loans includes a single bank loan in the amount of $37,000 to be repaid over 36 months.

10. Owner's equity contributions amount to $10,000 in cash.

11. Total Sources of cash is the sum of lines 8 through 10.

12–13. Used for headings only.

14. Cash expenses includes all expense items except for depreciation (income statement line 18–line 16).

15. Principal portion of loan payments is derived from the amortization schedule in Appendix I.

16. Computer system estimated cost is $4,000. See page 12 of the business plan for further information.

17. Delivery van cost is expected to be $18,000 as discussed in the business plan on page 14.

18. Furniture and fixtures total $15,000. For a detailed breakdown, see page 16 of the business plan.

19. Deposits include the following:

Rental deposit	$ 800
Utilities deposits	400
Total	$1,200

20–22. Used for headings only.

23. Current Period Cashflow is equal to the difference between the total sources and the total uses of cash (line 11–line 22 of the cashflow statement).

24. Cumulative Cash Position is an estimate of projected cash in bank and on hand and is computed as the sum of the previous period's cumulative cash position plus (or minus) the current period cashflow.

The cashflow statement illustration shows one way to handle the use of line explanations when the statements are shown on a prenumbered form. As suggested above, the preferable method is to number the lines yourself and number only those containing financial data. Also, note the references to other statements and reports. This method allows readers to answer immediately any questions they may have about the financial statement contents.

15.3 FINANCIAL STATEMENT FOOTNOTES

After the business has been operating for a period of time, most of the financial statements have become historical in nature, reporting what has actually happened rather than projecting what is expected to occur. Business professionals understand where all of the numbers in the historical financial statements come from, and so line explanations are no longer needed. Sometimes, though, unusual events occur that call for an explanation of the numbers reported in the financial statements, especially in the balance sheet. These explanations are handled through the use of *financial statement footnotes*.

Footnotes are not only a good idea, they are required in many instances where the statements must conform to generally accepted accounting principles (GAAP). The Financial Accounting Standards Board and other official accounting entities issue opinions and standards which comprise GAAP. These documents spell out in considerable detail the circumstances under which a footnote is required. To create effective, professional footnotes, you need to remember to write clearly, concisely, and conservatively. There is no need for elaborate descriptions or imagery. The excerpt from an annual report shown in the figure below illustrates good footnote form.

NOTES TO CONSOLIDATED FINANCIAL STATEMENTS
PFIZER INC. AND SUBSIDIARY COMPANIES
(EXCERPTS)

SIGNIFICANT ACCOUNTING POLICIES

The consolidated financial statements include the accounts of Pfizer Inc. and all significant subsidiaries (the "Company"). Material intercompany transactions are eliminated. Certain reclassifications have been made to the 1994 and 1993 financial statements to conform to the 1995 presentation, including classification of the food science business as a discontinued operation in the statement of income. See the footnote "Discontinued Operations" on page 55.

The preparation of the consolidated financial statements requires management to make estimates and assumptions that affect reported amounts and disclosures in these financial statements. Actual results could differ from these estimates.

The Company is subject to certain risks and uncertainties as a result of changes in the health care environment, competition, foreign exchange, and tax reform as discussed in "Prospective Information" beginning on page 36. . . .

DISCONTINUED OPERATIONS

In December 1995, the Company agreed to sell substantially all the net assets of its food science business to Cultor Ltd., a publicly held international nutrition company based in Finland, for approximately $350 million in cash. The sale was completed in January 1996. Disposal of the remaining assets, which are not material to the food science business, is expected to be completed over several years. The food science business has been reported as a discontinued operation.

The Company recorded a loss on disposal of the food science business of $3.0 million after provisions for direct transaction costs and estimated charges including exit costs, employee severance benefits, and professional fees. . . .

LEASE COMMITMENTS

Rent expense, net of sublease rentals, for the years ended December 31, 1995, 1994, and 1993 amounted to approximately $118.1, $94.4, and $87.2 million, respectively. Total future minimum rental commitments under all noncancelable leases for the years 1996 through 2000 and thereafter are approximately $28.2, $22.6, $16.7, $8.8, $6.8, and $185.9 million, respectively.

Under the more significant lease agreements, the Company must either pay directly for taxes, insurance, maintenance, and other operating expenses or pay higher rentals when such expenses increase. . . .

Source: Pfizer, Inc. 1995 Annual Report. Pfizer, Inc., 235 East 42nd Street, New York, NY.

15.4 AUDITORS' OPINIONS

The purpose of an audit is to let the clients know whether their own estimate of their financial situation, as reflected in their financial situation, is accurate. As you will learn in your auditing courses, the auditor first determines the financial condition of the client under audit and his or her records, then fashions a report by selecting the appropriate auditors' opinion and repeating it, usually verbatim, from the appropriate auditing standards report or, for accounting students, from the auditing textbook.

You may need to modify the standard unqualified report. Your auditing text will provide you with most of the verbiage you need to construct a proper report for each situation you may face as an auditor. Three such opinions are shown in the figures below. The first opinion is the *standard unqualified opinion,* the second is a *qualified opinion* including a "going-concern qualification," and the third is an *adverse opinion.* Except in your auditing course, you will probably never have occasion to write an adverse opinion throughout your auditing career, but accountants frequently find the prospect of doing so interesting.

Unqualified Independent Auditors' Report

INDEPENDENT AUDITOR'S REPORT

To the Board of Directors of The Marilou Flower Corporation:

We have audited the accompanying balance sheet of The Marilou Flower Corporation as of December 31, 1997, and the related statements of income, retained earnings, and cashflows for the year then ended. These financial statements are the responsibility of the Company's management. Our responsibility is to express an opinion on these financial statements based on our audit.

We conducted our audit in accordance with generally accepted auditing standards. Those standards require that we plan and perform the audit to obtain reasonable assurance about whether the financial statements are free of material misstatement. An audit includes examining, on a test basis, evidence supporting the amounts and disclosures in the financial statements. An audit also includes assessing the accounting principles used and significant estimates made by management, as well as evaluating the overall financial statement presentation. We believe that our audit provides a reasonable basis for our opinion.

In our opinion, the financial statements referred to above present fairly, in all material respects, the financial position of The Marilou Flower Corporation as of December 31, 1997, and the results of its operations and its cashflows for the year then ended, in conformity with generally accepted accounting principles.

Signed _____

Date _____

Independent Auditors' Report Containing a Going-Concern Qualification

INDEPENDENT AUDITOR'S REPORT

To the Board of Directors of Bobbie's Shears, Incorporated:

We have audited the accompanying balance sheet of Bobbie's Shears, Incorporated, as of December 31, 1997, and the related statements of income, retained earnings, and cashflows for the year then ended. These financial statements are the responsibility of the Company's management. Our responsibility is to express an opinion on these financial statements based on our audit.

We conducted our audit in accordance with generally accepted auditing standards. Those standards require that we plan and perform the audit to obtain reasonable assurance about whether the financial statements are free of material misstatement. An audit includes examining, on a test basis, evidence supporting the amounts and disclosures in the financial statements. An audit also includes assessing the accounting principles used and significant estimates made by management, as well as evaluating the overall financial statement presentation. We believe that our audit provides a reasonable basis for our opinion.

In our opinion, the financial statements referred to above present fairly, in all material respects, the financial position of Bobbie's Shears, Incorporated, as of December 31, 1997, and the results of its operations and its cashflows for the year then ended, in conformity with generally accepted accounting principles.

The accompanying financial statements have been prepared assuming that the Company will continue as a going concern. As discussed in Note 11 to the financial statements, the Company has suffered recurring losses from operations and has a net capital deficiency that raises substantial doubt about its ability to continue as a going concern. Management's plans in regard to these matters also are described in Note 11. The financial statements do not include any adjustments that might result from the outcome of this uncertainty.

Signed _____

Date _____

Independent Auditors' Report Containing an Adverse Opinion

INDEPENDENT AUDITOR'S REPORT

To the Board of Directors of The Delta Bowl Company:

We have audited the accompanying balance sheet of The Delta Bowl Company as of December 31, 1997, and the related statements of income, retained earnings, and cashflows for the year then ended. These financial statements are the responsibility of the Company's management. Our responsibility is to express an opinion on these financial statements based on our audit.

We conducted our audit in accordance with generally accepted auditing standards. Those standards require that we plan and perform the audit to obtain reasonable assurance about whether the financial statements are free of material misstatement. An audit includes examining, on a test basis, evidence supporting the amounts and disclosures in the financial statements. An audit also includes assessing the accounting principles used and significant estimates made by management, as well as evaluating the overall financial statement presentation. We believe that our audit provides a reasonable basis for our opinion.

As set forth in Note 2, land owned by the Company is stated in the accompanying balance sheet at appraised value, which is $7,000,000 in excess of cost. Had this land been stated at cost, in accordance with generally accepted accounting principles, property and equipment and stockholders' equity would be reduced by this amount as of December 31, 1997. The recording of appraisal value has no effect on the statements of income, retained earnings, and cashflows.

In our opinion, because of the significant effect of recording appraised value as discussed in the preceding paragraph, the balance sheet referred to above does not present fairly the financial position of The Delta Bowl Company as of December 31, 1997. However, in our opinion, the statements of income, retained earnings, and cashflows present fairly, in all material aspects, the results of operations and cashflows for the year ended December 31, 1997, in conformity with generally accepted accounting principles.

Signed _____

Date _____

The message to be stressed here is a simple one: copy the opinions word for word, including all punctuation, spelling, and capitalization wherever possible. Only in extremely rare circumstances is any creativity whatsoever allowed in the writing of auditors' opinions. Once on the job, you will find that your auditing firm will provide you with numerous examples of wording that will cover nearly every conceivable circumstance. While you are a student, you may find that you must construct a paragraph or two as a class assignment. In such assignments, you are best advised to find an example in your textbook or in the library of an auditors' report for a situation as close as possible to that assigned to you, then copy that report word for word, changing only the words you must to make the report fit your assignment.

References

Adler, Bill, and Bill Adler, Jr. 1985. *The Wit and Wisdom of Wall Street*. Homewood, IL: Dow Jones-Irwin.

Agassiz, Louis. 1958. *A Scientist of Two Worlds: Louis Agassiz*. Ed. Catherine Owens Pearce. Philadelphia: Lippincott.

Dunn, S. W., and A. M. Barban. 1986. *Advertising: Its Role in Modern Marketing*. 6th ed. Chicago: Dryden Press.

Hartwell, Patrick. 1985. "Grammar, Grammars, and the Teaching of Grammar." *College English* 47:105-127.

Henderson, Bruce D. 1973. *The Experience Curve—Reviewed. IV. The Growth Share Matrix of the Product Portfolio*. Perspectives No. 135. Boston: The Boston Consulting Group.

Iacocca, Lee. 1989. *Talking Straight*. New York: Bantam.

Jackman, Michael, ed. 1984. *The Macmillan Book of Business and Economics Quotations*. New York: Macmillan.

Kent, Robert W., ed. 1985. *Money Talks*. New York: Facts on File.

Lunsford, Andrea, and Robert Connors. 1992. *The St. Martin's Handbook*. 2nd ed. Annotated Instructor's Ed. New York: St. Martin's.

Lynch, Peter. 1989. *One Up on Wall Street*. New York: Simon and Schuster.

"Manufacturers Expect Slower Growth To Continue, But Builders Are Upbeat." 1997. *Wall Street Journal,* 8 January.

Molloy, John T. 1977. *The Woman's Dress for Success Book*. Chicago: Follet Publishing Co.

Molloy, John T. 1988. *John T. Molloy's New Dress for Success.* New York: Warner Books.

Porter, Michael E. 1980. *Competitive Strategy*. New York: The Free Press.

Siegel, Eric S., Loren A. Schultz, and Brian R. Ford. 1987. *The Arthur Young Business Plan Guide*. New York: John Wiley.

Index